Practical Text Mining
With Perl

WILEY SERIES ON METHODS AND APPLICATIONS IN DATA MINING

Series Editor: **Daniel T. Larose**

Discovering Knowledge in Data: An Introduction to Data Mining • Daniel T. LaRose

Data-Mining on the Web: Uncovering Patterns in Web Content, Structure, and Usage • Zdravko Markov and Daniel Larose

Data Mining Methods and Models • Daniel Larose

Practical Text Mining with Perl • Roger Bilisoly

Practical Text Mining
With Perl

Roger Bilisoly
Department of Mathematical Sciences
Central Connecticut State University

WILEY

A JOHN WILEY & SONS, INC., PUBLICATION

Library of Congress Cataloging-in-Publication Data:

Bilisoly, Roger, 1963–
  Practical text mining with Perl / Roger Bilisoly.
     p. cm.
  Includes bibliographical references and index.
  ISBN 978-0-470-17643-6 (cloth)
  1. Data mining. 2. Text processing (Computer science) 3. Perl (Computer program language) I. Title.
  QA76.9.D343.B45 2008
  005.74—dc22   2008008144

Printed in the United States of America.

10 9 8 7 6 5 4 3 2 1

*To my Mom and Dad & all
their cats.*

Contents

List of Figures

List of Tables

Preface

What This Book Covers

This book introduces the basic ideas of text mining, which is a group of techniques that extracts useful information from one or more texts. This is a practical book, one that focuses on applications and examples. Although some statistics and mathematics is required, it is kept to a minimum, and what is used is explained.

This book, however, does make one demand: it assumes that you are willing to learn to write simple programs using Perl. This programming language is explicitly designed to work with text. In addition, it is open-source software that is available over the Web for free. That is, you can download the latest full-featured version of Perl right now, and install it on all the computers you want without paying a cent.

Chapters 2 and 3 give the basics of Perl, including a detailed introduction to regular expressions, which is a text pattern matching methodology used in a variety of programming languages, not just Perl. For each concept there are several examples of how to use it to analyze texts. Initial examples analyze short strings, for example, a few words or a sentence. Later examples use text from a variety of literary works, for example, the short stories of Edgar Allan Poe, Charles Dickens's *A Christmas Carol*, Jack London's *The Call of the Wild*, and Mary Shelley's *Frankenstein*. All the texts used here are part of the public domain, so you can download these for free, too. Finally, if you are interested in word games, Perl plus extensive word lists are a great combination, which is covered in chapter 3.

Chapters 4 through 8 each introduce a core idea used in text mining. For example, chapter 4 explains the basics of probability, and chapter 5 discusses the term-document matrix, which is an important tool from information retrieval.

This book assumes that you want to analyze one or more texts, so the focus is on the practical. All the techniques in this book have immediate applications. Moreover, learning a minimal amount of Perl enables you to modify the code in this book to analyze the texts that interest you.

The level of mathematical knowledge assumed is minimal: you need to know how to count. Mathematics that arises for text applications is explained as needed and is kept to the minimum to do the job at hand. Although most of the techniques used in this book were created by researchers knowledgeable in math, a few basic ideas are all that are needed to read this book.

Although I am a statistician by training, the level of statistical knowledge assumed is also minimal. The core tools of statistics, for example, variability and correlations, are explained. It turns out that a few techniques are applicable in many ways.

The level of prior programming experience assumed is again minimal: Perl is explained from the beginning, and the focus is on working with text. The emphasis is on creating short programs that do a specific task, not general-purpose text mining tools. However, it is assumed that you are willing to put effort into learning Perl. If you have never programmed in any computer language at all, then doing this is a challenge. Nonetheless, the payoff is big if you rise to this challenge.

Finally, all the code, output, and figures in this book are produced with software that is available from the Web at no cost to you, which is also true of all the texts analyzed. Consequently, you can work through all the computer examples with no additional costs.

What Is Text Mining?

The *text* in *text mining* refers to written language that has some informational content. For example, newspaper stories, magazine articles, fiction and nonfiction books, manuals, blogs, email, and online articles are all texts. The amount of text that exists today is vast, and it is ever growing.

Although there are numerous techniques and approaches to text mining, the overall goal is simple: it discovers new and useful information that is contained in one or more text documents. In practice, text mining is done by running computer programs that read in documents and process them in a variety of ways. The results are then interpreted by humans.

Text mining combines the expertise of several disciplines: mathematics, statistics, probability, artificial intelligence, information retrieval, and databases, among others. Some of its methods are conceptually simple, for example, concordancing where all instances of a word are listed in its context (like a Bible concordance). There are also sophisticated algorithms such as hidden Markov models (used for identifying parts of speech). This book focuses on the simpler techniques. However, these are useful and practical nonetheless, and serve as a good introduction to more advanced text mining books.

This Book's Approach to Text Mining

This book has three broad themes. First, text mining is built upon counting and text pattern matching. Second, although language is complex, some aspects of it can be studied by considering its simpler properties. Third, combining computer and human strengths is a powerful way to study language. We briefly consider each of these.

First, text pattern matching means identifying a pattern of letters in a document. For example, finding all instances of the word *cat* requires using a variety of patterns, some of which are below.

cat Cat cats Cats cat's Cat's cats' cat, cat. cat!

It also requires rejecting words like *catastrophe* or *scatter*, which contain the string *cat*, but are not otherwise related. Using regular expressions, this can be explained to a computer, which is not daunted by the prospect of searching through millions of words. See section 2.2.1 for further discussion of this example and chapter 2 for text patterns in general.

It turns out that counting the number of matches to a text pattern occurs again and again in text mining, even in sophisticated techniques. For example, one way to compute the similarity of two text documents is by counting how many times each word appears in both documents. Chapter 5 considers this problem in detail.

Second, while it is true that the complexity of language is immense, some information about language is obtainable by simple techniques. For example, recent language reference books are often checked against large text collections (called *corpora*). Language patterns have been both discovered and verified by examining how words are used in writing and speech samples. For example, *big*, *large*, and *great* are similar in meaning, but the examination of corpora shows that they are not used interchangeably. For example, the following sentences: "he has big feet," "she has large feet," and "she has great insight" sound good, but "he has big insight" or "she has large insight" are less fluent. In this type of analysis, the computer finds the examples of usage among vast amounts of text, and a human examines these to discover patterns of meanings. See section 6.4.2 for an example.

Third, as noted above, computers follow directions well, and they are untiring, while humans are experts at using and interpreting language. However, computers have limited understanding of language, and humans have limited endurance. These facts suggest an iterative and collaborative strategy: the results of a program are interpreted by a human who, in turn, decides what further computer analyses are needed, if any. This back and forth process is repeated as many times as is necessary. This is analogous to exploratory data analysis, which exploits the interplay between computer analyses and human understanding of what the data means.

Why Use Perl?

This section title is really three questions. First, why use Perl as opposed to an existing text mining package? Second, why use Perl as opposed to other programming languages? Third, why use Perl instead of so-called pseudo-code? Here are three answers, respectively.

First, if you have a text mining package that can do everything you want with all the texts that interest you, and if this package works exactly the way you want it, and if you believe that your future processing needs will be met by this package, then keep using it. However, it has been my experience that the process of analyzing texts suggests new ideas requiring new analyses and that the boundaries of existing tools are reached too soon in any package that does not allow the user to program. So at the very least, I prefer packages that allow the user to add new features, which requires a programming language. Finally, learning how to use a package also takes time and effort, so why not invest that time in learning a flexible tool like Perl.

Second, Perl is a programming language that has text pattern matching (called *regular expressions* or *regexes*), and these are easy to use with a variety of commands. It also has a vast amount of free add-ons available on the Web, many of which are for text processing. Additionally, there are numerous books and tutorials and online resources for Perl, so it is easy to find out how to make it do what you want. Finally, you can get on the Web and download full-strength Perl right now, for free: no hidden charges!

Larry Wall built Perl as a text processing computer language. Moreover, he studied linguistics in graduate school, so he is knowledgeable about natural languages, which influenced his design of Perl. Although many programming languages support text pattern matching, Perl is designed to make it easy to use this feature.

Third, many books use pseudo-code, which excels at showing the programming logic. In my experience, this has one big disadvantage. Students without a solid programming background often find it hard to convert pseudo-code to running code. However, once Perl is installed on a computer, accurate typing is all that is required to run a program. In fact, one way to learn programming is by taking existing code and modifying it to see what happens, and this can only be done with examples written in a specific programming language.

Finally, personally, I enjoy using Perl, and it has helped me finish numerous text processing tasks. It is easy to learn a little Perl and then apply it, which leads to learning more, and then trying more complex applications. I use Perl for a text mining class I teach at Central Connecticut State University, and the students generally like the language. Hence, even if you are unfamiliar with it, you are likely to enjoy applying it to analyzing texts.

Organization of This Book

After an overview of this book in chapter 1, chapter 2 covers regular expressions in detail. This methodology is quite powerful and useful, and the time spent learning it pays off in the later chapters. Chapter 3 covers the data structures of Perl. Often a large number of linguistic items are considered all at once, and to work with all of them requires knowing how to use arrays and hashes as well as more complex data structures.

With the basics of Perl in hand, chapter 4 introduces probability. This lays the foundation for the more complex techniques in later chapters, but it also provides an opportunity to study some of the properties of language. For example, the distribution of the letters of the alphabet of a Poe story is analyzed in section 4.2.2.1.

Chapter 5 introduces the basics of vectors and arrays. These are put to good use as term-document matrices, which is a fundamental tool of information retrieval. Because it is possible to represent a text as a vector, the similarity of two texts can be measured by the angle between the two vectors representing the texts.

Corpus linguistics is the study of language using large samples of texts. Obviously this field of knowledge overlaps with text mining, and chapter 6 introduces the fundamental idea of creating a text concordance. This takes the text pattern matching ability of regular expressions, and allows a researcher to compare the matches in a variety of ways.

Text can be measured in numerous ways, which produces a data set that has many variables. Chapter 7 introduces the statistical technique of principal components analysis (PCA), which is one way to reduce a large set of variables to a smaller, hopefully easier to interpret, set. PCA is a popular tool among researchers, and this chapter teaches you the basic idea of how it works.

Given a set of texts, it is often useful to find out if these can be split into groups such that (1) each group has texts that are similar to each other and (2) texts from two different groups are dissimilar. This is called clustering. A related technique is to classify texts into existing categories, which is called classification. These topics are introduced in chapter 8.

Chapter 9 has three shorter sections, each of which discusses an idea that did not fit in one of the other chapters. Each of these is illustrated with an example, and each one has ties to earlier work in this book.

Finally, the first appendix gives an overview of the basics of Perl, while the second appendix lists the R commands used at the end of chapter 5 as well as chapters 7 and 8. R is a statistical software package that is also available for free from the Web. This book uses it for some examples, and references for documentation and tutorials are given so that an interested reader can learn more about it.

ROGER BILISOLY

New Britain, Connecticut
May 2008

Acknowledgments

Thanks to the Department of Mathematical Sciences of Central Connecticut State University (CCSU) for an environment that provided me the time and resources to write this book. Thanks to Dr. Daniel Larose, Director of the Data Mining Program at CCSU, for encouraging me to develop Stat 527, an introductory course on text mining. He also first suggested that I write a data mining book, which eventually became this text.

Some of the ideas in chapters 2, 3, and 5 arose as I developed and taught text mining examples for Stat 527. Thanks to Kathy Albers, Judy Spomer, and Don Wedding for taking independent studies on text mining, which helped to develop this class. Thanks again to Judy Spomer for comments on a draft of chapter 2.

Thanks to Gary Buckles and Gina Patacca for their hospitality over the years. In particular, my visits to The Ohio State University's libraries would have been much less enjoyable if not for them.

Thanks to Dr. Edward Force for reading the section on text mining German. Thanks to Dr. Krishna Saha for reading over my R code and giving suggestions for improvement. Thanks to Dr. Nell Smith and David LaPierre for reading the entire manuscript and making valuable suggestions on it.

Thanks to Paul Petralia, senior editor at Wiley Interscience who let me write the book that I wanted to write.

The notation and figures in my section 4.6.1 are based on section 1.1 and figure 1.1 of *Word Fequency Distributions* by R. Harald Baayen, which is volume 18 of the "Text, Speech and Language Technology" series, published in 2001. This is possible with the kind permission of Springer Science and Business Media as well as the author himself.

Thanks to everyone who has contributed their time and effort in creating the wonderful assortment of public domain texts on the Web. Thanks to programmers everywhere who have contributed open-source software to the world.

I would never have gotten to where I am now without the support of my family. This book is dedicated to my parents who raised me to believe in following my interests wherever they may lead. To my cousins Phyllis and Phil whose challenges in 2007 made writing a book seem not so bad after all. In memory of Sam, who did not live to see his name in print. And thanks to the fun crowd at the West Virginia family reunions each year. See you this summer!

Finally, thanks to my wife for all the good times and for all the support in 2007 as I spent countless hours on the computer. Love you!

R. B.

CHAPTER 1

INTRODUCTION

1.1 OVERVIEW OF THIS BOOK

This is a practical book that introduces the key ideas of text mining. It assumes that you
have electronic texts to analyze and are willing to write programs using the programming
language Perl. Although programming takes effort, it allows a researcher to do exactly what
he or she wants to do. Interesting texts often have many idiosyncrasies that defy a software
package approach.

Numerous, detailed examples are given throughout this book that explain how to write
short programs to perform various text analyses. Most of these easily fit on one page, and
none are longer than two pages. In addition, it takes little skill to copy and run code shown
in this book, so even a novice programmer can get results quickly.

The first programs illustrating a new idea use only a line or two of text. However, most of
the programs in this book analyze works of literature, which include the 68 short stories of
Edgar Allan Poe, Charles Dickens's *A Christmas Carol*, Jack London's *The Call of the Wild*,
Mary Shelley's *Frankenstein*, and Johann Wolfgang von Goethe's *Die Leiden des jungen
Werthers*. All of these are in the public domain and are available from the Web for free.
Since all the software to write the programs is also free, you can reproduce all the analyses
of this book on your computer without any additional cost.

This book is built around the programming language Perl for several reasons. First,
Perl is free. There are no trial or student versions, and anyone with access to the Web
can download it as many times and on as many computers as desired. Second, Larry Wall
created Perl to excel in processing computer text files. In addition, he has a background in

linguistics, and this influenced the look and feel of this computer language. Third, there are numerous additions to Perl (called modules) that are also free to download and use. Many of these process or manipulate text. Fourth, Perl is popular and there are numerous online resources as well as books on how to program in Perl. To get the most out of this book, download Perl to your computer and, starting in chapter 2, try writing and running the programs listed in this book.

This book does not assume that you have used Perl before. If you have never written any program in any computer language, then obtaining a book that introduces programming with Perl is advised. If you have never worked with Perl before, then using the free online documentation on Perl is useful. See sections 2.8 and 3.9 for some Perl references.

Note that this book is not on Perl programming for its own sake. It is devoted to how to analyze text with Perl. Hence, some parts of Perl are ignored, while others are discussed in great detail. For example, process management is ignored, but regular expressions (a text pattern methodology) is extensively discussed in chapter 2.

As this book progresses, some mathematics is introduced as needed. However, it is kept to a minimum, for example, knowing how to count suffices for the first four chapters. Starting with chapter 5, more of it is used, but the focus is always on the analysis of text while minimizing the required mathematics.

As noted in the preface, there are three underlying ideas behind this book. First, much text mining is built upon counting and text pattern matching. Second, although language is complex, there is useful information gained by considering the simpler properties of it. Third, combining a computer's ability to follow instructions without tiring and a human's skill with language creates a powerful team that can discover interesting properties of text. Someday, computers may understand and use a natural language to communicate, but for the present, the above ideas are a profitable approach to text mining.

1.2 TEXT MINING AND RELATED FIELDS

The core goal of text mining is to extract useful information from one or more texts. However, many researchers from many fields have been doing this for a long time. Hence the ideas in this book come from several areas of research.

Chapters 2 through 8 each focus on one idea that is important in text mining. Each chapter has many examples of how to implement this in computer code, which is then used to analyze one or more texts. That is, the focus is on analyzing text with techniques that require little or modest knowledge of mathematics or statistics.

The sections below describe each chapter's highlights in terms of what useful information is produced by the programs in each chapter. This gives you an idea of what this book covers.

1.2.1 Chapter 2: Pattern Matching

To analyze text, language patterns must be detected. These include punctuation marks, characters, syllables, words, phrases, and so forth. Finding string patterns is so important that a pattern matching language has been developed, which is used in numerous programming languages and software applications. This language is called regular expressions.

Literally every chapter in this book relies on finding string patterns, and some tasks developed in this chapter demonstrate the power of regular expressions. However, many tasks that are easy for a human require attention to detail when they are made into programs.

For example, section 2.4 shows how to decompose Poe's short story, "The Tell-Tale Heart," into words. This is easy for someone who can read English, but dealing with hyphenated words, apostrophes, conventions of using single and double quotes, and so forth all require the programmer's attention.

Section 2.5 uses the skills gained in finding words to build a concordance program that is able to find and print all instances of a text pattern. The power of Perl is shown by the fact that the result, program 2.7, fits within one page (including comments and blank lines for readability).

Finally, a program for detecting sentences is written. This, too, is a key task, and one that is trickier than it might seem. This also serves as an excellent way to show several of the more advanced features of regular expressions as implemented in Perl. Consequently, this program is written more than once in order to illustrate several approaches. The results are programs 2.8 and 2.9, which are applied to Dickens's *A Christmas Carol*.

1.2.2   Chapter 3: Data Structures

Chapter 2 discusses text patterns, while chapter 3 shows how to record the results in a convenient fashion. This requires learning about how to store information using indices (either numerical or string).

The first application is to tally all the word lengths in Poe's "The Tell-Tale Heart," the results of which are shown in output 3.4. The second application is finding out how often each word in Dickens's *A Christmas Carol* appears. These results are graphed in figure 3.1, which shows a connection between word frequency and word rank.

Section 3.7.2 shows how to combine Perl with a public domain word list to solve certain types of word games, for example, finding potential words in an incomplete crossword puzzle. Here is a chance to impress your friends with your superior knowledge of lexemes.

Finally, the material in this chapter is used to compare the words in the two Poe stories, "Mesmeric Revelations" and "The Facts in the Case of M. Valdemar." The plots of these stories are quite similar, but is this reflected in the language used?

1.2.3   Chapter 4: Probability

Language has both structure and unpredictability. One way to model the latter is by using probability. This chapter introduces this topic using language for its examples, and the level of mathematics is kept to a minimum. For example, Dickens's *A Christmas Carol* and Poe's "The Black Cat" are used to show how to estimate letter probabilities (see output 4.2).

One way to quantify variability is with the standard deviation. This is illustrated by comparing the frequencies of the letter *e* in 68 of Poe's short stories, which is given in table 4.1, and plotted in figures 4.3 and 4.4.

Finally, Poe's "The Unparalleled Adventures of One Hans Pfaall" is used to show one way that text samples behave differently from simpler random models such as coin flipping. It turns out that it is hard to untangle the effect of sample size on the amount of variability in a text. This is graphically illustrated in figures 4.5, 4.6, and 4.7 in section 4.6.1.

1.2.4   Chapter 5: Information Retrieval

One major task in information retrieval is to find documents that are the most similar to a query. For instance, search engines do exactly this. However, queries are short strings of text, so even this application compares two texts: the query and a longer document. It turns out that these methods can be used to measure the similarity of two long texts.

The focus of this chapter is the comparison of the following four Poe short stories: "Hop Frog," "A Predicament," "The Facts in the Case of M. Valdemar," and "The Man of the Crowd." One way to quantify the similarity of any pair of stories is to represent each story as a vector. The more similar the stories, the smaller the angle between them. See output 5.2 for a table of these angles.

At first, it is surprising that geometry is one way to compare literary works. But as soon as a text is represented by a vector, and because vectors are geometric objects, it follows that geometry can be used in a literary analysis. Note that much of this chapter explains these geometric ideas in detail, and this discussion is kept as simple as possible so that it is easy to follow.

1.2.5   Chapter 6: Corpus Linguistics

Corpus linguistics is empirical: it studies language through the analysis of texts. At present, the largest of these are at a billion words (an average size paperback novel has about 100,000 words, so this is equivalent to approximately 10,000 novels). One simple but powerful technique is using a concordance program, which is created in chapter 2. This chapter adds sorting capabilities to it.

Even something as simple as examining word counts can show differences between texts. For example, table 6.2 shows differences in the following texts: a collection of business emails from Enron, Dickens's *A Christmas Carol*, London's *The Call of the Wild*, and Shelley's *Frankenstein*. Some of these differences arise from narrative structure.

One application of sorted concordance lines is comparing how words are used. For example, the word *body* in *The Call of the Wild* is used for live, active bodies, but in *Frankenstein* it is often used to denote a dead, lifeless body. See tables 6.4 and 6.5 for evidence of this.

Sorted concordance lines are also useful for studying word morphology (see section 6.4.3) and collocations (see section 6.5). An example of the latter is phrasal verbs (verbs that change their meaning with the addition of a word, for example, *throw* versus *throw up*), which is discussed in section 6.5.2.

1.2.6   Chapter 7: Multivariate Statistics

Chapter 4 introduces some useful, core ideas of probability, and this chapter builds on this foundation. First, the correlation between two variables is defined, and then the connection between correlations and angles is discussed, which links a key tool of information retrieval (discussed in chapter 5) and a key technique of statistics.

This leads to an introduction of a few essential tools from linear algebra, which is a field of mathematics that works with vectors and matrices, a topic introduced in chapter 5. With this background, the statistical technique of principal components analysis (PCA) is introduced and is used to analyze the pronoun use in 68 of Poe's short stories. See output 7.13 and the surrounding discussion for the conclusions drawn from this analysis.

This chapter is more technical than the earlier ones, but the few mathematical topics introduced are essential to understanding PCA, and all these are explained with concrete examples. The payoff is high because PCA is used by linguists and others to analyze many measurements of a text at once. Further evidence of this payoff is given by the references in section 7.6, which apply these techniques to specific texts.

1.2.7 Chapter 8: Clustering

Chapter 7 gives an example of a collection of texts, namely, all the short stories of Poe published in a certain edition of his works. One natural question to ask is whether or not they form groups. Literary critics often do this, for example, some of Poe's stories are considered early examples of detective fiction. The question is how a computer might find groups.

To group texts, a measure of similarity is needed, but many of these have been developed by researchers in information retrieval (the topic of chapter 5). One popular method uses the PCA technique introduced in chapter 7, which is applied to the 68 Poe short stories, and results are illustrated graphically. For example, see figures 8.6, 8.7 and 8.8.

Clustering is a popular technique in both statistics and data mining, and successes in these areas have made it popular in text mining as well. This chapter introduces just one of many approaches to clustering, which is explained with Poe's short stories, and the emphasis is on the application, not the theory. However, after reading this chapter, the reader is ready to tackle other works on the topic, some of which are listed in the section 8.4.

1.2.8 Chapter 9: Three Additional Topics

All books have to stop somewhere. Chapters 2 through 8 introduce a collection of key ideas in text mining, which are illustrated using literary texts. This chapter introduces three shorter topics.

First, Perl is popular in linguistics and text processing not just because of its regular expressions, but also because many programs already exist in Perl and are freely available online. Many of these exist as modules, which are groups of additional functions that are bundled together. Section 9.2 demonstrates some of these. For example, there is one that breaks text into sentences, a task also discussed in detail in chapter 2.

Second, this book focuses on texts in English, but any language expressed in electronic form is fair game. Section 9.3 compares Goethe's novel *Die Leiden des jungen Werthers* (written in German) with some of the analyses of English texts computed earlier in this book.

Third, one popular model of language in information retrieval is the so-called bag-of-words model, which ignores word order. Because word order does make a difference, how does one quantify this? Section 9.4 shows one statistical approach to answer this question. It analyzes the order that character names appear in Dickens's *A Christmas Carol* and London's *The Call of the Wild*.

1.3 ADVICE FOR READING THIS BOOK

As noted above, to get the most out of this book, download Perl to your computer. As you read the chapters, try writing and running the programs given in the text. Once a program runs, watching the computer print out results of an analysis is fun, so do not deprive yourself of this experience.

How to read this book depends on your background in programming. If you never used any computer language, then the subsequent chapters will require time and effort. In this case, buying one or more texts on how to program in Perl is helpful because when starting out, programming errors are hard to detect, so the more examples you see, the better. Although learning to program is difficult, it allows you to do exactly what you want to do, which is critical when dealing with something as complex as language.

If you have programmed in a computer language other than Perl, try reading this book with the help of the online documentation and tutorials. Because this book focuses on a subset of Perl that is most useful for text mining, there are commands and functions that you might want to use but are not discussed here.

If you already program in Perl, then peruse the listings in chapters 2 and 3 to see if there is anything that is new to you. These two chapters contain the core Perl knowledge needed for the rest of the book, and once this is learned, the other chapters are understandable.

After chapters 2 and 3, each chapter focuses on a topic of text mining. All the later chapters make use of these two chapters, so read or peruse these first. Although each of the later chapters has its own topic, these are the following interconnections. First, chapter 7 relies on chapters 4 and 5. Second, chapter 8 uses the idea of PCA introduced in chapter 7. Third, there are many examples of later chapters referring to the computer programs or output of earlier chapters, but these are listed by section to make them easy to check.

The Perl programs in this book are divided into *code samples* and *programs*. The former are often intermediate results or short pieces of code that are useful later. The latter are typically longer and perform a useful task. These are also boxed instead of ruled. The results of Perl programs are generally called *outputs*. These are also used for R programs since they are interactive.

Finally, I enjoy analyzing text and believe that programming in Perl is a great way to do it. My hope is that this book helps share my enjoyment to both students and researchers.

CHAPTER 2

TEXT PATTERNS

2.1 INTRODUCTION

Did you ever remember a certain passage in a book but forgot where it was? With the advent of electronic texts, this unpleasant experience has been replaced by the joy of using a search utility. Computers have limitations, but their ability to do what they are told without tiring is invaluable when it comes to combing through large electronic documents. Many of the more sophisticated techniques later in this book rely on an initial analysis that starts with one or more searches.

Before beginning with text patterns, consider the following question. Since humans are experts at understanding text, and, at present, computers are essentially illiterate, can a procedure as simple as a search really find something unexpected to a human? Yes, it can, and here is an example. Anyone fluent in English knows that *the* precedes its noun, so the following sentence is clearly ungrammatical.

$$\text{Dog the is hungry.} \tag{2.1}$$

Putting the *the* before the noun corrects the problem, so sentence 2.2 is correct.

$$\text{The dog is hungry.} \tag{2.2}$$

A systematically collected sample of text is called a *corpus* (its plural form is *corpora*), and large corpora have been collected to study language. For example, the *Cambridge International Corpus* has over 800 million words and is used in Cambridge University

Press language reference books [26]. Since a book has roughly 500 words on a page, this corresponds to roughly 1.6 million pages of text. In such a corpus, is it possible to find a noun followed by *the*? Our intuition suggests no, but such constructions do occur, and, in fact, they do not seem unusual when read. Try to think of an example before reading the next sentence.

$$\text{Dottie gave the small dog the large bone.} \qquad (2.3)$$

The only place *the* appears adjacent to a noun in sentence (2.3) is after the word *dog*. Once this construction is seen, it is clear how it works: *the small dog* is the indirect object (that is, the recipient of the action of giving), and *the large bone* is the direct object (that is, the object that is given.) So it is the direct object's *the* that happens to follow *dog*.

A new generation of English reference books have been created using corpora. For example, the *Longman Dictionary of American English* [74] uses the Longman Corpus of Spoken American English as well as the Longman Corpus of Written American English, and the *Cambridge Grammar of English* [26] is based on the Cambridge International Corpus. One way to study a corpus is to construct a concordance, where examples of a word along with the surrounding text are extracted. This is sometimes called a KWIC concordance, which stands for *Key Word In Context*. The results are then examined by humans to detect patterns of usage. This technique is useful, so much so that some concordances were made by hand before the age of computers, mostly for important texts such as religious works. We come back to this topic in section 2.5 as well as section 6.4.

This chapter introduces a powerful text pattern matching methodology called *regular expressions*. These patterns are often complex, which makes them difficult to do by hand, so we also learn the basics of programming using the computer language Perl. Many programming languages have regular expressions, but Perl's implementation is both powerful and easy to invoke. This chapter teaches both techniques in parallel, which allows the easy testing of sophisticated text patterns. By the end of this chapter we will know how to create both a concordance and a program that breaks text into its constituent sentences using Perl. Because different types of texts can vary so much in structure, the ability to create one's own programs enables a researcher to fine tune a program to the text or texts of interest. Learning how to program can be frustrating, so when you are struggling with some Perl code (and this will happen), remember that there is a concrete payoff.

2.2 REGULAR EXPRESSIONS

A text pattern is called a *regular expression*, often shortened to *regex*. We focus on regexes in this section and then learn how to use them in Perl programs starting in section 2.3. The notation we use for the regexes is the same as Perl's, which makes this transition easier.

2.2.1 First Regex: Finding the Word *Cat*

Suppose we want to find all the instances of the word *cat* in a long manuscript. This type of task is ideal for a computer since it never tires, never becomes bored. In Perl, text is found with regexes, and the simplest regex is just a sequence of characters to be found. These are placed between two forward slashes, which denotes the beginning and the end of the regex. That is, the forward slashes act as delimiters. So to find instances of *cat*, the following regex suggests itself.

```
/cat/
```

However, this matches all character strings containing the substring "cat," for example, *caterwaul*, *implicate*, or *scatter*. Clearly a more specific pattern is needed because /cat/ finds many words not of interest, that is, it produces many *false positives*.

If spaces are added before and after the word *cat*, then we have / cat /. Certainly this removes the false positives already noted, however, a new problem arises. For instance, *cat* in sentence (2.4) is **not** found.

Sherby looked all over but never found the cat.   (2.4)

At first this might seem mysterious: *cat* is at the end of the sentence. However, the string " *cat*." has a period after the *t*, not a blank, so / cat / does not match. Normal texts use punctuation marks, which pose no problems to humans, but computers are less insightful and require instructions on how to deal with these.

Since punctuation is the norm, it is useful to have a symbol that stands for a word boundary, a location such that one side of the boundary has an alphanumeric character and the other side does not, which is denoted in Perl as \b. Note that this stands for a location between two characters, not a character itself. Now the following regex no longer rejects strings such as "*cat*." or "*cat*,".

```
/\bcat\b/
```

Note that alphanumeric characters are precisely the characters *a-z* (that is, the letters *a* through *z*), *A-Z*, 0-9 and _. Hence the pattern /\bcat\b/ matches all of the following:

"cat." "cat," "cat?" "cat's" "-cat-"   (2.5)

but none of these:

"cat0" "9cat." "cat_" "implicate" "location"   (2.6)

In a typical text, a string such as "*cat0*" is unlikely to appear, so this regex matches most of the words that are desired. However, /\bcat\b/ does have one last problem. If *Cat* appears in a text, it does **not** match because regexes are case sensitive. This is easily solved: just add an i (which stands for case *insensitive*) after the second backslash as shown below.

```
/\bcat\b/i
```

This regex matches both "*cat*" and "*Cat*." Note that it also matches "*cAt*," "*cAT*," and so forth.

In English some types of words are inflected, for example, nouns often have singular and plural forms, and the latter are usually formed by adding the ending *-s* or *-es*. However, the pattern /\bcat\b/, thanks to the second \b, cannot match the plural form *cats*. If both singular and plural forms of this noun are desired, then there are several fixes. First, two separate regexes are possible: /\bcat\b/i and /\bcats\b/i.

Second, these can be combined into a single regex. The vertical line character is the logical operator *or*, also called *alternation*. So the following regex finds both forms of *cat*.

Regular Expression 2.1 A regex that finds the words *cat* and *cats*, regardless of case.

```
/\bcat\b|\bcats\b/i
```

Other regexes can work here, too. Alternatively, there is a more efficient way to search for the two words *cat* and *cats*, but it requires further knowledge of regexes. This is done in regular expression 2.3 in section 2.2.3.

2.2.2   Character Ranges and Finding Telephone Numbers

Initially, searching for the word *cat* seems simple, but it turns out that the regex that finally works requires a little thought. In particular, punctuation and plural forms must be considered. In general, regexes require fine tuning to the problem at hand. Whatever pattern is searched for, knowledge of the variety of forms this pattern might take is needed. Additionally, there are several ways to represent any particular pattern.

In this section we consider regexes for phone numbers. Again, this seems like a straightforward task, but the details require consideration of several cases. We begin with a brief introduction to telephone numbers (based on personal communications [19]).

For most countries in the world, an international call requires an International Direct Dialing (IDD) prefix, a country code, a city code, then the local number. To call long-distance within a country requires a National Direct Dialing (NDD) prefix, a city code, then a local number. However, the United States uses a different system, so the regexes considered below are not generalizable to most other countries. Moreover, because city and country codes can differ in length, and since different countries use differing ways to write local phone numbers, making a completely general international phone regex would require an enormous amount of work.

In the United States, the country code is 1, usually written +1; the NDD prefix is also 1; and the IDD prefix is 011. So when a person calls long-distance within the United States, the initial 1 is the NDD prefix, not the country code. Instead of a city code, the United States uses area codes (as does Canada and some Caribbean countries) plus the local number. So a typical long-distance phone number is 1-860-555-1212 (this is the information number for area code 860). However, many people write 860-555-1212 or (860) 555-1212 or (860)555-1212 or some other variant like 860.555.1212. Notice that all these forms are not what we really dial. The digits actually pressed are 18605551212, or if calling from a work phone, perhaps 918605551212, where the initial 9 is needed to call outside the company's phone system. Clearly, phone numbers are written in many ways, and there are more possibilities than discussed above (for instance, extensions, access codes for different long-distance companies, and so forth). So before constructing a regex for phone numbers, some thought on what forms are likely to appear is needed.

Suppose a company wants to test the long-distance phone numbers in a column of a spreadsheet to determine how well they conform to a list of formats. To work with these numbers, we can copy the column into a text file (or *flat* file), which is easily readable by a Perl program. Note that it is assumed below that each row has exactly one number. The goal is to check which numbers match the following formats: an initial optional 1, the three digits for the area code within parentheses, the next three digits (the exchange), and then the final four digits. In addition, spaces may or may not appear both before and after the area code. These forms are given in table 2.1, where d stands for a digit. Knowing these, below we design a regex to find them.

To create the desired regex, we must specify patterns such as three digits in a row. A range of characters is specified by enclosing them in square brackets, so one way to specify a digit is [0123456789], which is abbreviated by [0-9] or \d in Perl.

To specify a range of the number of replications of a character, the symbol {m,n} is used, which means that the character must appear at least m times, and at most n times

Table 2.1　Telephone number formats we wish to find with a regex. Here d stands for a digit 0 through 9.

```
1 (ddd) ddd-dddd
1(ddd) ddd-dddd
1(ddd)ddd-dddd
(ddd) ddd-dddd
(ddd)ddd-dddd
```

(so $m \leq n$). The symbol $\{m,m\}$ is abbreviated by $\{m\}$. Hence \d{3} or [0-9]{3} or [0123456789]{3,3} specifies a sequence of exactly three digits. Note that $\{m,\}$ means m or more repetitions. Because some repetitions are common, there are other abbreviations used in regexes, for example, $\{0,1\}$ is denoted ? and is used below.

Finally, parentheses are used to identify substrings of strings that match the regex, so they have a special meaning. Hence the following regex is interpreted as a group of three digits, not as three digits in parentheses.

/(\d{3})/

To use characters that have special meaning to regexes, they must be escaped, that is, a backslash needs to precede them. This informs Perl to consider them as characters, not as their usual meaning. So to detect parentheses, the following works.

/\(\d{3}\)/

Now we have the tools to specify a pattern for the long-distance phone numbers. The regex below finds them, assuming they are in the forms given in table 2.1.

/(1 ?)?\(\d{3}\) ?\d{3}-\d{4}/

This regex is complicated, so let us take it apart to convince ourselves that it is matching what is claimed. First, "1 ?" means either "1 " or "1", since ? means zero or one occurrence of the character immediately before it. So (1 ?)? means that the pattern inside the parentheses appears zero or one time. That is, either "1 " or "1" appears zero or one time. This allows for the presence or absence of the NDD prefix in the phone number. Second, there is the area code in parentheses, which must be escaped to prevent the regex as interpreting these as a group. So the area code is matched by \(\d{3}\). The space between the area code and the exchange is optional, which is denoted by " ?", that is, zero or one space. The last seven digits split into groups of three and four separated by a dash, which is denoted by \d{3}-\d{4}.

Unfortunately, this regex matches some unexpected patterns. For instance, it matches (ddd) ddd-ddddd and (ddd) ddd-dddd-ddd. Why is this true? Both these strings contain the substring (ddd) ddd-dddd, which matches the above regex. For example, the pattern (ddd) ddd-ddddd matches by ignoring the last digit. That is, although the pattern -\d{4} matches only if there are four digits in the text after the dash, there are no restrictions on what can come after the fourth digit, so any character is allowed, even more digits. One way to rule this behavior out is by specifying that each number is on its own line.

Fortunately, Perl has special characters to denote the start and end of a line of text. Like the symbol \b, which denotes not a character but the location between two characters, the symbol ^ denotes the start of a new line, and this is called a *caret*. In a computer, text is actually one long string of characters, and lines of text are created by newline characters, which is the computer analog for the carriage return for an old-fashioned typewriter. So ^ denotes the location such that a newline character precedes it. Similarly, the $ denotes the end of a line of text, or the position such that the character just after it is a newline. Both ^ and $ are called *anchors*, which are symbols that denote positions, not literal characters. With this discussion in mind, regular expression 2.2 suggests itself.

Regular Expression 2.2 A regex for testing long-distance telephone numbers.

```
/^(1 ?)?\(\d{3}\) ?\d{3}-\d{4}$/
```

Often it is quite hard to find a regex that matches precisely the pattern one wants and no others. However, in practice, one only needs a regex that finds the patterns one wants, and if other patterns can match, but do not appear in the text, it does not matter. If one gets too many false positives, then further fine-tuning is needed.

Finally, note there is a second use of the caret, which occurs inside the square brackets. When used this way, it means the negation of the characters that follow. For example, [^abc] means all characters other than the lowercase versions of *a*, *b*, and *c*. Problem 2.3 gives a few examples (but it assumes knowledge of material later in this chapter).

We have seen that although identifying a phone number is straightforward to a human, there are several issues that arise when constructing a regex for it. Moreover, regex 2.2 is complex enough that it might have a mistake. What is needed is a way to test regexes against some text. In the next section we see how to use a simple Perl script to read in a text file line by line, each of which is compared with regex 2.2. To get the most out of this book, download Perl now (go to http://www.perl.org/ [45] and follow their instructions) and try running the programs yourself.

2.2.3 Testing Regexes with Perl

Many computer languages support regexes, so why use Perl? First, Perl makes it easy to read in a text document piece by piece. Second, regexes are well integrated into the language. For example, almost any computer language supports addition in the usual form 3+5 instead of a function call like plus(3,5). In Perl, regexes can be used like the first form, which enables the programmer to employ them throughout the program. Third, it is free. If you have access to the Internet, you can have the complete, full-feature version of Perl right now, on as many computers as you wish. Fourth, there is an active Perl community that has produced numerous sources of help, from Web tutorials to books on how to use it.

Other authors feel the same way. For example, Friedl's *Mastering Regular Expressions* [47] covers regexes in general. The later chapters discuss regex implementation in several programming languages. Chapter 2 gives introductory examples of regexes, and of all the programming languages used in this book, the author uses Perl because it makes it easy to show what regexes can do.

This book focuses on text, not Perl, so if the latter catches your interest, there are numerous books devoted to learning Perl. For example, two introductory texts are Lemay's *Sams Teach Yourself Perl in 21 Days* [71] and Schwartz, Phoenix, and Foy's *Learning Perl* [109]. Another introductory book that should appeal to readers of this book is Hammond's *Programming for Linguists* [51].

To get the most out of this book, however, download Perl to your computer (instructions are at http://www.perl.org/ [45]) and try writing and running the programs that are discussed in the text. To learn how to program requires hands-on experience, and reading about text mining is not nearly as fun as doing it yourself.

For our first Perl program, we write a script that reads in a text file and matches each line to regular expression 2.2 in the previous section. This is one way to test the regex for mistakes. Conceptually, the task is easy. First, open a file for Perl to read. Second, loop through the file line by line. Third, try to match each line with the regex, and fourth, print out the lines that match. This program is an effective regex testing tool, and, fortunately, it is not hard to write.

Program 2.1 performs the above steps. To try this script yourself, type the commands into a file with the suffix .pl, for example, call it test_regex.pl. Perl is case sensitive, so do **not** change from lower to uppercase or the reverse. Once Perl is installed on your computer, you need to find out how to use your computer's command line interface, which allows the typing of commands for execution by pressing the enter key. Once you do this, type the statement below on the command line and then press the enter key. The output will appear below it.

```
perl test_regex.pl
```

```
open(FILE, "testfile.txt");
while (<FILE>) {
  if ( /^(1 ?)?\(\d{3}\) ?\d{3}-\d{4}$/ ) {
    print;
  }
}
```

Program 2.1 Perl script for testing regular expression 2.2.

Semicolons mark the end of statements, so it is critical to use the them correctly. A programmer can put several statements on one line (each with its own semicolon), or write one statement over several lines. However, it is common to use one statement per line, which is usually the case in this book. Finally, as claimed, the code is quite short, and the only complex part is the regex itself. Let us consider program 2.1 line by line.

First, to read a file, the Perl program needs to know where the file is located. Program 2.1 looks in the same directory where the program itself is stored. If the file "testfile.txt" were in another directory, the full path name is required, for example, "c:/dirname/testfile.txt". The open statement is a function that acts on two values, called *arguments*. The first argument is a name, called a *filehandle*, that refers to the file, the name of which is the second argument. In this example, FILE is the filehandle of "testfile.txt", which is read in by the while loop.

Second, the while loop reads the contents of the file designated by FILE. Its structure is as follows.

Code Sample 2.1 Form of a while loop.

```
while (<FILE>) { # commands }
```

The angle brackets around FILE indicate that each iteration returns a piece of FILE. The default is to read it line by line, but there are other possibilities, for example, reading paragraph by paragraph, or reading the entire file at once. The curly brackets delimit all the commands that are executed by the while loop. That is, for each line of the file, the commands in the curly brackets are executed, and such a group of commands is called a *block*. Note that program 2.1 has only an if statement within the curly brackets of the while loop. Finally, the # symbol in Perl denotes that the rest of the line is a comment, which allows a programmer to put remarks in the code, and these are ignored by Perl. This symbol is called a *number sign* or sometimes a *hash* (or even an *octothorp*). Hence code sample 2.1 is valid Perl code, although nothing is done as it stands.

Third, the if statement in program 2.1 tests each line of the file designated by FILE against the regex that is in the parentheses, which is regular expression 2.2. Note that these parentheses are required: leaving them out produces a syntax error. If the line matches the regex, then the commands in the curly brackets are executed, which is only the print statement in this case.

Finally, the print prints out the value of the current line of text from FILE. This can print out other strings, too, but the default is the current value of a variable denoted by $_, which is Perl's generic default variable. That is, if a function is evaluated, and its argument is not given, then the value of $_ is used. In program 2.1, each line read by the while loop is automatically assigned to $_. Hence the statement print; is equivalent to the following.

```
print "$_";
```

Assuming that Perl has been installed in your computer, you can run program 2.1 by putting its commands into a file, and save this file under a name ending in .pl, for example, test_regex.pl. Then create a text file called testfile.txt containing phone numbers to test against regular expression 2.2. Remember that this regex assumes that each line has exactly one potential phone number. Suppose that table 2.2 is typed into testfile.txt. On the command line enter the following, which produces output 2.1 on your computer screen.

```
perl test_regex.pl
```

Table 2.2   Telephone number input to test regular expression 2.2.

(000) 000-0000
(000)000-0000
000-000-0000
(000)0000-000
1-000-000-0000
1(000)000-0000
1(000) 000-0000
1 (000)000-0000
1 (000) 000-0000
(0000)000-0000
(000)0000-0000
(000)000-00000

Output 2.1 Output from the program `test_regex.pl` using table 2.2 as input.

```
(000) 000-0000
(000)000-0000
1(000)000-000
1(000) 000-0000
1 (000)000-0000
1 (000) 000-0000
```

Regular expression 2.2 is able to find all the forms in table 2.1. It also matches the pattern 1 `(ddd)ddd-dddd`, which is not in table 2.1, but it is a reasonable way to write a phone number.

Program 2.1 prints out the matches, but it is also informative to see what strings do not match the regex. This can be done by putting the logical operator `not` in front of the regex. See problem 2.2 for more on this.

Returning to old business in section 2.2.1, we can now simplify regular expression 2.1 as promised. Instead of using the vertical bar (which denotes the logical operator `or`), we can use the zero or one symbol (denoted by a question mark. This is shown in regular expression 2.3. It turns out that this regex is more efficient than the original version. Instead of checking for both *cat* and *cats* independently, now the regex just checks for *cat* and when this is found, it checks for an optional *s* character.

Regular Expression 2.3 Another regex that finds the words *cat* and *cats*.

```
/\bcats?\b/i
```

2.3 FINDING WORDS IN A TEXT

In the last section we saw that a little Perl is useful. This section starts with a review of regexes that we covered so far. Then we consider the task of identifying the words of a text, and our eventual goal is to write a Perl script that finds and prints these words without punctuation. That is, the words in a text are *segmented*, and this is often the initial step in more complicated analyses, so it is useful later in this book.

2.3.1 Regex Summary

Table 2.3 summarizes parts of regexes already seen as well as a few additional, related patterns. Remember that regexes search for substrings contained in a string that match the pattern. For example, \d stands for a single digit, so as long as there is one digit somewhere in the string, there is a match. Hence "The US NDD prefix is 1." matches \d since there is a digit in that string. What the string is depends on how the Perl code is set up. For example, in program 2.1, each line of the input file is the string. If a pattern runs across two different lines of the input file, then it does **not** match the regex. However, there are ways to deal with multiple lines of text at one time, one of which is discussed in table 2.5 in section 2.5.

Recall that $\{0,1\}$ is denoted ?, and we see that $\{1,\}$ is denoted + and $\{0,\}$ is denoted *, where $\{m,n\}$ stands for at least m repetitions and at most n repetitions. Also remember

Table 2.3   Summary of some of the special characters used by regular expressions with examples of strings that match.

Regex	Description	Example of a Match
/cat/	Specified substring	"cat" or "scatter"
/[BT]erry/	Choice of characters in [ ]	"Berry" or "Terry"
/cat|dog/	| means or	"cats" or "boondoggle"
/\d/	Short for [0123456789] or [0-9]	"1963" or "(860)"
/\D/	Not \d, i.e., [^0-9]	"(860)" or "Lucy"
/\w/	Alphanumeric: [0-9a-zA-Z_]	"Daisy!" or "Pete??"
/\W/	[^0-9a-zA-Z_]	"Dog!" or "Taffy??"
/\s/	Whitespace: space, tab, newline	"Hello, Hattie"
/\S/	Not whitespace	"Hello, Wally"
/\b/	Word boundary	"Dave!" or "Pam's"
/\B/	Not a word boundary	"Brownie" or "Annie's"
/./	Any character	Any nonempty string
/^Cat/	^ denotes the start of a string	"Catastrophic"
/Cat$/	$ denotes the end of a string	"The Cat"
/cats?/	? matches 0 or 1 occurrences	"scat" or "scats"
/Gary's+/	+ matches 1 or more occurrences	"Gary's" or "Gary'sss"
/Gina's*/	* matches 0 or more occurrences	"Gina'" or "Gina'sss"
/cat(cat)?/	( ) denotes grouping	"ssscat" or "catcatty"

that unless surrounding characters are explicitly specified, the restrictions of {m,n} are seemingly broken. For example, /\d{3}/ matches both "000" and "0000." However, /-\d{3}-/ matches "-000-" but not "-0000-." The latter regex demands a pattern of a hyphen, then exactly three digits, then another hyphen, while the former regex only looks for a substring of three digits, which can be found in a string of four digits. Finally, note that the caret inside square brackets signifies negation, so [^0-9] (also denoted by \D) means any character except a digit. However, the caret outside the brackets means the start of a string (see problem 2.3 for further examples of how to use a caret). Problem 2.4 has further regex examples.

   In the discussion of phone numbers, it is seen that parentheses have special meaning to a regex. Specifically, parentheses specify subpatterns. For example, (1 ?)? in regular expression 2.2 means that the substring (1 ?) is subject to the second ?. That is, the parentheses designate (1 ?) as a unit, and the second ? says that this unit appears zero or one time. It turns out that parentheses do more than specify parts: they also store whatever matches each part into match variables that are available for later use in the program (see section 2.3.4).

   As already noted, to match against a range of characters, square brackets are used. For example, lowercase letters are represented by [a-z]. However, certain characters have special meanings in regexes, for example, the question mark means zero or one instance of the preceding character. To match a literal question mark in a text, one has to use an escaped version , which is done by placing a backslash in front of the question mark as follows: \?. However, to include this character in a range of values, the escaped version is **not** needed, so [?!] means either a question mark or an exclamation point. Conversely, a hyphen is a special symbol in a range, so [a-z] means only the lowercase letters and does not match the hyphen. To include a hyphen in the square brackets, just put it first (or last), so [-a] matches either the letter *a* or a hyphen. However, the hyphen has no special meaning elsewhere in a regex. For example, /\d{3}-\d{4}/ matches a U.S.-style seven-digit phone number.

We have now seen the basic components of regexes: parentheses for grouping; {m,n} for repetition; characters and anchors; and | for alternation. These, however, do not have equal weight in Perl. In fact, Perl considers these in the order just given. That is, grouping is considered first, repetition second, characters and anchors third, and alternation last. For example, a|b+ means either the letter a or one or more copies of the letter b. So + is considered first, and only then |. This ordering is called the *precedence* of these regex components.

2.3.2 Nineteenth-Century Literature

A general, all-purpose regex would be great to have, but, in practice, different types of texts vary too much. For example, compared to formal business letters, a file of emails has many more abbreviations, misspellings, slang words, jargon, and odd symbols like smiley faces. What might work for analyzing business letters probably fails for emails, and vice versa. However, even documents from the same source sometimes have systematic differences. In text mining it always pays to examine the texts at the beginning of a project.

To test the word regexes that we develop below, we use literary texts. These have several advantages. First, literature comes in a variety of lengths, from short stories to novels. Second, if older texts are used, for instance, nineteenth-century literature, then public domain versions are often available from the Web. It is true that these versions may not be definitive, but they are certainly satisfactory for testing out text mining techniques. For this task of segmenting words, the short stories of Edgar Allan Poe are used. These stories are generally short and put all together still fit in one book. Plus Poe wrote in a variety of styles: although he is most famous for his horror stories (or as he called them, *Tales of the Grotesque and Arabesque*), he also wrote detective stories, early science fiction, and parodies of other genres. Finally, some of his fiction has unusual words in it. For example, Poe is fond of quoting foreign languages, and several of his stories have dialog with people using heavy dialects. With the goal of segmenting words for motivation, we need to learn a few more Perl tools to test our regexes.

2.3.3 Perl Variables and the Function split

Program 2.1 assumes that a line of text contains just one phone number and nothing more. A file with a Poe short story has many words per line, and so a way to break this into words is needed. However, the spaces in text naturally break a line into substrings, and Perl has a function called split that does this. The results require storage, and using variables and arrays are an effective way to do this, which is the next topic.

Programming languages use variables to store results. In Perl, *scalar* variables (variables that contain a single value) **always** start with a dollar sign. Consider the following statement.

```
$x = "They named their cat Charlie Brown.";
```

Perl stores this sentence in the variable $x. Later in the code $x is available for use or modification. We are interested in taking a line of text and breaking it into substrings that are potential words. These are tested against a regex, and the substrings that match the regex are labeled as words, and the nonmatches are declared nonwords. The initial substrings are stored in variables so that they can be later tested against the regex. One complication, however, is that the number of words per line of text varies, and it is not known beforehand. This requires the ability to store a variable number of substrings, which is easily done with arrays.

An *array* is an ordered collection of variables with a common name that starts with an @ character. Each variable in an array is indexed by the nonnegative numbers 0, 1, 2, ... Code sample 2.2 gives an example. Since the text "The sun is rising." has three blanks, it splits into four substrings, and "The" is stored in $word[0], "sun" in $word[1], "is" in $word[2], and "rising." in $word[3]. The array @word refers to this collection of four variables as a single unit. One convenient feature of Perl is that the programmer does not need to specify how big the array is beforehand. So the output of the function split can be stored in an array despite that the number of substrings produced is unknown beforehand.

Code Sample 2.2 An example of an array as well as string interpolation.

```
$line = "The sun is rising.";
@word = split(/ /,$line);
print "$word[0],$word[1],$word[2],$word[3]";
```

The first line of code sample 2.2 stores the string in the variable $line. The function split in the second line has two arguments: a regex and a string for splitting into pieces. In this case, the regex is a blank between two forward slashes, which splits at every place where there is a single space. The string for splitting is the second argument, which is $line. Finally, the print statement shows the results. Because the string in the print statement has double quotes, each variable in the this string is replaced by its value. That is, $word[0] is replaced by its value, as is true for the other three. In Perl, scalar variables in strings with double quotes are replaced by their values, which is called *interpolation*. Note that this does not happen for strings in single quotes.

The regex / / in the function split is not flexible: it only splits on exactly one space. If the text has two spaces instead of one between words, this causes an unexpected result which is seen by running code sample 2.3, and the results are output 2.2.

Code Sample 2.3 Note what happens to the double space between the words *The* and *sun*.

```
$line = "The  sun is rising.";
@word = split(/ /,$line);
print "$word[0],$word[1],$word[2],$word[3]";
```

Output 2.2 Output for code sample 2.3.

```
The,,sun,is
```

When split on / /, the double space is split so that the first piece is "The", the second piece is "" (the empty string), and the third piece is "sun", and so forth. This empty string produces the two commas in a row in the output. One way to fix this behavior is by changing the regex in the function split to match all the whitespace between words, as is done in code sample 2.4.

Code Sample 2.4 Now the double space is treated as a unit, unlike code sample 2.3.

```
$line = "The  sun is rising.";
@word = split(/\s+/,$line);
print "$word[0],$word[1],$word[2],$word[3]\n";
```

Recall from table 2.3 that \s stands for whitespace (space, tab, or newline) and the + means one or more of the preceding character, which is one or more whitespace characters in this case. Running this code produces output 2.3, which is what we expect.

Output 2.3 Output for code sample 2.4.

```
The,sun,is,rising.
```

Now that we can break a line of text into substrings and store these in an array, these substrings are tested against a regex. In program 2.1, the if statement has the following form.

```
if ( /$regex/ ) { # commands }
```

Although no variable is explicitly mentioned, Perl understands that the default variable, denoted $_, is compared with $regex, which contains a string denoting a regex. This is another example of Perl interpolation: the contents of this variable is used as the regex. One can use other variables with the following syntax.

```
if ( $x =~ /$regex/ ) { # commands }
```

Now the variable $x, not $_ is compared with the regex. Note that $_ can be written out explicitly instead of suppressing it, so the following is valid syntax.

```
if ( $_ =~ /$regex/ ) { # commands }
```

When testing a regex, it is useful to examine which strings match and which do not match the regex. Using an if-else construction is one way to do this, so if the regex matches, one set of commands is executed, and if there is no match, then another set is executed. The form is given in code sample 2.5.

Code Sample 2.5 The structure of an if statement.

```
if ( $x =~ /$regex/ ) {
   # commands for a match
} else {
   # commands for no match
}
```

Now we can split a line of text as well as test a variable against a regex. However, splitting text produces an array, not just one variable, so we need to test each component of the array. Just as the while loop can access the lines of a file, the foreach loop can access the values of an array by using the following syntax.

Code Sample 2.6 The structure of a `foreach` loop.

```
foreach $x (@word) {
  # commands
}
```

```
$line = "The  sun is rising.";
@word = split(/\s+/, $line);
foreach $x (@word) {
  if ( $x =~ /\w+/ ) {
    print "$x matches; ";
  } else {
    print "$x does not match; ";
  }
}
```

Program 2.2 Code for reading a string a word at a time.

Here the variable `$x` takes on each value of the array `@word`. The commands in the curly brackets then can use these `$x` values. For example, compare each one against a regex.

Let us put together the individual parts just discussed to create program 2.2. Here the `split` function splits on one or more whitespace characters, and the regex in the `if` statement matches strings having one or more alphanumeric characters. So there are four matches, as expected. Note that the semicolons inside the double quotes are characters, not Perl end-of-the-line delimiters. The output is as follows.

```
The matches; sun matches; is matches; rising. matches;
```

Finally, it is sometimes useful to undo `split`, and Perl has a function to do this called `join`. Code sample 2.7 has a short example, and it prints out the same sentence that is in `$line1`, except that the double space is replaced by a single space. Note that the first argument can be any string. For example, using the string `' + '` produces `The + sun + is + rising`.

Code Sample 2.7 The function `join` undoes the results of the function `split`.

```
$line1 = "The  sun is rising.";
@word = split(/\s+/, $line1);
$line2 = join(' ', @word);
print "$line2";
```

In the next section we learn how to access the substring that matches a regex. For example, in program 2.2 we do not know which characters actually do match `/\w+/`.

2.3.4 Match Variables

The content of parentheses in a regex is a unit. However, parentheses also store the substring that matches this unit in a variable. These are called *match* variables, and they are written

$1, $2, and so forth. The first, $1, matches the first set of parentheses, $2 matches the second set of parentheses, and so forth.

Using a match variable we can modify program 2.2 by adding parentheses to \w+. Now the part of the string that matches this is stored in the match variable $1, and this is a substring composed completely of alphanumeric characters. In particular, it does not match punctuation, so this seems like a promising regex for extracting words from a text. Let us try it out in the script below.

```
$line = "The  sun is rising.";
@word = split(/\s+/, $line);
foreach $x (@word) {
  if ( $x =~ /(\w+)/ ) {
    print "$1 ";
  }
}
```

Program 2.3 Code for removing nonalphanumeric characters.

```
The sun is rising
```

Program 2.3 produces the above output. Indeed, the period has been removed. If this code is placed into a while loop that goes through a file line by line, then we can see how well punctuation is removed for a longer text. Keep in mind that in text mining, promising initial solutions often have unexpected consequences, so we may need to patch up the regex used in program 2.3.

2.4 DECOMPOSING POE'S "THE TELL-TALE HEART" INTO WORDS

As noted earlier, public domain versions of Poe's short stories are available on the Web and are not hard to find using a search engine. Our goal here is to decompose "The Tell-Tale Heart" [94] into words. This task is called word *segmentation*. Program 2.3 suggests that this is not too hard, but there are many details to consider if we are to do this task well.

To extract words from text, punctuation must be removed. The discussion below covers the basics, but this is not the complete story. The following two references give more details and background on the grammar of English. First, section 506 of the *Cambridge Grammar of English* [26] gives a short synopsis of punctuation use. Second, section 4.2.2 of *Foundations of Statistical Natural Language Processing* [75] discusses some issues of the tokenization of a string into words.

Before discussing code, there are two more Perl functions that are useful here. Although text in files looks like it is stored in lines, in fact, it is stored as one long string of characters. The lines are created by the program displaying the text, which knows to put them in wherever a newline character exists. So the last word in a line ends with a newline character, which is not how humans think of the text. Therefore, it is useful to cut off this newline character, which is what the following command does.

```
chomp;
```

Note that this function has no explicit argument, which implies it is using the default variable of Perl, $_. In a while loop, each line read is automatically stored in $_, so chomp in a while loop cuts off the newline character at the end of each line.

The second function is die, which is often used to test for a failure in opening a file. In Perl, or is the logical operator of the same name, and it has a clever use in the following command.

```
open(FILE, "The Tell-Tale Heart.txt") or die("File not found");
```

If the file opens successfully, `open` returns the value `true` and `die` is not executed. If the file fails to open, then `die` runs, which halts Perl and prints out a warning that starts with the string in its argument, namely, "File not found." See problem 2.5 for why this happens.

Now let us consider a Perl script to remove punctuation from the short story "The Tell-Tale Heart." Note that this code assumes that the file `"The Tell-Tale Heart.txt"` exists in the same directory as the program itself, which if not true, then the name of the directory that contains the file requires specification, for example, `open(FILE, "C:/Poe/story.txt");`.

```
open (FILE, "The Tell-Tale Heart.txt") or die("File not found");

while (<FILE>) {
  chomp;
  @word = split(/\s+/);
  foreach $x (@word) {
    if ( $x =~ /(\w+)/ ) {
      print "$1 ";
    }
  }
}
```

Program 2.4 Code for extracting words.

Let us consider program 2.4 line by line. First, the `open` command makes FILE the filehandle for this short story, and the `die` command stops execution and prints a warning if the `open` command fails to work. Second, the `while` command loops through the story line by line. Third, `@word` is an array with one entry for each substring created by the `split` command, which splits on one or more whitespace characters. Note that `while` splits on newlines, so the `split` function only has spaces and tabs left for it.

With each line of text split into substrings, the `foreach` loop goes through each of these, which are stored in the variable `$x` in the body of the loop, that is, for the commands within the curly brackets. In this case, there is only one command, an `if` statement, which itself contains one command, a `print` statement. The `if` statement tests `$x` against the regex `/(\w+)/`, and the substring that matches is stored in the variable `$1`. For example, testing "dog." puts "dog" in `$1`, since only these characters are alphanumeric. Finally, `$1` is printed out, so that the output should have no punctuation.

If you obtain a copy of "The Tell-Tale Heart" and run program 2.4, the punctuation seems entirely removed at first glance. However, depending on the public domain version you choose, there are exceptions, five of which are shown in table 2.4. The first line should have the word *watch's*, but the apostrophe and the ending *-s* are both removed, which also happens in line 2. The hyphenated word *over-acuteness* is reduced to *over* in the third line, and *o'clock* is truncated to the letter *o* in the fourth. Finally, the last line has underscores since this character is included in `\w`, and it is commonly used to denote italics in electronic texts.

Hence, there is a major problem with program 2.4. The regex `/(\w+)/` matches all the alphanumeric characters of a word only if it has no internal punctuation. Otherwise, only the first group of contiguous alphanumeric characters are matched, and the rest is ignored, which happened in the first four lines of this table. So problems are caused by contractions, possessive nouns, and hyphenated words.

Table 2.4   Removing punctuation: a sample of five mistakes made by program 2.4.

A watch minute hand moves more quickly
Who there
madness is but over of the sense
it was four o still dark as midnight
I now grew _very_ pale

An additional problem not appearing in this version of "The Tell-Tale Heart" are dashes that are written as double hyphens such that they abut the words on either side of it. For example, this happens in sentence 2.7. Since punctuation does occur within words, let us consider the cases noted above one at a time.

$$\text{Cheryl saw Dave–he wore black–and she ran.} \tag{2.7}$$

2.4.1   Dashes and String Substitutions

Dashes are written in several ways. My version of "The Tell-Tale Heart" uses a single hyphen with one space on each side, that is, " - ". As long as the dash is written with spaces on each side of the dash, that is, " - " or " -- ", then splitting on whitespace never produces a word attached to a dash.

If there are no spaces between the adjacent words and the dash, then the form of the latter must be "--", otherwise a dash is indistinguishable from a hyphen. There are two ways to deal with this situation. First, if dashes are not of interest to the researcher, then these can be replaced with a single space. Second, if dashes are kept, then "--" can be replaced with " -- ".

Perl has string substitutions. For example, s/dog/cat/ replaces the first instance of the string "dog" with "cat". Note that the letter s stands for *substitution*. To replace every instance, just append the letter g, which stands for *global*. For example, see code sample 2.8, which produces the output below. Note that using s/--/ /g instead of s/--/ -- /g replaces each dash with a single space, thereby removing them altogether.

Code Sample 2.8 This adds spaces around the dashes in the string stored in the variable $line.

```
$line = "Cheryl saw Dave--he wore black--and she ran.";
$line =~ s/--/ -- /g;
print "$line\n";
```

```
Cheryl saw Dave -- he wore black -- and she ran.
```

So dashes are not hard to work with. Unfortunately, sometimes -- is used in other ways. For example, Poe sometimes wrote a year as "18--" in his short stories. But such special cases are detectable by regexes, and then a decision on what to do can be made by the researcher. For example, the following code finds all instances of "--", and notes the nonstandard uses, which means not having a letter or whitespace adjacent to the front and the back of the dash.

```
$line = "It was 18--, early April--some snow still lingered.";
@word = split(/\s+/, $line);
foreach $x (@word) {
  if ( $x =~ /--/ ) {
    if ( $x =~ /[a-zA-Z ]--[a-zA-Z ]/ ) {
      print "Standard dash: \"$x\" ";
    } else {
      print "Non-standard dash: \"$x\" ";
    }
  }
}
```

Program 2.5 Code to search for -- and to decide if it is between two words or not.

```
Non-standard dash: "18--," Standard dash: "April--some"
```

Program 2.5 produces the above output. The first dash is nonstandard since it has a number on its left, while the second dash is between two words, and so is standard. Looking at this Perl program, much of the syntax has already been introduced above. A string of text to test is stored in $line. The results of splitting on whitespace is stored in the array @word, and the foreach statement loops over the substrings stored in this array. The first if statement tests for any instance of --, while the second if tests if a space or a letter is both before and after the dash. If this is the case, then the first print statement is executed, otherwise the second one is. Finally, note that the print statements print out strings that contain a double quote, yet the strings themselves are delimited by them. To put one in a string, it must be escaped, that is, a backslash precedes the double quotes inside the string. Next we consider hyphens.

2.4.2 Hyphens

Hyphens are used in two distinct ways. First, many published works use justified typesetting; that is, the text is aligned on both its margins so that its width is constant. In order to do this, some words are broken into two pieces: the first ends a line of text and is followed by a hyphen, and the second starts the next line. However, for electronic texts, this is typically not done because the raw text can be entered into a word processing or typesetting program, which can convert it into justified text. For example, this book was originally written as a LaTeX text file, which includes typesetting commands.

Second, some words are hyphenated because they are built up from two or more words. For example, *mother-in-law*, *forty-two*, and *self-portrait* are written with hyphens. So, in practice, electronic text generally only uses hyphens for words that are themselves hyphenated.

Unfortunately, not everyone agrees on which words should be hyphenated. For example, is it *e-mail* or *email*? Both are used now (the latter is easier to type, so it should win out.) Moreover, three or more words are combinable. For example, *one-size-fits-all* is sometimes written with hyphens.

For many text mining applications, words are counted up as part of the analysis. Should we count a hyphenated word as one, or as more than one? Note that its components may or may not be words themselves. For example, *e-mail* is not a combination of two words. Even if the components are all words, their individual meanings can differ from the collective meaning. For example, *mother-in-law* is composed of *mother*, *in*, and *law*. However, the connotations of the noun *law* or the preposition *in* have little to do with the concept *mother-in-law*. Finally, a word like *once-in-a-lifetime* is roughly equivalent to its four constituent words. So there is no easy answer to whether a hyphenated word should be counted as one or several words. In this book, we take the former approach, which is simpler.

Hence, /(\w+)/ used in program 2.3 only matches up to the first hyphen. Because \w matches digits and underscores, specifying only letters with [a-zA-Z] is helpful. Since the hyphen is used to denote a range of characters, it must be first or last in the square brackets, for example, [a-zA-Z-]. So a first attempt at a regex is made by specifying exactly these characters, one or more times. Consider code sample 2.9, which produces the output below.

Code Sample 2.9 First attempt at a regex that finds words with hyphens.

```
$line = "Her sister-in-law came--today---and -it- is a-okay!";
@word = split(/\s+/, $line);
foreach $x (@word) {
  if ( $x =~ /([a-zA-Z-]+)/ ) {
    print "$1 ";
  }
}
```

```
Her sister-in-law came--today---and -it- is a-okay
```

This is not what we want. The dashes remain as well as three or more hyphens in a row, but both can be removed by the substitution in code sample 2.8.·

In addition, the hyphens of -it- require removal, but sister-in-law cannot be changed. This can be accomplished by thinking in terms of groups of characters. Hyphenated words start with one or more letters, then one hyphen, then one or more letters, perhaps another hyphen, then one or more letters, and so forth. To include words with no hyphens, make the first one optional. So the regex starts with ([a-zA-Z]+-?), which says that any word (hyphenated or not) must start with one or more letters followed by zero or one hyphen. Now if we specify that this pattern happens one or more times, which is done by adding a + after the parentheses, then this matches hyphenated words as well as regular words. Running code sample 2.10 produces the output below.

Code Sample 2.10 Second attempt at a regex that finds words with hyphens.

```
$line = "Her sister-in-law came--today---and -it- is a-okay!";
$line =~ s/--+/ /g;
@word = split(/\s+/, $line);
foreach $x (@word) {
  if ( $x =~ /(([a-zA-Z]+-?)+)/ ) {
    print "$1 ";
  }
}
```

```
Her sister-in-law came today and it- is a-okay
```

This almost works. The only problem is that it matches a group of letters ending in a hyphen, so −it− still ends in one in the output. This is easily fixed by specifying the last character as a letter. Code sample 2.11 does this, which produces the desired output below.

Code Sample 2.11 This code extracts words at least two letters long, including hyphenated ones.

```perl
$line = "Her sister-in-law came--today---and -it- is a-okay!";
$line =~ s/--+/ /g;
@word = split(/\s+/, $line);
foreach $x (@word) {
  if ( $x =~ /(([a-zA-Z]+-?)+[a-zA-Z])/ ) {
    print "$1 ";
  }
}
```

```
Her sister-in-law came today and it is a-okay
```

Although this test is successful, there is one problem with code sample 2.11. It won't match words that are exactly one letter long. This is an example of why testing is paramount: it is easy to make a change that fixes one problem only to discover that a new one arises. Upon reflection, this regex requires at least two letters because the part in the inner parentheses requires at least one letter, and the requirement of a final letter forces a potential match to have at least two. This is not hard to fix, and the solution is given in code sample 2.12. Note that the word *I* is matched in the output below.

Code Sample 2.12 This code extracts hyphenated and one-letter words.

```perl
$line = "Her sister-in-law came--today---and I -am- a-okay!";
$line =~ s/--+/ /g;
@word = split(/\s+/, $line);
foreach $x (@word) {
  if ( $x =~ /(([a-zA-Z]+-)*[a-zA-Z]+)/ ) {
    print "$1 ";
  }
}
```

```
Her sister-in-law came today and I am a-okay
```

Remember that ∗ means zero or more occurrences, so this regex matches zero or more groups of letters followed by exactly one hyphen, and which ends in one or more letters. This now matches one-letter words. Finally, suppose $line is set to the string "She received an A- on her paper." This regex now improves the grade. This is an example of the difficulties of writing for the general case instead of for a particular group of texts.

Our work, however, is not quite done. Now that we have considered both dashes and hyphens, we next discuss the apostrophe.

2.4.3 Apostrophes

Apostrophes are problematic because they serve more than one purpose. First, they are used to show possession, for example, *Gary's dog*. Second, they are also used for contractions, for example, *Gina's going home*. Third, they are used for quotation marks; see section 488 of [26]. In addition, quotes within quotations use the other type of quotation marks: for example, if double quotes are used for direct speech, then direct speech that quotes another person uses single quotes. An example of this is the following sentence.

$$\text{Katy said, "I thought he said, 'Sam,' but I was wrong."} \qquad (2.8)$$

Moreover, all three uses of the apostrophe are combinable. This is seen in the following example.

$$\text{Bart said, "I thought he said, 'That's Scoot's,' but I was wrong."} \qquad (2.9)$$

When processing sentence 2.9, unless care is taken, it is easy to match *'That'*, as the inner quotation. Although humans can easily use symbols in multiple ways depending on the context, this makes pattern matching more difficult for a computer.

Two further possible complications are worth noting. First, contractions can have an initial apostrophe, for example, *'twas*. And nouns ending in *-s* are made into a possessive noun by adding an apostrophe at the end of the word, for example, *my parents' cats*. If single quotes are used for direct speech, then these examples become harder to deal with.

For the short story "The Tell-Tale Heart," however, double quotes are used, and there are no quotes within direct speech. So all the single quotes are either contractions or possessive nouns. If the regex in code sample 2.12 has the single quote added to it, then using this new regex in program 2.4 extracts the words from this particular short story, which is done in program 2.6. However, putting the single quote in the range of characters also allows multiple single quotes in a row, which may or may not be desired.

```
open (FILE, "The Tell-Tale Heart.txt") or die("File not found");

while (<FILE>) {
  chomp;
  s/--/ -- /g;
  @word = split(/\s+/);
  foreach $x (@word) {
    if ( $x =~  /(([a-zA-Z']+-)*[a-zA-Z']+)/ ) {
      print "$1 ";
    }
  }
}
```

Program 2.6 Improved version of program 2.4 for extracting words.

Looking at the output of program 2.6, the problems in table 2.4 are corrected. Hence, *over-acuteness* appears, as do *watch's*, *Who's*, and *four o'clock*. Finally, *_very_* is changed to *very*. Therefore, this program works, at least for the input "The Tell-Tale Heart."

2.5   A SIMPLE CONCORDANCE

Sections 2.3 and 2.4 give us some tools to extract words from a text. We use these to create a concordance program in Perl. That is, we want to write code that finds a target word, and then extracts the same number of characters of text both before and after it. These extracts are then printed out one per line so that the target appears in the same location in each line. For example, output 2.4 shows four lines of output for the word *the* in Poe's "The Tell-Tale Heart," which is produced by program 2.7. This kind of listing allows a researcher to see which words are associated with a target word. In this case, since *the* is a determiner, a class of words that modify nouns, it is not surprising that *the* precedes nouns in this output.

Output 2.4 Four lines of concordance output for Poe's "The Tell-Tale Heart."

```
say that I am mad?  The disease had sharpen
hem.  Above all was the sense of hearing ac
heard all things in the heaven and in the e
n the heaven and in the earth.  I heard man
```

Conceptually, a concordance program is straightforward. When the first instance of the target word is found, its location is determined, and then the characters surrounding the target are printed out. Starting just after the target, the search continues until the next instance is found. This repeats until all instances are discovered.

We have already used regexes to find the target word. Here is a second approach. Perl has a function `index` that locates a substring within a string, and the function `substr` extracts a substring given its position. We first learn how these two functions work, and then apply them to the concordance program.

Code Sample 2.13 Example of the string function `index`.

```
$line = "He once lived in Coalton, West Virginia.";
$target = "lived";
$position = index($line, $target, 0);
print "The word \"$target\" is at position $position.";
```

For a first example, consider the code sample 2.13. Here `index` looks for the string in `$target` within `$line` starting at position 0 (given by the third argument), which is the beginning of `$line`. If this string is not found, then `$position` is assigned the value −1; otherwise the position of the start of the target string is returned. Running this code produces the following output.

Output 2.5 Results of code sample 2.13.

```
The word "lived" is at position 8.
```

Counting from the first letter of `$line` such that H is 0, e is 1, the blank is 2, and so forth, we do find that the letter l, the first letter of `lived`, is number 8.

Notice that `index` only finds the first instance after the starting position. To find the second instance, the starting position must be updated after the first match. Since the word lived is at position 8, then the following command finds the second instance of this word, if any.

```
$position = index($line, $target, 9);
```

If the value 8 is used instead, then $position is still 8 since the next instance of $target is, in fact, at that position. Updating the starting position is achievable as follows. Here old value of $position is used in the function index, and then it is updated to the result returned by index.

```
$position = index($line, $target, $position+1);
```

Code Sample 2.14 This searches for all instances of the target word *she*.

```
$line = "She was, she is, and she will be.";
$target = "she";
$position = index($line, $target, 0);
print "The word \"$target\" is at position(s): ";
while ($position > -1) {
  print "$position ";
  $position = index($line, $target, $position+1);
}
```

By repeatedly using this updating of $position, all instances of the target word are found by code sample 2.14. Running this produces the values 9 and 21, but not the value 0. However, the reason for this is simple: the first *she* is capitalized, and so it is not a match. Unfortunately, the function index does not take a regex for its argument, so we cannot find all the instances of *she* by putting the regex /she/i into $target. However, applying the function lc to the string in $line changes all the letters to lowercase. So replacing the third line in code sample 2.14 to the statement below and making the analogous change to the seventh line finds all three instances of *she*, regardless of case.

```
$position = index(lc($line), $target, 0);
```

The heart of code sample 2.14 is the while loop, which keeps going as long as $position is greater than −1. This is true as long as instances of the target word are found. Once this does not happen, index returns the value −1, which halts this loop. If the text has no instance of the target, then the value of $position before the while loop begins is −1, which prevents the loop from executing even once.

Finally, let us consider the function substr, which extracts substrings from text. It is easy to use: the first argument is the string, the second is the starting position, and the third is the length of the substring to be extracted. So the following line prints Nell.

```
print substr("I saw Nell on A level.", 6, 4);
```

Combining index and substr can produce a concordance program for a fixed string. However, regexes are more powerful, so we return to this approach using the ideas just discussed. Consider the following syntax.

```
while ( $var =~ /$target/g ) { # commands }
```

The letter g means to match globally, that is, all matches are found. Each one causes the commands in the curly brackets to execute once. However, how is the location of the match determined? Is there a function analogous to index for a regex? Yes, there is. Perl has pos, which returns the position of the character after the regex match. This is seen in code sample 2.15, which prints out the numbers 4 and 7. The former is the position of the space after the word *This*, which is the first occurrence of the letters *is*. The latter is the position of the space after the word *is*. These ideas are put into action in code sample 2.16.

Code Sample 2.15 An example of the pos function. When run, this code prints out the numbers 4 and 7.

```
$test = "This is a test.";
while ( $test =~ /is/g ) {
  $pos = pos($test);
  print "$pos ";
}
```

Code Sample 2.16 Core code for a concordance.

```
$line = "Cat, cat, cat, catastrophe.";
$target = "(cat)";

while ( $line =~ /$target/gi ) {
  $pos = pos($line);
  print "$1 $pos ";
}
```

The target word, *cat*, is made into a simple regex, and the parentheses store the matched text in $1. The variable $pos has the location of the character right after the matched text. The output has four matches as seen below.

```
Cat 3 cat 8 cat 13 cat 18
```

Note that the letter i after the regex makes the match case insensitive, hence the first *Cat* is matched. This also can be done in the regex, for example, using /[Cc]at/. As discussed above, finding the substring cat is necessary but not sufficient. For example, the word *catastrophe* has the substring cat, but it is not the word *cat*. However, since $target can have any regex, this is easily fixed. For example, the regex /\b[Cc]at\b/ rules out words that merely contain the letters *cat*. Similarly, the regex /\b[Cc]ats?\b/ finds both the word *cat* and its plural. This ability to find regexes as opposed to fixed strings makes it easy to match complex text patterns. Hence, while the function index is useful, the while loop in code sample 2.16 is much more flexible.

Up to now the text has been stored in the variable $line, which has been short. For a longer text like Poe's "The Tell-Tale Heart," it is natural to read it in with a while loop. However, the default is to read it line by line, which can prevent the concordance program from getting sufficient text surrounding the target. One way around this is to change the unit of text read in, for example, reading in the entire document at once. This is possible and is called the *slurp* mode. However, if the text is very long, this can slow the program down.

A compromise is to read in a text paragraph by paragraph. Many electronic texts use blank lines between paragraphs, and Perl knows this convention and can read in each paragraph if these are separated by blank lines. Changing the default only requires changing the value of the Perl variable $/. Table 2.5 gives some common values, but any string is possible.

Table 2.5   Some values of the Perl variable $/ and their effects.

$/ = undef;	Slurp mode
$/ = "";	Paragraph mode
$/ = "\n";	Line-by-line mode
$/ = " ";	Almost word-by-word mode

The reason that $/ set to a blank is not quite a word by word mode is that the last word of a line of text has a newline character after it, not a space. This combines the last word of a line with a newline character and then with the first word of the next line.

Now we have the tools to write program 2.7, which creates concordances. Remember that programming comments follow a #. It is good practice to comment your programs because it is surprisingly easy to forget the logic of your own code over time. If the program is used by others, then it is especially helpful to put in comments to explain how it works.

Program 2.7 builds on the discussions above on the index function and the trick of a while loop that iterates over all the matches of a regex. However, there are several additional points worth making. First, note that this program requests no input from the person running it, which restricts it to a concordance just for the "The Tell-Tale Heart" and for the target *the*. However, it is easy to modify <FILE> to refer to any other specific text file, and the target word can be any regex, not just a specific string. It is also straightforward to enable this code to accept arguments on the command line. This technique is discussed in section 2.5.1.

Second, note the use of parentheses in the string assigned to $target. This stores the matching substring in the Perl variable $1, which is then stored in $match. This is later used to ensure that the number of characters extracted before and after the matched substring have the precise length given in $radius. If no parentheses were used, then each line printed has exactly the number of characters in $width instead of length($target) + $width.

Third, the first while loop goes through the text paragraph by paragraph. For each of these paragraphs, the second while loop goes through each match found by the regex in $target. This is not the only way to go through the entire text, but it is one that is easy for a person to grasp.

Fourth, the if statement checks whether or not there are as many characters as $radius before the matched text. If not, then $start is negative, and spaces are added to the beginning of the concordance line, that is, to $extract. The operator x shown below creates a string of blanks that has length equal to the value of -$start.

```
" " x -\$start
```

However, this is not the only way to add spaces to $extract. The function sprintf creates a string with a specified format, which can be constructed by the program to make it the correct length. See problem 2.6 for more details.

Finally, running the program produces 150 lines of output, one for each *the* in "The Tell-Tale Heart." The first 10 lines of the output are displayed in output 2.6. Remember that the first 4 lines of this are displayed above in output 2.4.

```
open (FILE, "The Tell-Tale Heart.txt") or die("File not found");

$/ = ""; # Paragraph mode for first while loop

# Initialize variables
$target = '\b(the)\b';
$radius = 20;
$width = 2*$radius; # Width of extract without target

# First while loop
while (<FILE>) {
  chomp;
  s/\n/ /g; # Replace newlines by spaces
  s/--/ -- /g; # Add spaces around dashes

  # Second while loop
  while ( $_ =~ /$target/gi ) {
    $match = $1;
    $pos = pos($_);
    $start = $pos - $radius - length($match);

    if ($start < 0) {
      $extract = substr($_, 0, $width+$start+length($match));
      $extract = (" " x -$start) . $extract;
      $len = length($extract);
    } else {
      $extract = substr($_, $start, $width+length($match));
    }

    # Print the next concordance line
    print "$extract\n";
  }
}
```

Program 2.7 A regex concordance program.

Program 2.7, although it is short, it is powerful, especially because of its ability to match regular expressions. Although concordance programs already exist, we know exactly how this one works, and it is modifiable for different types of texts and tasks. For example, if a concordance for long-distance phone numbers were desired, then the work of section 2.2.3 provides a regex for this program. Then a document containing such numbers is analyzable to determine in what contexts these appear. This ability to adapt to new circumstances is one major payoff of knowing how to program, and when dealing with the immense variety and complexity of a natural language, such flexibility is often rewarded.

One drawback of program 2.7 is that to change the target regex, the code itself requires modification. Changing code always allows the possibility of introducing an error. So enabling the program to accept the regex as input is worth doing. We know how to open a

Output 2.6 First 10 lines of the output of program 2.7.

```
 say that I am mad? The  disease had sharpen
them. Above all was the  sense of hearing ac
heard all things in the  heaven and in the e
n the heaven and in the  earth. I heard many
lmly I can tell you the  whole story.
le to say how first the  idea entered my bra
e was none. I loved the  old man. He had nev
it was this! He had the  eye of a vulture -
up my mind to take the  life of the old man
to take the life of the  old man, and thus r
```

file so that its contents are read into the program, but for something short, this is overkill. The next section introduces an easy way to give a program a few pieces of information when it starts.

2.5.1 Command Line Arguments

Perl is run by using the command line. If text is placed after the name of the program, then there is a way to access this within the program. For instance, consider the following command.

```
perl program.pl dog cat
```

The two words after the program name are put into the array called @ARGV. The value of $ARGV[0] is dog, and $ARGV[1] is cat. Clearly this becomes tedious if many strings are needed, but it is quite useful for only a few values.

As an application, let us modify program 2.7 so that it expects three strings: a word to match, the size of the radius of the extract, and a file to open. For example, suppose all the instances of *and* in the file text.txt are desired along with the 30 characters before and after it. The modified version finds these by typing the following on the command line.

```
perl program.pl and 30 text.txt
```

This is easy to do. In program 2.7, remove all the code before the first while loop and replace it with code sample 2.17. One point to note: the definition of $target requires two backslashes before the b since a single backslash is interpreted as the word boundary, \b. That is, the backslash must be escaped by adding another backslash. Note that the use of single quotes does not require escaping the backslash, but then $ARGV[0] would not be interpolated.

This is enough for now on extracting words, but this task is essential since it is typically the first step of many text mining tasks. An implementation of command line arguments for a regex concordance is done in section 3.7: see program 3.2.

2.5.2 Writing to Files

For a large text, a concordance program can produce much output, and scrolling through this on a computer screen is a pain. It is often more convenient to store the output to a text file, which is doable in three ways.

Code Sample 2.17 Replace the code prior to the first `while` loop in program 2.7 with the commands here to make that program run as described above.

```
open(FILE, "$ARGV[2]") or die("$ARGV[2] not found");

$/ = ""; # Paragraph mode for first while loop

$target = "\\b($ARGV[0])\\b";
$radius = $ARGV[1];
$width = 2*$radius; # Width of extract
```

First, the function `open` can open a file for output as well as input. Code sample 2.18 gives two examples. Note that `OUT1` is a filehandle for `filename1.txt`. The greater than sign means that this file is written to. If this file already exists, then the original contents are lost.

Second, the use of two greater than signs means to append to the file. So in this case, if `filename2.txt` already exists, then the original contents are appended to, not overwritten.

Code Sample 2.18 How to write or append to a text file.

```
open (OUT1, ">filename1.txt") or die;
open (OUT2, ">>filename2.txt") or die;
# commands
print OUT1 "$x, $y, etc.\n";
print OUT2 "$x, $y, etc.\n";
```

Third, redirecting the output from the command line is possible. For example, the following command stores the output from the program to `filename3.txt`. In addition, using a double greater than sign appends the output to the file listed on the command line.

```
perl program.pl > filename3.txt
```

Although this is rarely discussed in this book's code examples, in practice, it is useful to store voluminous outputs in a file. Now we turn to a new problem in the next section: a first attempt to identify sentences using regexes.

2.6   FIRST ATTEMPT AT EXTRACTING SENTENCES

The general problem of extracting strings from a text is called *tokenization*, and the extracts are called *tokens*. This is a useful term since it covers any type of string, not just words, for example, telephone numbers, Web addresses, dollar amounts, stock prices, and so forth. One challenge of extracting words is how to define what a word is, and this is a complex issue. For example, in this book, sections 2.4.2 and 2.4.3 discuss the issues of hyphens and apostrophes, respectively. See section 4.2.2 of *Foundations of Statistical Natural Language Processing* [75] for further discussion on defining a word. Moreover, many other specialized cases come to mind with a little thought. For example, this book has regexes and computer code, and each of these have unusual tokens. However, we usually focus on tokens arising from literature.

Words are joined to create phrases, which are joined to form clauses, which are combined into sentences. So sentences inherit the complexity of words, plus they have their own structure, ranging from simple one-word exclamations up to almost arbitrarily long constructions. An early statistical paper on sentences by Yule in 1939 [128] starts out by noting that one difficulty he had in his analysis is deciding exactly what constituted both a word and a sentence. In fact, there is no definitive answer to these questions, and since language changes over time, any proposed definition becomes out of date. So the general issues are complex and are not dealt with in this book in detail, but see section 4.2.4 of the *Foundations of Statistical Natural Language Processing* [75] and sections 269 through 280 of the *Cambridge Grammar of English* [26] for further discussion on sentences. Fortunately, breaking a particular text into sentences might be easy because the author uses only certain kinds of punctuation and syntax. And even if a text cannot be broken into sentences perfectly, if the error rate is small, the results are useful.

Finally, note that written English and spoken English have many significant differences; for example, the former typically uses sentences as a basic unit. However, analyses of speech corpora have revealed that sentences are **not** the best unit of study for a discourse among people. Section 83 of the *Cambridge Grammar of English* [26] states that clauses are the basic unit of conversations. Although some texts analyzed in this book have dialogs, these are more structured than what people actually say when they talk to one another. Due to both its complexity and the lack of public domain transcriptions, this book does not analyze transcribed spoken English.

2.6.1   Sentence Segmentation Preliminaries

Another term for finding sentences is *sentence segmentation*. This is equivalent to detecting sentence boundaries; however, there is no built-in regex command analogous to \b for sentences. One reason for this difference is that (in English) whitespace typically separates words. Although there are exceptions, for example, *once-in-a-lifetime* can be written either with or without the hyphens, these are not typical. Sentences, however, are combinable in numerous ways so that a writer has a choice between using many shorter sentences, or a few medium length sentences, or just one long sentence. The examples in table 2.6 show several ways to combine the sentences *He woke up* and *It was dark*.

Table 2.6   A variety of ways of combining two short sentences.

He woke up, and it was dark.
He woke up, but it was dark.
He woke up when it was dark.
When he woke up, it was dark.
Although he woke up, it was dark.
He woke up; it was dark.
He woke up: it was dark.
He woke up–it was dark.

The freedom of choice in combining adjacent sentences is not the only consideration. First, sentences can be combined by nesting. For example, this is common in depicting dialog in a novel (see sentence 2.10 below). Second, sentence ending punctuation marks can be ambiguous because they serve more than one purpose. We discuss the basics of both of these below, but many details are left out. For an in depth discussion of this, see chapters 5, 10, and 14 of *The Chicago Manual of Style* [27].

First, sentences can be nested, that is, one sentence can interrupt the other as in sentence 2.10.

$$\text{“When I drive to Enfield," Dave said, “I take I-91."} \tag{2.10}$$

Here the direct quote is interrupted by the sentence *Dave said*. A similar situation occurs with parenthetical remarks, such as sentence 2.11. Here the sentence *I do it daily* interrupts the first sentence.

$$\text{“When I drive to Enfield–I do it daily–I take I-91."} \tag{2.11}$$

From the examples just discussed, nested sentences are not uncommon. However, ambiguous punctuation is even more of a problem for sentence segmentation. Sentences end in question marks, exclamation points, and periods. Unfortunately, all of these symbols have other uses than terminating sentences.

In many types of texts, question marks and exclamation points are used primarily for marking the end of a sentence, although we have seen that direct quotes make the situation more complicated as shown in sentence 2.12.

$$\text{She said, “You named your cat Charlie Brown?" to me.} \tag{2.12}$$

However, some types of texts use these two punctuation marks for other purposes. For example, this book also uses the question mark as a regex symbol. In addition, a book on chess uses the question mark to denote a poor move and an exclamation point to denote a good move, and a calculus text uses the exclamation point to denote the factorial function. However, for many kinds of texts, both the question mark and the exclamation point do not serve any other purpose besides ending a sentence.

Periods, however, have several uses besides ending a sentence, and all these can easily appear in many types of texts. First, periods are commonly used in numbered lists, right after the numeral. Second, periods are used as decimal points within numerals. Third, the ellipsis, used to indicate missing material in a quotation is written with three periods in a row. But there is another common, alternative use of the period: abbreviations.

Using periods with abbreviations is common, especially in American English. For example, a person's name is often accompanied by a social title such as *Mr.*, *Mrs.*, or *Dr.* There are many other titles, too: *Capt.*, *Prof.*, or *Rev.* Academic degrees are sometimes added to a name, for example, *B.A.* or *Ph.D.* Instead of the full name, many times parts of a name are replaced by an initial, for example, *John X. Doe.* But this is just a start, and after some thought, numerous other abbreviations come to mind: *U.S.* for the United States, *Ave.* for avenue, *A.D.* for *anno Domini*, *in.* for inches, *Co.* for company, and so forth. Of course, not all abbreviations use periods, for instance, one can use either *U.S.* or *US*, and the symbols for the chemical elements never use them. Yet enough abbreviations do use it that one should never ignore this possibility. Finally, note that a period can mark the end of a sentence and denote an abbreviation at the same time. For example, this is true of "I live in the U.S."

So creating a general-purpose sentence segmentation tool requires more than a few simple rules. Nonetheless, in the 1990s, error rates below 1% were achieved, for example, see Palmer's paper on SATZ [85], which is his software package to do sentence segmentation (note that *Satz* is the German word for *sentence*).

However, an imperfect program is still useful, and a regexes written for a particular set of texts might be quite good at detecting sentences. With the above discussion in mind, we now try to write such a program.

2.6.2 Sentence Segmentation for *A Christmas Carol*

Sentence segmentation is an interesting challenge for a regex. We try to solve it in several different ways for Charles Dickens's *A Christmas Carol* [39]. This lacks generality, but the process of analyzing this novel's sentence structure to create the regex also increases one's familiarity with this text, which is a worthwhile payoff.

Common sense suggests a sentence begins with a capital letter and ends with either a period, an exclamation point, or a question mark. Let us call these *end punctuation*, although as noted above, they do not always mark the end of a sentence.

Since program 2.7 is a regex-based concordance maker, we can easily analyze *A Christmas Carol* on its use of end punctuation with minor changes to this program. For instance, the filehandle FILE must be linked to the file containing this novel. Then just changing $target to the strings '(.)', '(?)', and '(!)', respectively, finds all instances of these three punctuation marks. Remember that the parentheses are needed to save the matched substring.

Output 2.7 A coding error fails to find just periods.

```
            MARLEY was dead: to begin with.
            MARLEY was dead: to begin with.
          MARLEY was dead: to begin with. T
         MARLEY was dead: to begin with. Th
        MARLEY was dead: to begin with. The
       MARLEY was dead: to begin with. Ther
      MARLEY was dead: to begin with. There
     MARLEY was dead: to begin with. There
    MARLEY was dead: to begin with. There i
   MARLEY was dead: to begin with. There is
```

Running program 2.7 with the change of FILE and with $target set to '(.)' produces output 2.7. Clearly something has gone wrong. In this case, the period has a special meaning in a regex. As stated in table 2.3, the period matches every character. So the reason why each line in output 2.7 moves over by one is that every single character matches, hence in the first line *M* is matched, and so is placed in the center. In the second line, *A* is matched, so it is placed in the center, which means that *M* has moved one space to the left, and so forth. Consequently, the regexes should be '(\.)' ,'(\?)', and '(!)' since both the period and the question mark have special meaning in regexes, but the exclamation point does not.

Changing $target to '(\.)' produces many lines, and output 2.8 shows the first 10. Note that the fifth and ninth lines are the end of the paragraph, which explains why there is no text after either period.

This program lists all uses of the period, but not all of these are of interest. In particular, the use of abbreviations is important for us to check. There are several ways to do this. First, find a list of abbreviations and check for these directly. Second, find a list of words and then flag tokens that do not match this list. However, both of these approaches require more

Output 2.8 First 10 periods in Dickens's *A Christmas Carol*.

```
MARLEY was dead: to begin with. There is no doubt whatever ab
s no doubt whatever about that. The register of his burial wa
ertaker, and the chief mourner. Scrooge signed it: and Scroog
ng he chose to put his hand to. Old Marley was as dead as a d
ley was as dead as a door-nail.
cularly dead about a door-nail. I might have been inclined, m
ce of ironmongery in the trade. But the wisdom of our ancesto
 it, or the Country's done for. You will therefore permit me
ley was as dead as a door-nail.
 he was dead? Of course he did. How could it be otherwise? Sc
```

advanced programming techniques, for example, the use of hashes (discussed in the next chapter), so a third approach is tried here. We search for periods followed by a lowercase letter.

A regex to do this needs to find a period followed by a single quote, or double quote or comma as well as zero or more whitespaces, and all of this is then followed by a lowercase letter. Remembering that the period and the single quote mark must be escaped, this regex is reasonably easy to write down: `/(\.[\s\'",]*[a-z])/`, which is assigned to `$target`. One more change is required: in the second `while` loop, the letters after the regex must be changed from `gi` to just `g`, otherwise the matches are case insensitive, but now we want to detect lowercase letters. After making these changes, running program 2.7 produces output 2.9, which shows exactly one match.

Output 2.9 All instances of a period followed by whitespace followed by a lowercase letter in *A Christmas Carol*.

```
his domestic ball broke up. Mr. and Mrs. Fezziwig took their st
```

This match occurs starting with the period in `Mr.` and ends with the first letter of `and`, which is in lowercase. So there are apparently no abbreviations in the interior of a sentence in this story. However, there are clearly social titles since `Mr.` and `Mrs.` do exist.

Changing `$target` to `'([MD]rs?\.)'` matches 3 common social titles. Making this change to program 2.7 now produces 45 lines, and the first 10 are given in output 2.10. Looking at the entire output, it turns out that there are no occurrences of `Dr.` While there are certainly other titles we might consider, familiarity with this story suggests that these should account for all of them.

Let us next look at the first 10 uses of either a question mark or a exclamation point by setting `$target` to `'([?!])'`. Recall that inside the square brackets, the question mark has no special meaning, so there is no need to escape it with a backslash here.

From output 2.11, we see that line 5 has an exclamation point followed by a lowercase letter, so this pattern needs to be checked by setting `$target` to `'([?!][\s\'",]*[a-z])'`. Now rerunning the program produces output 2.12, which shows that this construction happens 182 times, the first 10 of which are shown. Not surprisingly, most of these examples are nested sentences arising from conversations in the novel.

Output 2.10 First 10 instances of *Mr.*, *Mrs.*, or *Dr.* in *A Christmas Carol*.

```
the pleasure of addressing Mr. Scrooge, or Mr. Marley?"
addressing Mr. Scrooge, or Mr. Marley?"
                          "Mr. Marley has been dead these
estive season of the year, Mr. Scrooge," said the gentlem
s First of Exchange pay to Mr. Ebenezer Scrooge or his or
fty stomach-aches. In came Mrs. Fezziwig, one vast substan
ig stood out to dance with Mrs. Fezziwig. Top couple, too;
tch for them, and so would Mrs. Fezziwig. As to her, she w
 And when old Fezziwig and Mrs. Fezziwig had gone all thro
is domestic ball broke up. Mr. and Mrs. Fezziwig took the
```

Output 2.11 The first 10 instances of exclamation points or question marks in *A Christmas Carol*.

```
                Mind! I don't mean to say that I
   Scrooge knew he was dead? Of course he did. How coul
. How could it be otherwise? Scrooge and he were partne
                        Oh! But he was a tight-fisted
at the grind-stone, Scrooge! a squeezing, wrenching, gr
ching, covetous, old sinner! Hard and sharp as flint, f
y dear Scrooge, how are you? When will you come to see
hen will you come to see me?" No beggars implored him t
an an evil eye, dark master!"
   But what did Scrooge care! It was the very thing he l
```

Output 2.12 First 10 instances of exclamation points or question marks followed by a lowercase letter in *A Christmas Carol*.

```
at the grind-stone, Scrooge! a squeezing, wrenching, gras
istmas, uncle! God save you!" cried a cheerful voice. It w
                    "Bah!" said Scrooge, "Humbug!"
 "Christmas a humbug, uncle!" said Scrooge's nephew. "You
r of the moment, said, "Bah!" again; and followed it up wi
      "Don't be cross, uncle!" said the nephew.
              "Uncle!" pleaded the nephew.
              "Nephew!" returned the uncle sternly,
            "Keep it!" repeated Scrooge's nephew. "
           "But why?" cried Scrooge's nephew. "Why
```

Note that the first line of this output does not have the exclamation point at the end of a quote. By dropping the double quotes in the regex, all instances like this first line are found, and all of these are shown in output 2.13. As far as sentence segmentation goes, note that many of these lines are ambiguous. For example, line 5 can be rewritten as "Rise and walk with me!" or "Rise! And walk with me!" However, as in output 2.12, usually the

lowercase letter after a question mark or exclamation point means that the sentence need not
end at either of these. Adopting this as a rule even for output 2.13 also produces reasonable
sentences, even though alternatives exist. Furthermore, this rule also applies to the period,
although there is only one instance of this in the novel.

Output 2.13 All instances of exclamation points or question marks followed by a lowercase
letter but not immediately followed by quote marks in *A Christmas Carol*.

```
at the grind-stone, Scrooge! a squeezing, wrenching, gras
reation. Humbug, I tell you! humbug!"
                          "Oh! captive, bound, and double-i
misused! Yet such was I! Oh! such was I!"
                        "Rise! and walk with me!"
d it off, God bless my soul! to save my life. As to measu
claimed the Ghost. "Come in! and know me better, man!"
                The Grocers'! oh, the Grocers'! nearly clo
 Grocers'! oh, the Grocers'! nearly closed, with perhaps
rooge. "Oh, no, kind Spirit! say he will be spared."
is poor man's child. Oh God! to hear the Insect on the le
              "Oh, Man! look here. Look, look, down
              "Spirit! are they yours?" Scrooge cou
such things, if he did. Ah! you may look through that sh
                    YES! and the bedpost was his own.
```

Based on the above discussion, the following steps for sentence segmentation suggest
themselves. First, for each case of *Mr.* or *Mrs.*, remove the period. After this is done,
assume that a sentence starts with a capital letter, has a string of symbols ending in a period,
question mark, or exclamation point only if one of these is followed by another capital letter.

Code Sample 2.19 A first attempt to write a simple sentence segmentation program.

```
$test = "Testing.  one, two, three.  Hello!  What?";
while ( $test =~ /([A-Z].*[.?!])\s*[A-Z]/g ) {
  print "$1\n";
}
```

The initial attempt to write a sentence segmentation program is given in code sample 2.19, which applies the regex to $test. Looking at the regex, the part in parentheses,
([A-Z].*[.?!]), finds a capital letter, zero or more characters, and finally one of the
three sentence-ending punctuation marks. Outside the parentheses, whitespace is matched
up to another capital letter. Note that this regex requires that a sentence be followed by an
uppercase letter, so just ending in a question mark, for example, is not sufficient by itself.
Finally, each match is printed on a separate line. When run, however, this program produces
exactly the one line given below, so there is exactly one sentence match, not three matches
as expected.

What went wrong? To answer this, we need to know more about how matching occurs
for a regex, which is the topic of the next section.

Output 2.14 Output of code sample 2.19, which did not run as expected.

```
Testing.  one, two, three.  Hello!
```

2.6.3 Leftmost Greediness and Sentence Segmentation

All regexes start looking for matches at the leftmost character, and if this fails, then it tries the next character to the right, and if this fails, then it tries the next character, and so forth. So the regex /(10+)/ applied to the string "10010000" matches the first three characters, "100", but not the last five.

Hence, the default for {m,n} is to find the first match going from left to right. If there is more than one match starting at the same location, the longest one is picked, which is called *greediness*. In particular, this applies to the three special cases of {m,n}, namely * (same as {0,}), + ({1,}), and ? ({0,1}). With this in mind, output 2.15 of code sample 2.20 is understandable because instead of matching the first word and period, the regex matches as much text as possible, which is the entire line. Note that the print statement produces one slash per iteration of the while loop. Therefore the number of slashes equals the number of sentences matched.

Code Sample 2.20 The regex matches as many characters as possible starting as far left as possible.

```
$test = "Hello. Hello. Hello. Hello.";
while ( $test =~ /(.*\.)/g ) {
  print "$1/"; # Matches separated by a forward slash
}
```

Output 2.15 Output of code sample 2.20. The single forward slash means that only one match is made.

```
Hello. Hello. Hello. Hello./
```

For sentence segmentation, a greedy match is not wanted. In fact, the shortest substring is desired. Fortunately, it is easy to denote this pattern in the regex: just append the question mark to the repetition operators. That is, *?, +?, ??, and {m,n}? match as short a substring as possible. Thus making code sample 2.20 nongreedy is simple: just add a question mark after the plus, which creates code sample 2.21, which produces output 2.16. Now each *Hello.* is a separate match. Although there are other considerations, usually the heuristic that a regex is greedy is accurate.

There is another way to fix code sample 2.20. If sentences end only with periods (and no periods used for abbreviations), then a sentence is precisely what is between two periods. A regex to match this is /[^.]*\./, which means search for as many nonperiods in a row as possible, then a period. Hence code sample 2.22 produces the same as output 2.16.

Now we can fix code sample 2.19 using the nongreedy zero or more match, which is given in code sample 2.23. The results are in output 2.17, but there is still only one line, meaning that there is only one sentence detected, not three. However, unlike output 2.14,

Code Sample 2.21 The regex matches as few characters as possible since *? is nongreedy.

```
$test = "Hello. Hello. Hello. Hello.";
while ( $test =~ /(.*?\.)/g ) {
  print "$1/"; # Matches separated by a forward slash
}
```

Output 2.16 Output of code sample 2.21. Four matches are found.

```
Hello./ Hello./ Hello./ Hello./
```

Code Sample 2.22 This regex searches for as many nonperiods as possible, then a period.

```
$test = "Hello. Hello. Hello. Hello.";
while ( $test =~ /([^.]*\.)/g ) {
  print "$1/"; # Matches separated by a forward slash
}
```

the output does give the first sentence correctly. Remember that the word after a period must be capitalized, so the first sentence does end with the word *three*. Before reading on, can you discover the cause of this problem?

Code Sample 2.23 A second attempt using nongreedy matches to write a simple sentence segmentation program.

```
$test = "Testing.  one, two, three.  Hello!  What?";
while ( $test =~ /([A-Z].*?[.?!])\s*[A-Z]/g ) {
  print "$1\n";
}
```

Output 2.17 Output of code sample 2.23, which still did not run as expected.

```
Testing.  one, two, three.
```

There are, in fact, two problems in this code. One is that after the first match is found, the regex searches for another match starting at the character immediately after the prior match. Since the regex in this case searches for a capital letter following a sentence-ending punctuation mark, the start of the search for the second match occurs at the letter *e* in the sentence *Hello!* Hence the second sentence is not found. However, why is the third sentence *What?* not discovered?

Here the problem is different. Since the regex looks for a capital letter following a sentence-ending punctuation mark, and because there is no text after the third sentence, it is undetected. One way to fix this code requires two changes. First, we need a way to backup where a search starts after a match. Second, the last sentence in a string requires a different pattern than the other ones.

When Perl finds a match for a regex, it stores the position of the character following the match, which is obtainable by using the function pos. Moreover, the value of pos can be changed by the programmer, which starts the next search at this new value. Applying these two ideas to code sample 2.23 produces code sample 2.24. Note that the first line within the while loop uses a shortcut. In general, -= decreases the variable on the left by the value on the right. So the statement below decreases $y by one, then assigns this value to $x.

```
$x = \$y -= 1;
```

In addition, the variable $loc is needed because when the while loop makes its last test, it fails (which ends the while loop's execution), and it resets the pos function. Finally, the substr function with only two arguments returns the rest of the string starting at the position given in the second argument. That is, starting from the position in $loc, the remainder of $test is printed.

Code Sample 2.24 A third attempt using nongreedy matches and the function pos to write a simple sentence segmentation program.

```
$test = "Testing.  one, two, three.  Hello!  What?";
while ( $test =~ /([A-Z].*?[.?!])\s*[A-Z]/g ) {
  $loc = pos($test) -= 1;
  print "$1\n";
}
print substr($test, $loc);
```

Output 2.18 Output of code sample 2.24, which succeeds in finding all three sentences.

```
Testing.  one, two, three.
Hello!
What?
```

Although using pos provides a second way to do sentence segmentation, it means that the programmer is doing the bookkeeping, and this is best left to Perl itself, if possible. Fortunately, there is a third technique that finds sentences: the use of character negation in square brackets. If periods are not used for abbreviations, then sentences are the longest strings not containing end punctuation, which is denoted by [^.?!]. This does not take into account lowercase letters after the end punctuation, but that can be tested for. So this is the idea: use greedy matches to find the longest substrings that do not have end punctuation. If the next character after one of these substrings is uppercase, then it is a sentence. Otherwise save and combine it with the next substring without end punctuation. Repeat this process until either an uppercase letter is found or the end of the paragraph is reached.

Code sample 2.25 uses this approach, and its code has two constructions worth noting. First, the variable $buffer stores the substrings that conclude with end punctuation but are followed by a lowercase letter. The two statements below do exactly the same thing: they concatenate $match to $buffer. Note that if $match has not been assigned anything, then $buffer is unchanged.

```
$buffer .= $match;
```

```
$buffer = $buffer . $match;
```

Second, this code also introduces a new Perl variable, $'. When a regex matches a substring, it is stored in the variable $&. The string up to the match is assigned to $` (using a backquote), and the last part of the string is saved in $' (using a single quote). Hence the regex matched against $' is checking either if the next character is a capital letter or if the end of the string has been reached (not counting whitespace).

Code Sample 2.25 Sentence segmentation by character class negation.

```
$test = "Testing.  one, two, three.  Hello!  What?";
$buffer = "";
while ( $test =~ /(\s*[^.?!]+[.?!])/g ) {
  $match = $1;
  # Note use of the Perl variable $'
  if ( $' =~ /^\s*[A-Z]|^\s*$/) {
    print "$buffer$match\n";
    $buffer = "";
  } else {
    $buffer .= $match;
  }
}
```

Running code sample 2.25 produces output 2.19. Notice that the initial spaces before the sentences are retained, which is why the second and third sentence are indented.

Output 2.19 Output of code sample 2.25, which succeeds in finding all three sentences.

```
Testing.  one, two, three.
 Hello!
 What?
```

Now we have the tools to go back to sentence segmentation in *A Christmas Carol*. One complication in this novel (and any novel with dialog) is that quotation marks are used, and exclamation points and question marks can go either inside or outside these (see sections 5.20 and 5.28 of *The Chicago Manual of Style* [27] for the details). For example, if a person is quoted asking a question, then the question mark goes inside the quotation marks, but if a question is asked about what a person says, then the question mark goes outside. But including the possibility of quotation marks is easy: just place ["']{0,2} in the appropriate places in the regex, which is shown in regular expression 2.4. This is needed in case there are quotes within quotes, which does happen in *A Christmas Carol*. The heart of this regex is the character class [^.?!]*, which matches as many nonend punctuation as possible. This is eventually followed by [.?!], so together these two pieces search for a substring having no end punctuation except at the end of the substring. Most of the rest of this regex is checking for possible quotation marks.

If regular expression 2.4 replaces the regex in the while statement of code sample 2.25, then quotation marks are taken into account. If we add a while loop that goes through *A Christmas Carol* paragraph by paragraph, then we have program 2.8, which performs sentence segmentation. This code has several features that are commented on below.

First, the default variable $_ is explicitly given to emphasize its role, although this is optional. Second, the beginning of the while loop has four simplifying substitutions,

Regular Expression 2.4 A regex that matches a substring up to end punctuation and that may contain either double or single quotes.

```
/(["']{0,2}[a-zA-Z][^.?!]*["']{0,2}[.?!]["']{0,2}\s*)/
```

```
open (FILE, "A Christmas Carol.txt") or die("File not found");

$/ = ""; # Paragraph mode for while loop
$regex =
   '(["\']{0,2}[a-zA-Z][^.?!]*["\']{0,2}[.?!]["\']{0,2}\s*)';

while ($_ = <FILE>) {
  chomp;
  s/\n/ /g;       # Replace newlines by spaces
  s/--/ -- /g;    # Add spaces around dashes
  s/Mr\./Mr/g;    # Remove period in Mr.
  s/Mrs\./Mrs/g;  # Remove period in Mrs.

  $buffer = "";
  while ( $_ =~ /$regex/g ) {
    $match = $1;
    if ( $' =~ /^"?[A-Z]/ ) {  # Check for capital letter
      print "$buffer$match\n"; # Print sentence
      $buffer = "";
    } else {
      $buffer .= $match;
      if ($' =~ /^\w*$/) { # Check for end of paragraph
        print "$buffer\n"; # Print sentence
      }
    }
  }
  print "\n";
}
```

Program 2.8 A simple sentence segmentation program.

for example, the periods in *Mr.* and *Mrs.* are removed so that they are not mistaken for end punctuation. Third, the if statement includes an else clause. This if-then-else statement checks whether or not a capital letter follows the match found in the while statement. Hence the underlying structure is given in code sample 2.26.

Running program 2.8 produces much output (hopefully all the sentences of *A Christmas Carol*). Visual inspection reveals that the program does a good job, but the results are not perfect. For example, one error is caused by the sentence in table 2.7. Try to figure out what went wrong: the solution is given in problem 2.7.

Program 2.8 has been created with *A Christmas Carol* in mind, so the results of this program with other texts probably requires further modifications. For more robust sentence rules see figure 4.1 of section 4.2.4 of the *Foundations of Statistical Natural Language*

Code Sample 2.26 The underlying structure of program 2.8.

```
while ($_ = <FILE>) { # Loop paragraph by paragraph

  # Make substitutions to simplify text

  while ( $_ =~ /$regex/g ) { # Loop over regex matches

    # Does a capital letter follow the regex match?
    #   If true, print out a sentence
    #   If false, add current match to \$buffer

  }
}
```

Table 2.7 Sentence segmentation by program 2.8 fails for this sentence.

```
But the great effect of the evening came after the Roast
and Boiled, when the fiddler (an artful dog, mind!  The sort
of man who knew his business better than you or I could
have told it him!)  struck up ''Sir Roger de Coverley."
```

Processing [75]. However, there is another point of view: this program is only 28 lines long (which counts every line, even the blank ones). Given experience with regexes, creating this code is not difficult, and the process of fine tuning it helps the programmer understand the text itself, a worthwhile payoff. As long as a programmer is facing a homogeneous group of texts, this approach is fruitful. To analyze a heterogeneous group of texts makes the programming challenge much harder.

Finally, in any programming language a given task can be done in several ways, and this is especially true in Perl. For another example of sentence segmentation using a different approach, see section 6.8 of Hammond's *Programming for Linguists* [51]. This author employs regexes to create arrays by using the functions push and splice. In addition, we return to sentence segmentation in section 2.7.3 after introducing the idea of *lookaround*. This solution is the most elegant. Finally, section 9.2.3 has one last approach to this task in Perl.

The next section introduces a few more Perl techniques for creating regexes. These examples highlight new programming ideas and syntax.

2.7 REGEX ODDS AND ENDS

This section goes over a few miscellaneous techniques. It is also a chance to review some of the earlier material discussed in this chapter.

However, there are techniques that we do not discuss, and an excellent book covering regexes in depth is Friedl's *Mastering Regular Expressions* [47]. Although this book discussions several programming language's implementations of regexes, chapters 2 and 7 focus on Perl, which pops up in several other chapters, too. Conversely, almost all books on Perl have at least one chapter on regexes. Historically, Perl has been at the forefront of regexes as both have evolved over the years, and this co-evolution is likely to continue.

2.7.1 Match Variables and Backreferences

We have already seen the match variables $1, $2, and so forth, which store the substrings that match the parts of a regex inside parentheses. These can be nested as in code sample 2.27. This program examines a list of plural nouns, and the regex matches the last letter of the base word as well as the final -s or -es, if any. This is a simple example of lexical morphology, the study of the structure of words, and using a larger list of plural nouns would uncover the rules of plural forms. For information on these rules, see sections 523–532 of *Practical English Usage* [114]. Notice that the order of the variables $1, $2, $3, and $4, is determined by the order of the leftmost parenthesis. Hence $1 is the entire word; $2 is the singular form of the noun; $3 is the last letter before the addition of either -s or -es; and $4 is one of these two letter groups. The results are given in output 2.20. Note that the code fails for the word *moose*, which has an irregular plural form. Finally, see problem 2.8 for two more comments on this code sample.

Code Sample 2.27 Example of nested parentheses and the associated match variables.

```
$text = "dogs, cats, wishes, passes, moose.";
while ( $text =~ /\b((\w+?(\w))(es|s)?)\b/g ) {
  print "$1, $2, $3, $4\n";
}
```

Output 2.20 Output of code sample 2.27.

```
dogs, dog, g, s
cats, cat, t, s
wishes, wish, h, es
passes, pass, s, es
moose, moose, e,
```

Backreferences are related to match variables. While the latter allows the programmer to use matched text outside of the regex, backreferences allow it to be used inside the regex itself. For example, given text, let us find the words with doubled letters, that is, two letters in a row that are the same. Since \w stands for [a-zA-Z_], the goal is to match a letter, then immediately afterwards, match that letter again. The backreferences \1, \2, ..., store the substring that matches the part of a regex in parentheses. Hence, the regex /(\w)\1/ matches a double letter since the \1 has the value of the previous character.

Code sample 2.28 tests this. The code breaks the string into words using the function split, and the results are stored in an array. Then the foreach loop tests each word in the array against this regex. The matches are then printed out, as shown in output 2.21.

Notice that testing $x against the regex informs the if statement whether or not there is a match. So a true or a false value is generated, which suggests that there is more going on in $x =~ /(\w)\1/ than meets the eye. These details are discussed in the next section.

Code Sample 2.28 Example of using the backreference \1 to detect double letters in words.

```
$text = "moose, lamp, truck, Nell, 911";
@word = split(/, /, $text);
foreach $x (@word) {
  if ($x =~ /(\w)\1/g ) {
    print "$x\n";
  }
}
```

Output 2.21 Output of code sample 2.28

```
moose
Nell
911
```

2.7.2   Regular Expression Operators and Their Output

Since $x =~ /$regex/ can be put into an if or while statement, both of which require logical values to operate, then the regex must produce a logical value. This raises the question of how Perl represents true and false.

Perl only has two types of variables: string and numerical, and we have seen that Perl is flexible even with these. For example, $x = "3" + "4" assigns the number 7 to $x. Logical values can be either strings or numbers, and there are exactly seven values that are equivalent to the logical value false as shown in table 2.8. Note that the empty parentheses stands for an array with no entries (see section 3.3 for information on arrays).

Table 2.8   Defining true and false in Perl.

0, '0', "0", '', "", (), undef	false
All other numbers and strings	true

If matching regexes returns something, then this can be assigned to a variable, which then can be printed out. Code sample 2.29 does exactly this using dashes as delimiters. The output is just --1-, so $result1 has the empty string (since there is nothing between the first two dashes), and $result2 has the string or number 1.

Code Sample 2.29 Proof that matching a text to a regex produces either a logical true or false.

```
$text = "How do I get to Lower Wacker Drive?";
$result1 = ($text =~ /upper/i);
$result2 = ($text =~ /lower/i);
print "-$result1-$result2-";
```

To see if a string does not match a regex is easily done by replacing =~ by !~. For example, the following is true for $text in code sample 2.29.

```
$text !~ /upper/i
```

There is an alternative way to write matching a regex, which is done by putting an m before the initial forward slash. That is, the two statements below are equivalent. This parallels the substitution notation, s///.

```
$x =~ /$regex/
```

```
$x =~ m/$regex/
```

We have seen two types of regex operators, matching and substitution, denoted m// and s///, respectively. Not only does the match operator return a value, so does substitution. For example, s/Mr\./Mr/g removes periods in the abbreviation *Mr.* However, it also returns the number of substitutions performed. If none are, then the empty string is returned, which is equivalent to `false`. Remember that any positive number returned is equivalent to `true`, so s/// can be used in both `if` and `while` statements, just like m//. Hence, in code sample 2.30, $result has the value 2, which means that *Mr.* appears twice in $text. This sort of flexibility is common in Perl, which makes it fun to program in but harder to understand the code.

Code Sample 2.30 Example of the substitution operator returning the number of substitutions made.

```
$text = "Mr. Scrooge and Mr. Marley";
$result = ($text =~ s/Mr\./Mr/g);
print "$result";
```

Besides matching and substitution, there is one more regex operator, *quote regex*, denoted qr//, and this allows precompilation of a regex, which can make the program run quicker. The syntax is similar to assigning a string representing a regular expression to a variable. The operator qr// takes this one more step as seen in code sample 2.31, where two regexes are precompiled and stored into two variables: the first matches *Mr.* and *Mrs.*, and the second matches a name. The output of code sample 2.31 is given below.

```
Mr. Dickens Mrs. Poe
```

Code Sample 2.31 Example of two quote regex operators.

```
$title = qr/(Mrs?\.)/;
$surname = qr/([A-Z][a-z]*)/;
$text = "Mr. Dickens and Mrs. Poe";
while ( $text =~ /$title $surname/g ) {
  print "$1 $2 ";
}
```

Finally, there is *translation* (or *transliteration*), denoted tr///, which does **not** allow regexes, but the structure is similar to the operators m//, s///, and qr//. See problem 2.9 for some discussion on this.

Now we discuss one last regex technique. This allows us to solve the sentence segmentation problem of *A Christmas Carol* in a new and better fashion.

2.7.3 Lookaround

Lookaround allows a regex to test whether or not a condition is true without affecting which characters are matched. For example, the word boundary, \b, is a location satisfying the condition that one side has a word character and the other side does not. This idea is also called a *zero-width assertion*. The concept of lookaround allows the programmer to test locations for more complex conditions.

Lookaround comes in four types. It can lookahead (forward in the text) or it can lookbehind (backward in the text), and the lookaround can search either for a regex (positive form) or the negation of a regex (negative form). Hence, for any regular expression, call it $regex, there is positive lookahead with the syntax (?=$regex), as well as negative lookahead, (?!$regex). In addition, there is positive lookbehind, (?<=$regex), as well as negative lookbehind, (?<!$regex). We consider only two examples: a simple introductory one and positive lookahead for sentence segmentation.

First, in HTML, many tags come in pairs, which surround text. For example, bold font is indicated by the tags <B> and </B>. One way to match text inside these is to use lookbehind and lookahead to ensure that the tags exist, but these are not included in the match. This is done in code sample 2.32, which prints out the word *think*. Note that lookaround is not required: the regex /<B>(.*)</B>/ does the same task and is simpler.

Code Sample 2.32 An example of lookahead and lookbehind.

```
$test = "Don't even <B>think</B> it!";
$test =~ /(?<=<B>)(.*)(?=<\/B>)/;
print "$1\n";
```

The second example is yet another approach to sentence segmentation. Suppose that no periods are used for abbreviations (or that this type of period has been removed). Suppose a sentence is required to start with a capital letter. Then a sentence starts with [A-Z] followed by one or more occurrences of [^.?!]*[.?!] and ends in whitespace followed by either a capital letter or the end of the string. Although code sample 2.24 tests for this, it matches up to and including the capital letter. Lookahead can test for this capital letter, which is not included in the match.

Consider the regex in code sample 2.33. It breaks into two pieces: regexes 2.5 and 2.6. The former matches the sentence, which is stored in $1. The latter looks ahead for either the following capital letter or the end of the string.

Code Sample 2.33 A simple sentence matching regex using positive lookahead.

```
$regex = '([A-Z]([^.?!]*[.?!])+?)(?=\s+[A-Z]|\w*$)';

$_ = 'Short. a test.  A test? a text? No problem!';

while ( $_ =~ /$regex/g ) {
  print "$1\n";
}
```

Regular Expression 2.5 First part of the regex in code sample 2.33.

```
([A-Z]([^.?!]*[.?!])+?)
```

Regular Expression 2.6 Second part of the regex in code sample 2.33.

```
(?=\s+[A-Z]|\w*$)
```

It is essential that the +? at the end of the first pair of parentheses is not greedy. If this is changed to ([^.?!]*[.?!])+), then only one line of output is produced, which implies that only one sentence is found. Output 2.22 shows the correct, nongreedy results.

Output 2.22 Output of code sample 2.33.

```
Short. a test.
A test? a text?
No problem!
```

As is, this regex does not take into account quotation marks, but including these is not hard. The result is program 2.9. Note that the qr// construction has been used. Here it shortens the length of the regex, and it allows the programmer to label the two pieces of this regex in a more understandable fashion.

```
open (FILE, "A Christmas Carol.txt") or die("File not found");

$/ = ""; # Paragraph mode for while loop
$lookahead = qr/(?=\s+[\'"]{0,2}[A-Z]|\w*$)/;
$sentence  = qr/([\'"]{0,2}[A-Z]([^.?!]*[.?!][\'"]{0,2})+?)/;

while ($_ = <FILE>) {
  chomp;
  s/\n/ /g;      # Replace newlines by spaces
  s/--/ -- /g;   # Add spaces around dashes
  s/Mr./Mr/g;    # Remove period in Mr.
  s/Mrs./Mrs/g;  # Remove period in Mrs.

  while( $_ =~ /$sentence$lookahead/g ) {
    print "$1\n";
  }
  print "\n";
}
```

Program 2.9 Using lookahead to segment *A Christmas Carol* into sentences.

Again the code is not perfect when applied to *A Christmas Carol*, but the problem arises from the text: there are sentences that do not end in one of three end punctuation marks. For example, at the end of the novel, after Mr. Scrooge gives a large sum of money to two gentlemen who are collecting funds for charity, one of the men replies, "I don't know what to say to such munifi–" This is the end of the paragraph, and there is no end punctuation, so program 2.9 does not print this out.

This is almost the end of sentence segmentation in this book. It turns out that code to do this has already been written for Perl and all a programmer needs to do is download a certain package (called a Perl *module*). This is discussed in section 9.2.3.

This is a long chapter, yet much about Perl and regexes have been left out. So before moving on to chapter 3, the last section lists some Perl references for your reading pleasure. In addition, more advanced references for Perl are given in section 3.9.

2.8 REFERENCES

This section gives some introductory references for Perl. These represent only a small portion of the documentation on Perl, but it gives the reader a place to start.

There are many books that introduce programming using Perl. Three good beginning books are *Learning Perl* by Randal Schwartz, Tom Phoenix, and brian d foy [109], *Sams Teach Yourself Perl in 21 Days* by Laura Lemay [71], and *Perl 5 Interactive Course* by Jon Orwant [83]. Finally, *Programming for Linguists: Perl for Language Researchers* by Michael Hammond [51] is a gentle introduction to both Perl and programming and is intended for people interested in natural languages.

All of the above books discuss regular expressions, but to learn much more about them, start with Andrew Watt's *Beginning Regular Expressions* [124], where Perl is covered in chapter 26. Then try *Mastering Regular Expressions* by Jeffrey Friedl [47]. Chapter 7 covers Perl's implementation in detail, and chapter 2 introduces regexes mostly using Perl, which also appears in a few other chapters. It gives the details on how regexes work, and how to optimize them. Chapter 2 of Daniel Jurafsky and James Martin's *Speech and Language Processing* [64] covers regexes, and the book covers many topics on natural language processing and computational linguistics. Finally, there is a mathematical theory of regular expressions. If this interests the reader, try John Hopcroft and Jeffrey Ullman's *Introduction to Automata Theory, Languages and Computation* [58].

Of course, the most up-to-date information on Perl is always online. Web sites change unpredictably, so only three of them are given here, all of which are by The Perl Foundation. Perl documentation is available at `http://perldoc.perl.org/` [3]; and `http://www.perl.org/` [45] maintains many great links for Perl. Third, the Comprehensive Perl Archive Network (known as CPAN) at `http://cpan.perl.org` [54] has numerous existing Perl programs for a vast number of applications, and all of these are free.

For more advanced references on Perl, see section 3.9. The next chapter describes Perl's data structures. These are useful for many tasks, including counting the matches made by a regex.

PROBLEMS

2.1 One way to learn a programming language is to copy a piece of code, modify it, and then rerun it. Try this with some of the Perl code in this chapter. What happens if a semicolon is removed? Try modifying a regex to find out what it matches after it is changed. Try adjusting the arguments of a function, for example, `index` or `substr`. Be adventuresome!

2.2 Program 2.1 finds the lines in table 2.2 that match regular expression 2.2. For this problem, print out the lines that do not match, which can be done in at least two ways.

First, put the logical operator `not` in front of the regex in the `if` statement as shown below. Try this modification of this program and run the resulting code.

```
if ( not /^(1 ?)?\(\d{3}\) ?\d{3}-\d{4}$/ ) { print "$_"; }
```

Second, the two statements below are equivalent. The default variable is now explicit in the second one. Replacing `=~` by `!~` makes the expression inside the parentheses true only if there is no match. That is, `!~` is the nonmatching regex operator. Again, try modifying program 2.1 in this way and run it.

```
if ( /^(1 ?)?\(\d{3}\) ?\d{3}-\d{4}$/ ) { print "$_"; }

if ( $_ =~ /^(1 ?)?\(\d{3}\) ?\d{3}-\d{4}$/ ) { print "$_"; }
```

2.3 As noted in section 2.2.2, the caret is used in two distinct ways in a regex. Outside square brackets, it stands for the start of a line, and when it is the first character inside square brackets, it means to match all characters except for those that follow. Some examples are given in code sample 2.34. Try to guess what each line of code prints out, and then check your guess by running this code in Perl.

Code Sample 2.34 The uses of the caret. This is for problem 2.3.

```
$test = "The wedge product is written as dx^dy.";
if ($test =~ /(d.\^d.)/)    { print "match = $1\n"; }
if ($test =~ /([dxyz^]+)/)  { print "match = $1\n"; }
if ($test =~ /([xyz^]+)/)   { print "match = $1\n"; }
if ($test =~ /([^^]+)/)     { print "match = $1\n"; }
if ($test =~ /([^xyz]+)/)   { print "match = $1\n"; }
if ($test =~ /(^.*\^)/)     { print "match = $1\n"; }
```

Finally, note that to match the caret outside the square brackets, it must be escaped with a backslash. However, to include a caret as a character inside square brackets, it does not require escaping, but it cannot be the first character.

2.4 In section 2.3.1, table 2.3 gives examples of regexes as well as strings that match each one. Sometimes, however, this is too inclusive, that is, too many matches are obtained. For example, if a researcher is looking for the word *cat*, then matching *Cat*, *cats*, and *cat's* are probably all desired, but matching *scatter* or *catastrophe* are false positives.

It is useful to think about what delimits a target string, that is, what characters might begin or end this string. Is there punctuation? whitespace? XML tags? the end or beginning of a line? In addition, what forms of the string are desired?

For this problem, create a regex for the examples below, which represent different parts of speech.

    a) Write a regex to find the noun *rat*. Remember to prevent matches like *vituperation*, but to allow *Rat*, *rat's*, *rats*.

    b) Write a regex to find the adjective *old*. Remember that adjectives have comparative and superlative forms, and do not forget about preventing words like *golden* from matching.

c) Write a regex to find the verb *jump* in all its forms (past tense, third person singular, and so forth). Remember to prevent matches like *jumper*, which is a noun.

d) Write a regex to find all the forms of the verb *sit*. This, unlike *jump*, is irregular. How does this change the task?

2.5 In section 2.4, the construction given below is used. It stops execution if the file does not open for any reason.

```
open(FILE, "filename.txt") or die("Message");
```

This problem discusses why this works. Recall that the statement *A or B* is true if either *A* is true or *B* is or both are. In particular, if *A* is true, then the status of *B* is irrelevant. For the Perl command, if *open* is successful, it returns the value `true` and then there is no need to evaluate the second part of the `or` statement. That is, there is no need to execute `die`. If the `open` statement fails, it returns `false` and then `die` is executed. So this command does what is desired: if the file opens, the program runs on; otherwise, the program is halted. Perl is famous for shortcuts like this, which is why having an advanced programming book on Perl is useful.

a) Try changing `or` to `and` to see what happens.

b) Try putting `die` first to see what happens.

2.6 In the discussion of program 2.7 it is noted that `sprintf` that acts like `print`, but it allows formatting and produces a string output. The function `printf` is like `print` except that the former allows formatting. Code sample 2.35 shows a simple example of both functions.

a) Change the numbers in the double quotes to see how the output changes.

b) Look up other types of formats in a Perl book or online.

c) Try modifying program 2.7 by replacing the existing string construction for `$extract` with the `sprintf` function instead.

Code Sample 2.35 Example of the functions `printf` and `sprintf`. For problem 2.6.

```
$x = 3.1415926535;

printf "%8.3f\n", $x;

$string = sprintf "%8.5f", $x;
print "$string\n";

$string = "This is a test";
printf "%s?\n", $string;
```

Output 2.23 Output of code sample 2.35.

```
   3.142
 3.14159
This is a test?
```

2.7   Program 2.8 does make mistakes. One way to tell this is by a word count (doable in Perl or in word processing program). Show that the output of this program has less words than the original story. As noted in the text, table 2.7 shows a sentence that is broken into two pieces by this program. Where is this sentence broken? Hint: the problem is due to nesting.

2.8   In code sample 2.27, a simple regex finds the letter just before the *-s* and *-es* in a small list of plural nouns. Whichever ending is appropriate is often determined by the last letter (or letters) of the noun. For example, nouns that end in *-s* generally have the plural form *-es*: *alias* becomes *aliases*; *loss* becomes *losses*; and *sinus* becomes *sinuses*. More complete rules are available in section 523 of the *Practical English Usage* [114].

a) Create or find a larger list of plural nouns and use them as input into this code sample. What patterns do you see?

b) The regex in this code sample uses a nongreedy version of + (that is, +?). The greedy version gives different results: try to predict what it does and then test it using Perl.

2.9   Translation, `tr///`, is character-by-character substitution. Suppose a programmer wants to change all letters in a text to lowercase. One way to do this is by using the function `lc`. A second way is to specify a letter-by-letter translation with `tr/A-Z/a-z/`. Note that no letter g is needed since translation is inherently global. See code sample 2.36 for an example. The value returned by this function is the number of translations made. If none are made, then the number 0 is returned. Like `s///`, this value can be used as a logical value, where true means one or more translations, and false means no translations. Hence, `$result` gets the number 4 because four capital letters are made into lowercase letters. Like substitution, translation can be used in `if` and `while` statements.

Code Sample 2.36 Example of the translation operator returning the number of translations made. For problem 2.9.

```
$text = "Mr. Scrooge and Mr. Marley";
$result = ($text =~ tr/A-Z/a-z/);
print "$result";
```

---

a) The Caesar cipher takes each letter and replaces it by the letter three places ahead where the alphabet is seen as cyclic (see section 1.1 of Abraham Sinkov's *Elementary Cryptanalysis* [110] for a discussion). Hence, *D* replaces *A*, *E* replaces *B*, ..., *B* replaces *Y*, and *C* replaces *Z*. Use `tr///` to accomplish this.

b) DNA are long molecules that contain sequences of four bases, which are abbreviated as A, T, C, and G. DNA is double stranded, and the bases in one strand have the following relationship with the bases in the other: A and T always pair up as well as C and G. For example, given the fragment ATTTCTG, then the other strand must be TAAAGAC. Try implementing this conversion in Perl using `tr/ACGT/TGCA/`. Note that the letter translations are all done in parallel.

Although the above DNA sequence is made up, there are vast amounts of real DNA sequences available at the National Center for Biotechnology Information (NCBI) via their Web page: `http://www.ncbi.nlm.nih.gov/` [81]. For information on using Perl to analyze DNA, see the excellent book *Perl for Exploring DNA* by Mark LeBlanc and Betsey Dexter Dyer [70].

c) Use `tr///` to count the number of vowels in Dickens's *A Christmas Carol*. Assume that these are *a*, *e*, *i*, *o*, and *u*.

d) How hard is it to find vowels if *y* is included? Remember that it is not always a vowel, for example, it is a consonant in *yellow*.

2.10   This problem illustrates how Perl combined with a word list can be applied to word recreations. Fortunately, there are word game word lists that are in the public domain, and we use Grady Ward's `CROSSWD.TXT`, which is one of the *Moby Word Lists* [123] available at Project Gutenberg. It contains all inflections; for example, nouns appear both in singular and plural forms; verbs appear in all their conjugated forms, and so forth.

Regexes find strings that have a certain pattern, and this is applicable to a word list. Program 2.10 shows a simple program that prints out all words that match a regex that is entered on the command line.

```
open(WORDS, "C:/CROSSWD.TXT") or die("No such file");

while (<WORDS>) {
  if ( $_ =~ /$ARGV[0]/i ) {
    print;
  }
}
```

Program 2.10 Searching for words that match a regex. For problem 2.10.

The name of the file `CROSSWD.TXT` suggests one use: filling in words in a crossword puzzle. Here the length of any word is known, and if there are one or more letters known, so are their positions. This is also the situation in the game hangman. To solve any puzzle of these types, create a regex such that each unknown letter is represented by `\w`, and each known letter is put into the regex at its proper place. Finally, anchor the start and end of the word. Note that using Perl for word games is also discussed further in section 3.7.2 of this book.

a) Find an eight-letter word where the middle two letters are *p* and *m*. By the above discussion, this corresponds to the following regex. Note the use of starting and ending anchors.

```
/^\w\w\wpm\w\w\w$/
```

It is possible to shorten this regex, for example, `\w{3}` can replace the three letters before and after pm. Try finding all such words using program 2.10. For example, *chipmunk* and *shipment* both match.

b) Find all four-letter words that start with *p* and end with *m*.

c) Code sample 2.28 shows how to find double letters. Generalize this to find triple letters, which are much rarer. Examples of words with three or more repeated letters in a row are given in section 32 of Ross Eckler's *Making the Alphabet Dance* [41].

d) The above puzzles just scratch the surface. The book *The Oxford A to Z of Word Games* by Tony Augarde [4] lists numerous games, many of which have the goal of finding as many words as possible with certain patterns of letters. Often the length of the word is not specified, but this makes it even easier to write the regex.

For example, find all words that contain the letters pm (in that order) using /pm/ in program 2.10. For instance, find all the words that end in mp (in that order) using /mp$/, which has an ending anchor. Tony Augarde also wrote a book on the history of a selection of word games, which is called *The Oxford Guide to Word Games* [5]. Both of his books are enjoyable and informative.

CHAPTER 3

QUANTITATIVE TEXT SUMMARIES

3.1 INTRODUCTION

There are a number of text mining techniques, many of which require counts of text patterns as their starting point. The last chapter introduces regular expressions, a methodology to describe patterns, and this chapter shows how to count the matches.

As noted in section 2.6, literary texts consist of tokens, most of which are words. One useful task is counting up the number of times each distinct token appears, that is, finding the frequency of *types*. For example, sentence 3.1 has five tokens but only four types because the word *the* appears twice, while the rest appear only once.

$$\text{The cat ate the bird.} \tag{3.1}$$

Although counting four types at once is not hard, it requires deeper knowledge of Perl to count thousands of patterns simultaneously. We begin this chapter by learning enough Perl to do this.

3.2 SCALARS, INTERPOLATION, AND CONTEXT IN PERL

We have already encountered scalar variables, which start with a dollar sign and store exactly one value. Several examples are given in code sample 3.1, which also contrasts the usage of single and double quotes for strings. First, notice that $a and $b have the same value because it does not matter which type of quote marks are used to specify a specific string.

Practical Text Mining with Perl. By Roger Bilisoly
Copyright © 2008 John Wiley & Sons, Inc.

However, $g and $h are different because when $a is in double quotes, it is replaced by its value, but this is not true with single quotes. This is another example of interpolation (see the discussion near code sample 2.2).

Code Sample 3.1 Ten examples of scalar variables. Each has only one value, either a number or a string.

```
$a = 'Text';
$b = "Text";
$c = 7;
$d = 7.00;
$e = "7";
$f = "";
$g = '$a';
$h = "$a";
$i = $e + 5;
$j = "twenty" . $c;
print "$a, $b, $c, $d, $e, $f, $g, $h, $i, $j";
```

Output 3.1 Output of code sample 3.1.

```
Text, Text, 7, 7, 7, , $a, Text, 12, twenty7
```

Second, $c, $d, $e all print out the value 7. If the two zeros after the decimal point are desired (for instance, if $d represents a dollar amount), there is a formatted print statement, printf, to do this. For an example, see problem 2.6.

Third, the string "7" acts like a number when it is added to 5 to compute $i. That is, Perl converts the string "7" to the number 7, and then adds these together to get 12. In general, Perl tries to determine what *context* is appropriate for any operation, and addition implies a numerical context. For a programmer used to declaring all variables before using them, this allows some unusual programming techniques. Here is another example using the period, which stands for string concatenation. When computing $j, Perl pastes the string twenty with $c, expecting the latter is a string. However, $c is a number, but it is in a string context, hence Perl converts it into one, and the final result is twenty7. Perl recognizes other contexts, for example, strings and numbers can be used as logical truth values as discussed in section 2.7.2 (see table 2.8). In the next section we discuss scalar and array contexts.

Finally, we have already seen in section 2.3.3 that when using split to break text into words, it is natural to store the results in an array because prior knowledge of the number of words is not needed. Arrays are useful in other ways, and the next section begins our study of them.

3.3 ARRAYS AND CONTEXT IN PERL

Arrays can be defined by putting values inside parentheses, which is called a *list*. This explicitly shows its values, for example, ("The", "Black", "Cat"). Looking at code sample 3.2, an array can have both numbers and strings as entries. Finally, note that the two print statements produce exactly the same text: both give the array entries in the same order.

Code Sample 3.2 Example of initializing an array. Note that both numbers and strings can be used in one array.

```
@array = ("the", 220, "of", 149);
print "$array[0] $array[1] $array[-2] $array[-1]\n";
print "@array\n";
```

Array numbering starts at 0, so that $array[1] is the second value in the list. Negative values start at the end of the array, so $array[-1] is the last entry, and $array[-2] is the next to last entry, and so forth. All scalars in Perl start with the dollar sign, so the entries of @array all start with a dollar sign, for example, $array[0].

An array is also interpolated in a string if double quotes are used, and the default is to separate its entries with a space. However, the separator is the value of the Perl variable $". For instance, the following code prints out the entries of @array with commas.

```
$" = ','; print "@array";
```

It is valid syntax to use `print @array;` but then the entries are printed without any separator at all. So the following two commands print 1234567, which does not allow a person to determine what the entries of this array are. Consequently, interpolation of an array by putting it into double quotes is usually what a programmer wants.

```
@array = (1, 2, 34, 56, 7);  print @array;
```

Just as there are string and number contexts, there are also scalar and array contexts. This allows various shortcuts, but it can lead to unexpected results for the unwary. For example, code sample 3.3 shows examples of assigning arrays to scalars and vice versa. Try to guess what each print statement produces before reading on.

Code Sample 3.3 An example of scalar and array contexts.

```
$scalar1 = ("Damning", "with", "faint", "praise");
@array1 = ("Damning", "with", "faint", "praise");
$scalar2 = @array1;
@array2 = $scalar1;
print "$scalar1, $scalar2, @array1, @array2";
```

The two scalar values are hard to guess unless one is familiar with Perl. First, $scalar1 is assigned the last element of a list of values. But if an array is assigned to a scalar, then the scalar context is in force. In this case, Perl assigns the length of the array to the scalar. Hence, $scalar1 has the string "praise", but $scalar2 has the number 4. Thinking that $scalar1 and $scalar2 both have the same value is reasonable, but it is not what Perl does. When trying to find errors in a program, knowing these sort of details prevents frustration.

Setting an array equal to a scalar forces the latter into an array context. The result, however, is not surprising. The array that is created has only one element, which is equal to the scalar. Hence @array2 has just the value of $scalar1.

When defining an array using a list of values, these can include variables, or even other arrays. Entries of an array are accessed by using an index in square brackets, and portions of an array are accessed by giving ranges of values. One shortcut for consecutive indices is the range operator, which is formed by two periods in a row. For example, (1..5) produces an array with the numbers 1 through 5, This also works for strings: ('a'..'e') produces an array with the letters *a* through *e*. If one array has indices in it, say @indices, then @array[@indices] consists of exactly the elements of @array with the indices of @indices. Examples are given in code sample 3.4.

Code Sample 3.4 Examples of making new arrays from parts of an existing array.

```
@array1 = ("Tip", "of", "the", "iceberg");
@array2 = ("Time", "is", "of", "the", "essence");
$scalar = "not";
@indices = (0..2);
@array3 = @array1[@indices];
@array4 = @array1[0,1,2];
@array5 = @array1[0..2];
@array6 = @array1[(0..2)];
@array7 = (@array1, @array2);
@array8 = (@array2[0..1], $scalar, @array2[2..4]);
print "@array3\n@array4\n@array5\n@array6\n@array7\n@array8\n";
```

This produces output 3.2. Note that @array3, @array4, @array5, @array6 are exactly the same. In addition, Perl *flattens* arrays, that is, constructing an array by including arrays (as done for @array7) still produces a one-dimensional array. Note that the print statement has arrays separated by newline characters, which makes the output easier to read.

Output 3.2 Output of code sample 3.4.

```
Tip of the
Tip of the
Tip of the
Tip of the
Tip of the iceberg Time is of the essence
Time is not of the essence
```

Keeping in mind that Perl is context driven, try to guess what code sample 3.5 prints out before reading further.

Perl does not treat an array like a vector, so the results are not what a mathematician expects. Since $x1 is a scalar, @vector1 is in scalar context, which means its value (in this context) is the length of the array, which is 6. Therefore Perl multiplies 6 by 2 to get 12. Of course, $x2, $x3 and $x4 are also scalars, so all the arrays on the right-hand side are converted to lengths. Hence, $x2 equals 11, and $x3 is set to 30. Finally, $x4 forces the right hand side into scalar context, and the period, which is the string concatenation

Code Sample 3.5 Examples of scalar context.

```
@vector1 = (1, 1, 2, 3, 5, 8);
@vector2 = (1, 3, 4, 7, 11);
$x1 = @vector1 * 2;
$x2 = @vector1 + @vector2;
$x3 = @vector1 * @vector2;
$x4 = @vector1 . @vector2;
print "$x1, $x2, $x3, $x4";
```

operator, interprets the lengths of the arrays as strings. The result is the concatenation of "6" and "5", which produces "65".

Lists can be used to create new arrays, and there is one rule to keep in mind: assignment takes place from left to right. This is illustrated in the examples of code sample 3.6.

Code Sample 3.6 Examples of assigning arrays to lists and scalars.

```
@array = ('a'..'g');
($first) = @array;
print "$first\n";

($first, $second, @rest) = @array;
print "$first, $second, @rest\n";

($first, $second) = ($second, $first);
print "$first, $second\n";

$first = @array;
print "$first\n";
```

The first line in output 3.3 is the first element of @array, which is an example of assignment going from left to right. With this rule in mind, the output of the second print statement is no surprise. These assignments are done as if in parallel, so the third print statement reveals that the values previously in $first and $second have been switched. Finally, ($first) is an array, while $first is a scalar. Consequently, the last print statement shows that the length of the array is stored in $first, which differs from the first print statement.

Output 3.3 Output of code sample 3.6.

```
a
a, b, c d e f g
b, a
7
```

Before moving to the next section, a word of caution. Perl allows the programmer to use the same name for both a scalar and an array. That is, it is valid to use both $name and

@name, and these are treated as unrelated variables. However, doing this is confusing, so it is not recommended.

3.4   WORD LENGTHS IN POE'S "THE TELL-TALE HEART"

Instead of learning more Perl syntax in this section, we analyze the word lengths of a text. To do this, we split the text into words, find their lengths, and tally these. Since arrays use numerical indices and these lengths are numbers, using an array to store the tallies is straightforward.

The goal of section 2.4 is to write a program that extracts words from "The Tell-Tale Heart" [94]. This culminates in program 2.6, which is the starting point for the counting task at hand. A length of a string is easily obtained by the function length. So consider code sample 3.7, which is described below.

Code Sample 3.7 A program to tally the lengths of words in "A Tell-Tale Heart."

```
open (FILE, "The Tell-Tale Heart.txt") or die("File not found");

# Segment words from text file
while (<FILE>) {
  chomp;
  s/--/ -- /g;
  @word = split(/\s+/);
  foreach $x (@word) {
    if ( $x =~ /(([a-zA-Z']+-)*[a-zA-Z']+)/ ) {
      $count[length($1)] += 1;
    }
  }
}

# Print out tallies for each word length
$i = 0;
while ( $i <= $#count ) {
  print "There are $count[$i] words of length $i\n";
  $i += 1;
}
```

The overall structure is simple. The first while loop goes through the "The Tell-Tale Heart" line by line, removes the punctuation marks, and breaks each line into words. The heart of the first while loop is the regular expression. Its parentheses store each word in $1. The length function computes the length of each word, which becomes the index of the array called @count, and $count[length($1)] is incremented by 1. The entries of this array are set to the empty string by default, but this is converted to 0 when addition is attempted, which is a case of a numeric context.

The second while loop prints out the number of times each word length appears. The variable $#count gives the largest index of @count, which is the upper limit of the variable $i. Finally, the print statement produces the final tallies, as shown in output 3.4. Note that the first line does not give a value for the number of words of length 0. This happens because $count [0] is never incremented, so that its value remains the empty string. Not printing a number, however, is not as clear as printing out a zero. There is an easy solution to this: before printing out the value of $count [$i], add zero to it. This does not change any of the numerical values, and it converts the empty string to zero, as desired.

Output 3.4 Output of code sample 3.7.

```
There are  words of length 0
There are 168 words of length 1
There are 335 words of length 2
There are 544 words of length 3
There are 408 words of length 4
There are 231 words of length 5
There are 167 words of length 6
There are 137 words of length 7
There are 69 words of length 8
There are 45 words of length 9
There are 23 words of length 10
There are 9 words of length 11
There are 6 words of length 12
There are 1 words of length 13
There are 3 words of length 14
```

In fact, besides adding zero to $count [$i], there are other ways to improve this code. First, counting something is a common task in programming, so there is a shorter way to do this than using +=1. The operator ++ placed before a variable does the same thing. Similarly, the operator -- placed before a variable decreases it by 1. These operators can also be placed after a variable, but they work slightly differently when this is done. Consult Day 3 of Lemay's *Perl in 21 Days* [71] for an explanation of this technical point.

Second, this program only works for the short story "The Tell-Tale Heart." As discussed in section 2.5.1, inputting information from the command line is easy. Instead of placing the filename in the open statement, the Perl variable $ARGV [0] can be used instead. If the name of the program were word_lengths.pl, then the command line looks like the following. Note that the quotes are required because this filename has blanks in it.

```
perl word_lengths.pl "The Tell-Tale Heart.txt"
```

Third, although the second while loop works fine, it is replaceable by a for loop, which is more compact. The while statement is used when the number of iterations is not known prior to running the code, but a for statement is often used when it is known. In this case, the number of iterations is unknown beforehand because it depends on the length of the longest word in the text, but it is stored in the Perl variable $#count, so a for loop makes sense.

The for loop requires an initial value for a variable, a logical test of an ending condition, and a way to change the value of this variable. For example, consider the following line of code.

```
for ($i = 0; $i <= $#count; ++$i) { # commands }
```

This for loop is equivalent to the while loop in code sample 3.7. The while loop initializes $i before the loop and changes $i inside the loop, but the for loop does all this in one place. Making these four changes in code sample 3.7 produces program 3.1. This revised version is more general and prints out 0 if there is no instances for a specific word length.

```
open (FILE, $ARGV[0]) or die("$ARGV[0] not found");

# Segment words from text file
while (<FILE>) {
  chomp;
  s/--/ -- /g;
  @word = split(/\s+/);
  foreach $x (@word) {
    if ( $x =~ /(([a-zA-Z']+-)*[a-zA-Z']+)/ ) {
      ++$count[length($1)];
    }
  }
}

# Print out tallies for each word length
for ($i = 0; $i <= $#count; ++$i) {
  print "There are ", $count[$i]+0, " words of length $i\n";
}
```

Program 3.1 A refined version of code sample 3.7.

Finally, the `print` statement is a function that can have multiple arguments, all of which are printed. In program 3.1 these are separated by commas.

The output of program 3.1 is exactly the same as output 3.4 except for one item. The first line has a zero, not an empty string. With this application finished, the next section discusses functions that use arrays for either input or output.

3.5 ARRAYS AND FUNCTIONS

In section 2.3.3 the functions `split` and `join` are introduced. The former breaks a string into the pieces that are between the matches of a regex, which form an array. The `join` function reverses this process: it takes an array and glues its entries to form a string. For a simple example, see code sample 2.7. Both of these commands involve arrays, and this section introduces more such functions.

3.5.1 Adding and Removing Entries from Arrays

An array is a one-dimensional list of entries indexed by nonnegative integers. It is possible to modify an array by adding or removing entries from either the right or left end of it. Perl has functions to do each combination of these modifications, which we now consider.

First, an array can be lengthened by appending an entry on the right. For example, code sample 3.8 adds the word *Cat* after the last entry of `@title`, so that the `print` statements produces The Black Cat.

Code Sample 3.8 The function push adds the word *Cat* to the end of @title.

```
@title = ("The", "Black");
push(@title, "Cat");
print "@title";
```

Note that push modifies its array argument, @title. Also notice that declaring arrays beforehand is not required. When elements are added to an array, Perl knows it must be lengthened. Finally, the first argument of push must be an array: using a list instead produces an error.

The function push can create an array from scratch. For example, suppose an array of square numbers (called *squares*) is desired. Recalling that a square equals an integer multiplied by itself, we can use push inside a for loop to create it, and this is done in code sample 3.9. The results are shown in output 3.5. Since the for loop makes $i go from 1 through 10, @squares contains the first 10 squares from lowest to highest.

Code Sample 3.9 This program creates an array containing the first 10 squares by using push.

```
@squares = ();
for ($i = 1; $i <= 10; ++$i) {
  push(@squares, $i**2);
}

print "@squares";
```

Output 3.5 Output of code sample 3.9.

```
1 4 9 16 25 36 49 64 81 100
```

Second, the left end of an array can be added to by using unshift. For example, the following commands change @title to ("The", "Black", "Cat").

```
@title = ("Black", "Cat"); unshift(@title, "The");
```

As with push, unshift can be used to create arrays. For example, code sample 3.10 replaces push in code sample 3.9 by unshift. This change still produces the first 10 square numbers, but in reverse order because the numbers are now added on the left, which is shown in output 3.6.

Third, instead of adding to an array, removal of entries is possible. To remove the last (rightmost) element of an array, use pop(@array). To remove the first (leftmost) element, use shift(@array).

As a final example of these four functions, consider the operation of taking the last element of an array and making it the first. This can be done by using pop followed by unshift. Similarly, taking the first element and making it the last can be done by using shift followed by push. These types of operations are sometimes called *rotations* or

Code Sample 3.10 This program creates an array with the first 10 squares in reverse order by using unshift.

```
@squares = ();
for ($i = 1; $i <= 10; ++$i) {
  unshift(@squares, $i**2);
}

print "@squares";
```

Output 3.6 Output of code sample 3.10.

```
100 81 64 49 36 25 16 9 4 1
```

cyclic permutations. See code sample 3.11 for an example of rotating an array. The first line of output 3.7 shows that the last three letters of the alphabet have been moved to the beginning, and the second line shows that the first three letters have been moved to the end. In both cases, three letters have been rotated, though in opposite directions.

Code Sample 3.11 Example of using pop and unshift as well as push and shift to rotate the alphabet by three letters.

```
# Rotating the alphabet by three letters
@letters = ('A'..'Z');
for ($i = 1; $i <= 3; ++$i) {
  unshift(@letters, pop(@letters));
}
print @letters, "\n";

# Rotating the alphabet in the opposite direction
@letters = ('A'..'Z');
for ($i = 1; $i <= 3; ++$i) {
  push(@letters, shift(@letters));
}
print @letters;
```

Output 3.7 Output of code sample 3.11.

```
XYZABCDEFGHIJKLMNOPQRSTUVW
DEFGHIJKLMNOPQRSTUVWXYZABC
```

In this section, functions that manipulate arrays one entry at a time are discussed. Sometimes subsets of an array are desired, and Perl has a function called grep that can select entries that match a given regular expression. Chapter 2 shows the utility of regexes, so this function is powerful, as seen in the next section.

3.5.2   Selecting Subsets of an Array

The syntax for grep is given below. It selects entries of a matrix that match a regex and is based on a utility of the same name.

```
grep(/$regex/, @array);
```

Recalling code sample 2.28, which uses a regex to check for double letters in a word, we create code sample 3.12. It also uses the qr// construction, which is demonstrated in code sample 2.31. For this task the regex can be placed in grep directly, but using qr// can speed up the code (the regex is precompiled), and this technique allows the programmer to build up complex patterns. Finally, note that $regex must be inside forward slashes, as shown in this code. When run, only the word *letters* is printed out.

Code Sample 3.12 Example of using grep to select a subset of an array.

```
@words = qw(A test for double letters);
$regex = qr/(\w)\1/;
@double = grep(/$regex/, @words);

print "@double";
```

The next section discusses how to sort an array. Perl has built-in functions to sort strings in alphabetical order and numbers in numerical order, but the function sort is able to use programmer-defined orders, too.

3.5.3   Sorting an Array

Not surprisingly, the Perl function sort does sorting. However, this function does have some surprising results, one of which is shown by code sample 3.13.

Code Sample 3.13 Two examples of sorting the entries of an array.

```
$data = "Four score and seven years ago";
@words = split(/ /, $data);   # Break the phrase into words
@sorted_words = sort(@words); # Sort the words
print "@sorted_words\n";

@numbers = (1, 8, 11, 18, 88, 111, 118, 181, 188);
@sorted_numbers = sort(@numbers);   # Sort the numbers
print "@sorted_numbers";
```

It seems obvious what the output should be for these two arrays when they are sorted. Unfortunately, the results in output 3.8 are unexpected.

Both arrays have been sorted using the order given by the American Standard Code for Information Interchange (ASCII) standard, where the numbers 0 through 9 precede the uppercase letters *A* through *Z*, which precede the lowercase letters *a* through *z*. These three ranges of characters are not contiguous in ASCII, but the others that come between are not

Output 3.8 Output of code sample 3.13.

```
Four ago and score seven years
1 11 111 118 18 181 188 8 88
```

present in these arrays, so they do not matter here. Hence Four precedes ago because the former word is capitalized, which precedes lowercase.

Moreover, dictionary order is used both for the words and the numbers. For example, even though both start with the same three letters, *bee* precedes *beech*. This is equivalent to adding spaces at the end of the shorter word and declaring that a space precedes all the alphanumeric characters (which is true for ASCII). Hence 1 comes before 11, which comes before 111. And 118 precedes 18 since both start with 1, but for the second character, 1 precedes 8.

Since numbers are usually sorted by numerical value, the default used by sort is typically not appropriate with them. It turns out, fortunately, that it is easy to make sort use other orders.

The general form of sort is as follows.

```
sort { code } @array;
```

Here code must use the arguments $a and $b, and it must return a numerical value. A positive value means $a comes after $b, and a negative value means $a comes before $b. Finally, 0 means that $a and $b are equivalent. This function is often <=> or cmp, which is discussed below, but it is possible to use an explicit block of code or a user-defined function. Creating the latter requires the use of subroutines, which is discussed in section 5.3.2.1. In this section, we focus on the first two methods and only give a short example of the third method in code sample 3.20.

The default of sort is cmp, which uses the dictionary order. It returns one of three values: −1, 0, and 1, and these have the effect described in the previous paragraph. Hence code sample 3.14 reproduces output 3.8.

Code Sample 3.14 This example is equivalent to the default use of sort in code sample 3.13.

```
$data = "Four score and seven years ago";
@words = split(/ /, $data);
@sorted_words = sort { $a cmp $b } @words;
print "@sorted_words";
```

Even with cmp, it is still the case that the word *Four* is put first because its first letter is in uppercase. But this is easy to fix by applying the function lc to $a and $b, so that all strings are changed into lowercase when compared. One can also use uc, which transforms text into uppercase, because the key is to have all text in the same case. Changing code sample 3.14 this way produces code sample 3.15.

Output 3.9 now shows the desired results. Note that @sorted_words contains the sorted words, but that the entries of @words are unchanged. Unlike pop or shift, sort does not modify its argument.

Switching $a and $b sorts in reverse order, so $a and $b are not interchangeable. The function reverse reverses the order of an array, so if reverse alphabetical order is desired, then either of the two methods in code sample 3.16 works.

Code Sample 3.15 This modification of code sample 3.14 produces the results one expects in output 3.9.

```
$data = "Four score and seven years ago";
@words = split(/ /, $data);
@sorted_words = sort { lc($a) cmp lc($b) } @words;
print "@sorted_words";
```

Output 3.9 Output of code sample 3.15.

```
ago and Four score seven years
```

Code Sample 3.16 Two ways to obtain reverse alphabetical order.

```
$data = "Four score and seven years ago";
@words = split(/ /, $data);

# Reverse alphabetical order, method 1
@reverse_sorted_words1 = sort { lc($b) cmp lc($a) } @words;

# Reverse alphabetical order, method 2
@reverse_sorted_words2 = reverse sort {lc($a) cmp lc($b)} @words;

print "@reverse_sorted_words1\n@reverse_sorted_words2";
```

Remember that code sample 3.13 did not sort the numbers into numerical order. The numerical analog of cmp is <=>, which is sometimes called the *spaceship* operator because of its appearance. Like its analog, it returns one of three values: -1, 0, and 1, which correspond to less than, equal to, and greater than, respectively. Code sample 3.17, which uses the spaceship operator, now sorts the numbers as expected: @sorted_numbers is identical to @numbers.

Code Sample 3.17 Example of a numerical sort.

```
@numbers = (1, 8, 11, 18, 88, 111, 118, 181, 188);
@sorted_numbers = sort{ $a <=> $b } @numbers;
print "@sorted_numbers";
```

We end this section with two types of sorts, each one of interest to anyone who enjoys word games. The first sorts an array of words in alphabetical order, but considering the letters from right to left. The second is a double sort: first sort by word length, and within the words of a fixed length, then sort by the usual alphabetical order. Although the output of the code shown below is not that informative, there are extensive word lists on the Web (for example, see Grady Ward's *Moby Word Lists* [123]), and if these two sorts are applied to such a list, that output is interesting.

To accomplish right to left alphabetical word order, we use the function `reverse`, which is used above to reverse the entries in an array. In scalar context, this function reverses the characters in a string. If applied to a number, the number is acted upon as if it were a string. Code sample 3.18 shows how to perform this sort.

Code Sample 3.18 Example of a right to left alphabetical word sort.

```
@words = qw(This is a list of words using qw);
@sorted_words = sort {lc(reverse($a)) cmp lc(reverse($b))} @words;
print "@sorted_words";
```

Note that `lc` is used so that case differences are ignored. Because writing a list of words, each with double quotes, is tedious, Perl has the operator `qw` that informs it that strings are involved. To remember this, think of the initial letters of *quote word*. Output 3.10 gives the results, which make sense if the ends of the words are considered.

Output 3.10 Output of code sample 3.18.

```
a of using words is This list qw
```

For the second example, we sort words first by using length, then by alphabetical order for all the words of a given length. Code sample 3.19 shows an example of this using the following logic. First, compare the lengths of $a and $b using the function `length` and the comparison operator `<=>`. If these lengths are the same, then compare the strings using `lc` and `cmp`.

Code Sample 3.19 Example of sorting strings first by length then by alphabetical order.

```
@words = qw(This is a list of words using qw);
@sorted_words =
  sort { $value = (length($a) <=> length($b));
    if ($value == 0) { return lc($a) cmp lc($b);
    } else { return $value }; }
  @words;

print "@sorted_words";
```

Output 3.11 Output of code sample 3.19.

```
a is of qw list This using words
```

Although it works, code sample 3.19 is becoming hard to read. This sorting code can be defined as a separate function, which is done in code sample 3.20. The technique is almost the same as making a user-defined function, except that the arguments are the special Perl variables $a and $b. Notice that the function name `lengthSort` is put between `sort` and the name of the array, and curly brackets are not needed. Finally, the output of this code sample is the same as output 3.11.

Code Sample 3.20 Rewriting code sample 3.19 using a subroutine for sorting.

```
@words = qw(This is a list of words using qw);
@sorted_words = sort byLength @words;
print "@sorted_words";

sub byLength {
  $value = (length($a) <=> length($b));
  if ($value == 0) {
    return lc($a) cmp lc($b);
  } else {
    return $value;
  }
}
```

3.6 HASHES

Arrays are excellent tools for storing a sequence of values. For example, when splitting a sentence into words, the order is important. However, suppose the goal is the following: for a specific text, determine what set of words are in it and then count the frequency of each of these. To use an array, each numerical index must represent a unique word, and the problem becomes how to keep track of which index represents which word.

Fortunately, there is a better way. Instead of indexing with the numbers 0, 1, 2, ..., it is more convenient to use the words themselves for indices. This idea is exactly what a *hash* does.

Just as arrays start with their own unique symbol (an @), hashes must begin with the percent sign, that is, %. Recall that the entries of @array are accessed by $array[0], $array[1], $array[2], ... Similarly, the entries of %hash are accessed by $hash{"the"}, $hash{"and"}, and so forth. The strings that have associated values are the *keys*. See table 3.1 for a summary of these points.

Table 3.1 Comparison of arrays and hashes in Perl.

Arrays	Hashes
@name	%name
$name[0]	$name{"string1"}
$name[1]	$name{"string2"}
Indices are numbers	Indices are strings
Uses square brackets	Uses curly brackets
Ordered	No inherit order

Like arrays, lists can be used to define a hash. Moreover, it is easy to convert a hash to an array, as well as the reverse. Examples of hashes and hash conversions to arrays are given in code sample 3.21. Unlike arrays, hashes cannot be interpolated in double quotes because they are unordered.

Note that %hash1 through %hash4 are identical. Although a hash can be defined using a list with all commas, its entries naturally come in key-value pairs, so Perl provides the

Code Sample 3.21 Examples of defining hashes and converting them into arrays.

```
%hash1 = ("the", 220, "of", 149);
%hash2 = ("the" => 220, "of" => 149);
%hash3 = (the, 220, of, 149);
%hash4 = (the => 220, of => 149);
%hash5 = (1..9);
@array1 = %hash1;
@array2 = %hash2;
@array3 = %hash3;
@array4 = %hash4;
@array5 = %hash5;
$" = ",";
print "@array1\n@array2\n@array3\n@array4\n@array5\n";
```

=> operator, which is equivalent to a comma, but it is easier to read. Perl also expects that the keys are strings, so quotes (either single or double) are optional as long as there are no embedded blanks. Since pairs of entries are the norm for a hash, a list usually has an even number of entries. However, %hash5 has an odd length, which means the key 9 has no value paired to it in the list. Whenever this happens, Perl assigns the empty string as the value.

Output 3.12 Output of code sample 3.21.

```
the,220,of,149
the,220,of,149
the,220,of,149
the,220,of,149
1,2,3,4,7,8,9,,5,6
```

The first four lines of output 3.12 contain no surprises. The arrays are identical to the hashes assigned to them. However, the fifth line shows that the hash has changed the order of some of the key-value pairs. In particular, key 5 has been moved to the last position. Hashes are ordered so that storage and retrieval of values are optimized.

As is the case with arrays, there are Perl functions that manipulate hashes. The most important of these are discussed in the next section.

3.6.1 Using a Hash

Hashes have no particular order, so functions such as push and pop do not make sense, and using them with a hash produces a compilation error. However, hashes do have keys and values, which are returned as arrays by the functions keys and values, respectively. The former is particularly useful for looping through a hash. We consider this next.

Consider code sample 3.22. The variable $sentence is a string, and the punctuation is removed by using the s/// operator. Then split extracts the individual words, which are put into the array @words. The foreach loop goes through this array one at a time, which are keys for the hash, %counts. Initially, each key has the empty string for its value, but the increment operator ++ forces this empty string into number context, where it acts like

0, so it works even for the first appearance of a word. Note that lc is used to put all the letters into lowercase, so that capitalization is ignored. For example, the words *The* and *the* are counted as the same.

Code Sample 3.22 This code counts the frequency of each word in the sentence by using a hash.

```
$sentence = "The cat that saw the black cat is a calico.";
$sentence =~ s/[.,?!;;'"(){}\[\]]//g; # Remove punctuation
@words = split(/ /,$sentence);
foreach $word (@words) {
  ++$counts{lc($word)};
}

foreach $word (keys %counts) {
  print "$word, $counts{$word}\n";
}
```

The second foreach loop prints out the frequencies of each word by looping over the array produced by keys. Remember that the order of these keys typically looks random to a human, as is the case in output 3.13. However, these keys can be sorted.

Output 3.13 Output of code sample 3.22.

```
the, 2
a, 1
that, 1
is, 1
cat, 2
saw, 1
black, 1
calico, 1
```

Alphabetical order is commonly used to list the keys of a hash. Since this is the default order of sort, it is easy to do: just put this function in front of keys in code sample 3.22, which produces code sample 3.23. This prints output 3.14.

Code Sample 3.23 Example of sorting the keys of the hash %counts, which is created in code sample 3.22.

```
foreach $word (sort keys %counts) {
  print "$word, $counts{$word}\n";
}
```

Suppose that the least frequent words in $sentence are of interest. In this case, listing the values of the hash in numerical order is desired, which is done by the following trick. The value of key $a is $counts{$a}, and an analogous statement is true for $b. Hence, we

Output 3.14 Output of code sample 3.23.

```
a, 1
black, 1
calico, 1
cat, 2
is, 1
saw, 1
that, 1
the, 2
```

apply the spaceship operator to $counts{$a} and $counts{$b}, which is done in code sample 3.24, which produces output 3.15.

Code Sample 3.24 The sort function puts the values of %counts (from code sample 3.22) into numerical order.

```
foreach $word (sort {$counts{$a} <=> $counts{$b}} keys %counts) {
  print "$word, $counts{$word}\n";
}
```

Output 3.15 Output of code sample 3.24.

```
a, 1
that, 1
is, 1
saw, 1
black, 1
calico, 1
the, 2
cat, 2
```

Although the values are in order, for a fixed value, the keys are not in alphabetical order. This is fixed by byValues in code sample 3.25, which is an extension of byLength in code sample 3.20. By using this user-defined function, this sort statement is much easier to read. Finally, the results of using this order is given in output 3.16.

We end this section with a quick mention of one additional Perl hash function. The function exists checks to see whether or not a key has a value in a hash. Here is an example of its use.

```
if ( exists($counts{$key}) ) { # commands }
```

Up to this point, much of this chapter discusses how to use arrays and hashes in Perl. Now it is time to apply this knowledge. The next section discusses two longer examples where we implement our new programming skills to analyze text.

Code Sample 3.25 The subroutine byValues first orders the values of %counts (from code sample 3.22) numerically and then by alphabetical order.

```
foreach $word (sort byValues keys %counts) {
  print "$word, $counts{$word}\n";
}

sub byValues {
  $value = $counts{$a} <=> $counts{$b};
  if ($value == 0) {
    return $a cmp $b;
  } else {
    return $value;
  }
}
```

Output 3.16 Output of code sample 3.25.

```
a, 1
black, 1
calico, 1
is, 1
saw, 1
that, 1
cat, 2
the, 2
```

3.7 TWO TEXT APPLICATIONS

This section discusses two applications, which are easy to program in Perl thanks to hashes. The first illustrates an important property of most texts, one that has consequences later in this book. The second develops some tools that are useful for certain types of word games. We have worked hard learning Perl, and now it is time to reap the benefits.

Before starting these applications, we generalize the concordance code, program 2.7, which is hard-coded to read in Charles Dickens's *A Christmas Carol* [39] and to find the word *the*. Section 2.5.1 discusses the command line, which is also used in program 3.1. The version here, program 3.2, uses the command line to read in a file name, a regex, and a text radius (to determine the size of the text extracts). This program proves useful below.

As for the code itself, note that the first two lines are comments, which tell the user about the code. The regex from the command line is put into parentheses when assigned to the variable $target, which causes the match to be stored in $1. If the parentheses are included on the command line, however, the code still works.

3.7.1 Zipf's Law for *A Christmas Carol*

This section determines which words are in Dickens's *A Christmas Carol* and how often each of these appears. That is, we determine all the word frequencies. This sounds like

```
# USAGE > perl regex_concordance.pl FileName.txt Regex Radius
# This program is case insensitive.

open (FILE, "$ARGV[0]") or die("$ARGV[0] not found");
$/ = ""; # Paragraph mode for first while loop

# Initialize variables
$target = "($ARGV[1])"; # Parentheses needed for $1 in 2nd while
$radius = $ARGV[2];
$width = 2*$radius;

while (<FILE>) {
  chomp;
  s/\n/ /g; # Replace newlines by spaces

  while ( $_ =~ /$target/gi ) {
    $match = $1;
    $pos = pos($_);
    $start = $pos - $radius - length($match);

    if ($start < 0) {
      $extract = substr($_, 0, $width+$start+length($match));
      $extract = (" " x -$start) . $extract;
      $len = length($extract);
    } else {
      $extract = substr($_, $start, $width+length($match));
    }

    print "$extract\n";
  }
}
```

Program 3.2 A concordance program that finds matches for a regular expression. The file name, regex, and text extract radius are given as command line arguments.

a straightforward task, but punctuation is trickier than one might expect. As discussed in sections 2.4.2 and 2.4.3, hyphens and apostrophes cause problems. Using program 3.2, we can find all instances of potentially problematic punctuation. These cases enable us to decide how to handle the punctuation so that the words in the novel change as little as possible.

First, we check for dashes in the novel and whether or not there are spaces between the dashes and the adjacent words. The following command produces output 3.17.

```
perl regex_concordance.pl A_Christmas_Carol.txt -- 30
```

Notice the name of the file containing the novel has no blanks in it. If it did, double quotes must be placed around this name (single quotes do not work).

The complete output has 82 lines, and the first 10 are shown here. Certainly *A Christmas Carol* does use dashes, and these are generally placed in between words without spaces, so

Output 3.17 Output from program 3.2, which prints out extracts containing dashes. Only the first 10 lines shown.

```
ut after dark in a breezy spot--say Saint Paul's Churchyard fo .
Paul's Churchyard for instance-- literally to astonish his son
              Once upon a time--of all the good days in the ye
 in the year, on Christmas Eve--old Scrooge sat busy in his co
 but it was quite dark already-- it had not been light all day
 it had not been light all day--and candles were flaring in th
 s time, when it has come round--apart from the veneration due
 g to it can be apart from that--as a good time; a kind, forgiv
 oge said that he would see him--yes, indeed he did. He went th
 stablishments I have mentioned--they cost enough; and those wh
```

the few spaces that do appear are typos. Substituting a space for each dash removes them, and this is easily done by s/--/ /g;.

Next we check for single hyphens, which should only appear in hyphenated words. The regex \w-\w detects them since it specifies a hyphen between two alphanumeric characters. This gives the following command, which produces 226 examples, the first 10 of which are given in output 3.18. Note that the regex is in double quotes, which are optional here, but are required if the regex has spaces or quotes.

```
perl regex_concordance.pl A_Christmas_Carol.txt "\w-\w" 30
```

Output 3.18 Output from program 3.2, which prints out extracts containing hyphenated words. Only the first 10 lines shown.

```
ld Marley was as dead as a door-nail.
 particularly dead about a door-nail. I might have been incline
ned, myself, to regard a coffin-nail as the deadest piece of ir
at Marley was as dead as a door-nail.
re would be in any other middle-aged gentleman rashly turning o
         Oh! But he was a tight-fisted hand at the grind-stone,
 tight-fisted hand at the grind-stone, Scrooge! a squeezing, wr
generous fire; secret, and self-contained, and solitary as an o
; he iced his office in the dog-days; and didn't thaw it one de
crooge sat busy in his counting-house. It was cold, bleak, biti
```

Since this text has just over 200 hyphenated words, we need to decide what to do with them. The 3 simplest choices are: leave them as is; split them into separate words; or combine them into one word. In this case, Dickens is an acknowledged great writer, so let us leave his text as is.

Third, and trickiest, are the apostrophes. This text uses double quotes for direct quotations. Apostrophes are used for quotes within quotations as well as for possessive nouns. The latter produces one ambiguity due to possessives of plural nouns ending in *s*, for example, *seven years'*. Another possible ambiguity is a contraction with an apostrophe at either the beginning or the end of a word. To check how common the latter is, the regex

`\w'\W` checks for an alphanumeric character, an apostrophe, and then a nonalphanumeric character. Running the following command creates output 3.19, which gives all 13 cases.

```
perl regex_concordance.pl A_Christmas_Carol.txt "\w'\W" 30
```

Output 3.19 Output from program 3.2, which matches words ending with '.

```
oes about with 'Merry Christmas' on his lips, should be boiled
uddy as they passed. Poulterers' and grocers' trades became a s
passed. Poulterers' and grocers' trades became a splendid joke:
last mention of his seven years' dead partner that afternoon. A
ave become a mere United States' security if there were no days
azing away to their dear hearts' content. There was nothing ver
f it went wrong. The poulterers' shops were still half open, an
l half open, and the fruiterers' were radiant in their glory. T
rapes, made, in the shopkeepers' benevolence to dangle from con
                The Grocers'! oh, the Grocers'! nearly clos
    The Grocers'! oh, the Grocers'! nearly closed, with perhaps t
ing their dinners to the bakers' shops. The sight of these poor
                "Are spirits' lives so short?" asked Scrooge
```

The only example other than a possessive noun is the first line, which is a quote within a quote that ends in the letter *s*. In particular, none of these are a contraction with an apostrophe at the end of the word. So if no single quotes after the final letter of a word are removed, only one error arises. If one error is unacceptable, then add a line of code to handle this exception.

Finally, there is the possibility of a contraction starting with an apostrophe, which does happen in this text. Using the regex `\W'\w`, we find all cases of this. This results in 24 matches, the first 10 of which are given in output 3.20.

Output 3.20 Output from program 3.2, which matches words starting with '. Only the first 10 lines shown.

```
d Scrooge's name was good upon 'Change, for anything he chose t
books and having every item in 'em through a round dozen of mon
very idiot who goes about with 'Merry Christmas' on his lips, s
              "Couldn't I take 'em all at once, and have it ove
fter sailing round the island. 'Poor Robin Crusoe, where have y
in, accompanied by his fellow-'prentice.
shutters--one, two, three--had 'em up in their places--four, fi
laces--four, five, six--barred 'em and pinned 'em--seven, eight
ve, six--barred 'em and pinned 'em--seven, eight, nine--and cam
rybody had retired but the two 'prentices, they did the same to
```

The only contractions that appear are *'Change* (short for the *Exchange*, a financial institution), *'em* (them), and *'prentices* (apprentices). Again we can check for these three cases, or we can always remove an initial single quote, and this produces only one ambiguity: it is not possible to distinguish between '*Change* and the word *change* (which does appear in this text). For more on contractions, see problem 3.1.

Turning the above discussion into Perl code, we get program 3.3. There are several points to note. First, there are two open statements. The first opens the text file containing *A Christmas Carol*. The second opens a file for the output, which is indicated by the greater sign at the start of the filename (see section 2.5.2 for more on this). Since this program produces many lines of output (one for each distinct word), this is easier to handle if it is in a file. To write to this, the `print` statement must have the filehandle immediately after it as shown in the last `foreach` loop.

```perl
open(TEXT, "A_Christmas_Carol.txt") or die("Text not found");
open(OUT, ">Word_Counts.csv");

while (<TEXT>) {
  chomp;
  $_ = lc;  # Convert to lowercase
  s/--/ /g; # Replace dash with space
  s/ +/ /g; # Replace multiple spaces to one space
  s/[.,:;?"!()]//g; # Remove punctuation (except ')

  @words = split(/ /);

  foreach $word (@words) {

    if ( /(\w+)'\W/ ) {
      if ( $1 eq 'Christmas' ) {
        $word =~ s/'//g; # Remove single quote
      }
    }
    if ( /\W'(\w+)/ ) {
      if ( ($1 ne 'change') and ($1 ne 'em') and
           ($1 ne 'prentices') ) {

        $word =~ s/'//g; # Remove single quote
      }
    }

    $dictionary{$word} += 1; # Increment count for $word
  }
}

foreach $word (sort byDescendingValues keys %dictionary) {
  print OUT "$word, $dictionary{$word}\n";
}
```

Program 3.3 This program counts the frequency of each word in *A Christmas Carol*. The output is sorted by decreasing frequencies.

Second comes the `while` loop. It starts with `chomp`, which removes the final newline character from the default variable, `$_`. Then `$_ = lc;` converts the default variable to lowercase. The next three lines are substitutions that remove all of the punctuation except for the single quote. Next, the line of text is split into words.

Third, the `foreach` loop inside the `while` loop decides whether or not to remove apostrophes. If it is inside the word itself, it is not removed. If it is at the end of the word, it is removed only if the word is *Christmas*, which is an odd rule, but one discovered by looking at output 3.19. If the single quote is at the start of the string, it is removed unless it is one of the following: *'change*, *'em*, or *'prentices*.

Fourth, since `$word` has no punctuation (except apostrophes), we use the hash `%dictionary` to increment the count associated with `$word`. Once the `while` loop is done, the last `foreach` loop prints out the results to the file `Word_Counts.csv`. The order of the `sort` is determined by `byDescendingValues`, which sorts by values, from largest to smallest. Code sample 3.26 gives the subroutine for this function, and the first 10 lines it produces are given in output 3.21. Note that the suffix of this file, `.csv`, stands for *comma-separated variables*. Many types of programs know how to read such a file, and they are a popular way to store data.

Code Sample 3.26 This subroutine sorts the values of `%dictionary` (computed by program 3.3) from largest to smallest.

```
sub byDescendingValues {
  $value = $dictionary{$b} <=> $dictionary{$a};
  if ($value == 0) {
    return $a cmp $b;
  } else {
    return $value;
  }
}
```

Output 3.21 First 10 lines of output from program 3.3, which uses code sample 3.26.

```
the, 1563
and, 1052
a, 696
to, 658
of, 652
in, 518
it, 513
he, 485
was, 427
his, 420
```

Finally, the file used for *A Christmas Carol* has chapter titles. These have been included in program 3.3. If a programmer wants to leave these out, this requires modifying this code.

Now we can state and illustrate Zipf's law. First, the words in the text are listed from most to least frequent. Then assign ranks for each word by numbering them 1, 2, 3, ...

For example, from output 3.21 we see that *the* is most common (appearing 1563 times), so it has rank 1. Since the sequence continues *and, a, to*, these words have ranks 2, 3, 4, respectively. If there are ties, then arrange these alphabetically, and rank them in that order. For example, *but* and *not* both appear 177 times, so give the former rank 24, and the latter rank 25. As the counts get smaller, the number of ties goes up. For instance, there are 2514 out of 4398 words that appear exactly once (just over 57%). Such words are called *hapax legomena*.

The total number of words in *A Christmas Carol* is determined by adding all the numbers produced by program 3.3, which is 28,514. We can also count the number of distinct words, or types. This is the number of lines of output, which equals 4398.

Once the ranks are given, each word has two values associated with it: its frequency and its rank. Zipf's law says that plotting the logarithm of the frequency against the logarithm of the rank produces an approximately straight line. Figure 3.1 shows such a plot, which is approximately straight. More importantly, since the horizontal lines in the lower right corner represent numerous ties, the conclusion is clear: the lower the frequency, the larger the number of ties, on average.

3.7.2 Perl for Word Games

Now we take a break for some fun. There are various types of word lists on the Web, and for word games we want one that includes inflected words. That is, nouns include both singular and plural forms; verbs include all the conjugated forms; adjectives include the comparative and superlative forms, and so forth. We use Grady Ward's CROSSWD.TXT from the *Moby Word Lists* [123]. This has more than 110,000 words total, including inflected forms.

In this section we consider three types of word games. First, in a crossword puzzle the length of a word is known. In addition, a few letters and their locations in the word can be known. Using CROSSWD.TXT, we find all words that match these two constraints. Second, given a group of letters, we find out if it is possible to rearrange them so that they form a word. For example, the letters *eorsstu* can form seven words: *estrous, oestrus, ousters, sourest, souters, stoures,* and *tussore*. Third, given a group of letters, what are all the possible words that can be formed from all or some of these letters? For example, using all or some of the letters in *textmining*, what words can be formed? There are many possibilities, some obvious like *text* and *mining*, and others that are harder to discover, like *emitting* and *tinge*.

3.7.2.1 *An Aid to Crossword Puzzles* Finding words to fit in a crossword puzzle is easy to do. Suppose the goal is to find a seven-letter word with a *j* in the third position and an *n* in the sixth. All the other letters must match \w, so the following regex works because CROSSWD.TXT has exactly one word per line, so the initial caret and ending dollar sign guarantee that the matches are exactly seven letters long.

```
/^\w{2}j\w{2}n\w$/
```

Program 3.4 is straightforward to create. For flexibility, it uses a command line argument to supply the regex, which is constructed by the qr// operator. The if statement prints out each word that matches this regex.

If we run the following command, we get output 3.22, assuming that program 3.4 is stored under the filename crossword.pl.

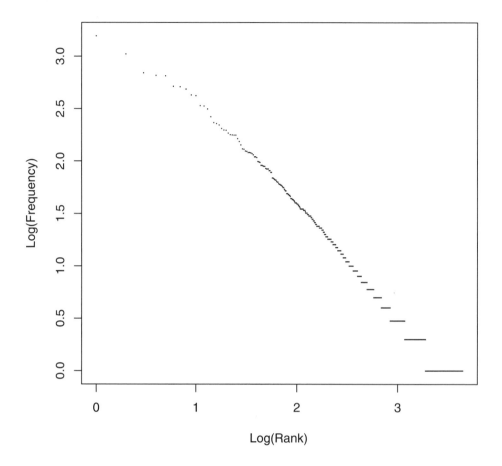

Figure 3.1   Log(Frequency) vs. Log(Rank) for the words in Dickens's *A Christmas Carol*.

```
perl crossword.pl "^\w{2}j\w{2}n\w$"
```

The usefulness of this program depends on the number of matches found. The extreme case is using something like the regex /^\w{7}$/, which returns all 21,727 seven-letter words, which is not much help in solving a crossword clue.

3.7.2.2   Word Anagrams   Here we create an anagram dictionary, which is a listing of words indexed by the letters of each word sorted in alphabetical order. For example, the word *abracadabra* has the index string *aaaaabbcdrr*. By making this index string a key, we can create a hash that stores the entire anagram dictionary. Unfortunately, `sort` does not have a string context, but the following approach works.

The function `split(//)` turns a string into an array, which `sort` can order. Finally, the function `join` turns the array back into a string. Its first argument is the text to place

```
# USAGE > perl crosswd.pl "regex"

open(WORDS, "CROSSWD.TXT") or die;
$regex = qr/$ARGV[0]/;

while (<WORDS>) {
  if ( /$regex/ ) {
    print;
  }
}
```

Program 3.4 Finding words fitting crossword-puzzle-type constraints.

Output 3.22 All matches from running program 3.4 as described in the text.

```
adjoins
adjoint
enjoins
rejoins
sejeant
```

---

between array entries, and if the empty string is used, then the entries of the array are concatenated together. So using these three functions can create the index string discussed above.

There is one last issue. Some keys work for more than one word. This requires checking to see if any value has been assigned to the current key. If so, then the program appends the new word to the old list using a comma as a separator. If not, then the current word becomes the value for this key. Using these ideas results in program 3.5. The first 10 lines produced by this program are given in output 3.23. Finally, note that this same technique is applicable to all sorts of strings, not just words. See problem 3.9 for an example.

3.7.2.3 Finding Words in a Set of Letters
The final task is harder because it requires considering not just a group of letters, but also all subgroups. Unfortunately, the number of nonempty subsets of n letters is $2^n - 1$, which grows quickly. For instance, eight letters has 255 subsets. Fortunately, there is a trick to avoid considering all these explicitly.

Suppose we want to find all the words that can be formed from some or all of the letters in the word *algorithm*. Sorting the letters of this word produces *aghilmort*. Now loop through all the keys of the anagram dictionary created by program 3.5. For each key, sort its letters, then create a regex from these by placing .* at the beginning, between each pair of letters, and at the end. For example, for the key *pull*, we sort to get *llpu*, and then create the regex /.*l.*l.*p.*u.*/. The only way that *aghilmort* can match this regex is that all the letters of *pull* are contained in the letters of *algorithm*. In this case, this is not true, so *pull* cannot be formed.

It is true that they are many keys, but computers are fast. Taking the logic of the last paragraph, and reusing the anagram dictionary code of program 3.5, we get program 3.6. In this code, $index contains the sorted letters of the string entered on the command line. The foreach loop sorts each key of %dictionary, creates a regex from these sorted letters

```
open(WORDS, "CROSSWD.TXT") or die;

while (<WORDS>) {
  chomp;
  @letters = split(//);
  $key = join('',sort(@letters));
  if ( exists($dictionary{$key}) ) {
    $dictionary{$key} .= ",$_";
  } else {
    $dictionary{$key} = $_;
  }
}

foreach $key (sort keys %dictionary) {
  print "$key, $dictionary{$key}\n";
}
```

Program 3.5 Creates an anagram dictionary.

Output 3.23 First 10 lines from running program 3.5

```
aa, aa
aaaaabbcdrr, abracadabra
aaaabcceeloprsttu, postbaccalaureate
aaaabcceelrstu, baccalaureates
aaaabcceelrtu, baccalaureate
aaaabdilmorss, ambassadorial
aaaabenn, anabaena
aaaabenns, anabaenas
aaaaccdiiklllsy, lackadaisically
aaaaccdiiklls, lackadaisical
```

as described above, then checks if $index matches. This technique is another example of interpolation, and it demonstrates how powerful it can be.

Finally, 10 lines of program 3.6 are given in output 3.24. Lines with more than one entry contain anagrams. For example, *algorithm* is an anagram of *logarithm*. Although the order of these words seems random, they are in alphabetical order of their keys.

In this section we have seen the power of hashes. In the next, we consider more complex data structures, which are essential later in this book.

3.8   COMPLEX DATA STRUCTURES

For a single text, hashes and arrays are sufficient. However, if a collection of texts are of interest, it is unwieldy to use numerous data structures, each with its own name. Fortunately, Perl supports complex data structures like arrays of arrays. But to understand how these work, we must learn about references, the topic of the next section.

```
# USAGE > perl subsetwords.pl string

open(WORDS, "CROSSWD.TXT") or die;

while (<WORDS>) {
  chomp;
  $key = join('',sort(split(//)));
  if ( exists($dictionary{$key}) ) {
    $dictionary{$key} .= ",$_";
  } else {
    $dictionary{$key} = $_;
  }
}

$index = join('',sort(split(//,$ARGV[0])));

foreach $key (sort keys %dictionary) {
  $regex = join('.*', split(//,$key) );
  $regex = '.*' . $regex . '.*';
  if ( $index =~ /$regex/ ) {
    print "$dictionary{$key}\n";
  }
}
```

Program 3.6 This program finds all words formed from subsets of a group of letters.

Output 3.24 First 10 lines from running program 3.6 with *algorithm* as the input.

```
hag
laigh
algorithm,logarithm
alright
alight
aright
ogham
garth
ghat
glioma
```

3.8.1   References and Pointers

So far, we have assigned values to variables. For example, the command below assigns the string the to the scalar $word.

```
$word = "the";
```

However, it is possible to assign not the value, but the memory location of the value, which is called a *reference*. For example, the command below now stores the location of the in the variable $wordref.

```
$wordref = \"the";
```

The backslash in front of the string indicates that a reference to that string is desired. Backslashes in front of arrays and hashes also produce references. Printing out $wordref on my computer produced SCALAR(0x184ba64), where the value in the parentheses is a memory location written out as a base 16 number (as indicated by the first two characters, 0x).

The actual memory location is not directly useful to a programmer, so a method to retrieve the value is needed, which is called *dereferencing*. A scalar reference is dereferenced by putting it inside the curly brackets of ${}. An example of this is given in code sample 3.27.

Code Sample 3.27 Example of referencing and dereferencing scalars.

```
$word = "the";
$wordref1 = \"the";
$wordref2 = \$word;
print "$wordref1, $wordref2\n";
print "${$wordref1}, ${$wordref2}\n";
print "$$wordref1, $$wordref2\n";
```

Running this code sample produces output 3.25. The print statements show that $wordref1 and $wordref2 have memory locations, and that ${$wordref1} and ${$wordref2} do access the values. In addition, these can be abbreviated to $$wordref1 and $$wordref2.

Output 3.25 Results of code sample 3.27.

```
SCALAR(0x1832824), SCALAR(0x18327f4)
the, the
the, the
```

Analogous examples can be created for both arrays and hashes. Code sample 3.28 shows an example for the array @sentence. Note that there are two ways to make an array reference. First, put the backslash operator in front of an array name. Second, use square brackets instead of parentheses for a list, which is also called an *anonymous array*. Note that putting a backslash in front of a list does not create an array reference.

Looking at output 3.26, putting the array reference inside @{} does work. That is, @{$sentenceref1} is an array, so, for example, @{$sentenceref1}->[0] or @{$sentenceref1}[0] accesses the first element of the array. However, this notation is a bit cumbersome, so two equivalent forms exist in Perl: $sentenceref1->[0] and $$sentenceref1[0]. References are also called *pointers*, and so a pointing arrow is an appropriate symbol. Notice that when $sentenceref1->[-1] is set to a different word, the original array, @sentence is itself changed. Hence changing a reference changes what it points to.

Finally, code sample 3.29 shows a hash example of referencing and dereferencing. As with arrays, there are two ways to specify a hash reference: using the backslash or using curly brackets, and the latter is called an *anonymous hash*. Again using either the arrow or the double dollar notations work with hash references, similar to arrays. The results of this code sample are given in output 3.27.

Code Sample 3.28 Example of referencing and dereferencing an array.

```
@sentence = qw(This is a sentence.);
$sentenceref1 = \@sentence;
$sentenceref2 = ["This", "is", "a", "sentence."];

print "$sentenceref1, $sentenceref2\n";
print "@{$sentenceref1}\n";
print "@{$sentenceref2}\n\n";

print "@{$sentenceref1}->[0]\n";
print "@{$sentenceref1}[0]\n";
print "$sentenceref1->[0]\n";
print "$$sentenceref1[0]\n\n";
print "$sentenceref1->[-1]\n";

$sentenceref1->[-1] = "banana";
print "@sentence\n";
```

Output 3.26 Results of code sample 3.28.

```
Arrays

ARRAY(0x1832974), ARRAY(0x2356f0)
This is a sentence.
This is a sentence.

This
This
This
This

sentence.
This is a banana
```

If you are new to programming, creating a reference to a memory location, and then dereferencing it to access its value may seem crazy. After all, why not just work with the value itself? It turns out that references are useful in more than one way, but we consider just one important application here.

Before stating this application, the need for it comes from one unfortunate fact about Perl: it only handles one-dimensional data structures. However, complex data structures like multidimensional arrays are possible in Perl, so how is this one-dimensional limitation overcome? Consider this concrete example: suppose a one-dimensional array $array2d contained references to other arrays. Then $array2d[0] is a reference to another array, as is $array2d[1], $array2d[2], and so forth. By dereferencing $array2d[0], we are able to access this new array, and the same is true for $array2d[1], $array2d[2], ... The

Code Sample 3.29 Example of referencing and dereferencing a hash.

```
%counts = (the => 1563, and => 1052, a => 696);
$countsref1 = \%counts;
$countsref2 = {the => 1563, and => 1052, a => 696};

print "$countsref1, $countsref2\n";
print "$countsref1->{and}\n";
print "$countsref2->{the}\n";
print "$$countsref2{the}\n";
```

Output 3.27 Results of code sample 3.29.

```
HASH(0x1832d04), HASH(0x1832ca4)
1052
1563
1563
```

result is a data structure that has two indices. In fact, it is more general than a traditional two-dimensional, rectangular array.

But before moving on, the following facts are useful to memorize. First, the backslash in front of a scalar variable, an array, or a hash creates a reference to these respective data structures, and this reference is a scalar in all cases (its scalar value is the memory location). Second, the dereferencing operators, ${}, @{}, %{} all start with the symbol that begins the respective names of the data structures. Third, anonymous arrays use square brackets, and array indices are put into square brackets. Similarly, anonymous hashes use curly brackets, and hash indices are put into curly brackets. In the next section we create an array of arrays, and see how it works in detail.

3.8.2   Arrays of Arrays and Beyond

The construction of an array of arrays discussed in the last section is straightforward. A one-dimensional array can be constructed by putting the entries inside parentheses. Array references can be created by listing entries inside square brackets, which are called anonymous arrays. So if we create a list of anonymous arrays, then that is an array of arrays. A simple example is done in code sample 3.30.

Code Sample 3.30 Example of an array of arrays using a list of anonymous arrays.

```
@data = ([1, 2, 3], ['a', 'b', 'c', 'd'], [3.3, 2.06]);

print "$data[0]\n";
print "@{$data[0]}\n";
print "$data[1]->[0]\n";
print "$data[2][1]\n";
```

The results from this code sample is given in output 3.28. The first line shows that $data[0] is indeed a reference to an array. By putting $data[0] into @{} this is dereferenced. Note that the following three expressions are equivalent, and all access an entry of an array of arrays. However, do not use double dollar signs in this situation.

```
@{$data[2]}->[1]
```

```
$data[2]->[1]
```

```
$data[2][1]
```

Knowing that two sets of square brackets imply the existence of the arrow between them, the last form is the easiest to use. However, it is prudent to remember that @data is not a two-dimensional array, but instead an array of references that happen to point to more arrays.

Output 3.28 Results of code sample 3.30.

```
ARRAY(0x18b12ac)
1,2,3
a
2.06
```

To get a complete listing of the elements of @data, one can use several techniques, two of which are shown in code sample 3.31. To understand the first method, remember that $#data gives the last index of @data, so the for loop iterates over the number of anonymous arrays in @data. The join function makes a string out of each dereferenced array using commas as separators. Finally, note that since @data has scalar entries that are references, the references must start with a dollar sign. Hence in join, the dereferencing operator @{} must contain the scalar variable $data[$i]. The second method iterates over the number of anonymous arrays, just like the first method. And the second for loop iterates over the length of each anonymous array since $#{} gives the value of the last index for the referenced array within the curly brackets. Output 3.29 shows the results.

Hashes of hashes are similar to arrays of arrays. In code sample 3.32, we see that arrows can be used, but similar to arrays of arrays, they are implied when two curly brackets are side by side. For printing out of all the values, notice that the first foreach loop iterates over the keys of %data, which is a hash of references. In the second foreach loop, $data{$i} is a reference, so it must start with a dollar sign, and it is dereferenced by %{}, which allows the use of keys. Finally, note that the order of the values printed by the two foreach loops in output 3.30 is not the order used in the definition of %data. Remember that Perl stores hashes using its own ordering.

Finally, arrays and hashes can be mixed together. An example of an array of hashes is seen in code sample 3.33, which produces output 3.31. Note that dropping the arrows is possible between square brackets and curly brackets, similar to the two cases above. Note that the for loop iterates through the array of hash references, and the foreach loop iterates through the keys of each hash.

Hashes of arrays are very similar to arrays of hashes. Moreover, it is possible to have more than two levels of references, for example, arrays of hashes of hashes, or even varying number of levels, for instance, @array where $array[0] refers to a hash, $array[1] refers to an array of arrays, $array[2] refers to a scalar, and so forth. For this book,

Code Sample 3.31 Two examples of printing out an array of arrays using `for` loops.

```
@data = ([1, 2, 3], ['a', 'b', 'c', 'd'], [3.3, 2.06]);

print "Method #1\n";
for ($i = 0; $i <= $#data; ++$i) {
  $line = join(', ',@{$data[$i]});
  print "$line\n";
}
print "\nMethod #2\n";

for ($i = 0; $i <= $#data; ++$i) {
  for ($j = 0; $j <= $#{$data[$i]}; ++$j) {
    print "$data[$i][$j], ";
  }
print "\n";
}
```

Output 3.29 Results of code sample 3.31.

```
Method #1
1, 2, 3
a, b, c, d
3.3, 2.06

Method #2
1, 2, 3,
a, b, c, d,
3.3, 2.06,
```

two levels suffice, but the above examples suggest how a programmer might proceed. For example, it is not surprising that `$data{$i}[$j][$k]` accesses a value of a hash of arrays of arrays.

There is more to know about references, but the material above suffices for the tasks in this book. Now we apply the tools discussed in this section to text. In the next section, we learn how to compare the words in two texts by using an array of hashes.

3.8.3 Application: Comparing the Words in Two Poe Stories

In this section we compare the vocabulary of Edgar Allan Poe's "Mesmeric Revelation" and "The Facts in the Case of M. Valdemar." With only two texts, two hashes can be used, but our goal is to use the techniques of the last section so that the code is generalizable to many texts, which is used in chapter 5.

We assume that the two stories are in one file, and the beginning of each story is marked by its title put between two XML tags as follows.

```
<TITLE> MESMERIC REVELATIONS </TITLE>
```

Code Sample 3.32 Examples of a hash of hashes and how to print out all its values.

```
%data = (order => {a => 1, b => 2, c => 3},
         length => {a => 1, b => 1, c => 1});
print "$data{order}->{b}\n";
print "$data{length}{c}\n";

print "\nListing\n";
foreach $i (keys %data) {
  foreach $j ( keys %{$data{$i}} ) {
    print "$i, $j, $data{$i}{$j}\n";
  }
}
```

Output 3.30 Results of code sample 3.32.

```
2
1

Listing
length, c, 1
length, a, 1
length, b, 1
order, c, 3
order, a, 1
order, b, 2
```

XML (eXtensible Markup Language) is related to HTML (HyperText Markup Language), which are the tags used in creating Web pages. XML and HTML are the most famous instances of SGML (Standard Generalized Markup Language). The need for XML in this case is modest: only title tags are used. Conveniently, we only need to know that XML tags come in matched pairs, as is shown above.

These title tags inform the program when one story ends and another one begins. The words of all the stories are stored in an array of hashes, one hash for each story. Notice that it is not necessary to know the number of stories in advance since hashes can be added as needed. Once Perl code exists to analyze one story, looping through all the stories is easy to do.

To create the array of hashes, a counter (just a variable that counts something up) is incremented each time a title tag is detected (by a regex, of course). This counter is also the current array index of the array of hashes. We already have segmented a text into words, so the first part of the program is familiar. Our first new task is to count the number of words shared by each pair of stories, which includes a story with itself (this equals the number of words in that story). Program 3.7 contains this code, which is described below.

After opening the input file and assigning it to the filehandle IN, the counter $nstory is initialized to -1. This counter is incremented in the while loop each time a title tag pair is matched, and it is also the index to the array @name.

Code Sample 3.33 Example of an array of hashes and how to print out all its values.

```
@data = ({a => 1, b => 2, c => 3}, {a => "first", b => "second"});

print "$data[0]\n";
print "$data[0]->{a}\n";
print "$data[0]{a}\n";
print "$data[1]{b}\n";

print "\nListing\n";
for ($i = 0; $i <= $#data; ++$i) {
  foreach $j ( keys %{$data[$i]} ) {
    print "$i, $j, $data[$i]{$j}\n";
  }
}
```

Output 3.31 Results of code sample 3.33.

```
HASH(0x1858d08)
1
1
second

Listing
0, c, 3
0, a, 1
0, b, 2
1, a, first
1, b, second
```

The if statement switches between two tasks. If a <TITLE> </TITLE> pair is detected, then the counter $nstory is incremented, and the story title is saved in the array @name. Otherwise, the line of text is processed: it is transformed into lowercase, dashes are removed, multiple spaces are reduced to one space, and then all punctuation except for the apostrophe is removed. It turns out that these two stories both use dashes, but one uses a single hyphen, the other a double hyphen. In addition, the only apostrophes used in both are either contractions or possessives. That is, none are single quotes used within quotations.

With the punctuation removed, since the default regex for split is one space, the words on each line are assigned to the array @words. The foreach loop goes through these one by one, and then two hashes are incremented. The first is the array of hashes, @dict. Note that ++$dict[$nstory]{$w} increments the count of $w in the story indexed by $nstory in @dict. Even though the text file used here has only two stories, this code works for any number as long as each one starts with XML title tags. The second hash, %combined, keeps track of word counts for all the stories combined, which is used in the next step.

When the while loop is finished, the raw data is in place. The two for loops after it keep track of each pair of stories, and then the foreach loop iterates through all the words in both stories (which are in the hash %combined). The if statement finally determines whether

```
open (IN, "PoeMesmerismStories.txt") or die;

$nstory = -1; # Counter for number of stories

while (<IN>) { # Read the file
  chomp;
  if ( $_ =~ /<TITLE> *(.*) *<\/TITLE>/ ) {
    $name[++$nstory] = $1; # Save the name of the story
    print "$1 detected.\n";
  } else {
    $_ = lc;     # Convert to lower case
    s/ -- / /g; # Remove double hyphen dashes
    s/ - / /g;  # Remove single hyphen dashes
    s/ +/ /g;    # Replace multiple spaces with one space
    s/[.,:;?"!_()\[\]]//g; # Remove punctuation

    @words = split;
    foreach $w (@words) {
      ++$dict[$nstory]{$w}; # Array of hashes for each story
      ++$combined{$w};  # Hash with all words
    }
  }
}

# Compute number of words in common between any two stories
for $i ( 0 .. $#dict ) {
  for $j (0 .. $#dict) {
    foreach $word (keys %combined) {
      if ( exists($dict[$i]{$word}) and exists($dict[$j]{$word}) )
        { ++$count[$i][$j] }
    }
  }
}

# Print results
for $i ( 0 .. $#dict ) {
  print "@{$count[$i]}\n";
}
```

Program 3.7 This program reads stories in from a file that has titles inside XML tags. Shared word counts are computed for each pair of stories, including a story with itself.

each word is a key for both hash references $dict[$i] and $dict[$j] by applying the function exists.

Finally, the last for loop prints out the counts between each pair of stories, and output 3.32 shows the results. The order of the stories is printed out, and the counts form a two-by-two table, which reveals that "Mesmeric Revelation" has 1004 types (distinct words), and "The Facts in the Case of M. Valdemar" has 1095. Finally, these two stories have 363 types in common.

Output 3.32 The results of program 3.7.

```
MESMERIC REVELATION   detected.
THE FACTS IN THE CASE OF M. VALDEMAR   detected.
1004,363
363,1095
```

Program 3.7 is easily modified to count the number of words in the first story but not the second. Code sample 3.34 shows the nested for loops that do this. It gives the answer 641, which is confirmed by output 3.32, since of the 1004 types in the first story, 363 are shared by the second, which leaves $1004 - 363 = 641$ types unique to the first.

Code Sample 3.34 If these for loops replace the analogous for loops in program 3.7, the resulting code computes the number of distinct words in the first story that are not in the second.

```perl
@count = undef; # Clear this array

for $i ( 0 .. $#dict-1 ) {
  for $j ($i .. $#dict) {
    foreach $word (keys %combined) {
      if ( exists($dict[$i]{$word}) and
           not exists($dict[$j]{$word}) )
        { ++$count[$i][$j] }
    }
  }
}
```

Thinking in terms of sets, program 3.7 computes the size of the intersection of the keys of two hashes, and code sample 3.34 computes the size of the complement of a hash. Finally, the keys of the hash %combined is the union of the keys of the hashes for each story. Recall that sets do not allow repeated elements, which is also true of hash keys. So these act like sets. For a discussion of working with sets in Perl see chapter 6 of *Mastering Algorithms with Perl* by Orwant et al. [84].

3.9 REFERENCES

Section 2.8 lists some introductory books on Perl and on regular expressions. This section lists some more advanced books on Perl programming as well as a few that apply Perl to text-mining-related topics.

Larry Wall created Perl, and he co-authored *Progamming Perl* with Tom Christiansen and Jon Orwant [120]. A companion volume to this book is the *Perl Cookbook* by Tom Christiansen and Nathan Torkington [28]. A third that covers the details of Perl is *Professional Perl Programming* by Peter Wainwright and six other authors [119].

If you want to learn about algorithms, try *Mastering Algorithms with Perl* by Jon Orwant, Jarkko Hietaniemi, and John Macdonald [84]. It covers many of the important tasks of computer science. Also, chapter 9 covers strings, and it gives the details on how regular expressions are actually implemented in Perl.

The book *Data Munging with Perl* by David Cross [36] focuses on how to use Perl to manipulate data, including text data. It is a good introduction to more advanced ideas such as parsing. One great source of text is the Web, which begs to be analyzed. A book that uses Perl to do just this is *Spidering Hacks* by Kevin Hemenway and Tara Calishain [53].

Genetics has discovered another type of text: the genome. This has an alphabet of four letters (A, C, G, T), and the language is poorly understood at present. However, looking for patterns in DNA is text pattern matching, so it is not surprising that Perl has been used to analyze it. For an introduction on this topic, try one of these three books: *Perl for Exploring DNA* by Mark LeBlanc and Betsey Dexter Dyer [70]; *Beginning Perl for Bioinformatics* by James Tisdall [116]; and *Mastering Perl for Bioinformatics* by James Tisdall [117].

There are many more areas of Perl that are useful to text mining but are not used in this book. Here are four example topics, each with a book that covers it. First, many Perl modules (bundled code that defines new functions; see section 9.2) are object oriented. Hence, this kind of programming is supported by Perl, and this can be learned from *Object Oriented Perl* by Damian Conway [33]. Second, a programmer can use Perl for graphics using the add-on package Perl/Tk. For more on this topic, see *Mastering Perl/Tk* by Steve Lidie and Nancy Walsh [72]. Third, text mining is related to data mining, which uses databases. There is a Perl DBI (Data Base Interface), which is covered in *Programming the Perl DBI* by Alligator Descartes and Tim Bunce [38]. Finally, text is everywhere on the Web, and the Perl module LWP can download Web pages into a running program. For more on this see *Perl & LWP* by Sean Burke [20]. Remember if you fall in love with Perl, these topics are just the beginning. A book search on the term Perl reveals many more.

3.10   FIRST TRANSITION

Chapter 2 introduces regular expressions and how to use them. This chapter introduces some data structures and how to implement these in Perl. Both of these together are an introduction to a subset of Perl that can do basic analyses of texts. The core of these analyses are text pattern matching (with regexes) and counting up matches in the text (which are kept track of by arrays and hashes). Working through these two chapters has taught you enough Perl to understand the programming after this point. If you started this book with no knowledge of Perl and little knowledge of programming, these two chapters required much thought and effort, and congratulations on getting this far.

At this point in this book, there is a transition. Prior to this, analyses of texts have been mixed with extensive discussions on how to use Perl. After this point, the focus is on analyzing texts with more complicated techniques, and Perl is more of a tool, not the focus of the discussion. However, if new features are used, these are pointed out and explained. But in general, the focus in the upcoming chapters is on text mining techniques, with Perl playing a supporting role.

PROBLEMS

3.1   Find all the words containing interior apostrophes in Dickens's *A Christmas Carol*. Hence, on each side of the apostrophe there is an alphanumeric character. There are quite a few of these, some familiar to today's reader (like *it's* or *I'll*), and some unfamiliar (like *thank'ee* or *sha'n't*). For each of these, find its frequency in the novel.

3.2   A *lipogram* is a text that is written without one or more letters of the alphabet. This is usually done with common letters because, for example, not using *q* is not much of a challenge. In English, many lipograms do not use the letter *e*, the most common letter. An impressive example is *A Void*, a translation into English from French by Gilbert Adair of Georges Perec's *La Disparition*. Both the original and the translation do not have the letter *e*.

Several people have written about the lipogram. See chapter 13 of Tony Augarde's *The Oxford Guide to Word Games* [5] for a history of lipograms. For a more detailed history, see the paper "History of the Lipogram" by Georges Perec [86], who is the same author noted in the above paragraph for writing a lipogrammic novel. Also see sections 11 and 12 of Ross Eckler's *Making the Alphabet Dance* [41]. For an example of a phonetic lipogram (the text is missing a particular sound), see pages 12–14 of Ross Eckler's *Word Recreations* [40].

The goal of this problem is to create a lipogram dictionary, that is, a list of words not containing some set of letters. This is not hard to do using a word list such as Grady Ward's CROSSWD.TXT from the *Moby Word Lists* [123]. Have Perl read in this file and test each word against the appropriate regex. For example, code sample 3.35 disallows the letter *e*. Modify this code sample to answer the questions below.

Code Sample 3.35 Assuming that WORDS is a filehandle to a word list, this prints out the words not containing the letter *e*. For problem 3.2.

```
$regex = qr/^[^e]+$/i;

while (<WORDS>) {
  if ( $_ =~ $regex ) {
    print;
  }
}
```

---

a) How many words do not have any of the letters *a, e, i, o*, and *u*?

b) How many words do not have any of the letters *a, e, i, o, u*, and *y*? Surprisingly, an exhaustive word list does have such words. For example there is *crwth*, which is borrowed from Welsh.

c) How many words require only the middle row of the keyboard? That is, how many words are composed of letters strictly from the following list: *a, s, d, f, g, h, j, k*, and *l*?

d) Compose a dictionary of words using only the vowel *u*. For discussion of this property, see section 12 of Ross Eckler's *Making the Alphabet Dance* [41].

e) Find words that have exactly the five vowels, each appearing once, for example, *facetious*. For examples of such words for every permutation of the vowels, see section 12 of Ross Eckler's *Making the Alphabet Dance* [41].

3.3   Section 3.7.2.2 discusses word anagrams, which are two (or more) words using the same group of letters, but with different orders. For example, *algorithm* is an anagram of *logarithm* since the former is a permutation of the latter.

Instead of allowing all permutations, one challenge is finding word anagrams limited to only certain types of permutations, examples of which are given below. Examples can be found by using a word list, for example, Grady Ward's CROSSWD.TXT from the *Moby Word Lists* [123].

a) The easiest permutation to check is reversing the letters because there is already a Perl function to do this, reverse. Find all the words that are also words when read backwards.

Hint: One way to do this is to create a hash, say %list, where its keys are the words in the word list. Then loop through the keys checking to see if the reversal of the word is also a key, as done in code sample 3.36. Note that this also finds palindromes, that is, words that are the same backwards as forwards, for example, *deified*.

Code Sample 3.36 A loop to find words that are still words when reversed. For problem 3.3.a.

```
foreach $x (sort %list) {
  if ( exists($list{reverse($x)}) ) {
    print "$x\n";
  }
}
```

b) Another simple permutation is taking the last letter and putting it first (sometimes called a rotation). Find words for which this rotation is also a word. For example, rotating *trumpets* produces *strumpet*, or rotating *elects* produces *select*.

Hint: Use the function rotate in code sample 3.37 instead of reverse in code sample 3.36.

Code Sample 3.37 A function to move the last letter of a word to the front for problem 3.3.b.

```
sub rotate {
  my $word = $_[0];
  my @letters = split(//, $word);
  unshift(@letters, pop(@letters));
  return join('', @letters);
}
```

c) Create a function that is a rotation in the opposite sense of rotate in code sample 3.37. Then find all words that are still words under this new rotation. For example, rotating *swear* in this way produces *wears*. Question: how does this list compare with the list from problem 3.3.b?

3.4   Using a word list, for example, Grady Ward's CROSSWD.TXT from the *Moby Word Lists* [123], find all the words where every letter appears exactly twice using a regex. For example, this is true of the word *hotshots*.

This property is called an *isogram*. For more information on these, see section 29 and figure 29c of Ross Eckler's *Making the Alphabet Dance* [41].

First hint: Sort the letters of each word into alphabetical order, then try to create a regex that matches pairs of letters. Note that `/^((\w)\1)+$/` seems promising, but does not work.

Second hint: define a pair of letters regex using `qr//` as shown below.

```
$pattern = qr/(\w)\1/;
```

Then use the regex `/^$pattern+$/`. This regex allows false positives (describe them). Is there a simple way to correct this?

3.5   One way to associate a numeric value to a word is as follows. Let $A = 1$, $B = 2$, $C = 3$, ..., and $Z = 26$, then for a given word, sum up its letter values, for example, *cat* produces $3 + 1 + 20$, or 24. This method is sometimes used in word puzzles, for example, see section 59 of Ross Eckler's *Making the Alphabet Dance* [41]. Here the goal is to write a function that takes a word and returns its number.

Code sample 3.38 shows one way to do this for all the numerical values at once using a hash of hashes. To figure out how the code works, refer back to section 3.8.2. The function ord changes an ASCII character into a number, which makes it easy to convert *a* to 1, *b* to 2, and so forth. The function map applies a function defined with `$_` as its argument to every entry in an array. For more information on this command, try looking it up online at `http://perldoc.perl.org/` [3]. Finally, note that using an array of hashes is another approach to this task.

Code Sample 3.38 Assuming that WORDS is a filehandle to word list, this code finds all words having the same numerical value using the procedure given in problem 3.5.

```
$baseline = ord('a')-1;

while (<WORDS>) {
  chomp;
  @letters = split(//);
  @values = map(ord($_)-$baseline, @letters);
  $total = 0;  foreach $x (@values) { $total += $x; }
  push( @{$list{$total}}, $_);
}

foreach $value (sort {$a <=> $b} keys %list) {
  print "$value\n";
  foreach $word ( @{$list{$value}} ) {
    print "$word ";
  }
  print "\n\n";
}
```

---

a) Perhaps this problem can be a start of a new type of pseudoscience. For your name, find out its value, then examine the words that share this value to discover possible clues to your personality (or love life, or career paths, ...). For example, the name *Roger* has the value 63, which is shared by *acetone*, *catnip*, and *quiche*. Not surprisingly, these words describe me quite well.

b) Another numerology angle arises by concatenating the letter values together to form a string. For example, *Roger* becomes 18157518. It can happen that some numbers are associated with more than one word. For example, *abode* and *lode* both have the number 121545. For this problem write a Perl program that finds all such words. See the article *Concatenating Letter Ranks* [13] for more information.

3.6   Transaddition is the following process: take a word, add a letter such that all the letters can be rearranged to form a new word. For example, adding the letter *t* to *learn* produces *antler* (or *learnt* or *rental*). A transdeletion is the removal of a letter so that what remains can be rearranged into a word, for example, removing *l* from *learn* produces *earn* (or *near*). For an extensive discussion on these two ideas, see sections 41 and 49 of Ross Eckler's *Making the Alphabet Dance* [41].

Code sample 3.39 shows how to take a word and find what words can be found by adding a letter and then rearranging all of them. Starting with this code, try changing it so that it can find transdeletions instead. Assume that WORDS is the filehandle for a word list.

Code Sample 3.39 Code to find all transadditions of a given word. For problem 3.6.

```perl
while (<WORDS>) {
  chomp;
  $key = join('',sort(split(//, $_)));
  if ( exists($list{$key}) ) {
    $list{$key} .= ",$_";
  } else {
    $list{$key} = $_;
  }
}

# Transaddition
$word = $ARGV[0];
@letters = split(//, $word);
foreach $x ('a' .. 'z') {
  @temp = @letters;
  push(@temp, $x);
  $key = join('', sort(@temp));
  if ( exists($list{$key}) ) {
    print "$list{$key}\n";
  }
}
```

3.7   Lewis Carroll created the game called Doublets, where the goal is to transform one word into another (of the same length) by changing one letter at a time, and such that each intermediate step is itself a word. For example, *red* can be transformed into *hot* as follows: *red, rod, rot, hot*.

One approach to this is to create a word network that shows all the one-letter-change linkages. The programming task of creating and storing such a network in a (complex) data structure is challenging because the network can be quite large (depending on the number of letters), and it is possible to have loops in the network (the network is not a *tree* in the graph-theoretic sense).

This problem presents an easier task: given one word, find all other words that are only a one-letter change from the given word. For example, the words *deashed*, *leached*, and *leashes* are all exactly one letter different from *leashed*.

Here is one approach. Create a hash from a word list (using, for example, Grady Ward's CROSSWD.TXT from the *Moby Word Lists* [123]). Then take the given word, replace the first letter by each letter of the alphabet. Check each of these potential words against the hash. Then do this for the second letter, and the third, and so forth. See code sample 3.40 to get started.

Code Sample 3.40 Hint on how to find all words that are one letter different from a specified word. For problem 3.7.

```
# $len = length of the word in $ARGV[0]
# The keys of %list are from a word list

for ($i = 0; $i < $len; ++$i) {
  foreach $letter ( 'a' .. 'z' ) {
    $word = $ARGV[0];
    substr($word, $i, 1) = $letter;
    if ( exists($list{$word}) and $word ne $ARGV[0]) {
      print "$word\n";
    }
  }
}
```

Finally, for more information on Doublets, see chapter 22 of Tony Augarde's *The Oxford Guide to Word Games* [5]. Moreover, sections 42 through 44 of Ross Eckler's *Making the Alphabet Dance* [41] give examples of word networks.

3.8 With HTML, it is possible to encode a variety of information by modifying the font in various ways. This problem considers one such example. Section 3.6.1 shows how to compute word frequencies. Given these frequencies, the task here is to convert them into font sizes, which are then used to write an HTML page.

Code sample 3.41 assumes that the hash %size contains font sizes in points for each word in Poe's "The Black Cat." The HTML is printed to the file BlackCat.html.

These font sizes are based on word counts using all of Poe's short stories, and $size{$word} was set to the function below.

```
int(1.5*log($freq)+12.5)
```

In this case, the frequencies went from 1 to 24,401, so the this function reduces this wide range of counts to a range appropriate for font sizes. Output 3.33 has the beginning of the HTML that is produced by this code.

For a text of your own choosing, create a word frequency list, and then modify the frequencies to create font sizes.

3.9 Section 3.7.2.2 shows how to find distinct words that have the same letters, but in different orders, which are called *anagrams*. The same idea is applicable to numerals. For example, are there many square numbers with anagrams that are also square numbers? Examples are the squares 16,384 (equals 128^2), 31,684 (178^2), 36,481 (191^2), 38,416

Code Sample 3.41 Code to vary font size in an HTML document. For problem 3.8.

```
open(STORY, "The_Black_Cat.txt");
open(OUT, ">BlackCat.html") or die;
print OUT "<html>\n<body>\n<marquee>\n";

while(<STORY>) {
  chomp;
  @words = split(/\s+/);
  if ( /^$/ ) {
    print OUT "\n</marquee><marquee>\n";
  } else {
    foreach $x (@words) {
      $x =~ /([\w-]+('s)?)/;
      if ( exists($size{lc($1)}) ) {
      print OUT "<span style=\"font-size:",
                "$size{lc($1)}pt\">$x</span>\n";
      } else { print "Missing Value for $1\n"; }
    }
  }
}
close(STORY);
print OUT "</marquee>\n</body>\n</html>\n";
```

Output 3.33 A few lines from code sample 3.41.

```
<html>
<body>
<marquee>
<span style="font-size:24pt">FOR</span>
<span style="font-size:27pt">the</span>
<span style="font-size:21pt">most</span>
<span style="font-size:19pt">wild,</span>
<span style="font-size:21pt">yet</span>
<span style="font-size:21pt">most</span>
<span style="font-size:12pt">homely</span>
<span style="font-size:16pt">narrative</span>
<span style="font-size:24pt">which</span>
```

(196^2), and 43,681 (209^2), and all five of these five-digit numbers use the same digits. This is called an *anasquare*.

Although word anagrams are not that common, this is not true for anasquares. See "Anasquares: Square anagrams of squares" [14] for a discussion of this.

3.10   As noted in problem 2.9.b, at present, there are plenty of DNA sequences available to the public at the National Center for Biotechnology Information (NCBI) at its Web page: http://www.ncbi.nlm.nih.gov/ [81].

Since DNA is text (though its words and grammar are mostly unknown), it makes sense to use Perl and regexes to analyze DNA, which is exactly the point made in *Perl for Exploring DNA* by Mark LeBlanc and Betsey Dexter Dyer [70]. Note that these authors also enjoy word games, and they introduce the idea of text patterns in DNA by analyzing letter patterns in English words. Even without a background in biology, the book is quite readable, and I recommend it.

For this problem, get a copy of LeBlanc and Dyer's book and see how they use Perl for DNA pattern finding. With the data of the NCBI, perhaps you can discover something notable.

CHAPTER 4

PROBABILITY AND TEXT SAMPLING

4.1 INTRODUCTION

Chapters 2 and 3 introduce and explain many features of Perl. Starting at this point, however, the focus shifts to using it for text analyses. Where new features are introduced, these are noted and explained, but the emphasis is on the texts.

This chapter focuses on some of the statistical properties of text. Unfortunately, some of the common assumptions used in popular statistical techniques are not applicable, so care is needed. This situation is not surprising because language is more complex than, for example, flipping a coin.

We start off with an introduction to the basics of probability. This discussion focuses on the practical, not the theoretical, and all the examples except the first involve text, keeping in the spirit of this book.

4.2 PROBABILITY

Probability models variability. If a process is repeated, and if the results are not all the same, then a probabilistic approach can be useful. For example, all gambling games have some element of unpredictability, although the amount of this varies. For example, flipping a fair coin once is completely unpredictable. However, when flipping a hundred coins, there is a 95% probability that the percentage of heads is between 40% and 60%.

Practical Text Mining with Perl. By Roger Bilisoly

Language has both structure and variability. For example, in this chapter, what word appears last, just before the start of the exercises? Although some words are more likely than others, and given all the text up to this point, it is still impossible to deduce this with confidence.

Even guessing the next word in a sequence can be difficult. For example, there are many ways to finish sentence 4.1.

$$\text{Crazed by lack of sleep, Blanche lunged at me and screamed ``....''} \qquad (4.1)$$

Because language is so complex, coin flipping is our first example, which introduces the basic concepts. Then with this in mind, we return to analyzing English prose.

4.2.1 Probability and Coin Flipping

First, we define some terms. A *process* produces *outcomes*, which are completely specified. How these arise need not be well understood, which is the case for humans producing a text. However, ambiguous outcomes are not allowed. For example, a person typing produces an identifiable sequence of characters, but someone writing longhand can create unreadable output, which is not a process in the above sense.

For processes, certain groups of outcomes are of interest, which are called *events*. For example, if a coin is flipped five times, getting exactly one head is an event, and this consists of the five outcomes HTTTT, THTTT, TTHTT, TTTHT, and TTTTH, where H stands for *heads* and T for *tails*. Notice that each of these sequences completely specifies the result of the process.

The *probability* of an event is a number that is greater than or equal to zero and less than or equal to one. For a simple process, probabilities can be computed exactly. For example, the probability of exactly one head in five flips of a fair coin is 5/32. However, because language is complex and ever changing, probabilities for text events are always approximate, and our interest is in computing *empirical* probabilities, which are estimates based on data.

For the first example, we estimate the empirical probability of heads from the results of computer-simulated coin flips. The simplest method for doing this is to count the number of events and divide by the number of results. Let n() be the function that returns the number of times its argument occurs, then equation 4.2 summarizes the above description.

$$P(\text{event}) = \frac{n(\text{events})}{n(\text{results})} \qquad (4.2)$$

We use this equation to estimate the probability of getting a head. Perl has a function called rand that returns a random number between 0 and 1. This can generate coin flips as follows: if rand is greater than 0.5, then the result is H, else it is T. Note that rand is not truly random (such computer functions are called *pseudorandom*), but we assume that it is close enough for our purposes. Using this idea, the following command line argument runs program 4.1 to simulate 50 flips.

```
perl flip.pl 50
```

The argument after the program name (50 in the above example) is stored in $ARGV[0], which determines the number of iterations of the for loop. When this is finished, the empirical probability estimate of getting a head is computed.

```
# USAGE > perl flip.pl value
# This program simulates flipping a coin $ARGV[0] times.

for ($n = 1; $n <= $ARGV[0]; ++$n) {
  if (rand > 0.5) {
    print "H";
    ++$count;
  } else {
    print "T";
  }
}

$proportion = $count/$ARGV[0]; # Empirical probability
print "\nProbability of heads = $proportion";
```

Program 4.1 This program simulates coin flips to estimate the probability of heads.

Output 4.1 shows one run of program 4.1 that produces 23 heads out of 50 flips, which is 46%. By equation 4.2, this proportion is the empirical probability estimate of getting a head. Clearly running this program a second time is likely to give a different estimate, so this estimate is an approximation.

Output 4.1 Output of program 4.1 for 50 flips.

```
HTHHHHHHHHTHHHTTTTHTHTHTTTTTHHTTTHTTHTHTTTHTTHTTTHHT
Probability of heads = 0.46
```

Because it is well known that the probability of heads is 0.5, program 4.1 might seem like a waste of time. But keep in mind two points. First, to estimate the probability of the word *the* occurring in some text, there is no theoretical solution, so we must use an empirical estimate. Second, even for coin tossing, there are events that are hard to compute from theory, and the empirical answer is useful either for an estimate or a check of the true probability. See problems 4.1 and 4.2 for two examples of this.

In addition, the above output can be used to estimate the probability of heads after the first flip, after the second flip, and so forth, until the last flip. If empirical estimates are useful, then as the number of flips increases, the probability estimates should get closer and closer to 0.5 (on average). Although this is tedious to do by hand, it is straightforward to modify program 4.1 to print out a running estimate of the probability of heads. This is done with the variable $proportion inside the for loop of program 4.2.

This program produces the running probability estimates shown in figure 4.1. Note that near the end of the 50 flips the estimates gets worse. Large deviations are always possible, but they are more and more unlikely as the number of flips increases. Finally, figure 4.2 shows an example of 5000 flips. Here the initial large deviations die out as the number of flips gets larger.

Although coins can be flipped more and more, samples of text have an upper limit. For example, Edgar Allan Poe is dead, and any new works are due to discovering previously unknown manuscripts, which is rare. Hence, it is often true with texts that either the sample

```
# USAGE > perl flip.pl value
# This program simulates flipping a coin $ARGV[0] times.

$record = "";

for ($n = 1; $n <= $ARGV[0]; ++$n) {
  if (rand > 0.5) {
    $record .= "H";
    ++$count;
  } else {
    $record .= "T";
  }
  $proportion = $count/$n;
  print "$proportion\n";
}

print "$record\n";
```

Program 4.2 Modification of program 4.1 that produces a running estimate of the probability of heads.

cannot be made larger, or it is labor intensive to increase its size. Unfortunately, there are measures of a text that do not converge to a fixed value as the sample size increases to its maximum possible value (see section 4.6). Hence working with texts is trickier than working with simpler random processes like coins.

4.2.2 Probabilities and Texts

Consider this problem: find an estimate of the probability of each letter of the alphabet in English. For a fair coin, assuming the probabilities of heads and tails are equal is reasonable, but for letters this is not true. For example, the letter a is generally more common than the letter z. Quantifying this difference takes effort, but anyone fluent in English knows it.

To estimate letter frequencies, taking a sample of text and computing the proportion of each letter is a reasonable way to estimate these probabilities. However, a text sample that is too short can give poor results. For example, sentence 4.3 gives poor estimates.

$$\text{Ed's jazz dazzles with its pizazz.} \tag{4.3}$$

Here z is the most common letter in this sentence comprising 7 out of the 27, or a proportion of almost 26%. Obviously, most texts do not have z occurring this frequently.

There is an important difference between the coin example in the last section and this example. In output 4.1, an estimate of 46% for the probability of heads is found by flipping a coin 50 times, which is close to the correct answer of 50%. However, there are 26 letters in the alphabet (ignoring case and all other characters), and letters are not used equally often. Such a situation requires larger sample sizes than coin flipping.

Note that sentence 4.3 has no bs, which is a proportion of 0%, but all the letters of the alphabet have a nonzero probability, so this estimate is too low. This reasoning is true for all the letters that do not appear in this sentence. Moreover, the existence of estimates that are too low imply that one or more of the estimated probabilities for the letters that do appear

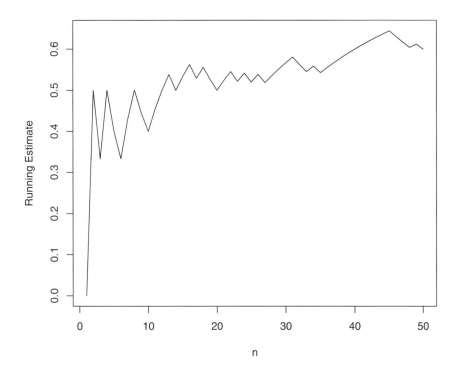

Figure 4.1   Plot of the running estimate of the probability of heads for 50 flips.

are too high. Having estimates that are known to be either too high or too low is called *bias*. The existence of zero counts produces biased probability estimates, and, to a lesser degree, so do very low counts.

Hence using proportions from samples as estimates of probabilities requires sample sizes that are large enough. Quantifying this depends on the size of the probabilities to be estimated, but if there are possible events that do not appear in the sample, then a larger sample is useful. However, as noted above, a larger example may not be possible with text.

Finally, coin flipping is not immune to the problem of bias. For instance, if we flip the coin only one time, the empirical probability of heads is either 0 or 1, and both of these answers are the furthest possible from 0.5. However, additional flips are easy to obtain, especially if a computer simulation is used. With the above discussion in mind, we estimate letter probabilities.

4.2.2.1 *Estimating Letter Probabilities for Poe and Dickens*   As noted in the last section, using sentence 4.3 to estimate the probability of each letter gives misleading results. However, a larger text sample should do better. Because counting letters by hand is tedious, this calls for Perl. It is easy to break a string into characters by using the function `split` with the empty regular expression as its first argument (empty meaning having no

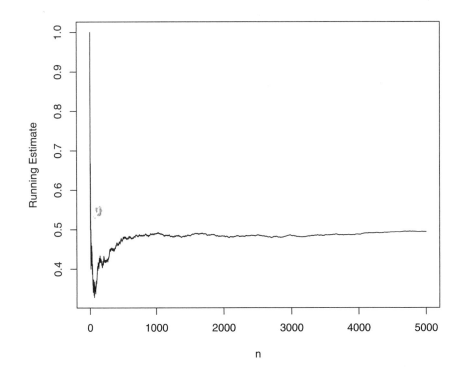

Figure 4.2 Plot of the running estimate of the probability of heads for 5000 flips.

characters at all). Keeping track of the character counts is done by using the hash `%freq` (see section 3.6 to review hashes).

To try out program 4.3, we first analyze Poe's "The Black Cat" [88] using the following command line statement.

```
perl count_characters.pl The_Black_Cat.txt
```

The output has two parts. First, all of the characters in the story are listed from most frequent to least frequent. Second, the frequencies of the letters a through z are listed in that order. It turns out that the blank is the most frequent (where newline characters within paragraphs are counted as blanks), with a frequency of 4068. The most frequent letter is e (appearing 2204 times), and the least frequent is z (6 times), which is out of a total of 17,103 letters. Hence, e appears almost 13% of the time, while z appears only 0.035% of the time.

The story "The Black Cat" is only a few pages long, so let us also try a longer work, Charles Dickens's *A Christmas Carol*, which can be done by replacing `The_Black_Cat.txt` with `A_Christmas_Carol.txt` in the open statement. Output 4.2 ranks the letters with respect to frequency for both these works of fiction. Although the orders do not match exactly, they are similar. For example, the letter e appears $2204/17,103 \approx 12.89\%$ of the time in "The Black Cat," as compared to $14,869/121,179 \approx 12.27\%$ for *A Christmas Carol*.

```
# USAGE > perl count_characters.pl FileName.txt
# This program is case insensitive.
# This program counts all characters, not just letters.

open (FILE, "$ARGV[0]") or die("$ARGV[0] not found");
$/ = ""; # Paragraph mode used

while (<FILE>) {
  chomp;
  s/\n/ /g; # Replace newlines by spaces
  $_ = lc; # Make letters lowercase
  @chars = split(//);

  foreach $char (@chars) {
    ++$freq{$char};
  }
}

$count = 0; # Stores total number of letters
foreach $char ( sort byReverseValues keys %freq ) {
  if ('a' le $char and $char le 'z') {
    $count += $freq{$char};
  }
  print "$char: $freq{$char}\n";
}

print "\nTotal number of letters: $count\n";

foreach $letter ( 'a'..'z' ) {
  print "$letter: $freq{$letter}\n";
}

sub byReverseValues {
  $value = $freq{$b} <=> $freq{$a};
  if ($value == 0) { return $a cmp $b;
      } else { return $value; };
}
```

Program 4.3 This program counts the frequency of each character in a text file.

Both of these are close to the value of 13% cited in Sinkov's *Elementary Cryptanalysis* [110], which is based on a larger text sample. These similarities suggest that these two works are representative of English prose with respect to letter frequencies.

This question of representativeness is key. In sampling, the researcher hopes that the sample is similar to the population from which it is taken, but he or she can always get unlucky. For example, Georges Perec wrote the novel *La Disparition* without using the letter *e*, which is the most common letter in French (and English). This novel was translated by Gilbert Adair into English with the title *A Void* [87]. He was faithful to the original in

Output 4.2 Output of program 4.3 for both Dickens's *A Christmas Carol* and Poe's "The Black Cat". Letters are listed in decreasing frequency.

e:	14869	e:	2204
t:	10890	t:	1600
o:	9696	a:	1315
a:	9315	o:	1279
h:	8378	i:	1238
i:	8309	n:	1121
n:	7962	h:	985
s:	7916	r:	972
r:	7038	s:	968
d:	5676	d:	766
l:	4555	l:	684
u:	3335	m:	564
w:	3096	f:	496
c:	3036	c:	488
g:	2980	u:	471
m:	2841	y:	387
f:	2438	w:	358
y:	2299	p:	329
p:	2122	g:	292
b:	1943	b:	286
k:	1031	v:	152
v:	1029	k:	80
x:	131	x:	33
j:	113	j:	16
q:	97	q:	13
z:	84	z:	6

that he also did not use the letter *e*. So if we pick the English version of this novel, the estimate of the probability of the letter *e* is 0%, which is clearly anomalous. However, *A Void* is not a representative sample of English prose. This kind of a literary work (one that does not use a specific letter) is called a *lipogram*.

Finally, output 4.2 shows that both stories use all the letters of the alphabet. Unfortunately, for more complex sets of strings that are of interest to linguistics, usually some are not represented in any given sample. For example, the next section shows that counting letter pairs produces many zero counts. As noted at the start of this section, these are underestimates, which makes at least some of the nonzero counts overestimates, both of which cause biases in the probability estimates.

4.2.2.2 *Estimating Letter Bigram Probabilities*

From single letters, the next step up in string complexity are pairs, which are called letter *bigrams*. These are ordered pairs, that is, the order of the letters matters. For example, the title "The Black Cat" has the following letter bigrams: *th*, *he*, *bl*, *la*, *ac*, *ck*, *ca*, and *at*. Here both case and the spaces between the words are ignored. Depending on the application, however, treating a space as a character can be useful. Also, a decision on whether to keep or to ignore punctuation is needed. For this section, nonletter characters are deleted, except for hyphenated words. In this case, the hyphens are replaced with spaces, for example, *self-evident* is split into *self* and *evident*.

To do this, first, substitute all nonletters with spaces with s/[^a-zA-Z]/ /g. Second, change multiple spaces into one space, which is done by another substitution. Third, convert all the letters to lowercase with the lc function. Then convert the text into words with the split function (splitting on whitespace), followed by splitting each word into letters. Finally, the letters are combined into pairs with the join function. All these steps are done in code sample 4.1, which produces output 4.3.

Code Sample 4.1 Code to find letter bigrams contained in the string stored in $_.

```
$_ = "Well!!!  No surprise, this.";

s/[^a-zA-Z]/ /g; # Substitute spaces for nonletters
s/ +/ /g;        # Substitute one space for many
$_ = lc;         # Convert to lowercase

@words = split(/\s/); # Split into words

foreach $word (@words) {
  @letters = split(//, $word); # Split into letters
  for ($i = 0; $i < $#letters; ++$i) {
    $bigram = join('', @letters[$i..($i+1)]);
    print "$bigram ";
  }
}
```

Output 4.3 The bigram output of code sample 4.1.

```
we el ll no su ur rp pr ri is se th hi is
```

Code sample 4.1 works for the test string, so we use it to construct a bigram counting program. The result is program 4.4, which uses byReverseValues from program 4.3.

Program 4.4 produces much more output than program 4.3 since there are $26^2 = 676$ possible bigrams. Applying this to *A Christmas Carol* produces 415 bigrams, the 10 most frequent are given in output 4.4. Note that $676 - 415 = 261$ bigrams that do not appear in this novel.

The fact that many bigrams are missing (a little more than a third) is not surprising. For example, it is difficult to think of a word containing *xx* or *tx*. However, such words exist. For example, for a list of 676 words that contains each of the 676 possible bigrams, see section 31 of *Making the Alphabet Dance* [41] by Eckler. However, words are not the only way these bigrams can appear. For example, *XX* is the roman numeral for 20 and *TX* is the postal code for Texas. Moreover, there are many other types of strings besides words that can be in a text. For example, a license plate can easily have one of these two bigrams. Hence, the missing bigrams are possible, so a proportion of 0% is an underestimate.

In general, with even long texts it is not hard to find words or phrases that are not unusual yet do not appear in the text. For example, of the days of the week, *Tuesday*, *Wednesday*,

```
# USAGE > perl count_bigrams.pl FileName.txt
# This program is case insensitive
# Nonletters are ignored

open (FILE, "$ARGV[0]") or die("$ARGV[0] not found");
$/ = ""; # Paragraph mode used

$count = 0;  # Tallies number of bigrams
while (<FILE>) {
  chomp;
  s/[^a-zA-Z]/ /g; # Substitute spaces for nonletters
  s/ +/ /g;        # Substitute one space for many
  $_ = lc;         # Convert to lowercase

  @words = split(/\s/);

  foreach $word (@words) {
    @letters = split(//, $word);
    for ($i = 0; $i < $#letters; ++$i) {
      $bigram = join('', @letters[$i..($i+1)]);
      ++$freq{$bigram};
      ++$count;
    }
  }
}

# Print out results
foreach $bigram ( sort byReverseValues keys %freq ) {
  print "$bigram: $freq{$bigram}\n";
}

print "\nTotal number of bigrams: $count";

sub byReverseValues {
  $value = $freq{$b} <=> $freq{$a};
  if ($value == 0) { return $a cmp $b;
          } else { return $value; };
}
```

Program 4.4 This program counts the frequency of each bigram in the text file specified on the command line.

and *Thursday* do not appear in *A Christmas Carol* (although *Friday* does appear, it refers to the character with that name in Robert Louis Stevenson's *Treasure Island*.) Unfortunately, this means the problem of having proportions that are 0% is generally unavoidable when working with texts.

Output 4.4 The 10 most frequent bigrams found by program 4.4 for Dickens's *A Christmas Carol*.

th:	3627
he:	3518
in:	2152
an:	2012
er:	1860
re:	1664
nd:	1620
it:	1435
ha:	1391
ed:	1388

Finally, before moving on, it is not hard to write a Perl program to enumerate letter triplets (or *trigrams*). See problem 4.4 for a hint on doing this. We now consider two key ideas of probability in the next section: conditional probability and independence.

4.3 CONDITIONAL PROBABILITY

The idea of *conditional probability* is easily shown through an example. Consider the following two questions. First, for a randomly picked four-letter word (from a list of English words), what is the probability that the second letter is *u*? Second, for a randomly picked four-letter word that starts with the letter *q*, what is the probability that the second letter is *u*?

Given a word list and a Perl program, these questions are answerable, and with regular expressions, it is not hard to create such a program. Grady Ward's *Moby Word Lists* [123] has the file CROSSWD.TXT, which has more than 110,000 total words, including inflected forms. Code sample 4.2 counts the following: all four-letter words, all four-letter words starting with *q*, all four-letter words with *u* as the second letter, and all four-letter words starting with *qu*. Note that chomp must be in the while loop: try running this code sample without it to see what goes wrong. Finally, the results are given in output 4.5.

Now we can answer the two probability questions. Since there are 3686 four-letter words, and 378 of these have *u* as their second letter, the probability that a randomly selected four-letter word has *u* as the second letter is 378/3686, which is close to 10%. But for the second question, only the 12 four-letter words starting with *q* are considered, and of these, 10 have *u* as the second letter, so the answer is 10/12, which is close to 83%.

Knowing English, it is no surprise that the most common letter following *q* is *u*. In fact, having an answer as low as 83% may be surprising (the two exceptions are *qaid* and *qoph*). Because *u* is typically the least common vowel (true in output 4.2 for "The Black Cat" and *A Christmas Carol*), it is not surprising that as little as 10% of four-letter words have *u* in the second position.

Although the above example is a special case, the general idea of estimating conditional probabilities from data does not require any more theory, albeit there is some new notation. However, the notation is simple, widely used, and saves time, so it is worth knowing.

Suppose A is an event. For example, let A stand for obtaining a head when flipping a coin once. Then $P(A)$ is the probability of event A happening, that is, the probability of

Code Sample 4.2 An analysis of four-letter words.

```
open(WORDS, "CROSSWD.TXT") or die;

while (<WORDS>) {
  chomp;
  if ( length == 4 ) {
    ++$n;
    ·if ( /q.../ ) { ++$n_q_first  }
    if ( /.u../ ) { ++$n_u_second }
    if ( /qu../ ) { ++$n_q_then_u }
  }
}

print "# 4 letter words = $n\n";
print "# 4 letter words with q first = $n_q_first\n";
print "# 4 letter words with u second = $n_u_second\n";
print "# 4 letter words starting with qu = $n_q_then_u\n";
```

Output 4.5 Word counts computed by code sample 4.2.

```
# 4 letter words = 3686
# 4 letter words with q first = 12
# 4 letter words with u second = 378
# 4 letter words starting with qu = 10
```

getting heads. In statistics, the first few capital letters are typically used for events. For example, let B stand for a randomly picked four-letter word with u as its second letter. Then, as discussed above, $P(B) = 378/3686$, at least for Grady Ward's CROSSWD.TXT word list.

In symbols, conditional probability is written $P(B|C)$, which means "the probability of event B happening given that event C has already happened." This is usually read as "the probability of B given C." For example, let B be the event defined in the preceding paragraph, and let C be the event that a randomly selected four-letter word has q as its first letter. Then $P(B|C)$ is the probability that the second letter is u **given** that the first letter of a randomly selected four-letter word is q. As computed above, $P(B|C) = 10/12$.

The general formula is straightforward. For any two events E and F, $P(E|F)$ assumes that F has, in fact, happened. So the computation requires two steps. First, enumerate all outcomes that comprise event F. Second, of these outcomes, find the proportion that also satisfies event E, which estimates $P(E|F)$. Equation 4.4 summarizes this verbal description as a formula, where *and* is used as in logic. That is, both events connected by *and* must happen.

$$P(E|F) = \frac{n(E \text{ and } F)}{n(F)} \tag{4.4}$$

For the example of four-letter words discussed above, "B and C" means that both B and C must occur at the same time, which means a four-letter word starting with qu. There are

10 words that satisfy this in the file CROSSWD.TXT (they are *quad, quag, quai, quay, quey, quid, quip, quit, quiz, quod*). This is out of all the four-letter words starting with *q* (which also includes *qaid* and *qoph* to make a total of 12). Finally, equation 4.4 says $P(B|C)$ is the ratio of these two numbers, so it is 10/12, as claimed above.

Here is one more way to think about conditional probability. Let n be the total number of possibilities. Then equation 4.5 holds.

$$P(E|F) = \frac{P(E \text{ and } F)}{P(F)} = \frac{n(E \text{ and } F)/n}{n(F)/n} = \frac{n(E \text{ and } F)}{n(F)} \qquad (4.5)$$

Using B and C as defined above, let us check this result. In equation 4.6, note that the number of four-letter words (3686) cancels out to get 10/12.

$$
\begin{aligned}
P(B \text{ and } C) &= \frac{n(B \text{ and } C)}{n(\text{four-letter words})} \\
&= \frac{10}{3686} \\
P(C) &= \frac{n(C)}{n(\text{four-letter words})} \\
&= \frac{12}{3686} \\
P(B|C) &= \frac{P(B \text{ and } C)}{P(C)} \\
&= \frac{10/3686}{12/3686} = \frac{10}{12}
\end{aligned}
\qquad (4.6)
$$

Finally, it is important to realize that order of events matters in conditional probability. That is, $P(B|C)$ is generally different from $P(C|B)$, and this is the case for B and C defined above. For these events, $P(C|B)$ is the probability of a randomly picked four-letter word having q as its first letter given that u is its second letter. Given this, there are many four-letter words that begin with letters other than q, for example, *aunt, bull, cups, dull, euro,* and *full*. Hence this probability should be much smaller than 83%, the value of $P(B|C)$. Using output 4.5, it is 10/378, or about 2.6%. Note that this numerator is the same as the one for $P(B|C)$, which is no accident since "B and C" is the same event as "C and B." However, the denominators of $P(B|C)$ and $P(C|B)$ are quite different, which makes these probabilities unequal.

Related to conditional probability is the concept of independence of events, which allows computational simplifications if it holds. With text, however, independence may or may not hold, so it must be checked. This is the topic of the next section.

4.3.1 Independence

Examples of two independent events are easy to give. For instance, as defined above, let A stand for a coin flip resulting in a head, and let B stand for a randomly picked four-letter word that has u as its second letter. Since coin flipping has nothing to do with four-letter words (unless a person has lost large sums of money betting on the coin), knowing that A has occurred should not influence an estimate of the probability of B happening. Symbolically, this means $P(B|A) = P(B)$, and, in fact, this can be used as the definition of independence of A and B. Moreover, since four-letter words do not influence coin flips, it is also true that $P(A|B) = P(A)$.

These two equalities and equation 4.5 imply that equation 4.7 holds when E and F are independent events. This result is called the multiplication rule.

$$\begin{aligned} P(E|F) &= \frac{P(E \text{ and } F)}{P(F)} \\ P(E|F) &= P(E) \\ \Rightarrow P(E) &= \frac{P(E \text{ and } F)}{P(F)} \\ \Rightarrow P(E \text{ and } F) &= P(E)P(F) \end{aligned} \qquad (4.7)$$

The closer $P(E \text{ and } F)$ is to $P(E)P(F)$, the more likely it is that E and F are independent. Returning to events B and C of the last section, we can check if these are independent, although intuition of English suggests that q at the beginning of a four-letter word and u in the second position are not independent. That is, they are *dependent*.

Fortunately, all the needed probabilities are already computed, which are summarized in equation 4.8. The two values are different by a factor of 8.1. Although the precise boundary that distinguishes dependence from independence is not obvious, a factor of 8.1 seems large enough to support the intuition that q and u are dependent. See problem 4.5 for a statistical test that strongly confirms this.

$$\begin{aligned} P(B \text{ and } C) &= \frac{10}{3686} \approx 0.002713 \\ P(B)P(C) &= \frac{378}{3686}\frac{12}{3686} \approx 0.0003339 \end{aligned} \qquad (4.8)$$

With the ideas of conditional probability and independence introduced, let us consider one more theoretical idea. In text mining, counting is a key step in many analyses. In the next section we consider the ideas of the mean and variance of a numeric measurement.

4.4   MEAN AND VARIANCE OF RANDOM VARIABLES

This section introduces *random variables*, which are widely used in the statistical literature. These are a convenient way to model random processes.

Random variables are written as uppercase letters, often toward the end of the alphabet, for example, X, Y, or Z. In this book, a random variable is a numeric summary of a sample of text. For example, let X be the number of times the word *the* appears in a randomly selected text.

Random variables look like algebraic variables and can be used in algebraic formulas. However, unlike algebraic equations, we do not solve for the unknown. Instead, think of random variables as random number generators. For text mining, random variables are often counts or percentages, and the randomness comes from picking a text at random.

As a second example, let Y be the proportion of the letter e in a text. Once a text is specified, then Y is computable. For example, in section 4.2.2.1 the letters of *A Christmas Carol* are tabulated. For this text Y equals 14,869/121,179, or about 0.1227. If the Poe short story "The Black Cat" were picked instead, then Y is 2204/17,103, or about 0.1289. Clearly Y depends on the text.

The hope of formulating this problem as a random variable is that as more and more texts are sampled, some pattern of the values becomes clear. One way to discover such a pattern is to make a histogram. For example, if all the values are close together, then an accurate estimate based on this sample is likely.

Let us consider the 68 Poe short stories from [96], [97], [98], [99] and [100] with respect to the proportion of the letter *e* in each one. For some hints on how to do this, see problem 4.6. The results are listed in table 4.1 and then plotted in figure 4.3. This histogram shows a clear peak just below 0.13, and all the values are between 0.11 and 0.14, except for an unusually low one of 0.0989. This comes from "Why the Little Frenchman Wears His Hand in a Sling," which is narrated in a heavy dialect with many nonstandard spellings. Otherwise, Poe is consistent in his use of the letter *e*.

Table 4.1   Proportions of the letter *e* for 68 Poe short stories, sorted smallest to largest.

0.0989	0.1245	0.1285	0.1309
0.1141	0.1247	0.1286	0.1310
0.1145	0.1248	0.1286	0.1312
0.1164	0.1260	0.1287	0.1317
0.1182	0.1263	0.1289	0.1318
0.1201	0.1264	0.1294	0.1320
0.1213	0.1267	0.1294	0.1323
0.1216	0.1271	0.1295	0.1325
0.1219	0.1273	0.1296	0.1326
0.1221	0.1273	0.1296	0.1329
0.1226	0.1274	0.1297	0.1329
0.1239	0.1274	0.1297	0.1342
0.1239	0.1281	0.1300	0.1343
0.1241	0.1283	0.1302	0.1356
0.1241	0.1284	0.1303	0.1357
0.1245	0.1284	0.1303	0.1372
0.1245	0.1285	0.1304	0.1385

The histogram in figure 4.3 is an empirical approximation of the proportion of *e*'s in Poe's short stories. It suggests that a normal distribution is a good model, which is supported by the good fit of the curve drawn in figure 4.4. The mean and standard deviation of this curve are estimated by the respective sample values, which are 0.1274 and 0.0060.

The standard deviation is one popular measure of variability. In general, to say precisely what it measures depends on the shape of the data. For distributions that are roughly bell-shaped (also called normally distributed), it can be shown that the mean and standard deviation provide an excellent summary of the shape.

Nonetheless, there are constraints and heuristics for this concept. For example, the standard deviation is a number greater than or equal to zero. Zero only occurs if there is no variability at all, which means that all the values in the data set are exactly the same. The larger the standard deviation, the more spread out the values, which makes the histogram wider. To say more than this, we need to know something about the shape of the data. Below we assume that the histogram is approximately bell-shaped.

First, we define some notation. Let the mean value of the data (called the *sample mean*) be denoted by a bar over the letter used for the associated random variable, or $\overline{Y}$ in this case. Second, let the standard deviation of the data (called the *sample standard deviation*) be denoted by the letter *s* with the random variable given as a subscript, for example, s_Y.

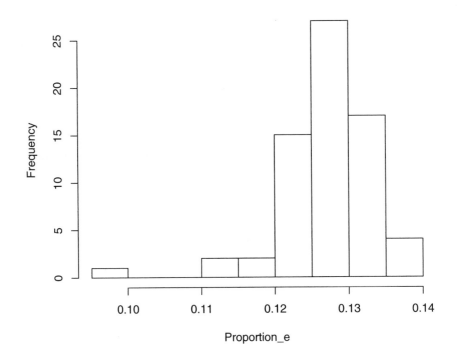

Figure 4.3   Histogram of the proportions of the letter *e* in 68 Poe short stories based on table 4.1.

Now we consider the range of values $\overline{Y} - s_Y$ to $\overline{Y} + s_Y$. This is an interval centered at $\overline{Y}$, and its length is $2s_Y$, a function of only the standard deviation. Assuming bell-shaped data, then about 68% of the values lie in this interval. A more popular interval is $\overline{Y} - 2s_Y$ to $\overline{Y} + 2s_Y$, which contains about 95% of the data. Note that the length of this is $4s_Y$, which makes it twice as wide as the first interval.

For the Poe stories, s_Y is 0.0060 (see equation 7.2 for a formula), and we can construct the two intervals given above, which is done in table 4.2. Note that 55 out of the 68 stories have *e* proportions in the smaller interval, and this is 80.9%, which is bigger than the predicted 68%. However, the second interval has 65 out of the 68 stories, which is 95.6%, or practically 95%. In general, data that looks roughly bell-shaped need not fit the theoretical normal curve perfectly, yet the predicted percentages are often close to the theoretical ones.

Finally, there are other types of intervals. The next section, for example, considers intervals to estimate the population mean.

4.4.1 Sampling and Error Estimates

One common framework in statistics is taking a sample from a population. The latter is a group of items of interest to the researcher, but measuring all of them is too expensive

Table 4.2 Two intervals for the proportion of e's in Poe's short stories using table 4.1.

Lower Limit	Upper Limit	Predicted	Actual
$\overline{Y} - s_Y = 0.1214$	$\overline{Y} + s_Y = 0.1334$	68%	55/68 = 80.9%
$\overline{Y} - 2s_Y = 0.1154$	$\overline{Y} + 2s_Y = 0.1394$	95%	65/68 = 95.6%

(either in time or resources or both). Measuring only a subset of these items is one way to reduce the costs. The smaller the sample, the cheaper the analysis, but also the larger the error in the estimates (on average). So there is always a trade-off between accuracy and cost in sampling.

Numerical properties of the population are called *parameters*. These can be estimated by constructing a list of the population and then selecting a random subset from this list. For this discussion, a random sample is a method of picking items so that every item has the same probability of selection, which is called a *simple random sample*. There are, however, many types of samples: see section 6.2.1 for an example.

Now reconsider the proportion of the letter e data from the last section. Suppose we believe that Poe's use of this letter is not something he tried to purposely manipulate. Then it is plausible that Poe has a typical proportion of its use. This value is an unknown parameter, and we want to estimate it by taking a sample of his works and computing its average. Since different stories use different words, the percentage of e in each work varies, and so an estimate of the standard deviation is also of interest. Again this is an unknown parameter of Poe, so we estimate it by computing the standard deviation of the sample. If the data in the sample is roughly bell-shaped, then the mean and the standard deviation is a good summary of the data. For more on what is meant by this, see problem 4.7.

For conciseness, let us introduce these symbols. First, let the unknown population mean be μ_p, where the p stands for Poe. This is estimated by computing the sample mean $\overline{Y}$. Second, let the unknown population standard deviation be σ_p. This is estimated by the sample standard deviation, s_Y.

If we believe our data model that the sample has a bell-shaped histogram, which is visually plausible in figure 4.4, then not only can μ_p be estimated, but its error is estimable, too. One way of doing this is to give an interval estimate of μ_p along with an estimate of the probability this interval contains μ_p. For example, equation 4.9 gives a 95% confidence interval for the population mean. That is, constructing such an interval successfully contains the true population mean 95% of the time, on average.

$$(\overline{Y} - 2\frac{s_Y}{\sqrt{n}}, \overline{Y} + 2\frac{s_Y}{\sqrt{n}}) \tag{4.9}$$

Using the sample mean and standard deviation of the Poe stories, this formula produces the interval 0.1259 to 0.1289. Notice that this is much smaller than the ones in table 4.2. This happens because predicting the mean of a population is more precise than predicting an individual value for a sample size of 68.

Another way to view this equation is that $\overline{Y}$ is the best estimate of the population mean, and that $2s_Y/\sqrt{n}$ is an error estimate of $\overline{Y}$. For more information on a variety of confidence intervals, see *Statistical Intervals: A Guide for Practitioners* by Hahn and Meeker [49].

Finally, we consider the randomness of the selection of the 68 Poe short stories used above, which are obtained from a public domain edition available on the Web. First, some of these are not short stories, for example, "Maelzel's Chess Player" [91] is an analysis of a

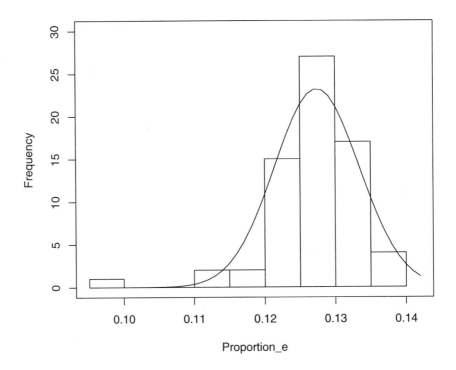

Figure 4.4   Histogram and best fitting normal curve for the proportions of the letter *e* in 68 Poe short stories.

touring mechanical device that was claimed to play chess (and Poe concludes correctly that it hid a human chess player). Second, not all of Poe's short stories are included in these five volumes, for example, "The Literary Life of Thingum Bob, Esq." is missing. However, most of them are represented. Third, Poe wrote many short pieces of nonfiction, for example, book reviews and opinion pieces. In fact, one of these is included, "The Philosophy of Furniture," in which he discusses his ideas on interior design. Hence, these 68 works are closer to the complete population of his short stories than to a random sample of these.

There is one more complication to consider. If Poe is thought of as a generator of short stories, then these 68 are just a subset of his potential short stories. With this point of view, the population is not clear. In addition, the idea that his existing stories are a random sample of this population is unlikely. For example, he might have written the stories he thought would sell better. Note that in either of these points of view, the stories analyzed are not a random sample of some population. For more on text sampling, see section 6.2.2.

Next we switch from letters to words in a text. Words can be studied themselves or as the building blocks of linguistic objects like sentences. The next section introduces an important, but limited, probability model for words.

4.5 THE BAG-OF-WORDS MODEL FOR POE'S "THE BLACK CAT"

In the next chapter the *bag-of-words* model is used. In this section we define it and discuss some of its limitations. However, in spite of these, it is still useful.

Analyzing a text by only analyzing word frequencies is essentially the bag-of-words model. Because any random permutation of the text produces the same frequencies as the original version, word order is irrelevant. Note that cutting out each word of a paper version of the text, putting them into a bag, and then picking these out one by one produces a random order. So the term *bag-of-words* is an appropriate metaphor.

Since the bag-of-words model completely ignores word order, it clearly loses important information. For example, using Perl it is not hard to randomize the words of a text. Output 4.6 contains the first few lines of a random permutation of "The Black Cat" by Poe. For a hint on how to do this, see problem 4.8.

Output 4.6 The first few lines of the short story "The Black Cat" after its words have been randomized and converted to lowercase.

```
hideous me at above this breast something fell impression had
the as between down a i body scream caresses the the on and
put night make or of has ascended been brute into similar blood
and bosom hit but from entire destroying and search evidence
frequent to could had and i they why investigation dislodged
and rid day inquiries from the time the steadily to oh me be
i and chimney the the old violence graven dared blow understand
was for appeared in i and of at feelings of took stood aimed hot
i the concealment of period trouble assassination the for better
off evident a him this shriek and nook immortal it easily wish
```

Although output 4.6 is ungrammatical, it does preserve some of Poe's writing style. For example, it is appropriate (though accidental) that it starts off with *hideous me*. And it does include many words with negative connotations: *hideous*, *scream*, *brute*, *blood*, *destroying*, and so forth. On the other hand, reading the original story is much more enjoyable.

An example of a word frequency text analysis is done in section 3.7.1, which illustrates Zipf's law applying program 3.3 to Dickens's novel *A Christmas Carol*. This program produces the counts needed to create figure 3.1.

Zipf's law implies words that appear once are the most common, which suggests that authors do not use all the words they know in a text (empirical evidence of this is given in the next section). Hence a text has many zero counts for words known by the author. As noted in section 4.2.2, this implies that these word frequencies have biases. This is an important conclusion, and one based on a bag-of-words model, which shows that a simplistic language model can produce interesting results.

Finally, to finish this chapter, we analyze how word frequencies depend on the size of the text used. This reveals an important difference between coin tossing and texts. Unfortunately, this difference makes the latter harder to analyze.

4.6   THE EFFECT OF SAMPLE SIZE

Section 4.2.1 shows an example of estimating the probability of getting heads by simulating coin flips. Although the results are not exact, as the number of flips increases, the accuracy of the estimate increases on average, as shown by figures 4.1 and 4.2. In this simulation, all the bigger deviations from 0.5 occur below 1000 flips. For coins, the exact answer is known, so an estimate based on simulation is easily checked. However, with a text sample, the exact answer is unknown, and so using samples to make estimates is the only way to proceed.

In the next section, we examine how the number of types is related to the number of tokens as the sample size increases. The texts used are Poe's "The Unparalleled Adventures of One Hans Pfaall" [95] and "The Black Cat" [88]. We find out below that coins are better behaved than texts. Finally, this example uses the approach described in section 1.1 of Harald Baayen's book *Word Frequency Distributions* [6], which analyzes Lewis Carroll's *Alice in Wonderland* and *Through the Looking Glass*. If word frequencies interest the reader, then read Baayen for an in-depth discussion of modeling them.

4.6.1   Tokens vs. Types in Poe's "Hans Pfaall"

In section 3.1, a distinction is made between *tokens* and *types*, which we now apply to words. First, as tokens, every word is counted, including repetitions. Second, as types, repetitions are ignored. Recall sentence 3.1: *The cat ate the bird*. It has five tokens, but only four types.

In this section we show that the number of types is a function of the number of tokens, which is the length of a text sample. Because some words are very common (for example, prepositions and pronouns), the number of tokens is generally much greater than the number of types. We consider just how much greater this is as a function of text size.

First, let us define some notation, which is almost the same as Baayen's [6] except that his Greek omega is changed to a *w* here. Let N be the size of the text sample, which is the number of tokens. Suppose the words of a text are known, say by using code similar to program 3.3. Label these words w_1, w_2, w_3, ... Although the order used here is not specified, for any particular example, it is determined by how the program works. Let $V(N)$ be the number of types in a text of size N. Let $f(w_i, N)$ be the frequency of word w_i in a text of size N. Finally, define the proportion of word w_i in a text of size N by equation 4.10.

$$p(w_i, N) = \frac{f(w_i, N)}{N} \tag{4.10}$$

Now that the notation is given, let us consider the concrete example of Poe's "The Unparalleled Adventures of One Hans Pfaall" [95], which is one of his longer short stories. To create samples of varying sizes, we select the first N words for a sequence of values. Then the results can be plotted as a function of N.

First, consider $V(N)$ as a function of N. Since there are only a finite number of types for an author to use, if the sample size were big enough, $V(N)$ should flatten out, which means that no new vocabulary is introduced. In practice, an author can coin new words or create new names (of characters, of locations, of objects, and so forth), so even for an enormous sample, $V(N)$ can keep increasing to the end. But the hope is that this rate of increase eventually becomes small. Mathematically speaking, this means that the slope decreases to near zero.

Programming this in Perl is straightforward. First, convert the text to lowercase, then remove the punctuation. Use `split` to break lines into words. The number of tokens is just the number of words, which can be used as hash keys. Then the size of the hash is the number of types at any given point. These ideas are implemented in program 4.5.

```perl
# USAGE > perl Pfaall_word_richness.pl

open(IN, 'Hans_Pfaall.txt') or die;
open(OUT, ">Pfaall_word_richness.csv") or die;

while(<IN>) {
  chomp;

  $_ = lc;             # Convert to lowercase
  s/[.,:;?"!()]//g;    # Remove most punctuation
  s/--//g;             # Remove dashes
  s/ +/ /g;            # Replace multiple spaces by one space

  if ( not /^$/ ) {    # Ignore empty lines
    @words = split(/ /);
    foreach $x (@words) {
      ++$tokens;
      ++$freq{$x};
    }
    $types = scalar keys %freq;
    $ratio = $tokens/$types;
    print OUT "$tokens, $types, $ratio\n";
  }
}
```

Program 4.5 This program computes the ratio of tokens to types for Poe's "The Unparalleled Adventures of One Hans Pfaall."

In this program, the size of the hash `%freq` is stored in `$types` as follows. The function keys returns the keys as an array. Then function `scalar` forces this array into a scalar context, but this is just the size of the array, which is the number of types in the text. So the combination `scalar keys` returns the size of the hash. Finally, the results are stored in a comma-separated variable file called `Pfaall_word_richness.csv`, which then can be imported to a statistical package for plotting (R is used in this book).

Figure 4.5 is the resulting plot, which clearly shows that $V(N)$ steadily increases as N increases, even at the end of the story. Although the rate of increase is slowing, it is never close to converging to some value. In fact, in the last thousand or so words the slope increases a little, so the limiting value of $V(N)$ is not yet reached. This suggests that Poe's vocabulary is much bigger than the vocabulary that is contained in this story.

Since $V(N)$ is an increasing function of N, we should take into account the sample size. For example, for coin tossing, the number of heads steadily increases as the number of flips increases, but the proportion of heads stabilizes around 0.5. This suggests that it might be useful to form a ratio of $V(N)$ with N. In section 1.1 of [6], Baayen suggests

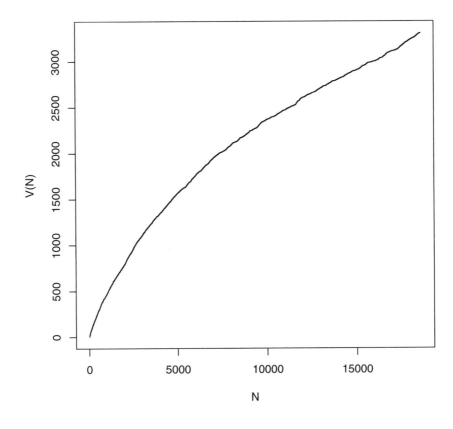

Figure 4.5   Plot of the number of types versus the number of tokens for "The Unparalleled Adventures of One Hans Pfaall." Data is from program 4.5. Figure adapted from figure 1.1 of Baayen [6] with kind permission from Springer Science and Business Media and the author.

using the *mean word frequency*, $N/V(N)$, which is the mean number of tokens per type. Program 4.5 already computes this, and the results are plotted in figure 4.6.

Unfortunately, this second plot does not flatten out either. In fact, the rate of increase (or slope) of the plot for N in the range of 3000 to 17,000 is close to constant. Although at the highest values of N the slope of the plot decreases somewhat, it is not clear that it is close to reaching a plateau.

This lack of convergence might be due to the small sample size. After all, this text is not even 20,000 words long, and perhaps longer texts behave as we expect. However, section 1.1 of Baayen [6] states that even for text samples on the order of tens of millions of words, the mean word frequency still does not converge to a fixed value.

This has practical consequences. Suppose we want to compare "The Black Cat" and "The Unparalleled Adventures of One Hans Pfaall" with respect to vocabulary diversity. The stories have different lengths, and it is tempting to believe that this can be taken into

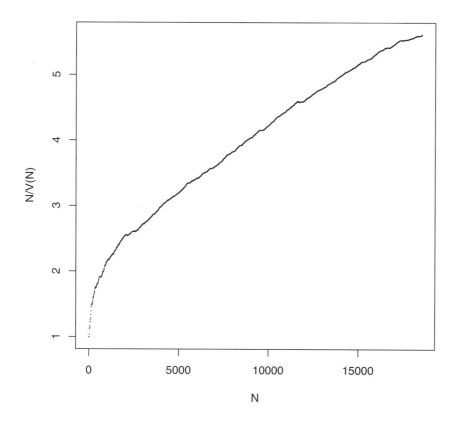

Figure 4.6 Plot of the mean word frequency against the number of tokens for "The Unparalleled Adventures of One Hans Pfaall." Data is from program 4.5. Figure adapted from figure 1.1 of Baayen [6] with kind permission from Springer Science and Business Media and the author.

account by computing the mean word frequency for both stories. The results seem quite significant: "The Black Cat" has an average of 3.17 tokens per type, while "Hans Pfaall" has a value of 5.61, which is about 75% higher.

However, the mean word frequency depends on sample size. So if we plot $N/V(N)$ vs. N for both stories on the same plot, then we can make a fairer comparison. Program 4.5 is easily modified to count up the number of tokens and types for "The Black Cat." Once this is done, the plots for both stories are put into figure 4.7 for comparison.

This figure shows that "The Black Cat" has the slightly higher mean word frequency when we compare both stories over the range of 1000 to 4000 (the latter is approximately the length of "The Black Cat"). Hence the initial comparison of 3.17 to 5.61 tokens per type is mistaken due to the effect of text length. Note that this approach compares the shorter story to the initial part of the longer story, so the two texts are not treated in a symmetric manner.

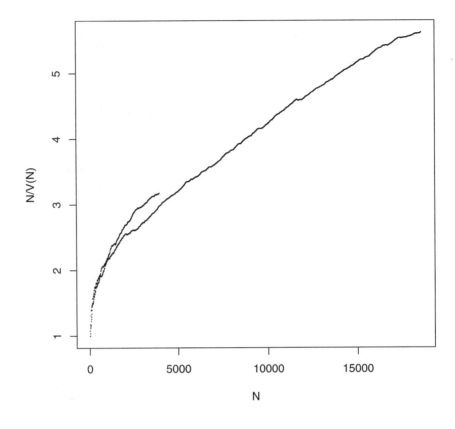

Figure 4.7   Plot of the mean word frequency against the number of tokens for "The Unparalleled Adventures of One Hans Pfaall" and "The Black Cat." Figure adapted from figure 1.1 of Baayen [6] with kind permission from Springer Science and Business Media and the author.

In corpus linguistics, researchers typically take samples of equal size from a collection of texts. This size is smaller than each text, so that all of them are analyzed in a similar fashion. The corpora built by linguists use this approach. For example, the Brown Corpus uses samples of about 2000 words. For more information on the construction of this corpus, see the *Brown Corpus Manual* [46].

4.7 REFERENCES

This chapter introduces the basics of probability using text examples. These ideas occur again and again in the rest of this book since counting and computing proportions of strings or linguistic items is often useful by itself and is a common first step for more sophisticated statistical techniques.

To learn more about statistics with an exposition intended for language researchers, there are several options. First, an excellent book devoted to this is Christopher Manning and Hinrich Schütze's *Foundations of Statistical Natural Language Processing* [75]. The first four chapters introduce the reader to statistical natural language processing (NLP), and chapter 2 introduces probability theory along with other topics.

Second, *Statistics for Corpus Linguistics* by Michael Oakes [] reviews statistics in its first chapter, then covers information theory, clustering, and concordancing. It is a good book both for reviewing statistics and seeing how it is useful in analyzing corpora.

Third, there is Brigitte Krenn and Christer Samuelsson's manual called "The Linguist's Guide to Statistics" [67], which is available for free online at CiteSeer [29]. It starts with an overview of statistics and then discusses corpus linguistics and NLP.

Fourth, for more advanced examples of probability models used in linguistics, see *Probabilistic Linguistics*, which is edited by Rens Bod, Jennifer Hay, and Stefanie Jannedy [17]. Each chapter shows how different areas in linguistics can benefit from probability models. Another book with probabilistic models for analyzing language is Daniel Jurafsky and James Martin's *Speech and Language Processing* [64]. For example, chapter 5 discusses a Bayesian statistical model for spelling, and chapter 7 covers hidden Markov models.

The next chapter introduces a useful tool from the field of information retrieval (IR), the *term-document matrix*. Think of this as a spreadsheet containing counts of words from a collection of texts. It turns out that geometry is a useful way of thinking about this. Although the next chapter is the first one so far to discuss geometric concepts, it is not the last.

PROBLEMS

4.1 A fair coin is flipped until either HHH or THH is obtained. If HHH occurs first, then Player A wins, and if THH occurs first, then Player B wins. For example, the sequence HTTTTHH is a win for Player B because THH occurs in the last three flips, but HHH does not appear. Although both sequences are equally likely when flipping a coin three times, one of the two players is a favorite to win. Write a Perl program to simulate this process, find who wins, and then estimate Player A's probability of winning.

This problem is just one case of a game described by Walter Penney. See pages 59–63 of John Haigh's *Taking Chances: Winning with Probability* [50] for a description of Penney's game and how it has counterintuitive properties.

4.2 Suppose two people are betting the outcome of a fair coin where Player A loses a dollar if the flip is tails and otherwise wins a dollar. A running tally of Player A's net winnings or loses is kept where the initial value is $0. For example, if the game starts off with HTTHT, then Player A has $1, $0, −$1, $0, −$1, respectively.

Write a Perl simulation of this game for 20 tosses, then compute the proportion of the flips where Player A is ahead or even. Then repeat this simulation 10,000 times. The result will be 10,000 proportions each based on 20 flips. One guesses that since the coin is fair, that Player A should be ahead about 50% of the time, but this is **not** true. Surprisingly, the most probable scenario is that Player A is either ahead or behind the entire game. See pages 64–69 of John Haigh's *Taking Chances: Winning with Probability* [50] for a discussion of this process. For a mathematical exposition, see section III.4 of *An Introduction to Probability Theory and Its Applications* by William Feller [44].

4.3 [Requires a statistical package] Output 4.2 gives the frequencies of the letters appearing in the fictional works *A Christmas Carol* and "The Black Cat." For this problem, focus on the former. The ranks of the letters in *A Christmas Carol* are easy to assign since these values are already in numerical order; that is, the letter on the first line (*e*) has rank 1, the letter on the second line (*t*) has rank 2, and so forth. Using a statistical package such as R, make a plot of the Log(Rank) vs. Log(Frequency) for the 26 letters. How does this compare to figure 3.1? In your opinion, how well does Zipf's law hold for letters?

4.4 Modify program 4.4 to make it enumerate trigrams. Hint: In the `foreach` loop that iterates over the array `@words`, modify the `join` statement so that it takes three instead of two letters in a row. A modification of the `for` loop's ending condition is needed, too.

4.5 [Mathematical] For four-letter words, equation 4.8 suggests that the events "first letter is a *q*" and "second letter is an *u*" are dependent as language intuition suggests. However, how strong is this evidence? This problem gives a quantitative answer to this.

The problem of independence of events can be solved with contingency tables. There are several ways to do this, and this problem applies Fisher's exact test. Equation 4.11 shows the computation needed, which gives the probability of seeing the counts in table 4.3 if independence were true. Since this answer is about six in a billion, the reasonable conclusion is that the two events are dependent.

Table 4.3 Counts of four-letter words satisfying each pair of conditions. For problem 4.5.

	1st is *q*	1st not *q*	Row Sums
2nd is *u*	10	368	378
2nd not *u*	2	3306	3308
Column Sums	12	3674	3686

$$\text{Probability of independence} = \frac{378!\,3308!\,12!\,3674!}{10!\,368!\,2!\,3306!\,3686!} = 6.17222 \times 10^{-9} \quad (4.11)$$

For this problem, find a statistics text that shows how to analyze categorical data. Then look up Fisher's exact test to see why it works. For example, see section 3.5.1 of Alan Agresti's *Categorical Data Analysis* [2].

4.6 In section 4.4, the proportions of the letter *e* in 68 Poe stories are given. Here are some steps to compute these values. First, download the five volumes from the Web, and get rid of the initial and ending text so that just the titles and stories are left. Second, although the titles are easy for a person to read, it helps to make them completely unambiguous. One common way to add information to a text is by XML tags. These work the same way as HTML tags except that they can stand for anything, not just how to display a Web page. Here we put the story titles in between two title tags, for example, <TITLE>The Black Cat</TITLE>. Third, scan these five files line by line using a `while` loop. Finally, use code sample 4.3 as a start for counting the total number of letters (in `$count`) and the number of *e*'s (in `$count_e`).

4.7 [Mathematical] For some distributions, the sample data can be summarized by a few *sufficient statistics* without loss of any information about the population parameters. However, this assumes that the data values are really generated by the assumed population distribution, which is rarely exactly true when working with a real data set. Hence, in practice, reducing the data to sufficient statistics can lose information about how well the population distribution fits the observed data.

Code Sample 4.3 Code sample for problem 4.6.

```
if (/<TITLE>(.*)<\/TITLE>/) {
  $title = $1;
  $count = 0;
  $count_e = 0;
} else {
  $_ = lc;
  s/[^a-z]//g;
  $count_e += tr/e/e/;
  $count += length;
}
```

Here is an example that is discussed in section 9.4.1. Equation 9.1 gives a sequence of 0's and 1's reproduced here as equation 4.12.

$$1111111111110000000011111 \tag{4.12}$$

Suppose we assume that this sequence is generated by a coin, where 1 stands for heads and 0 for tails. Assume that the probability of heads is p, which we wish to estimate. Assuming that this model is true, then the sufficient statistic for p is estimated by the number of 1's divided by the number of flips, which gives $17/25 = 68\%$.

However, this data set does not look like it comes from flipping a coin because the 0's and 1's tend to repeat. For this problem, compute the probability of getting the data in equation 4.12 assuming that a coin with $p = 0.68$ is, in fact, used.

If this probability is low, then the assumption of a biased coin model is cast into doubt. However, reducing the data set to the sufficient statistic for p makes it impossible to decide on the validity of this coin model; that is, information is lost by ignoring the original data in favor of the estimate $p = 0.68$.

Hint: see section 9.4.1 for one approach of estimating the probability observing equation 4.12 if seventeen 1's and eight 0's can appear in any order with equal probability.

For more on sufficient statistics see chapter 10 of Lee Bain and Max Engelhardt's *Introduction to Probability and Mathematical Statistics* [7]. In addition, the point that the data set does have more information than the sufficient statistic is made in section 8.7 of John A. Rice's *Mathematical Statistics and Data Analysis* [106].

For the normal distribution, the sample mean and sample standard deviation are sufficient for the population mean and population standard deviation. See theorem 7.1.1 of James Press's *Applied Multivariate Analysis* [103] for a proof.

4.8 To randomize the words in a story requires two steps. First, they must be identified. Second, they are stored and then permuted. The task of identifying the words is discussed in section 2.4 (and see program 2.6). So here we focus on rearranging them. For each word, store it in a hash using a string generated by the function rand as follows.

```
$permutation{rand()} = $word;
```

Then print out the hash %permutation by sorting on its keywords (either a numerical or an alphabetical sort works). Since the keywords are randomly generated, the sort randomly permutes the values of this hash.

CHAPTER 5

APPLYING INFORMATION RETRIEVAL
TO TEXT MINING

5.1 INTRODUCTION

Information retrieval (IR) is the task of returning relevant texts for a query. The most famous application is the online search engine where the texts are Web pages. The basic underlying concept is simple: a measure of similarity is computed between the query and each document, which are then sorted from most to least relevant.

The details of search engines are more complex, of course. For example, Web pages must be found and indexed prior to any queries. For an introduction to this, see chapter 1 of *Data Mining the Web* by Markov and Larose [77]. For details of how the computations are made, see *Google's PageRank and Beyond* by Langville and Meyer [68].

We are interested in using the similarity scores from IR to compare two texts. With these scores a number of statistical techniques can be employed, for example, clustering, the topic of chapter 8.

IR has a number of approaches, and we consider only one: the *vector space model*. *Vector space* is a term from linear algebra, but our focus is the specific application of this model to texts, and all the required mathematics is introduced in this chapter. This includes geometric ideas such as angles.

5.2   COUNTING LETTERS AND WORDS

To keep the focus on text, not mathematics, we study the distribution of third-person pronouns by gender in four Edgar Allan Poe short stories. Section 4.6.1 shows that the length of a text influences the estimates, so these four stories are picked because they are approximately the same length: all are between 3529 and 3607 words long. These are: "Hop Frog" [90], "A Predicament" [93], "The Facts in the Case of M. Valdemar" [89], and "The Man of the Crowd" [92].

Before concentrating on the pronouns, we first discuss what programming techniques are needed to count all the words in these stories. This reviews some of the material in the earlier chapters and provides another example of dealing with the quirks of a text analysis.

5.2.1   Counting Letters in Poe with Perl

To extract words, the punctuation must be removed, which requires knowing which ones are present. So we first run a program that determines all the different characters used in these four stories. To inform the computer on where each story starts, the tags <TITLE> and </TITLE> are used to enclose the titles, as shown below.

```
<TITLE>Hop Frog</TITLE>
```

These are XML tags, which are similar to the HTML tags used in Web pages. However, the former are used to indicate information, not page layouts. For another example, see problem 4.6.

The hash %freq keeps track of the character counts in program 5.1. This reveals which nonalphanumeric characters are among the four stories. These counts are printed out in descending order in table 5.1 using multiple columns for compactness.

Table 5.1   Character counts for four Poe stories combined. Computed by program 5.1.

, 13219	m, 1723	;, 117	8, 2
e, 8526	f, 1601	q, 97	1, 1
t, 5921	w, 1429	j, 87	ê, 1
a, 5056	p, 1294	!, 82	>, 1
o, 4668	,, 1251	', 65	-, 1
i, 4573	g, 1248	(, 36	æ, 1
n, 4465	y, 1242	), 36	è, 1
s, 3885	b, 935	z, 34	0, 1
h, 3816	v, 670	?, 27	3, 1
r, 3738	., 641	:, 21	9, 1
d, 2893	-, 490	_, 4	
l, 2587	k, 392	[, 3	
c, 1774	", 140	], 3	
u, 1742	x, 122	2, 2	

Note that the space is the most common character, and the famous ordering ETAOIN SHRDLU almost appears after it: see problem 5.1 for more information. Double quotes and single quotes are both present, and the concordance program (program 3.2 in section 3.7) confirms that double quotes are used for quotations. Poe likes to use dashes, and these

```
open(IN, "Poe_4_Stories.txt") or die;

while (<IN>) {
  chomp;
  if ( /<TITLE>(.*)<\/TITLE>/ ) {
    print "$1\n";
  } else {
    $_ = lc;
    if ( not /^$/ ) {
      @characters = split(//);
      foreach $char (@characters) {
        ++$freq{$char};
      }
    }
  }
}

# Print out character counts in decreasing order
foreach $char (sort { $freq{$b} <=> $freq{$a} } keys %freq) {
  print "$char, $freq{$char}\n";
}
```

Program 5.1 This program counts every instance of each character in four Poe short stories. Note that uppercase letters are changed to lowercase.

stories are no exception. This program reveals, however, that double hyphens are used in all the stories except "The Man of the Crowd," which uses a single hyphen.

There are a few odd characters found by program 5.1, which can be checked, if desired. For instance, a greater sign (>) appears, and it turns out that it comes from the string the "PL> 0 BDT ,B,L, which makes no sense. By checking a book of Poe's writings, it turns out that this should be the Greek phrase: $\alpha\chi\lambda\upsilon\sigma\ \eta\ \pi\rho\iota\nu\ \epsilon\pi\eta\epsilon\nu$, which was mangled when the electronic document was created. Besides the zero from this string, the other numbers come from the strings 1839, a year, and [page 228:], a reference of some sort.

Finally, this text uses apostrophes for both contractions and quotations. A simple way to handle these is to always keep them within a word, and to always remove them at the start or end of a word. This is not a perfect solution due to contractions that start or end with an apostrophe, but this is uncommon.

Putting the above ideas together produces program 5.2. Note that each story's word counts are stored in the same hash of hashes, a data structure discussed in section 3.8. The story names are used as keys. Finally, note that removing the initial and ending apostrophes is done with a nongreedy regular expression. See problem 5.2 for why this is necessary.

As program 5.2 stands, it prints out the counts for all the words for all four stories, which requires many lines of output. Adding the counts for a story produces the total number of words in it, and the story lengths quoted above are obtained in this way. But remember our original goal: to study the use of masculine and feminine pronouns, so only a small subset of this output is needed.

```
open(IN, "Poe_4_Stories.txt") or die;

while (<IN>) {
  chomp;
  if ( /<TITLE>(.*)<\/TITLE>/ ) {
    $title = $1; print "TITLE = $title\n";
  } else {
    if ($title eq '') { print "NULL TITLE\n"; }
    $_ = lc;   # Change letters to lowercase
    s/--/ /g;  # Remove dashes
    s/ - / /g; # Remove dashes
    s/[,.";!()?:_\[\]]//g; # Remove non-apostrophes
    s/\s+/ /g; # Replace multiple spaces with one space
    s/^\s+//g; # Remove spaces at the start of a line
    @words = split(/ /);
    foreach $word (@words) {
      if ($word =~ /^'?(.*?)'?$/) { # Must be non-greedy
        $word = $1; # Remove initial and final apostrophes
        ++$freq{$title}{$word};
      }
    }
  }
}

foreach $title (sort keys %freq) {
  foreach $word ( sort keys %{$freq{$title}} ) {
    print "$title, $word, $freq{$title}{$word}\n";
  }
}
```

Program 5.2 This program keeps track of word counts for four Poe stories.

5.2.2 Counting Pronouns Occurring in Poe

Of the four Poe stories that we are considering, we start with "A Predicament," since its narrator talks about both males and females. In program 5.2, replace the final `foreach` loop with code sample 5.1. This now prints out the counts for just the words in the array `@pronouns`.

Output 5.1 gives the pronoun counts for "A Predicament." Both genders are represented, but not equally. However, there are differences in the grammar of the pronouns by gender, which we review now.

The forms *he* and *she* are used when the pronoun is the subject of the sentence. When the pronoun is the object of the sentence, then *him* and *her* are used. To indicate possession of an object, the terms *his* and *her* are used. For example, a person can say *her bike* or *his book*. Used in this way, *his* and *her* are called *possessive determiners*. Finally, a person can say *the bike is hers* or *the book is his*. These are examples of *possessive pronouns*. For a detailed explanation of these grammatical ideas see sections 198 and 201 of the *Cambridge Grammar of English* [26].

Code Sample 5.1 This prints out the pronoun counts when placed at the end of program 5.2.

```
@pronouns = qw(he she him her his hers himself herself);

foreach $title (sort keys %freq) {
  foreach $word ( @pronouns ) {
    $freq{$title}{$word} += 0;  # In case of empty strings
    print "$title, $word, $freq{$title}{$word}\n";
  }
}
```

Output 5.1 Output of program 5.2 and code sample 5.1 for Poe's "A Predicament."

```
he, 19
she, 9
him, 7
her, 13
his, 22
hers, 0
himself, 1
herself, 2
```

With this terminology, the asymmetry in gender can be specified. The masculine forms of the possessive determiner and the possessive pronoun are identical, but the feminine forms differ: *her* versus *hers*, respectively. However, the feminine forms of the object form and the possessive determiner are identical, but the masculine forms differ: *him* versus *his*, respectively. Finally, recall that if the gender of a person is not known, generally the masculine pronoun is used, which can inflate these counts.

These facts complicate the interpretation of output 5.1. Note that *he* and *she* counts are directly comparable since both are subject forms of the pronoun and nothing else. However, does *her* outnumber *him* because the former serves two roles and the latter only one? The analogous statement is possible for *his* and *hers*.

One way to avoid this issue is to combine counts. For example, compare *he* versus *she* and *himself* versus *herself*, but combine the counts for *his* and *him*, which is compared to the combined counts for *her* and *hers*. Another solution is to combine all four counts for each gender; that is, compare the total numbers of masculine and feminine pronouns.

The most involved solution is using a person to classify each use of an ambiguous pronoun and record these with XML tags in the text, as is done in sentence 5.1.

$$\text{Is that <PD>his</PD> book? Yes, it's <PP>his</PP>.} \qquad (5.1)$$

Here PD stands for possessive determiner and PP for possessive pronoun. For a shorter text this is doable by using the concordance program 3.2, which can find all the uses of the pronouns in question and print out each context. Then a person can decide which is the case. For a longer text, there are Perl programs that tag words by parts of speech, but not without errors. See section 9.2.4 for how to do this. Returning to these counts, we now introduce the mathematical concepts of vectors and matrices.

5.3 TEXT COUNTS AND VECTORS

Output 5.1 is a convenient way to display the results of counting up masculine and feminine pronouns. In this section, we introduce vectors and matrices to do the same thing. If unfamiliar with linear algebra, then the advantages of this are not apparent at first, but there is a practical payoff.

The numbers of output 5.1 are easily written in vector notation by thinking of it as a list of values in parentheses. This is also how Perl creates an array as shown below.

```
@vector = (19, 9, 7, 13, 22, 0, 1, 2);
```

In mathematical notation, letters are often used to denote vectors. A linear algebra book writes the following.

$$\mathbf{x} = (19, 9, 7, 13, 22, 0, 1, 2) \tag{5.2}$$

The order of the entries in a vector is important. But there is one drawback: equation 5.2 records pronoun counts, but how does one know which counts go with which pronouns? This requires stating the order explicitly in the definition of this vector. That is, while output 5.1 makes it clear which counts are which, if equation 5.2 is given without any explanation, then a person can only guess at what the numbers represent.

Horizontal vectors such as equation 5.2 are called *row* vectors. Vectors can also be written vertically, which are called *column* vectors. For example, equation 5.3 has the same entries as equation 5.2, but is written as a column.

$$\mathbf{x} = \begin{pmatrix} 19 \\ 9 \\ 7 \\ 13 \\ 22 \\ 0 \\ 1 \\ 2 \end{pmatrix} \tag{5.3}$$

As far as information content, it does not matter whether a vector is written as a row or a column. But for mathematical manipulations, it does matter. We follow the mathematical convention that a vector denoted just by a letter is a column. However, it is convenient to have an operator that transforms column to row vectors and the reverse. This is denoted with a superscript T, which stands for *transpose*. For example, equation 5.3 can be rewritten as equation 5.4.

$$\mathbf{x}^T = (19, 9, 7, 13, 22, 0, 1, 2) \tag{5.4}$$

If notation were the only contribution of mathematics to vectors, then it is not worth learning since Perl's array notation is both workable and ready for programming. However, mathematics has methods of comparing two vectors, which is useful in text mining. In particular, geometric ideas are applicable.

The next section introduces a key geometric idea, which is the concept of the angle between two vectors. Fortunately, angles are relatively easy to compute, and we discuss how to do this. For a mathematical introduction to the geometry underlying linear algebra, my favorite book is Strang's *Linear Algebra and Its Applications* [113].

5.3.1 Vectors and Angles for Two Poe Stories

For this section, we focus on two Poe stories: "A Predicament" and "The Man of the Crowd." Let the pronoun counts be represented by two vectors given in equation 5.5.

$$\mathbf{x}^T = (19, 9, 7, 13, 22, 0, 1, 2), \quad \mathbf{y}^T = (33, 0, 17, 3, 32, 0, 1, 0) \tag{5.5}$$

These vectors have eight entries (since there are eight pronouns under consideration). The number of entries is called the *dimension* of the vector, so these vectors are eight-dimensional. Finally, remember that these two stories have almost the same number of words, so that the differences in the counts reflect differences in usage.

Comparing two numbers just means determining which is bigger. However, comparing vectors is not as simple. First, let us use the notation in equation 5.6. Note that the indices start with 1, not 0 as done in Perl.

$$\mathbf{x}^T = (x_1, x_2, x_3, x_4, x_5, x_6, x_7, x_8), \quad \mathbf{y}^T = (y_1, y_2, y_3, y_4, y_5, y_6, y_7, y_8) \tag{5.6}$$

Unlike numbers, there are eight entries to compare, and in this case some entries of $\mathbf{x}$ are bigger than the respective entries of $\mathbf{y}$, some are smaller and some are ties. For example, $x_1 < y_1, x_2 > y_2, x_3 < y_3$, and $x_6 = y_6$. So it is not clear how these two vectors compare.

One solution is to compute the angle between the two vectors. The more similar the two vectors are, the closer this angle is to zero. Notice this converts comparing eight entries to the easier task of considering one angle.

To compute angles, it turns out that only one technique is needed, which is called either the *inner product* or the *dot product*. Fortunately, the formula for this operation is simple. For two vectors that have the same number of entries, multiply the first entries of each vector, and add this to the product of the second entries, then add this to the product of the third entries, and repeat this until all the entries are included.

For the two vectors given in equation 5.5, the inner product is shown in equation 5.7. As suggested by the first row, there are two different notations. First, as a row vector adjacent to a column vector, where the row vector **must** go first. Second, with a dot between the two vectors, which is called the dot product.

$$
\begin{aligned}
\mathbf{x} \cdot \mathbf{y} \equiv \mathbf{x}^T \mathbf{y} &= \\
19 * 33 + 9 * 0 + 7 * 17 + 13 * 3 + 22 * 32 + 0 * 0 + 1 * 1 + 2 * 0 &= \\
627 + 0 + 119 + 39 + 704 + 0 + 1 + 0 &= \\
1490 &
\end{aligned}
\tag{5.7}
$$

Since counts are always at least zero, they are *nonnegativeinxxnonnegative*. This implies that the inner product is also nonnegative for these types of vectors. Note that for other applications, negative entries are possible, in which case the inner product can be negative, too.

Before computing angles, we need to compute vector lengths, which is denoted $|\mathbf{x}|$. The square of the length of a vector is its inner product with itself, that is, $|\mathbf{x}|^2 = \mathbf{x}^T \mathbf{x}$. Equation 5.5 gives an example.

$$
\begin{aligned}
\mathbf{x} \cdot \mathbf{x} \equiv \mathbf{x}^{\mathrm{T}}\mathbf{x} &= \\
19*19 + 9*9 + 7*7 + 13*13 + 22*22 + 0*0 + 1*1 + 2*2 &= \\
361 + 81 + 49 + 169 + 484 + 0 + 1 + 4 &= \\
1149 &
\end{aligned}
\tag{5.8}
$$

Since each number in the sum is a square, the result is always at least zero. To get the length of a vector, take the square root as shown in equation 5.9. So the length of $\mathbf{x}$ in equation 5.8 is $\sqrt{1149}$, or about 33.9. Check that the length of $\mathbf{y}$ is $\sqrt{2412}$.

$$
|\mathbf{x}| = \sqrt{\mathbf{x}^{\mathrm{T}}\mathbf{x}}
\tag{5.9}
$$

Although eight-dimensional vectors sound esoteric, it reflects the source of the data: the counts of the eight pronouns *he*, *she*, *him*, and so forth. Even the length computation is based on a simple mathematical idea, which is illustrated with an example. Suppose the length of the two-dimensional vector $(4, 3)$ is desired. This can be interpreted as the hypotenuse of a right triangle by dropping the perpendicular to the x-axis, which is shown in figure 5.1. By the Pythagorean theorem, the square of the hypotenuse equals the sum of the squares of the other two sides, and this triangle has sides of length 4 and 3. Hence $|(4, 3)|^2 = 4^2 + 3^2 = 16 + 9 = 25$, which implies $|(4, 3)| = \sqrt{25} = 5$. But taking the dot product of this vector with itself gives $4*4 + 3*3 = 16 + 9 = 25$. That is, for two dimensions the inner product method is the same as the Pythagorean theorem. For more than two dimensions, inner products are equivalent to applying the Pythagorean theorem multiple times.

Finally, we are in a position to define angles between two vectors (with equal dimensions). Let this angle be denoted θ (the lowercase Greek letter *theta*). Then equation 5.10 gives the formula to compute the cosine of θ.

$$
\cos\theta = \frac{\mathbf{x}^{\mathrm{T}}\mathbf{y}}{|\mathbf{x}||\mathbf{y}|}
\tag{5.10}
$$

To get θ itself, apply the arccos function to this equation. For some insight on why the inner product is related to the $\cos\theta$, see problem 5.3.

Word counts are one source of vectors in text mining, and even a short text can have thousands of them. Hence high-dimensional vectors are common, and computing these by hand is not feasible. One solution is obvious: use Perl. After all, it produced the counts in the first place. The next section shows how to do this.

5.3.2 Computing Angles between Vectors

Perl has many useful functions, but it does not have an inner product or a cosine function for vectors. However, Perl allows the programmer to create new functions by writing *subroutines*. Note that this technique is used for the function sort; for example, see code sample 3.20. So first we discuss writing subroutines and then create one that computes cosines.

5.3.2.1 Subroutines in Perl The function lc changes letters to lowercase. How this is done is usually not of interest to the programmer: what matters is that a certain task is done. If Perl is missing a function, then a programmer can write a subroutine to do it. The payoff is that once written, this can be reused.

Subroutines are created by the sub declaration followed by a block of code contained in curly brackets. As an introductory example, code sample 5.2 has a subroutine called

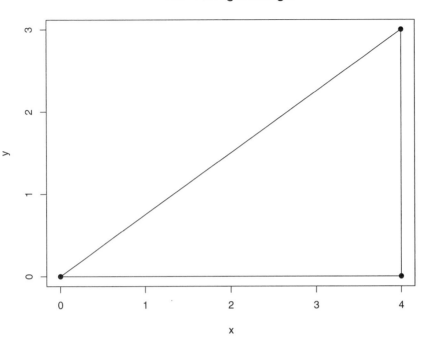

Figure 5.1 The vector (4,3) makes a right triangle if a line segment perpendicular to the *x*-axis is drawn to the *x*-axis.

print_hello that prints "Hello." Since this is in a `for` loop, it is executed 10 times. The code outside the subroutines is called the *main* program. In this case, the subroutine is at the end, but it can be placed anywhere.

Code Sample 5.2 A subroutine that only prints out the string "Hello."

```
for ($i = 0; $i < 10; ++$i) {
   print_hello();
}

sub print_hello {
   print "Hello.\n"
}
```

Note that print_hello() has parentheses, but since it needs no argument, the parentheses contain nothing. There are other ways to write a subroutine, which is discussed in problem 5.4.

Arguments are put inside the parentheses, and these are passed to the subroutine in an array called @_, which is analogous to the array @ARGV that passes values to a program from the command line. Finally, the subroutine can return a value using `return`.

Our first example of a function returns the length of a vector. The last section shows how to do this computation, so creating code sample 5.3 is straightforward.

Code Sample 5.3 A subroutine that returns the length of a vector.

```
@vector = (19, 9, 7, 13, 22, 0, 1, 2);
$length = vector_length(@vector);
print "Length of vector = $length\n";

sub vector_length {
  my $sum = 0;
  for(my $i = 0; $i <= $#_; ++$i) {
    $sum += $_[$i]*$_[$i];
  }
  return(sqrt($sum));
}
```

This program prints out the value 33.9 (when rounded to one decimal place), which equals the value found earlier. Notice that within the subroutine, the array @_ appears in the forms $#_ (the value of the last array index) and $_[]. Finally, $sum keeps a running sum of the squares of the entries of @_, and the square root is taken inside the function `return`.

The first time $sum and $i appear, they are preceded by my. Doing this is optional, but it is good practice. This makes the variables in the subroutine *local*. For example, if $i were used in the subroutine without my, and if it were used in the main program, then both of these variables would refer to the same memory location. This allows interactions that can cause perplexing errors, so it is a good habit to make all variables local in subroutines. See problem 5.5 for an example of not using my.

Based on code sample 5.3, creating a function to compute the inner product of two vectors seems straightforward. However, there is one complication. It is tempting to invoke this function as `inner_product(@vector1, @vector2)`. However, these two vectors are first combined into @_ so the first half consists of @vector1, and the rest consists of @vector2.

The array @_ can be split into two pieces to recover the original array, but this assumes that the two input arrays are equal in length. Although this should be true, it is certainly possible that the lengths are different due to an error, so this should be checked. Hence another approach is needed.

Since Perl passes all arguments to the array @_, it seems that we are stuck. But there is a solution: instead of using arrays, references to them can be used instead. Then @_ has two values, both of which point to an array, so after dereferencing with the @{} operator, these are now available to the subroutine. To review references, see section 3.8.1.

Using references, code sample 5.4 shows the function `dot`, which computes the dot product of two vectors. Notice the two dereferences just before the `if` statement. The result is 1490, confirming the calculations made above.

With the idea of passing references to the subroutine, along with a subroutine to compute the dot product, we are ready to convert equation 5.10 into Perl code, which is done in the next section.

Code Sample 5.4 A subroutine that returns the dot product of two vectors.

```
@x = (19, 9, 7, 13, 22, 0, 1, 2);
@y = (33, 0, 17, 3, 32, 0, 1, 0);
$answer = dot(\@x, \@y);
print "Dot product = $answer\n";

sub dot {
  my ($vector_ref1, $vector_ref2) = @_;
  my $sum_cross = 0;
  my @vector1 = @{$vector_ref1}; # Dereference pointer
  my @vector2 = @{$vector_ref2}; # Dereference pointer

  if ($#vector1 == $#vector2) { # Ensure vectors have same length
    for (my $i=0; $i <= $#vector1; ++$i) {
      $sum_cross += $vector1[$i]*$vector2[$i];
    }
    return($sum_cross);
  }
}
```

5.3.2.2 *Computing the Angle between Vectors*   Using subroutine dot from code sample 5.4, we write another one to compute the cosine of the angle between two vectors using equation 5.10. In general, breaking a complicated programming task down into smaller pieces makes it easier to do, which is done in program 5.3.

Note that the if statement checks to see if the vectors have the same length. If they are not, then the string Error is returned to the main program. Running this produces 0.89503 for the cosine. This corresponds to an angle of 0.46230 radians, which is about 26.5°.

We know that the closer this angle is to zero, the higher the similarity between the two vectors. However, this heuristic does not indicate how close 26.5° is to zero. In general, it is not enough to quantify a measurement, a researcher also needs to calibrate it.

We do not have any calibration for 26.5°, which requires either (1) a model of the variability of angles or (2) an empirical analysis of a group of texts. In the next section we do the latter for four Poe stories and then compare the six resulting angles. This analysis also introduces the term-document matrix, an important tool in IR and text mining.

5.4   THE TERM-DOCUMENT MATRIX APPLIED TO POE

Program 5.2 and code sample 5.1 compute the counts of eight pronouns for all 4 Poe stories mentioned at the start of section 5.2. Our goal is to compare each pair of stories by computing the angle between each pair of pronoun count vectors.

Table 5.2 gives the counts for each pronoun and each story. These counts clearly show a bias toward the masculine pronouns, with "The Facts in the Case of M. Valdemar" as the most lop-sided with no feminine pronouns at all.

It is easy to convert this table into a term-document matrix because it only requires putting the numbers between large parentheses and dropping the pronouns on the left and

```
$answer = cosine(\@x, \@y);
print "Cosine = $answer\n";

sub cosine {
  # This uses the subroutine dot
  my ($vector_ref1, $vector_ref2) = @_;
  my @vector1 = @{$vector_ref1};
  my @vector2 = @{$vector_ref2};

  if ($#vector1 == $#vector2) { # Do vectors have the same length?
    my $length1 = sqrt(dot(\@vector1, \@vector1));
    my $length2 = sqrt(dot(\@vector2, \@vector2));
    my $answer = dot(\@vector1, \@vector2)/($length1*$length2);
    return($answer);
  } else {
    return('Error');
  }
}
```

Program 5.3 A subroutine that returns the cosine of the angle between the two vectors in equation 5.5. This uses subroutine dot from code sample 5.4.

Table 5.2 Pronoun counts from program 5.2 and code sample 5.1 for 4 Poe stories.

	Predicament	Hop-Frog	Valdemar	Crowd
he	19	27	24	33
she	9	5	0	0
him	7	10	28	17
her	13	11	0	3
his	22	55	35	32
hers	0	0	0	0
himself	1	4	3	1
herself	2	0	0	0

the story titles on the top, which is done in equation 5.11. The relationship of this matrix to the table is obvious.

$$
\begin{pmatrix}
19 & 27 & 24 & 33 \\
9 & 5 & 0 & 0 \\
7 & 10 & 28 & 17 \\
13 & 11 & 0 & 3 \\
22 & 55 & 35 & 32 \\
0 & 0 & 0 & 0 \\
1 & 4 & 3 & 1 \\
2 & 0 & 0 & 0
\end{pmatrix}
\tag{5.11}
$$

In equation 5.11, each row stands for a pronoun, and each column stands for a document. The size of a matrix is called its dimensions, which are just the number of rows and columns. For example, this is an 8 by 4 matrix.

In this book, a term-document matrix typically has rows representing words and columns representing documents, so the dimensions are the number of words by the number of documents. However, some authors reverse the role of the rows and columns, so pay attention to how such a matrix is defined when reading an article. Although the example given in equation 5.11 is small, these matrices can be enormous. For example, if there are rows for each word in a document, then tens of thousands of rows are possible.

There are two ways to consider a term-document matrix such as equation 5.11. First, each column is a vector of pronoun counts occurring in a particular story. For example, the first column is the same vector given in equation 5.3. Second, each row represents counts for a particular pronoun. For example, the first row represents *he*. Both of these points of view can be useful in analyzing a collection of texts.

To finish this section, we compute the angles between each pair of columns in equation 5.11 by using program 5.2 to count all the types and saving these in the hash of hashes %freq. Then code sample 5.5 computes the angles (in degrees) for all pairs of stories by using program 5.3 (which itself uses code sample 5.4).

Code Sample 5.5 The computation of cosines assuming that the hash of hashes %freq has already been computed by program 5.2. This requires program 5.3, which uses code sample 5.4.

```
# Angles are in degrees
# Requires subroutines cosine() and dot()
# Requires the existence of the hash %freq

use Math::Trig;  # Load all trig functions and pi

@pronouns = qw(he she him her his hers himself herself);

foreach $story (keys %freq) { # Print out the story names
  print "$story\n";
}

print "\nCOSINE ANGLES\n\n";
foreach $story1 (keys %freq) {
  foreach $story2 (keys %freq) {
    %hash1 = %{$freq{$story1}};
    %hash2 = %{$freq{$story2}};
    @vector1 = @hash1{@pronouns};
    @vector2 = @hash2{@pronouns};
    $angle = acos(cosine(\@vector1, \@vector2))/pi*180;
    printf " %.1f", $angle;
  }
  print "\n";
}
```

Notice that code sample 5.5 has three new features. First, it uses printf, which is a formatted print statement, similar to the one in the programming language C. The %.1f means that only one decimal place is printed out, which makes the output more readable.

Second, the trigonometric function `acos` is not part of Perl's core functions. However, when downloading Perl, a number of additional packages (called *modules*) are provided, and these are loaded by using the command `use`. The syntax is as follows.

```
use PackageName;
```

Many packages have a two-part name (but one or three is not uncommon), with each part separated by double colons. In particular, there are many packages that go under the name `Math`, and `Math::Trig` is the one that supplies all the usual trigonometric functions. Moreover, `use` can define constants as well as other items. For this code sample, `pi` is the famous value from geometry and is used by the program to convert radians to degrees. For more examples of Perl modules and how to use them, see section 9.2.

Third, remember that `%freq` has word counts for all the words that appear among the four stories, but we are interested only in the eight pronouns. These can be obtained all at once by the following trick. First, `%hash1` stores the part of `%freq` corresponding to one of the four stories (the current one selected by the `foreach` loop). Note that the following Perl statement writes the hash with an `@` symbol, but still uses curly brackets.

```
@vector1 = @hash1{@pronouns};
```

The result is that `@vector1` stores the values corresponding to the keys in `@pronouns` from `%hash1`. This is a useful trick.

Output 5.2 shows the results of code sample 5.5. The story names are printed out to show the order of the stories in the hash `%freq`. Remember that this order need not be the original order in the text file. The *main* diagonal goes from the upper left to the lower right of the matrix. All these entries have $0°$ since this is the angle between a story and itself.

The rest of the entries come in pairs. For example, the value in the second row and fourth column is the same as the one in the fourth row and second column. This makes the matrix symmetric about the main diagonal.

Output 5.2 Output of code sample 5.5.

```
THE FACTS IN THE CASE OF M. VALDEMAR
THE MAN OF THE CROWD
HOP-FROG
A PREDICAMENT

0.0 17.1 27.4 34.4
17.1 0.0 23.3 26.5
27.4 23.3 0.0 22.5
34.4 26.5 22.5 0.0
```

This symmetry leaves six distinct angles, one for each pair of stories. For example, the angle between "The Man of the Crowd" and "A Predicament" is $26.5°$. These are the two stories represented in equation 5.5, and this angle agrees with the value computed in section 5.3.2.2.

Putting these six angles into order produces: $17.1°$, $22.5°$, $23.3°$, $26.5°$, $27.4°$, $34.4°$. Although this is a small sample, we do get some sense of the size of $26.5°$, namely, it is close to the median angle, so it is not unusually small or large. However, "The Man of the Crowd," which is narrated by a man who decides to follow another man, and "A Predicament," which is narrated by a woman about her misadventure with a male servant and her female dog, have dissimilar literary plots. This suggests an angle larger than average, yet this is not true of $26.5°$. However, looking at only four of the 68 short stories is a small sample, so it is rash to read too much into this result. See section 7.4.3 for a pronoun analysis of all his stories.

The examples above show that vectors and matrices are numbers displayed in a rectangular layout. However, their power comes from geometric ideas. Although the mathematics of these objects has been extensively analyzed in linear algebra, we require only a few basic tools to analyze text. The most important of these is matrix multiplication, which is based on the inner (or dot) product and is the topic of the next section.

5.5   MATRIX MULTIPLICATION

Vectors are a special type of matrix. For example, equation 5.12 has a row and a column vector. The first is also a 1 by 8 matrix, the second is 8 by 1. Since these have the same number of entries, the inner product is possible. The result is $1 * 19 + 1 * 9 + ... + 1 * 2 = 73$. Now viewing these two vectors as matrices, the matrix product is the same as the inner product for this special case. Finally, note that since the row vector has all 1's, this result is the sum of the entries of the column vector, which is the total number of these pronouns in "A Predicament." This is the first example of how matrix multiplication can perform useful tasks in text analysis.

$$(\ 1 \ 1 \ 1 \ 1 \ 1 \ 1 \ 1 \ 1 \ ) \begin{pmatrix} 19 \\ 9 \\ 7 \\ 13 \\ 22 \\ 0 \\ 1 \\ 2 \end{pmatrix} \tag{5.12}$$

For an inner product to exist, the number of entries of both vectors must be the same. Likewise, for the matrix product to exist, there are constraints on the dimensions. To multiply the matrices M_1 and M_2, the number of columns of M_1 must be the same as the number of rows of M_2, and no other restrictions are required.

When matrix multiplication is permitted, the product of two matrices is a matrix. Even in equation 5.12, although the final result is a number, it is also a 1 by 1 matrix (containing the value 73). Suppose that the product of M_1 and M_2 is the matrix P. The value of the entry in the ith row and jth column of P equals the inner product of row i of M_1 and column j of M_2, which requires this row and column have the same number of entries. However, the length of the rows of M_1 is its number of columns, and the length of the columns of M_2 is its number of rows, and the preceding paragraph requires that these are the same.

$$\begin{pmatrix} 1 & 2 & 3 \\ 4 & 5 & 6 \end{pmatrix} \begin{pmatrix} 60 & 50 \\ 40 & 30 \\ 20 & 10 \end{pmatrix} = \begin{pmatrix} 200 & 140 \\ 560 & 410 \end{pmatrix} \tag{5.13}$$

Let us do a small, concrete example to see how this works. Equation 5.13 shows a 2 by 3 matrix and a 3 by 2 matrix. Since the number of columns of the first matrix equals the number of rows of the second matrix, these can be multiplied. A common notation is to represent the ith row and jth column of matrix P by P_{ij}. Hence P_{11} is the inner product of $(1, 2, 3)$ and $(60, 40, 20)^{\mathrm{T}}$, which equals $1 * 60 + 2 * 40 + 3 * 20 = 200$. Continuing, $P_{12} = 1 * 50 + 2 * 30 + 3 * 10 = 140$, $P_{21} = 4 * 60 + 5 * 40 + 6 * 20 = 560$ and $P_{22} = 4 * 50 + 5 * 30 + 6 * 10 = 410$.

Note that a 2 by 3 times a 3 by 2 matrix results in a 2 by 2 matrix. In general, an m by n matrix times an n by p matrix produces an m by p matrix, so the two n's "cancel." In addition, the order of the two matrices count. For example, an n by p matrix cannot be multiplied by an m by n matrix unless $p = m$. For another example, see problem 5.6. For an example of applying matrix multiplication to texts, see the next section.

5.5.1 Matrix Multiplication Applied to Poe

In this section we find the angles between pairs of stories by using matrix multiplication. Doing this by hand is tedious, so we use the statistical package R. Like Perl, it is freely available on the Web, so you can download it right now and try the computations yourself. The commands and output given below is discussed briefly, and it is used again in the last three chapters, but this book does not teach R beyond a few specific applications. Hopefully these examples show that R is both powerful and relatively easy to use.

To compute angles from a term-document matrix, first *normalize* each column; that is, each entry is divided by the length of its column. This changes its length to 1, which makes it a *unit vector*. Call this new matrix N (for *Normalized*). Second, by problem 5.3, the cosine of the angle between unit vectors is their inner product. Computing $N^{\mathrm{T}}N$ obtains all of these at the same time. Doing these two steps shows how to work with matrices in R, but note that there are faster ways to get the final results. For example, the function `scale()` is useful: see problem 5.9. Moreover, chapter 7 shows a connection between angles and correlations, and the latter are easy to compute in R.

Output 5.3 Output from the statistical package R. M is the term-document matrix for the eight pronouns analyzed in the text.

```
> M = matrix(c(19,9,7,13,22,0,1,2,27,5,10,11,55,0,4,0,24,0,28,0,
                35,0,3,0,33,0,17,3,32,0,1,0),nrow=8,ncol=4)
> M
      [,1] [,2] [,3] [,4]
[1,]   19   27   24   33
[2,]    9    5    0    0
[3,]    7   10   28   17
[4,]   13   11    0    3
[5,]   22   55   35   32
[6,]    0    0    0    0
[7,]    1    4    3    1
[8,]    2    0    0    0
```

Note that R is interactive, and the $>$ shows where to type in each line of code, which is run after the enter key is pressed. Output 5.3 defines the term-document matrix M, which is constructed by `matrix()` from a vector that is defined by listing its entries within `c()`. Note that the default in R is to construct a matrix using columns, not rows. However, the latter can be done by using `byrow=T` as shown in problem 5.8.

Also note that the following convention for R is used throughout this book. Since Perl does not require parentheses for its functions, when these are named in the text, they are not used, for example, `keys`. However, R does require them, so they are written with parentheses, for example, `matrix()`. This distinguishes functions between these two computer languages.

Output 5.4 Computing the matrix product $M^T M$.

```
> product = t(M) %*% M
> product
      [,1] [,2] [,3] [,4]
[1,] 1149 1985 1425 1490
[2,] 1985 4016 2865 2858
[3,] 1425 2865 2594 2391
[4,] 1490 2858 2391 2412
```

The matrix product $M^T M$ is shown in output 5.4. Note the diagonal entries are the squared length of each column (do you recognize the [1,1] and [4,4] entries?). Because we want to multiply each column of M by the reciprocal of its length, these diagonal entries are used below. Finally, `%*%` is the matrix multiplication operator in R.

Output 5.5 Each diagonal entry is the reciprocal of the respective column length of M.

```
> solve(diag(sqrt(diag(product))))
            [,1]       [,2]       [,3]       [,4]
[1,] 0.02950122 0.00000000 0.00000000 0.00000000
[2,] 0.00000000 0.01577986 0.00000000 0.00000000
[3,] 0.00000000 0.00000000 0.01963428 0.00000000
[4,] 0.00000000 0.00000000 0.00000000 0.02036157
```

Output 5.5 shows a matrix with only diagonal entries, which is called a *diagonal matrix*. Each nonzero entry is the reciprocal of the corresponding column length. For example, the first entry is $0.02950122 = 1/\sqrt{1149}$. The R function `diag()` has two uses. First, it extracts the diagonal elements from a matrix to form a vector. Second, it takes a vector and makes a diagonal matrix out of it (that is, the vector becomes the main diagonal, and the other entries are all zeros). In addition, `solve()` computes the inverse of a matrix. When this is diagonal, it is equivalent to taking the reciprocal of the nonzero entries.

The column-normalized version of M, denoted by N, is computed in output 5.6. Now each column has length 1, which means the sum of the squares of the column entries must be 1. For example, the first column satisfies $0.56052319^2 + 0.26551099^2 + \cdots + 0.05900244^2 = 1$ (up to round-off error).

Output 5.7 computes the cosines of the angles. Finally, the R function `t()` returns the transpose of a matrix, which is obtained by interchanging the rows and the columns of a matrix. A special case of this is the transpose of a vector, which is done in equations 5.3 and 5.4.

The conversion from cosines to angles is done in output 5.8. Most of the functions are used to print the results with one decimal place. Comparing this to output 5.2, we see that all the values are the same, but the order is different. This happens because the Perl hash changed the order of the stories.

Output 5.6 Matrix N equals M with its columns normalized to have length 1.

```
> N = M %*% solve(diag(sqrt(diag(product))))
> N
          [,1]       [,2]       [,3]       [,4]
[1,]  0.56052319 0.42605622 0.47122276 0.67193194
[2,]  0.26551099 0.07889930 0.00000000 0.00000000
[3,]  0.20650854 0.15779860 0.54975988 0.34614676
[4,]  0.38351587 0.17357846 0.00000000 0.06108472
[5,]  0.64902685 0.86789230 0.68719985 0.65157037
[6,]  0.00000000 0.00000000 0.00000000 0.00000000
[7,]  0.02950122 0.06311944 0.05890284 0.02036157
[8,]  0.05900244 0.00000000 0.00000000 0.00000000
```

Output 5.7 $N^{\mathrm{T}}N$ is the matrix of cosines of the columns of M.

```
> cos_matrix = t(N) %*% N
          [,1]      [,2]      [,3]      [,4]
[1,]  1.0000000 0.9240674 0.8254103 0.8950300
[2,]  0.9240674 1.0000000 0.8876521 0.9182834
[3,]  0.8254103 0.8876521 1.0000000 0.9558856
[4,]  0.8950300 0.9182834 0.9558856 1.0000000
```

Output 5.8 The cosines of output 5.7 are converted to degrees.

```
> matrix(as.numeric(sprintf("%.1f",acos(cos_matrix)/pi*180)),4,4)
       [,1] [,2] [,3] [,4]
[1,]    0.0 22.5 34.4 26.5
[2,]   22.5  0.0 27.4 23.3
[3,]   34.4 27.4  0.0 17.1
[4,]   26.5 23.3 17.1  0.0
```

With these ideas, the next section discusses two tasks. First, how two entire texts are compared. The examples up to this point use only a few words at a time. Second, the examples so far use counts. However, this can cause problems, and one solution is discussed.

5.6 FUNCTIONS OF COUNTS

So far in this chapter, unmodified word counts are used (called *raw counts*). However, there is a downside to this, which is shown by a simple example. Suppose we analyze the four Poe stories with respect to the two words *the* and *city*. This is easily done by reusing code sample 5.5, replacing @pronouns by an array containing just these two words.

Once this modification is made, then the `foreach` prints out the counts for the four stories. The results are given in output 5.9. Since there are only two words, these can be plotted to visually compare the four vectors, which is done in figure 5.2.

Output 5.9 Counts of the words *the* and *city*, respectively.

```
THE FACTS IN THE CASE OF M. VALDEMAR
231,0
THE MAN OF THE CROWD
236,4
HOP-FROG
302,0
A PREDICAMENT
242,7
```

The two axes of the plot in figure 5.2 are **not** drawn on the same scale: the *y*-axis should be about three times more compressed, but this makes the plot too thin to read. Hence the angles shown are about three times too big. In fact, the largest is only 1.66°. These vectors are so close to the *x*-axis because *the* has high counts (it is the most common word in English), and *city* only appears 7 times at most. Hence, all the vectors are nearly horizontal.

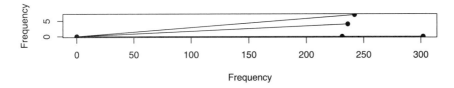

Figure 5.2   Comparing the frequencies of the word *the* (on the *x*-axis) against *city* (on the *y*-axis). Note that the *y*-axis is not to scale: it should be more compressed.

However, *city* is a useful word for distinguishing these stories. Both "The Man of the Crowd" and "A Predicament" take place in an urban environment as the narrator walks around. In the other two stories, all the action takes place inside. The fact that *city* splits these stories into two groups is disguised by the large counts of *the*.

High-frequency words are often used for grammatical purposes. For example, *the* is used with nouns to emphasize a particular instance of that noun, as in *the picture*. So words like *that*, *this*, *is*, and so forth, are common, but add little to the imaginative, creative part of a text. These are called *function* words.

There are two common solutions to the problem of high-frequency function words. First, these can be ignored. All such words are called a *stoplist* (see section 9.2.2 for further discussion). For the above analysis, instead of using *the* and *city*, the former can be replaced with a more interesting word.

Second, using functions of the counts is common. For example, if f is a term frequency, then this can be replaced by $\log(f + 1)$. This compresses the values together. Now *the* goes from 0 to 6, and *city* from 0 to 2, so these scales are more comparable. In addition, the largest angle in figure 5.3 is now 20.7°, compared to 1.60° before. The four stories are now clearly split into two groups, so applying $\log(f + 1)$ is helpful in this case.

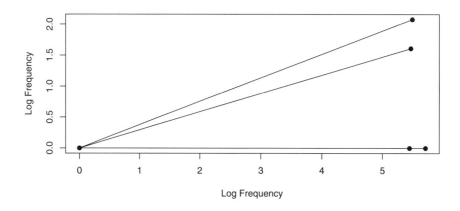

Figure 5.3   Comparing the logarithms of the frequencies for the words *the* (on the *x*-axis) and *city* (on the *y*-axis).

In the next section, we consider a popular similarity function from IR that penalizes common words. This is applied to the four Poe stories in their entirety, not just a small subset of words such as pronouns.

5.7 DOCUMENT SIMILARITY

The core application in information retrieval is returning the documents most similar to a query. For example, a person goes to a search engine and enters "text mining." The results are Web pages that are listed in order from most to least similar based on a numerical score.

In the case of search engines, this score is a combination of similarity and a Web link analysis. The latter assumes that the importance of a Web page is a function of both the number and the importance of the other pages that link to this page. The importance of these other in-linking pages is determined by the same idea, so the importance of all Web pages must be computed simultaneously. Because the number of pages on the Web is quite large, this makes for a massive computation, but one that is doable using linear algebra and many computers. For the details of link analysis, see Langville and Meyer's *Google's PageRank and Beyond* [68].

However, for this book, documents do not have any linkages. The preceding section shows how to compute the cosine of the angle between two vectors, and there are no constraints on how many entries these vectors can have. Hence angles between two long texts are computable using the same idea. First, find all the words that appear in both texts. Second, create vectors where each entry is the frequency of a word. Third, use the technique given in the last section to compute the angle between these two vectors.

To make this idea clear, here is a simple example of the angle between sentence 5.14 and sentence 5.15.

$$\text{The gray cat is called Misty.} \tag{5.14}$$

$$\text{Ashford is the gray and white cat.} \tag{5.15}$$

The set of words (in alphabetical order) that appear in at least one sentence is: *and, Ashford, called, cat, gray, is, Misty, the,* and *white*. A frequency vector for sentence 5.14 is given by equation 5.16. Equation 5.17 is the vector for the other sentence. Each number is the count with respect to the order of the words just given.

$$(0, 0, 1, 1, 1, 1, 1, 1, 0) \tag{5.16}$$

$$(1, 1, 0, 1, 1, 1, 0, 1, 1) \tag{5.17}$$

Remember that these vectors do not record the order of the words in the original sentences. For example, equation 5.16 is also the vector for sentence 5.18 as well as any other permutation of these words.

$$\text{The cat called Misty is gray.} \tag{5.18}$$

Finally, the cosine of the angle between these two vectors is $4/(\sqrt{6}\sqrt{7})$, which is about 0.617. This is an angle of $51.9°$.

In this example, raw frequencies are used. In the last section, the function $\log(f + 1)$ is applied to the entries of the vectors, but in this case, this transformation does not change the angle. See problem 5.10 for why this is so. In general, $\log(f + 1)$ is useful when the counts vary a lot, and by Zipf's law (see section 3.7.1) this is typical, for example, a few words like *the* are extremely common, but the most common situation is that words only appear once.

So far, the only modification of counts attempted is $\log(f + 1)$, but this is only one function among many. The next section discusses another, the inverse document frequency.

5.7.1 Inverse Document Frequency

This section introduces the *inverse document frequency* (IDF), which provides information about how a term is distributed among a collection of texts. It is another technique to modify counts.

The less a term appears in a collection of documents, the higher its value of IDF. Specifically, let N be the total number of documents in the collection, and let N_t be the total number of documents containing the term t. Then the IDF of t is given in equation 5.19.

$$\text{IDF}_t = \log \frac{N}{N_t} \tag{5.19}$$

As N_t gets larger, the IDF of a term gets smaller. In fact, if $N_t = N$, then $\text{IDF}_t = 0$, so words like *the* are given no weight whatsoever. This effectively puts these words on a stoplist.

For an example, we compute the IDFs for the words in sentences 5.14 and 5.15 of the last section, treating each one as a text. Hence, $N = 2$ and N_t is either 1 or 2 for any word that appears. Finally, when $N_t = 1$, $IDF_t = \log(2)$, and when $N_t = 2$, $IDF_t = \log(1) = 0$. Note that the base of the logarithm is not critical since changing it only multiplies the result by a constant, which is removed by making the columns have unit length.

In practice, the term weight (or a function of it) is multiplied by the IDF to produce the term frequency-inverse document frequency or TF–IDF. The resulting weights are commonly normalized because unit vectors make computing angles easier. However, there are numerous ways proposed in the research literature on how to combine term frequencies and IDFs. For additional weightings and combinations, see section 15.2 of Manning and Schütze's *Foundations of Statistical Natural Language Processing* [75], and for an overview, see section 3.2 of Berry and Browne's *Understanding Search Engines* [10].

5.7.2   Poe Story Angles Revisited

This section recalculates the angles between pairs of Poe's stories using TF-IDF. This is done in Perl using the following steps. First, all the words are counted, which produces the term frequencies. Second, the number of stories in which each word appears is counted, which are the document frequencies. Third, the TF-IDF values are computed. Fourth, the document vectors are normalized; and, fifth, the cosines are computed by taking the inner products. These five steps are done in programs 5.4 and 5.5, which must be run together. They are split into two pieces so that each fits on one page.

In program 5.2, the word frequencies are stored in a hash of hashes, where the title of each story is used as the key. However, hashes typically change the order of the index strings as they are constructed, so in this case, the order of the four stories in the file `Poe_4_stories.txt` is probably not the order used in the hash of hashes `%freq`. This reordering can be prevented by using an array of hashes, although which number corresponds to which story must be remembered. Hence the word counts (term frequencies) are stored in `$tf[$nstory]{$word}`.

In step 1, the term frequencies for each story are stored in the array of hashes, `@tf`, while the hash `%granddict` stores the frequencies for all the stories combined. Step 2 computes and stores the document frequencies in `%df`.

In step 3, the array of hashes `@weight` stores the TF-IDFs. The first `foreach` loop in step 4 computes the square of the length of the hash `@weight[$i]`, and the second divides each `@weight[$i]` by this length, so that the result, when viewed as a vector, has unit length. Then step 5 takes the dot product of these normalized vectors, which equals the cosine of the angle between each story.

Finally, running programs 5.4 and 5.5 together produces the list of story names in the order they appear in the file `Poe_4_Stories.txt`, which is also the order they appear in the array of hashes, `@tf`. Output 5.10 produces a four by four array of cosines, where each row and each column represents a story. Besides the zeros on the diagonal, there are six cosines: 0.0277, 0.0214, 0.0323, 0.0270 ,0.0442, 0.0224. These represent angles from $87.5°$ to $88.8°$. Comparing these with output 5.2, there are differences in how pairs of stories are ranked. For example, the smallest angle in output 5.2 ($17.1°$) is between "The Facts in the Case of M. Valdemar" and "The Man of the Crowd." In output 5.10 the largest cosine is 0.0442 (corresponding to the smallest angle $87.5°$), and this is between "A Predicament" and "The Man of the Crowd." Hence the IDF part of TF-IDF does make a difference in rankings. It clearly enlarges the angles, too: all the stories are now nearly orthogonal.

```
open(IN, "Poe_4_Stories.txt") or die;
$nstory = -1;

# Step 1: Compute the term frequencies
while (<IN>) {
  chomp;
  if ( /<TITLE>(.*)<\/TITLE>/ ) {
    $title = $1;
    ++$nstory;
    print "Title of story $nstory = $title\n";
  } else {
    if ($title eq '') { print "NULL TITLE\n"; }
    $_ = lc;   # Change letters to lowercase
    s/--/ /g;  # Remove dashes
    s/ - / /g; # Remove dashes
    s/[,.";!()?:_\[\]]//g; # Remove non-apostrophes
    s/\s+/ /g; # Replace multiple spaces with one space
    s/^\s+//g; # Remove spaces at the start of a line
    @words = split(/ /);

    foreach $word (@words) {
      if ($word =~ /^'?(.*?)'?$/) { # Must be non-greedy
        $word = $1; # Remove initial and final apostrophes
        ++$tf[$nstory]{$word};
        ++$granddict{$word};
      }
    }
  }
}

# Step 2: Compute the document frequencies
foreach $word ( sort keys %granddict ) {
  $sum = 0;
  for $i ( 0 .. $#tf ) {
    if ( $tf[$i]{$word} > 0 ) {
      ++$sum;
    }
    $df{$word} = $sum;
  }
}
```

Program 5.4 Part 1 of computing the cosine similarities between Poe stories.

```
# Step 3: Compute the tf-idf weights
$n = $#tf + 1; # number of stories
foreach $word ( sort keys %granddict ) {
  for $i ( 0 .. $#tf ) {
    $weight[$i]{$word} = $tf[$i]{$word}*log($n/$df{$word})/log(2);
  }
}

# Step 4: Normalize the columns of weights
for $i ( 0 .. $#tf ) {
  $len2 = 0;
  foreach $word ( sort keys %granddict ) {
    $len2 += $weight[$i]{$word}**2;
  }
  $len = sqrt($len2);
  foreach $word ( sort keys %granddict ) {
    $unit[$i]{$word} = $weight[$i]{$word}/$len;
  }
}

# Step 5: Compute cosine similarities between each pair of stories
for $i ( 0 .. $#tf ) {
  for $j (0 .. $#tf) {
    $sum = 0;
    foreach $word ( sort keys %granddict ) {
      $sum += $unit[$i]{$word} * $unit[$j]{$word};
    }
    $cosine[$i][$j] = $sum;
  }
}

# Print out the cosine similarities
print "\n";
for $i ( 0 .. $#tf ) {
  for $j ( 0 .. $#tf ) {
    printf "%.4f ", $cosine[$i][$j];
  }
  print "\n";
}
```

Program 5.5 Part 2 of computing the cosine similarities between Poe stories.

Output 5.10 Output of programs 5.4 and 5.5. Values are cosines of angles between pairs of stories.

```
Title of story 0 = THE FACTS IN THE CASE OF M. VALDEMAR
Title of story 1 = A PREDICAMENT
Title of story 2 = HOP-FROG
Title of story 3 = THE MAN OF THE CROWD


1.0000 0.0277 0.0214 0.0323
0.0277 1.0000 0.0270 0.0442
0.0214 0.0270 1.0000 0.0224
0.0323 0.0442 0.0224 1.0000
```

To understand these six values better, using more Poe stories for more comparisons is needed. In addition, using these similarities for input to other statistical techniques is often profitable. For instance, this can be done with clustering algorithms, which are discussed in chapter 8.

5.8 REFERENCES

This chapter focuses on one small part of IR. The three main ideas discussed are (1) the term-document matrix, a natural way to analyze the words in a collection of texts; (2) the idea of representing texts by vectors, and then applying geometric concepts; and (3) the TF-IDF for computing similarities between texts.

Of course, IR has many other ideas and techniques beyond the vector space model. For further information on IR, here are three introductory books. First, Michael Berry and Murray Browne's *Understanding Search Engines* [10] has an excellent introduction to the vector space model. Second, David Grossman and Ophir Frieder's *Information Retrieval* [48] has a good overview of the many approaches of IR. Third, Dominic Widdows's *Geometry and Meaning* [126] is a fascinating book that considers how to use geometry to analyze language, and his level of mathematics is similar to this book. Finally, for more information on linear algebra itself, my favorite book is Gilbert Strang's *Linear Algebra and Its Applications* [113].

In the next chapter, we turn to corpus linguistics, which studies language through the computer analysis of *corpora* (plural of *corpus*). These are collections of texts representative of an aspect of language.

PROBLEMS

5.1 In table 5.1, the most common letters in the four Poe stories are almost ETAOIN SHRDLU. This sequence of letters is relatively famous, and originally arose in Linotype keyboards because printers believed this was the true frequency order of letters. Also compare this order to the results in output 4.2. How well does it fit?

ETAOIN SHRDLU has taken a life of its own. Try searching the Web for this term. Here are two examples of this phrase in the literature. First, read the dialog called *SHRDLU, Toy of Man's Designing* in Douglas Hofstadter's excellent book *Gödel, Escher, Bach: An Eternal Golden Braid* [55]. This dialog includes the characters Eta Oin and SHRDLU. Second, read problem 112, called *ETAOIN SHRDLU*, of Dmitri Borgmann's *Beyond Language:*

Adventures in Word and Thought [18]. Its answer section gives some background on this phrase.

5.2   In program 5.2, the following line appears.

```
if ($word =~ /^'?(.*?)'?$/) { # Must be non-greedy
```

Why must this be nongreedy? One way to understand this is to change .*? to .* and see what happens. Or try to figure it out from first principles, keeping in mind the following two points. First, .* is greedy, so it matches as much as possible including apostrophes. Second, '? is greedy and means zero or one apostrophe. How do these two greedy operators act when put together?

5.3   [Mathematical] Why is there a connection between the inner product and the cosine of the angle between two vectors? The first time a person sees equation 5.10, it is often unclear why this formula works. Using linear algebra, this problem offers some geometric insight.

First, when a vector is divided by its length, the result is a unit vector. Because equation 5.10 is rewritable as equation 5.20, it is sufficient to consider just unit vectors.

$$\cos \theta = \frac{\mathbf{x}^T \mathbf{y}}{|\mathbf{x}||\mathbf{y}|} = \left(\frac{\mathbf{x}}{|\mathbf{x}|} \right)^T \frac{\mathbf{y}}{|\mathbf{y}|} \tag{5.20}$$

Second, suppose the unit vectors are two-dimensional, and suppose these are $(1, 0)$ and (x_1, x_2). Remember that $\cos \theta$ for a right triangle equals the length of the adjacent side over the length of the hypotenuse. For example, in figure 5.1, the cosine of the angle at the origin = 4/5. So for these two vectors, the cosine equals $x_1/1 = x_1$. But the dot product also equals x_1, so we have confirmed the result for this special case.

Third, consider two unit vectors of arbitrary dimension. These still lie in a two-dimensional plane, so by a (high-dimensional) rotation, these two vectors can be brought to the (x, y)-plane so that one of the vectors is $(1, 0, 0, ..., 0)$ and the other is arbitrary, say $(x_1, x_2, 0, 0, ..., 0)$. By the reasoning in the previous paragraph, $\cos \theta = x_1$, but this is again the inner product.

Finally, as long as both vectors are rotated in the same way, the angle between them is not affected. So the inner product of the original two vectors is the same as the inner product of the rotated vectors, which, by the previous paragraph, equals $\cos \theta$.

If the above is not clear to you, find a text on linear algebra. My favorite is Gilbert Strang's *Linear Algebra and Its Applications* [113] because it is well-written and emphasizes the underlying geometry. See chapter 3 for an explanation of the above ideas.

5.4   Like scalars, arrays, and hashes, there is an initial symbol to denote a subroutine, which is the ampersand. In addition, parentheses can be used or left out. This makes four possibilities, which are shown in code sample 5.6.

Run this code to see what happens. Which form of the subroutine call must come before its use in the main program? Why is this true?

5.5   Run code sample 5.7. Then remove the my statement in interference to see how it modifies the variable $i in the main code. How does this effect the for loop?

5.6   Reversing the two matrices in equation 5.13 gives us a 3 by 2 times a 2 by 3 matrix multiplication and now the result is a 3 by 3 matrix, not a 2 by 2 matrix as before. Carry out the multiplication of equation 5.21 to find the entries of this 3 by 3 matrix.

Hint: $P_{11} = 60 * 1 + 50 * 4 = 260$.

Code Sample 5.6 For problem 5.4.

```
$x1 = yes;
$x2 = yes();
$x3 = &yes;
$x4 = &yes();
print "$x1, $x2, $x3, $x4\n";

sub yes { return "jawohl"; }

$x1 = yes;
$x2 = yes();
$x3 = &yes;
$x4 = &yes();
print "$x1, $x2, $x3, $x4\n";
```

Code Sample 5.7 For problem 5.5.

```
for ($i = 0; $i < 10; ++$i) {
  print "$i\n";
  interference();
}

sub interference {
  my $i;
  if (rand() > 0.5) {
    ++$i;
  } else {
    --$i;
  }
}
```

$$
\begin{pmatrix} 60\ 50 \\ 40\ 30 \\ 20\ 10 \end{pmatrix} \begin{pmatrix} 1\ 2\ 3 \\ 4\ 5\ 6 \end{pmatrix} \tag{5.21}
$$

5.7   Make sure that you understand how the matrix manipulations are done in section 5.5.1. Do this by verifying by hand the following results given by R.

   a) In output 5.4 verify the first row of the product $M^{\mathrm{T}}M$.

   b) In output 5.6 verify that the first column shown is the first column of M multiplied by the [1, 1] entry of output 5.5.

   c) Verify the second column of the cosines in output 5.7.

5.8   The default for R is to treat matrices as columns; for example, see output 5.3. However, the option byrow=T changes this to working with rows as seen in output 5.11. With this example in mind, rewrite output 5.3 so that the matrix M is defined by a vector that contains its rows, not its columns.

Output 5.11 Creating a matrix row by row with option `byrow=T` for problem 5.8.

```
> matrix(c(1,2,3,4,5,6), 2, 3, byrow=T)
     [,1] [,2] [,3]
[1,]   1    2    3
[2,]   4    5    6
```

5.9   In section 5.5.1, a series of matrix multiplications are done to compute the cosine of the angles between column vectors in a matrix. This problem shows a shortcut. Try to understand why the method given in output 5.12 has the same result as the method given in this chapter. In particular, why is the matrix product divided by 7? What is the connection between 7 and the size of the matrix, M?

Output 5.12 A shortcut method to compute the cosine of the angles between column vectors of a matrix. Note that this agrees with output 5.7. For problem 5.9.

```
> out=scale(M,center=F,scale=T)
> t(out) %*% out/7
          [,1]       [,2]       [,3]       [,4]
[1,] 1.0000000 0.9240674 0.8254103 0.8950300
[2,] 0.9240674 1.0000000 0.8876521 0.9182834
[3,] 0.8254103 0.8876521 1.0000000 0.9558856
[4,] 0.8950300 0.9182834 0.9558856 1.0000000
```

5.10   [Mathematical] The vectors in equations 5.16 and 5.17 have only zeros and ones as entries. Show that the angle between two vectors with only zeros and ones is the same as the angle between these vectors after the transformation by $\log(f+1)$.

Hint: Consider the vector in equation 5.16. Applying $\log(f+1)$ to each entry of $(0,0,1,1,1,1,1,1,0)$ produces $(0,0,\log 2,\log 2,\log 2,\log 2,\log 2,\log 2,0)$, but this new vector is the original vector multiplied by $\log 2$. Hence both vectors point in the same direction (in nine-dimensional space). Since the angle between two vectors is only a function of the directions, not the lengths, the angle for vectors of only zeros and ones is not affected by the transformation $\log(f+1)$. For readers with a mathematical background, convert this argument into a general proof.

CHAPTER 6

CONCORDANCE LINES AND CORPUS LINGUISTICS

6.1 INTRODUCTION

A *corpus* (plural *corpora*) is a collection of texts that have been put together to research one or more aspects of language. This term is from the Latin and means *body*. Not surprisingly, *corpus linguistics* is the study of language using a corpus.

The idea of collecting language samples is old. For example, Samuel Johnson's dictionary was the first in English to emphasize how words are used by supplying over 100,000 quotations (see the introduction of the abridged version edited by Lynch [61] for more details). Note that his dictionary is still in print. In fact, a complete digital facsimile of the first edition is available [62].

In the spirit of Samuel Johnson, a number of large corpora have been developed to support language references, for example, the *Longman Dictionary of American English* [74] or the *Cambridge Grammar of English* [26]. To analyze such corpora, this chapter creates concordances.

The next section introduces a few ideas of statistical sampling, and then considers how to apply these to text sampling. The rest of this chapter discusses examples of concordancing, which provide ample opportunity to apply the Perl programming techniques covered in the earlier chapters.

6.2   SAMPLING

Sampling replaces measuring all of the objects in a population with those from a subset. Assuming that the sample is representative of the population, then estimates are computable along with their accuracy. Although taking a subset loses information, it also requires less resources to measure. For example, asking questions of a thousand adults in the United States is cheaper and faster than contacting all the adults across America. Hence, sampling is a trade-off between accuracy and costs. The next section introduces a few basic ideas of sampling, and while reading this, think about how these ideas might apply to text.

6.2.1   Statistical Survey Sampling

This section gives one example of statistical survey sampling, which is compared to text sampling in the next section. The former is a well-researched area and many methods of sample selection have been proposed and analyzed.

We consider this example: for an upcoming statewide election, the percentage of voters for Candidate X is desired. A survey is the usual way to answer this question.

The underlying idea of a survey is straightforward. Some unknown properties (called *parameters*) of a *population* are desired. Measuring all the members is too expensive (in time or money or both), so a *sample* of the population is taken. The members of this are measured, which are used to compute an estimate of the population parameters.

In this election survey, the population is all people who do, in fact, vote on election day. However, it is not known who these voters are prior to that time. Although there exist lists of registered voters, even if these were without error, they only indicate who can vote, not who will vote on election day. Let us call the actual voters in the upcoming election the *target population*, while the registered voters are the *frame population*. The percentage of target voters in favor of Candidate X over Candidate Y is the desired parameter, but we must sample the frame population to make an estimate.

A good sample is representative of the population. A variety of *demographic* variables such as gender and marital status have been measured by region, for example, by ZIP codes. Assume that these two variables are available for registered voters, say from a marketing firm. Then the sample can be selected to ensure that its demographics match those of the registered voters.

Consider the following sampling design. A subset of the registered voter lists (the frame population) is taken so that every person on it has an equal chance of selection, which is called a *simple random sample*. When these people are contacted, each person is asked if he or she plans to vote in the next presidential election. If the answer is no, then the questioning ends. Otherwise, three more questions are asked. First, "What is your gender?" Second, "Are you single, married, or divorced?" Third, "Who do you prefer: Candidate X or Candidate Y?" Quotas for gender and marital status are established prior to the survey, and once each category is filled, no more responses from people in that category are used in the analysis. For example, if the quota for single females were 250, then only the first 250 contacted are asked about the candidates. Once all the quotas are filled, then the percentage of people (in the sample) who said that they will vote for Candidate X on election day is computed, which is the estimate of the election day results.

The above sampling design is *stratified*. The strata are all the combinations of demographic variables, for example, single females, single males, married females, and so forth. In general, strata are picked because they are important in making the sample representative of the target population. In addition, the strata must not overlap, that is, a person is not a member of two strata at once, which is the case above.

The above description ignores many practical considerations. For example, what should be done about all the people picked from the frame population who are unreachable? In the question "Who do you prefer: Candidate X or Candidate Y?" does the order of the candidates matter? However, these issues are not pertinent to text sampling, so we ignore them. See problem 6.1 for another sampling design applicable to this situation. For a much more detailed discussion on statistical sampling, see Thompson's book *Sampling* [115]. With this example in mind, let us consider text.

6.2.2   Text Sampling

Language comes in two forms: written and spoken. Speech is transcribable, but not without simplifications. For example, intonation, body language, and speed of speaking are generally not recorded but convey important information. To simplify matters a little, this book only analyzes written language.

Suppose we want to study a sample of written American English. As in statistical sampling, it should be representative of some form of language, but what is the target population? There are nonfiction and literary texts. The latter includes short stories and novels, and these come in a variety of genres including romance, detective, historical, fantasy, mysteries, children's, and science fiction. Moreover, nonfiction texts cover an immense number of topics and come in many forms including books, magazines, newspapers, journal articles, Web pages, letters, emails, and pamphlets. Finally, all the texts have to be accessible to the researchers, which suggests using a library database to construct the frame population.

Although registered voter lists exist, the situation varies for texts. Most books have International Standard Book Numbers (ISBN), and most periodicals have International Standard Serial Numbers (ISSN). However, no such lists exist for emails, product catalogs, graffiti, and so forth. And there are texts between these two extremes, for instance, many Web pages are cataloged by search engines, but not the deep Web.

Since there is no hope of a complete list of all texts, the specification of the target population requires some thought. One simplification is to limit texts to those that are cataloged in some way. This underrepresents certain categories, but the alternative is to create one's own list of unusual texts, which requires effort, and the idea of sampling is to decrease the amount of work.

The key question for a corpus is to decide exactly what it is sampling. Should it focus on a very narrow type of usage? For example, English is the official language of international air traffic control, but this type of English is limited to discussions about aviation. Another example is an English as a Second Language (ESL) program that creates a collection of student essays in order to study typical mistakes. In fact, this has been done, and for more information on such a corpus, see the Web page of the *Cambridge Learner Corpus* [24], which is part of the *Cambridge International Corpus* [23].

However, a broader focus is possible. For example, English is spoken in many countries, and each has its own peculiarities, so it makes sense to speak of American English, British English, Australian English, and so forth. In addition, it is both written and spoken. How a person talks depends upon what he or she is doing, for example, speaking to a friend in a bar is different from discussing work with one's boss over the phone. These changes in use due to circumstances are called *registers*. Already this makes three ways to classify English (country, written/spoken and register), and a corpus can be made for any combination of these three, for example, American written English as it appears in newspaper business stories.

The divisions in the preceding paragraph are strata. That is, a researcher can stratify by countries, written/spoken language, registers, and so forth. This is a useful way to approach a corpus that is representative of many types of English. Such a corpus might first divide texts by country. Then for each country, written and spoken examples are collected, and each of these can be further broken down. The end result are strata that are narrow enough in scope so that it is possible to gather a representative collection of texts. If enough are found, then the result is representative of a wide variety of English.

There exist giant copora that are representative of a large swath of Englishes, for example, the *Cambridge International Corpus* of English [23]. This combines other corpora owned by Cambridge University Press. For a detailed description of the construction of a corpus that is representative of American English, see the *Brown Corpus Manual* [46]. This explains many details, including the strata used, and the sizes of each text sample.

Although survey sampling and text sampling have similarities, there is one important difference: many texts have copyrights. Researchers must request permission to use copyrighted texts in their corpus, but permission need not be given. For a discussion of this issue, see unit A9 of McEnery, Xiao, and Tono's *Corpus-Based Language Studies* [78]. Note that the issue of copyright is why this book uses texts that are in the public domain, which explains the preponderance of pre–World War I literary works.

With the above discussion of both survey and text sampling in mind, we are ready to consider corpus linguistics. The next section introduces the first of several uses of corpora.

6.3   CORPUS AS BASELINE

A common statistical task is deciding whether or not a measurement is typical. For example, output 3.4 gives counts of the word lengths for the story "The Tell-Tale Heart." On average, are these unusually long? unusually short? Without a standard of comparison, it is hard to say.

If a corpus is representative of some part of the English language, it can be used as a baseline for comparison. For example, the most ambitious to date are the giant corpora such as the *Cambridge International Corpus* [23], which have been built to study English as a whole. Text that deviate from this kind of corpus are likely to be atypical in some way.

Unfortunately, even smaller, less ambitious corpora are labor intensive, and although many exist, few are in the public domain. For example, the *Linguistic Data Consortium* [73] has many available, but most of them cost money to obtain. Note that many older texts are in the public domain and are available online, so a researcher can create certain types of corpora without obtaining copyright permissions. For example, to create a corpus of 19th-century novels, many texts are available, so the frame population is clear. However, care is needed to define the target population as well as choosing texts that are representative of this.

This section compares three novels to a large, public domain corpus consisting of Enron emails released to the public by the Federal Energy Regulatory Commission during its investigation of the company [31]. This is called the EnronSent corpus, and it was prepared for public distribution by the CALO Project [76], created by SRI International's Artificial Intelligence Center. This corpus is distributed as 45 files, each containing from 1.5 to 2.5 megabytes of text (uncompressed). However, the analysis here is based on just one file, enronsent00, for simplicity.

Although the novels and emails are both in English, clearly these types of texts have differences. A more appropriate corpus might be made from public domain literary novels of the 19th century, but as noted above, this requires time and effort. However, this comparison shows the use of a corpus as a baseline.

We compare three novels with the EnronSent corpus with regards to word frequencies. Since the latter is composed of email, it is wise to check its contents for odd characters. Table 6.1 shows the frequencies for `enronsent00`, which are obtained from program 4.3. Note that the original output is changed from one column to three to save space.

Table 6.1   Character counts for the EnronSent email corpus.

: 377706	v: 14816	): 2310
e: 169596	k: 13619	(: 2244
t: 128570	,: 12423	q: 1858
o: 114242	1: 8808	>: 1805
a: 112451	-: 8459	$: 1575
i: 102610	2: 8428	": 1345
n: 100985	/: 5613	z: 1129
s: 89229	3: 5609	@: 867
r: 88811	=: 5592	<: 802
l: 61438	5: 4908	!: 711
h: 59689	*: 4907	+: 614
d: 50958	:: 4726	&: 512
c: 45425	j: 4375	~: 501
u: 43439	x: 4222	%: 448
m: 38346	': 4162	#: 419
p: 34210	9: 4035	[: 353
y: 31347	4: 3642	]: 353
f: 29674	7: 3269	;: 218
g: 29336	?: 3250	': 95
w: 27443	6: 2807	|: 88
.: 24821	tab: 2695	\: 11
b: 21606	8: 2661	}: 2
0: 15875	_: 2600	

Not surprisingly, there are some unusual characters, for example, 4907 asterisks and 1805 greater than signs. Using the regex concordance (program 2.7), it is easy to print out all the lines that match some pattern, which gives insight into how the special symbols are used.

In section 2.4, it is noted that the dash, hyphen, and apostrophe can cause complications. For the EnronSent corpus, we remove dashes, but leave all the hyphenated words in place. To decide what to do with the apostrophes, we examine them using program 2.7. Output 6.1 shows a selection of the 270 matches for the regex (\w'\W|\W'\w), which finds all the apostrophes at the beginning or the end of a word. Note the initial output line numbers, which start at 1.

Output 6.1 clearly shows a variety of uses of the apostrophe. For example, in lines 2 and 41, it is used to form a possessive noun, while in lines 5, 6, and 196, it forms contractions. In lines 7 and 87, single quotes are used to highlight a phrase, but in line 19 it is used to indicate length in feet. Notice that lines 75, 129, and 136 have typos, which is common in emails. In line 109, two apostrophes are used to make double quotes, as is true in line 157

Output 6.1 Selected concordance lines matching an apostrophe in the EnronSent corpus.

```
  2           Can you pull Tori K.'s and Martin Cuilla's resum
  5  from shockwave.com, stick 'em in your Shockmachine and
  6  ~~~~~~~~~~~~~~~~~~~~~ The '80s may not have left many
  7  nish,  simply click on the 'Reply With History' button
 19  e overall dimensions are 55' X 40'.  For a total of 440
 41              CA legislators' suit against FERC.
 75  tting out of that-john who 's getting squeezed on the m
 87  ow.  Was it 'Blue Men Group' that you recommended we se
109  ply goofed, setting up a  ''dysfunctional'' system. It
129   you gotta love heffner...'if we take out the jan 31 l
136                  I cant' seem to make my gambling p
157  look on India to ''negative'' from ''stable.'' Fitch sa
196              Buying for nothin' and your commissions for f
233  '; and commercial paper 'F2'. Pipeline subsidiary 'A-'
```

except that the initial double quote is made with back-quotes. Finally, line 233 shows the back-quote, apostrophe pair to highlight a term.

Since there are many patterns of typos to fix (like cant' and who 's), and because changing nothin' to nothin is still comprehensible, all apostrophes at both ends of a word are removed in the word counting program. This creates some ambiguities, such as changing 55' to 55, but these are not that common (after all, there are only 270 total matches.)

To count the words in this corpus, all the nonalphanumeric characters shown in table 6.1 are removed, as are two single quotes in a row and single quotes either at the beginning or the end of a word. With these in mind, it is straightforward to rewrite program 3.3 and code sample 3.26 to create code sample 6.1.

The output from code sample 6.1 is quite long, but we focus on the 20 most frequent words, which are shown in the first column of table 6.2. These word frequencies are used as a baseline for comparisons, which assumes that similarities or differences from this corpus are of interest.

We compare the Enronsent corpus with the following literary works: Charles Dickens's *A Christmas Carol* (compare with output 3.21), Jack London's *The Call of the Wild*, and Mary Shelley's *Frankenstein*. The results for these three novels have been combined in table 6.2.

Notice that there are both similarities and differences among the four columns. First, the same word is at the top of each column, *the*, which is the case for most texts. Second, the top five words in the first column are highly ranked in all four columns. These are common function words.

Third, the first column has *is*, *are*, and *have*, but these do not appear in the other three columns (although these words are in the three novels, their ranking is below 20). On the other hand, *was*, *were*, and *had* are in the last three columns but are not in the first. So there is a difference in verb tense of the auxiliary verbs *to be* and *to have*: the novels prefer the past, the emails prefer the present.

Fourth, character names appear in the second and the third columns. For example, *Scrooge* is the protagonist of *A Christmas Carol* as is *Buck* for *The Call of the Wild*. Not surprisingly, *Scrooge* does not appear in the corpus or the other two novels. However, *buck*

Code Sample 6.1 Computes word frequencies for the EnronSent corpus.

```
open(FILE, "C:/enronsent00") or die;
open(OUT, ">counts.csv") or die;

sub byDescendingValues {
  $value = $freq{$b} <=> $freq{$a};
  if ($value == 0) {
    return $a cmp $b;
  } else {
    return $value;
  }
}

while(<FILE>) {
  chomp;
  $_ = lc($_);
  s/--+/ /g;
  s/''//g;
  s/(\W)'(\w)/$1$2/g; # Remove apostrophes at start of a word
  s/(\w)'(\W)/$1$2/g; # Remove apostrophes at end of a word
  s/[.,\/=*:?_)(>\$"\@<!+&~%\#\[\];`|\\}{]//g;
  @word = split(/\s+/);
  foreach $x (@word) {
    ++$freq{$x};
  }
}

foreach $x (sort byDescendingValues keys %freq) {
  print OUT "$x, $freq{$x}\n";
}
```

is in the corpus (both as a name and as a word) as well as in *A Christmas Carol* (though not as a name). Nonetheless, it appears infrequently in these works.

Finally, the rate of use of *I* varies greatly among the columns. It is twelfth in *A Christmas Carol*, but is 121st in *The Call of the Wild*. Both of these novels have narrators who are not characters in the stories they tell, so lower ranks are not surprising. However, Buck is a dog and does not use this pronoun. Checking with the concordance program, all the uses of *I* in *The Call of the Wild* appear in direct quotes where humans are speaking.

In contrast, *I* is third in *Frankenstein*, which is told in a series of first-person accounts. For example, Robert Walton writes letters to his sister of his expedition to the North Pole, during which he sees the monster and then meets Victor Frankenstein. The latter eventually tells Walton his tale of creating the monster that he is currently pursuing. This tale also includes other first-person narratives, for example, the monster's story. All this explains the high frequencies of first-person pronouns.

Even though the above analysis only requires finding and counting words, these top 20 counts do reveal differences. That is, even though table 6.2 represents a tremendous loss

Table 6.2   Twenty most frequent words in the EnronSent email corpus, Dickens's *A Christmas Carol*, London's *The Call of the Wild*, and Shelley's *Frankenstein* using code sample 6.1.

the, 14485	the, 1563	the, 2274	the, 4193
to, 9372	and, 1052	and, 1536	and, 2976
and, 5785	a, 696	of, 867	i, 2850
a, 5487	to, 658	he, 814	of, 2641
of, 5423	of, 652	was, 696	to, 2094
you, 4903	in, 518	to, 675	my, 1776
i, 4376	it, 513	a, 662	a, 1391
in, 4184	he, 485	his, 559	in, 1128
is, 3821	was, 427	in, 537	was, 1021
for, 3601	his, 420	it, 370	that, 1017
on, 3150	that, 338	buck, 313	me, 867
that, 2668	i, 335	that, 307	but, 687
this, 2496	scrooge, 314	with, 304	had, 686
be, 2375	with, 265	him, 290	with, 667
have, 2197	you, 233	they, 287	he, 608
we, 2170	as, 228	had, 274	you, 575
are, 2113	said, 221	as, 258	which, 558
will, 2036	had, 205	for, 237	it, 547
it, 2027	him, 198	on, 226	his, 535
with, 1995	for, 197	were, 217	as, 528

of information, enough is left to draw interesting conclusions. Hence reductive techniques like word counting can be informative.

6.3.1 Function vs. Content Words in Dickens, London, and Shelley

Words can be split into two classes: *function* and *content*. The former are often frequent and provide grammatical information. Examples of this are *the*, *to*, and *and*, which are the three most frequent words in the EnronSent corpus. The latter provide content. For instance, the sentence "The prancing blue cat is on a snowboard" is evocative because of its four content words (*cat*, *snowboard*, *blue*, and *prancing*) and is grammatical because of its four function words (*the*, *is*, *on*, and *a*).

Function words are common in a *stoplist*, which is a collection of terms to ignore in an analysis. For example, *the* is seen to distort the angles between word count vectors in section 5.6. Since *the* serves a grammatical role, but has little meaning to contribute, decreasing its influence is reasonable, and removing it completely is the most extreme way of achieving this.

However, this distinction between function words and content words is not so clear-cut. For example, consider table 6.3, which contains eight examples of phrasal verbs using *up*, which is a common preposition and is called a *particle* when used this way. First, note that adding *up* changes the meaning of these verbs, for example, *to throw up* is much different than *to throw*. Second, the meaning of *up* ranges from literal to idiomatic. For example, *to walk up a hill* implies that a person has increased his or her elevation, but *to screw something up* is an idiomatic phrase. See section 235 of the *Cambridge Grammar of English* [26] for an explanation of the grammar of multiword verbs, which include phrasal verbs.

Table 6.3   Eight phrasal verbs using the preposition *up*.

Phrasal Verb	Rough Meaning
Screw up	Make a mistake
Shape up	Exercise
Wake up	Awaken
Shut up	Be quiet
Speak up	Talk louder
Throw up	Vomit
Walk up	Ambulate upward or toward
Pick up	Lift upward

In the last section, the pronouns *I* and *my* are informative. The narrative structure of the novel *Frankenstein* is reflected by the higher than expected proportion of these two pronouns. Hence, ignoring these words does lose information. For more on stoplists, see section 15.1.1 of *Foundations of Statistical Natural Language Processing* [75]. Also see section 9.2.2 for one way to obtain stoplists for a variety of natural languages using Perl.

The preceding section shows that examining the most frequent words in a text is informative, even when these are function words. Code sample 6.1 prints out the word frequencies from highest to lowest, and as it decreases, the proportion of content words increases.

For example, in *The Call of the Wild*, the word *dogs* appears 111 times (ranks 33rd) and *dog* appears another 57 times. Since the novel is a narrative about the dog, Buck, this is not surprising. Furthermore, most of the story takes place in the outdoors of far north of Canada, and this is reflected in the ranks of *sled* (58th), *camp* (71st), and *trail* (88th). In addition, the names of the important characters in the story appear frequently. For example, *Buck* is in the top 20, *Thorton* (44th) is the human Buck loves most before he joins the wolves at the end of the book, and *Spitz* (58th) dislikes Buck so much that the two of them fight it out to the death.

Hence, studying word frequency lists does give insight to a novel. However, considering how a word is used in a text provides additional information, which is easy to do by running a concordance program. This technique combines the computer's ability to find text with a human's ability to understand it, which is both simple and powerful and is the topic of the next section.

6.4 CONCORDANCING

Concordancing is also called *Key Word In Context* (KWIC). The goal is to find all instances of a regex, and print these out along with the surrounding text for the researcher to inspect. Section 2.5 discusses how this is done in Perl, which culminates with program 2.7.

We first use the concordance program to check the accuracy of the word frequencies found in the last section. For example, applying program 2.7 with the regex (\bbuck\b) to *The Call of the Wild* results in 360 matches, which is 47 more than the 313 noted in table 6.2. Using (\bhe\b), there are 817 matches compared to 814. Finally, using (\bthe\b), both the table and the program report 2274 matches. This is a reminder that a programmer must be careful when using regexes. Try to think of what causes the counts to differ in these cases before reading the next paragraph.

Since the concordance counts are always at least as big as those in table 6.2, code sample 6.1 can miss instances of words. One possibility is that the programs treat capitalization differently. However, code sample 6.1 uses lc, so all letters are converted to lowercase, and program 2.7 uses the regex /$target/gi, which is case indifferent. Hence, both programs ignore capitalization, although they use different means to achieve this.

The answer is due to the boundary condition, \b. Putting this before and after the target only matches nonalphanumeric characters before and after it, and punctuation satisfies this condition. However, do both programs take into account all punctuation? Not quite: the apostrophe and hyphen match \b, but they are not removed in code sample 6.1.

It turns out that there are 47 *Buck's* and 3 *he's* in *The Call of the Wild*, which cause the discrepancies noted above. Another potential problem are hyphenated words because the hyphens match the boundary condition. Now we are ready to consider how to sort concordance lines, which is the topic of the next section.

6.4.1 Sorting Concordance Lines

The output of program 2.7 shows the matches in the order they appear in the input text. However, other arrangements can be useful.

We consider three kinds of orders in this section. First, since the text that matches a regex can, in general, produce a variety of strings, sorting these in alphabetical order can be interesting. For example, the regex (\bdogs?\b) matches both the singular and plural forms of *dog*, and sorting these means that all the concordance lines with *dog* come first, and then all the lines with *dogs*.

Second, one way to create table 6.3 is by looking at concordance lines that match the word *up*. Output 6.2 does exactly this, which finds many phrasal verbs, for example, *wrap up*, *take up*, and *pent up*. This output, however, is easier to use if the word immediately before *up* were alphabetically sorted. Moreover, some of the verbs are not adjacent to *up*, for example, *takin' 'm up* and *licked some up*. Hence, sorting two or three words before *up* is also useful.

Output 6.2 First 10 concordance lines matching the word *up* in *The Call of the Wild*.

```
              "You might wrap up the goods before you deli
     struggle. "I'm takin' 'm up for the boss to 'Frisco.
   ere they keeping him pent up in this narrow crate?  He
   ur men entered and picked up the crate.  More tormento
   o long, and Buck crumpled up and went down, knocked ut
   riously, then licked some up on his tongue.  It bit li
   the bone for three inches up and down. Forever after B
   strils, and there, curled up under the snow in a snug
   snarl he bounded straight up into the blinding day, th
   e in harness and swinging up the trail toward the Dyea
```

Third, the prepositions that go with a phrasal verb can be studied. For example, output 6.3 shows the first 10 matches of *sprang* in *The Call of the Wild*. This reveals several phrasal verbs: *to spring at*, *to spring for*, *to spring to*, and so forth. Now sorting the lines by the word right after the match is of interest. With these types of sorts in mind, we implement them in the next section.

Output 6.3 First 10 concordance lines matching the word *sprang* in *The Call of the Wild*.

```
breath.  In quick rage he sprang at the man, who met him h
a kidnapped king. The man sprang for his throat, but Buck
times during the night he sprang to his feet when the shed
 the first meal.  As Buck sprang to punish him, the lash o
ething very like mud.  He sprang back with a snort.  More
ggled under his feet.  He sprang back, bristling and snarl
e beast in him roared. He sprang upon Spitz with a fury wh
ing, and when the two men sprang among them with stout clu
, terrified into bravery, sprang through the savage circle
bristling with fear, then sprang straight for Buck. He had
```

6.4.1.1 *Code for Sorting Concordance Lines*   We start with sorting concordance lines by the strings that match the regex. Program 2.7 finds these lines, and only two additional ideas are needed. First, instead of immediately printing out the lines, store them in an array, say @lines. Second, once stored, use sort to order them.

Code sample 6.2 prints its output in the order the lines are found, and adding subroutines to this program enables the types of sorts discussed above. Compared to program 2.7, program 6.1 has several advantages. First, it allows the programmer to enter the regex and the radius on the command line. Second, $radius is padded with spaces so that the final string always has $extract characters both before and after the regex match, which makes sorting the concordance lines easier. Third, these are stored in the array @lines. Fourth, sorting is achieved by replacing (@lines) with (sort byOrder @lines) in the final foreach loop.

One detail to remember is that all characters have an order, which has two consequences. First, the order of words containing punctuation can be surprising. For example, *don't* comes before *done* because the single quote comes before all the letters of the alphabet. This is solved by removing all the punctuation within the sort function (except that a dash adjacent to words is replaced by a space), which is done by removePunctuation in code sample 6.3. Note that the function lc is required because capital letters come before lowercase letters. Otherwise *Zebra* comes before *aardvark*.

Second, a function to order the concordance lines is required. Recall that the lines have exactly $radius characters before and after the match. Hence, given a line, the match is recoverable by removing these characters, which can be done by substr. This is the reason that program 6.1 adds spaces to each line if they are short due to paragraph boundaries. What remains is processed by removePunctuation and sorted by cmp. Code sample 6.4 does this.

Finally, changing the foreach loop of code sample 6.2 to the following reorders the output as discussed above.

```
foreach $x (sort byMatch @lines)
```

Combining code samples 6.2, 6.3, and 6.4 with program 6.1 accomplishes our original goal of sorting by regex matches. See problem 6.5 for some simple punctuation searches to try. The next section discusses some applications.

```perl
# EXAMPLE: perl concordance.pl regex radius
open (FILE, "Call of the Wild.txt") or die("File not found");

$/ = ""; # Paragraph mode for while loop
$target = "($ARGV[0])";
$radius = $ARGV[1];
$width = 2*$radius;

$count = 0;
while (<FILE>) {
  chomp;
  s/\n/ /g; # Replace newlines by spaces
  s/\b--\b/ -- /g; # Add spaces around dashes adjacent to words

  while ( $_ =~ /$target/gi ) {
    $match = $1;
    $pos = pos;
    $start = $pos - $radius - length($match);

    # Extracts are padded with spaces if needed
    if ($start < 0) {
      $extract = substr($_, 0, $width+$start+length($match));
      $extract = (" " x -$start) . $extract;
    } else {
      $extract = substr($_, $start, $width+length($match));
      $deficit = $width+length($match) - length($extract);
      if ($deficit > 0) {
        $extract .= (" " x $deficit);
      }
    }
    $lines[$count] = $extract;
    ++$count;
  }
}
```

Program 6.1 Core concordance code for use with code samples 6.2, 6.3, 6.4, 6.7, 6.8, 6.9, and 6.10.

6.4.2 Application: Word Usage Differences between London and Shelley

Lexicography is the study of words. Recent dictionaries like the *Longman Dictionary of American English* [74] use proprietary corpora representative of written and spoken English. However, any corpus can be used to study the language it contains. For example, the EnronSent corpus gives insight into the register of corporate emails.

When studying usage, even though English has relatively few inflected forms, it does have some. For example, many nouns have singular and plural forms, and verbs have conjugated forms. Hence, to study a word often requires finding several forms, which are collectively called a *lemma*. Fortunately, finding multiple patterns is easy for a regex.

Code Sample 6.2 Code to print out the concordance lines found by program 6.1.

```
$line_number = 0;

foreach $x (@lines) {
  ++$line_number;
  printf "%5d", $line_number;
  print " $x\n";
}
```

Code Sample 6.3 A function to remove punctuation, which is used in code sample 6.4.

```
sub removePunctuation {
  # USAGE: $unpunctuated = removePunctuation($string);
  my $string = $_[0];
  $string = lc($string);    # Convert to lowercase
  $string =~ s/[^-a-z ]//g; # Remove non-alphabetic characters
  $string =~ s/--+/ /g;     # Replace 2+ hyphens with a space
  $string =~ s/-//g;        # Remove hyphens
  $string =~ s/\s+/ /g;     # Replace whitespaces with a space
  return($string);
}
```

Code Sample 6.4 A function to sort concordance lines by the strings that match the regex. This is used in program 6.1.

```
sub byMatch {
  my $middle_a = substr($a, $radius, length($a) - 2*$radius);
  my $middle_b = substr($b, $radius, length($b) - 2*$radius);
  $middle_a = removePunctuation($middle_a);
  $middle_b = removePunctuation($middle_b);
  $middle_a cmp $middle_b;
}
```

For the first example, we consider how the pronoun *I* is used in *The Call of the Wild*. This word ranks 121st most frequent, and it is that low because it is only used by the humans in the novel, not by Buck, the dog protagonist.

Although *I* has no inflected forms, it is often used in contractions. Hence the regex $(\bi('\w+)?\b)$ is used, where the innermost parentheses match any potential contractions (as long as only one apostrophe is used). Output 6.4 gives the first 10 occurrences of *I* in addition to all its contractions. Note that the first line matched the roman numeral *I*, not the pronoun.

Although some of these lines are too short to know for sure, most of them include double quotes. In fact, the last 42 lines are direct quotations of human characters in the novel. Also, as promised, the matches are in alphabetical order, that is, all the occurances of *I* are first, then all instances of *I'll*, *I'm*, and *I've*, in that order.

Output 6.4 Representative lines containing *I* in *The Call of the Wild*.

```
 1                    Chapter I
 2                "All I get is fifty for it," he
 3 or it," he grumbled; "an' I wouldn't do it over for a
 4  his lacerated hand.  "If I don't get the hydrophoby-
 5  dog-breakin', that's wot I say," one of the men on t
 6 e learned your place, and I know mine.  Be a good dog
 7 uck, heem pool lak hell.  I tich heem queek as anyt'i
 8 led his appearance.  "Wot I say?" the dog-driver crie
 9 s rejoinder.  "All de tam I watch dat Buck I know for
10 l de tam I watch dat Buck I know for sure.  Lissen: s
31  high.  Be a bad dog, and I'll whale the stuffin' outa y
32         "The lazy brutes, I'll show them," he cried, pre
33 ou strike that dog again, I'll kill you," he at last man
34 .  "Get out of my way, or I'll fix you. I'm going to Daw
35 to one!" he proclaimed.  "I'll lay you another thousand
36  the Skookum Bench king. "I'll give you a thousand for h
37  the sounds of struggle. "I'm takin' 'm up for the boss
38 d; "and he's worth it, or I'm a squarehead."
39  my way, or I'll fix you. I'm going to Dawson."
40                          "I'm not hankering to be the m
41 "Though it's little faith I'm having, John, that the be
42  so that all could hear, "I've got a thousand dollars th
43                          "I've got a sled standing outsi
```

It is easy to confirm that the usage of *I* in the EnronSent corpus is much different, which agrees with common sense. A person writing an email commonly uses the first-person pronoun, but without using quotation marks. Nonetheless, there are examples in this corpus where the person quoted uses *I*, for example, some emails include news reports that include first-person direct quotes. However, these are rare.

Hence, these two texts differ in the grammatical use of the pronoun *I*. *The Call of the Wild* always uses this word in direct quotations of the human characters. However, the EnronSent corpus rarely uses direct quotations.

This example, however, is somewhat crude. Concordance lines can be used to discover which meanings a word has in a text. To illustrate this, we compare the word *body* as it is used in the novels *The Call of the Wild* and *Frankenstein* by searching for matches to the regex (\bbod(y|ies)\b). Both texts use the word about the same number of times, but not in the same way.

The extracts in tables 6.4 and 6.5 are found by the concordance program, but are edited to fit on the page. The numbering does not start at 1 because the initial lines match the word *bodies*. In the former table, all the lines refer to Buck's body except 11 (Perrault's) and 14 (a primitive man's). Note that all 10 lines refer to living bodies. *The Call of the Wild* is an adventure story of the dog, Buck, and the emphasis is on physical action. Although a few of the characters in the novel die, the focus is on what they did, not their corpses.

In the second novel, however, the story revolves around Victor Frankenstein's successful attempt to animate a dead body. Although his experiment succeeds, he abandons his monster, who through ill treatment grows to hate men, especially the man who created him. This

Table 6.4   First 10 lines containing the word *body* in *The Call of the Wild*.

5 an opening sufficient for the passage of Buck's body.
6 he received a shock that checked his body and brought his teeth together
7 With drooping tail and shivering body, very forlorn indeed,
8 In a trice the heat from his body filled the confined space
9 The muscles of his whole body contracted spasmodically
10 blood carried it to the farthest reaches of his body
11 it fell each time across the hole made by his body,
12 his splendid body flashing forward, leap by leap,
13 and every hair on his body and drop of blood in his veins;
14 but on his body there was much hair.

Table 6.5   First 10 lines containing the word *body* in *Frankenstein*.

4 I commenced by inuring my body to hardship.
5 His limbs were nearly frozen, and his body dreadfully emaciated by fatigue
6 in a state of body and mind whose restoration
7 No word, no expression could body forth the kind of relation
8 I must also observe the natural decay and corruption of the human body.
9 renew life where death had apparently devoted the body to corruption.
10 for the sole purpose of infusing life into an inanimate body.
11 where the body of the murdered child had been afterwards found.
12 When shown the body, she fell into violent hysterics
13 If she had gone near the spot where his body lay,

leads to the monster systematically killing the friends and family of Victor until both of them die in the frozen wastelands of the arctic.

Unlike *The Call of the Wild*, where the word *body* is consistently used to refer to a living body doing something, the uses of *body* in table 6.5 are more diverse. Line 4 is written by Robert Walton about his preparations to explore the arctic. He refers to his body in a matter of fact way that is reminiscent of *The Call of the Wild*.

Lines 5 and 6 refer to Victor Frankenstein, who is discovered by Walton in the arctic. Line 7, however, uses *body* as a verb, not as a noun, which is a very different use of this word. And lines 8, 9, and 10 refer to Frankenstein's research of animating the dead. In all three cases, the discussion is about abstract science, not physical deeds, and *body* is replaceable by *corpse*.

In lines 11, 12, and 13, all three uses of *body* refer to the corpse of William Frankenstein, Victor's brother. The murderer is the monster, but he also planted evidence on Justine Moritz, who is accused, found guilty, and executed for the crime. Finally, some of the lines not shown introduce other meanings, for example, "the phenomena of the heavenly *bodies* ...," which refers to astronomical bodies.

The differences in the usage of *body* in the two novels reflects the different genres of these stories. In *Call of the Wild*, the emphasis is on Buck's physical adventures as fate prepares him to answer the call of the wild. However, in *Frankenstein*, Victor pays the price for daring to create life. He sees his friends and family killed one by one until he himself dies at the end. While this story also has adventures (Walton's arctic explorations, for instance), the focus is on the life and death of the body, not the physical deeds that it can perform.

In general, by looking at many examples of word usage in many texts, patterns are discovered, which are studied by lexicographers to create dictionary definitions. Although finishing a dictionary requires an immense amount of research, the spirit of this process is captured in the idea of concordancing.

6.4.3 Application: Word Morphology of Adverbs

The preceding section examines concordance lines to explore word usage, which is a task of corpus linguistics. This section shows that word forms are also amenable to this approach.

English is famous for irregular spelling. Nonetheless, there are still many patterns that can be written as a regex. For example, plural nouns often follow the pattern of adding either an -*s* or an -*es* to the singular form, and which one it is depends on the end of the word. For example, nouns that end in *s* usually form a plural by adding -*es*. However, there are irregular plurals, for example, it is "one *mouse*," but "many *mice*." See problem 2.8 for more on this.

This section finds adverbs formed from adjectives by adding -*ly*. For example, consider sentences 6.1 and 6.2. The former uses *quick* to modify the proper noun *Scoot*, while the latter uses *quickly* to modify the verb *runs*.

$$\text{Scoot is quick.} \tag{6.1}$$

$$\text{Scoot runs quickly.} \tag{6.2}$$

The above pattern does not cover all adverbs. In fact, sentence 6.3 uses *quick* as an adverb. However, even a rule that is applicable some of the time has value.

$$\text{Run here, Scoot, and be quick about it.} \tag{6.3}$$

A simplistic idea is to search for all words that end in -*ly*, which is easy to do. Using the regex (\b\w+ly\b), and sorting the concordance lines alphabetically by the matches produces output 6.5.

Output 6.5 First 10 lines in alphabetical order of words that end in -*ly*. Text is *The Call of the Wild*.

```
 1 , who had been trembling abjectly, took heart at this open
 2  very forlorn indeed, he aimlessly circled the tent.  Sudde
 3 the progress down-stream amazingly rapid.  From below came
 4 ved at Skaguay they were apparently on their last legs.  The
 5 uck, over whose limp and apparently lifeless body Nig was se
 6 enting a front which was apparently unbroken so swiftly did
 7 ck, his four feet waving appealingly in the air, and refused
 8 . Billee wagged his tail appeasingly, turned to run when he s
 9  avail, and cried (still appeasingly) when Spitz's sharp teet
10         Buck watched them apprehensively as they proceeded to tak
```

In this output, all the matches are adverbs. For example, in line 5, *apparently* modifies the adjective *lifeless*. However, looking at the entire output, there are matches that are not adverbs, for example, *belly* (a noun), *Curly* (a name of a dog), and *silly* (an adjective). Hence there are false positives. One idea is to find words ending in *-ly* such that removing this still results in a word: perhaps these are more likely to be adverbs. However, sometimes adding *-ly* changes the final letter, so investigating this possibility first is useful.

Using the Grady Ward CROSSWD.TXT word list, code sample 6.5 finds all the words that end in *-ly* such that when this is removed, the result is no longer a word.

Code Sample 6.5 Finding words that end in *-ly* that are not words when this ending is removed.

```
open(WORDS, "C:/CROSSWD.TXT") or die;

while(<WORDS>) {
  chomp;
  ++$dict{$_};
}

foreach $word (sort keys %dict) {
  if ($word =~ /(^\w+)ly$/) {
    if (not exists $dict{$1}) {
      print "$word ";
    }
  }
}
```

Running this code produces many words, which reveal several patterns. First, adjectives that end in *-y* change to *-ily*, hence *happily* is an adverb, yet *happi* is not a word. Second, there are words like *seasonable* and *incredible* where the *-ble* changes to a *-bly*. Third, words like *automatic* change to *automatically*. All these patterns can be removed with an if statement coupled with substr, which is done by code sample 6.6.

Running this produces output 6.6. It turns out that there are still word patterns that produce false positives, for example, words that end in *-ll* change to *-lly*, or words that end in *-le* change to *-ly* (which includes the *-ble* words noted above). It also turns out that there are gaps in the original word list, for example, *analogous* and *deceptive* are missing.

Note that the process of trying to find exceptions to a potentially useful rule reveals morphological patterns for some adverbs, although some unrelated words also appear, for example, *anomaly*, *apply*, and *billy*.

The next step is to remove the not in the if statement of code sample 6.5. This produces a long list of words, which must be examined to determine how many of them are adverbs. This is not done here, but see problem 6.6 for the first few words of output.

The above example shows that language is complex, and that a back-and-forth programming approach is helpful. That is, the researcher programs an idea, which is found to have exceptions. This program is revised, and then new exceptions might appear. However, in practice, this process usually ends after several iterations with code that has an acceptably low error rate. Moreover, this process itself teaches the programmer about the texts under analysis.

A final lesson is to realize that data sets often have errors. In the above case, two words that should not have been in output 6.6 did appear: *analogously* and *deceptively*.

Code Sample 6.6 Variant of code sample 6.5 that removes certain patterns of words.

```
open(WORDS, "C:/Grady Ward/CROSSWD.TXT") or die;

while(<WORDS>) {
  chomp;
  ++$dict{$_};
}

foreach $word (sort keys %dict) {
  if ($word =~ /(^\w+)ly$/) {
    if (substr($word, -3) ne "ily" and
        substr($word, -4) ne "ably" and
        substr($word, -4) ne "ibly" and
        substr($word, -4) ne "ally") {
          if (not exists $dict{$1}) {
            print "$word ";
          }
      }
    }
  }
}
```

Output 6.6 Initial 10 lines of output from code sample 6.6.

```
agly analogously anomaly antimonopoly apetaly aphylly apply
assembly beauteously bialy bihourly billy biweekly biyearly
blackfly blowfly botfly brambly bristly brolly bubbly buirdly
bully burbly butterfly catchfly chilly cicely coly contumely
crinkly cuddly cully dayfly deceptively deerfly dhooly dicycly
dilly dimply dooly doubly doyly drizzly drolly dully duly
duopoly eely emboly epiboly feebly felly firefly fly folly
freckly frilly fully gadfly gallfly giggly gilly gingelly
gingely girly glowfly goggly golly googly gorbelly greenfly
grisly grizzly grumbly hepatomegaly hillbilly hilly holly
```

Unfortunately, errors are always a possibility. Even the act of finding and correcting these can introduce new errors. Instead of expecting no errors, it is wise for any data analyst to assume that errors exist and try to detect them.

For another example of morphology, see section 3.2 of *Corpus Linguistics* by Biber, Conrad, and Reppen [11]. That section studies proportions of nominalizations, which are classes of nouns that are formed by using particular endings. For example, *happy* is an adjective, and *happiness* is a noun formed by adding the suffix *-ness* (and changing *y* to *i*, which also happens with *happily*).

This reference also states how the authors approach their task. What computer tools do they use to study nouns ending in these suffixes? As they note on page 59 of *Corpus Linguistics*, although some concordance programs can do what they want, they find it easier to write their own computer code. These authors are linguists, not computer scientists, yet they realize the flexibility of programming is worth the effort.

In the next section we move from sorting the regex matches of concordance lines to sorting the words near these matches. This can be applied to collocations.

6.5   COLLOCATIONS AND CONCORDANCE LINES

Table 6.3 shows examples of verbs that change their meaning when used with *up*. For example, *to throw your lunch into the sink* means something completely different than *to throw up your lunch into the sink*. However, there are examples where the meaning of a phrase is solely determined by its constituent words. For example, a *green phone* is a phone that is green.

Certain words occur together more often than chance, and these are called *collocations*. For example, *throw up* is a collocation, as is *blue moon*, but *green phone* is not. Recall from section 4.3.1 that the probability of two independent words is the product of the probabilities of each word. However, the probability of a collocation is higher than this product, as stated below.

$$P(\text{green phone}) \approx P(\text{green})P(\text{phone})$$
$$P(\text{blue moon}) > P(\text{blue})P(\text{moon})$$
$$P(\text{throw up}) > P(\text{throw})P(\text{up})$$

Note that the words in a collocation can be separated by other words, for example, *he threw his hands up into the air*, where *his hands* separates *threw* and *up*. In addition, there are some words that avoid each other. For example, people say *brag about something* but not *brag up something* nor *brag something up*.

For further information on collocations, see chapter 5 of Barnbrook's *Languages and Computers* [9]. In addition, see section A10.2 of *Corpus-Based Language Studies* by McEnery et al. [78]. In the latter, on page 81, the authors note that native speaker intuition about collocations is not that reliable. Hence there is a need for analyzing language data.

Before we analyze collocations, the next section extends the sorting capabilities of the concordance program used above. It shows how to replace code sample 6.4 with functions that can sort the concordance lines by the words near the regex match instead of the regex match itself.

6.5.1   More Ways to Sort Concordance Lines

This section shows how to sort concordance lines by the words neighboring the regex matches. For example, suppose the regex matches *up*, then sorting by the words that appear immediately to the left produces output 6.7. This helps identify potential collocations.

Doing this requires a function that takes a concordance line and returns the word that is a specified distance away from the regex match. For example, in output 6.7, a function that returns the word to the left of *up* is used with `sort` to order the lines. This requires a few steps. First, take the characters up to but not including the match. Since `$radius` has the number of characters the come before (and after) the match, this is easy to do. Second, use `removePunctuation` given in code sample 6.3. Third, split the result into an array of words. Fourth, pick the last word of this array, which is the closest to *up*.

Output 6.7 Ten concordance lines from *The Call of the Wild* with the word *up*. These are sorted in alphabetical order of the word immediately to the left of *up*.

```
 1  heem chew dat Spitz all up an' spit heem out on de
 2 across his shoulders and up his neck, till he whimpe
 3  at it again.  He backed up Spitz with his whip, whi
 4  whip, while Buck backed up the remainder of the tea
 5 ond day saw them booming up the Yukon well on their
 6  was the pride that bore up Spitz and made him thras
 7 not like it, but he bore up well to the work, taking
 8 ed in to the bank bottom up, while Thornton, flung s
 9  boats against the break-up of the ice in the spring
10 eek bed, till he brought up against a high gravel ba
```

The general case is no more difficult. Let $ordinal be the number of words to go to the left. For example, setting $ordinal to 1 corresponds to output 6.7. Each of four lines of Perl code in code sample 6.7 corresponds to the four steps in the last paragraph. Remember that a negative index counts from the end of the array, for example, $word[-1] is the last entry.

Code Sample 6.7 A function that returns a word to the left of the regex match in a concordance line.

```
sub onLeft {
  # USAGE: $word = onLeft($string, $radius, $ordinal);
  my $left = substr($_[0], 0, $_[1]);
  $left = removePunctuation($left);
  my @word = split(/\s+/, $left);
  return($word[-$_[2]]);
}
```

With the function onLeft, defining an order is easy. Use it to select the word, which is changed to lowercase, then sort these using cmp. This is done in code sample 6.8.

Code Sample 6.8 An ordering for sort. It uses the function onLeft defined in code sample 6.7.

```
sub byLeftWords {
  my $left_a = onLeft($a, $radius, $ordinal);
  my $left_b = onLeft($b, $radius, $ordinal);
  lc($left_a) cmp lc($left_b);
}
```

The same logic applies to sorting on words to the right of the match. The function onRight and the ordering byRightWords are both shown in code sample 6.9.

With program 6.1 and the above code samples, there are only two details left. First, code sample 6.10 prints out the results. Second, set $ordinal to $ARGV[2].

Code Sample 6.9 Subroutines to sort concordance lines by a word to the right of the match.

```
sub onRight {
  # USAGE: $word = onRight($string, $radius, $ordinal);
  my $right = substr($_[0], -$_[1]);
  $right = removePunctuation($right);
  $right =~ s/^\s+//;        # Remove initial space
  my @word = split(/\s+/, $right);
  return($word[$_[2]-1]);
}

sub byRightWords {
  my $right_a = onRight($a, $radius, $ordinal);
  my $right_b = onRight($b, $radius, $ordinal);
  lc($right_a) cmp lc($right_b);
}
```

Code Sample 6.10 Commands to print out the sorted concordance lines.

```
$line_number = 0;
foreach $x (sort byLeftWords @lines) {
  ++$line_number;
  printf "%5d", $line_number;
  print " $x\n";
}

$line_number = 0;
foreach $x (sort byRightWords @lines) {
  ++$line_number;
  printf "%5d", $line_number;
  print " $x\n";
}
```

By putting code samples 6.7, 6.8, 6.9, and 6.10 together with program 6.1, we have a concordance program able to sort by words near the regex match. This produces output 6.7. The next section shows some applications.

6.5.2 Application: Phrasal Verbs in *The Call of the Wild*

Let us apply the programming of the last section to phrasal verbs. Our first task is to recreate output 6.7, and all the pieces are in place.

Start with program 6.1 and add removePunctuation defined in code sample 6.3. Second, add code sample 6.7, which defines the subroutine onLeft. This is used by the subroutine byLeftWords in code sample 6.8, which defines the ordering of the concordance lines. Finally, the first foreach loop of code sample 6.10 prints out the sorted results.

Combining the above parts into one file and running it produces output 6.7. There are 104 total lines, so it is convenient to summarize these by listing the words that appear immediately to the left of *up*, along with their frequencies. By using code sample 3.26, these frequencies are sorted in descending order. Putting code sample 6.11 at the end of the code described in the preceding paragraph produces output 6.8 (words appearing once are not shown.)

Code Sample 6.11 Code to print out the sorted frequencies of words to the left of the match. This uses code sample 3.26.

```
$line_number = 0;
foreach $x (sort byLeftWords @lines) {
  ++$line_number;
  printf "%5d", $line_number;
  print " $x\n";
  ++$dict{onLeft($x, $radius, $ordinal)};
}

print "\n\n";
foreach $x (sort byDescendingValues keys %dict) {
  print "$x, $dict{$x}\n";
}
```

Output 6.8 Frequencies of the words immediately to the left of *up* in *The Call of the Wild*.

```
get, 8
him, 4
harness-, 3
straight, 3
went, 3
backed, 2
bore, 2
curled, 2
it, 2
made, 2
picked, 2
team, 2
took, 2
```

This output contains more than verbs. Looking at the concordance lines reveals the reason for this. For example, lines 41, 43, and 44 are all phrasal verbs where *him* is between the verb and the preposition. However, in line 42 *up* is part of the prepositional phrase *up to Buck* as shown in the quote of the entire sentence.

> At another time Spitz went through, dragging the whole team after him up to Buck, who strained backward with all his strength, his fore paws on the slippery edge and the ice quivering and snapping all around.

While sorting on the word immediately to the left of *up* is certainly helpful in finding phrasal verbs, intervening words cause problems. Even if words were labeled by their part

Output 6.9 The four concordance lines with *him up*, which are counted in output 6.8.

```
41 ancois's whip backed him up, Buck found it to be che
42 the whole team after him up to Buck, who strained ba
43 s. Francois followed him up, whereupon he again retr
44 rior weight, and cut him up till he ceased snapping
```

of speech (see section 9.2.4 for a way to do this), finding the first verb to the left can fail as shown in the above sentence.

Clearly, creating a fully automated phrasal verb finder is difficult. However, by combining a concordance program with a human, shorter texts like a novel are analyzable.

Phrasal verbs can be studied by analyzing the words that come after a verb. In fact, there are dictionaries that do this such as *NTC's Dictionary of Phrasal Verbs and Other Idiomatic Verbal Phrases* [111]. The subroutines onRight and byRightWords in place of onLeft and byLeftWords, respectively, perform this task.

As an example, output 6.3 is redone so that the lines are sorted into alphabetical order by the first word after the verb *sprang*. The complete results are in output 6.10.

Output 6.10 Concordance lines sorted by the word after *sprang* in *The Call of the Wild*.

```
 1             The dogs sprang against the breast-bands
 2 ng, and when the two men sprang among them with stout cl
 3 r-holes formed, fissures sprang and spread apart, while
 4 reath.  In quick rage he sprang at the man, who met him
 5 a frenzy to destroy.  He sprang at the foremost man (it
 6 the yelp of the pack and sprang away into the woods.  Th
 7 thing very like mud.  He sprang back with a snort.  More
 8 gled under his feet.  He sprang back, bristling and snar
 9  kidnapped king. The man sprang for his throat, but Buck
10           One night he sprang from sleep with a start,
11 ending death.  Then Buck sprang in and out; but while he
12 ristling with fear, then sprang straight for Buck. He ha
13  terrified into bravery, sprang through the savage circl
14  sound heard before.  He sprang through the sleeping cam
15 imes during the night he sprang to his feet when the she
16 the first meal.  As Buck sprang to punish him, the lash
17 . And when, released, he sprang to his feet, his mouth l
18 ke an electric shock, He sprang to his feet and ran up t
19  general insubordination sprang up and increased. Dave a
20  beast in him roared. He sprang upon Spitz with a fury w
21 Spitz's opportunity.  He sprang upon Buck, and twice his
22 at this open mutiny, and sprang upon his overthrown lead
23 forgotten code, likewise sprang upon Spitz.  But Francoi
24 best lead-dog left. Buck sprang upon Sol-leks in a fury,
25 an animal, John Thornton sprang upon the man who wielded
26 uck dashed into camp and sprang upon him in a frenzy of
```

By inspection, *sprang upon* is the most common preposition (lines 21–26) followed by *sprang to* (lines 15–18). As noted above, collocations should occur higher than chance. For example, equation 6.4 should hold for the suspected collocation *sprang upon*.

$$P(\text{sprang upon}) > P(\text{sprang})P(\text{upon}) \tag{6.4}$$

The output shows *sprang* occurs 26 times, and it is easy to check with the concordance program that *upon* occurs 79 times. The total number of words in the novel is 31,830, so by equation 4.2, equation 6.5 shows that *sprang upon* is a collocation because the left-hand side equals 0.00022, which is much bigger than the right-hand side of 0.00000203.

$$P(\text{sprang upon}) = \frac{7}{31,830} > \frac{26}{31,830} \times \frac{79}{31,830} = P(\text{sprang})P(\text{upon}) \tag{6.5}$$

Although *sprung upon* is a collocation for *the Call of the Wild*, this may or may not be true for other texts. For example, the same analysis for *Frankenstein* gives equation 6.6. Here the left hand side is zero, so it is certainly not bigger than the right hand side. So for this text, *sprung upon* is not a collocation. In retrospect, that a story about the adventures of a dog contains many scenes of springing upon objects is not a surprise.

$$P(\text{sprang upon}) = \frac{0}{75,065} < \frac{4}{75,065} \times \frac{126}{75,065} = P(\text{sprang})P(\text{upon}) \tag{6.6}$$

Unfortunately, the zero count of *spring upon* in *Frankenstein* is all too common. The next section comments on this phenomenon.

6.5.3 Grouping Words: Colors in *The Call of the Wild*

Counts from texts can vary by large amounts. For example, output 4.2 counts letters in *A Christmas Carol*, and *e* occurs 14,869 times while *z* appears only 84. Zipf's law (see section 3.7.1) shows the same phenomenon with words, for example, in *The Call of the Wild*, *the* appears 2274 times, but about half the words appear exactly once.

Unfortunately, analyzing linguistic objects two at a time when many of them are rare often produces zero counts, which are hard to work with. For example, program 4.4 analyzes letter bigrams, and finds that roughly a third of the possibilities do not appear at all.

If letter bigrams are rare, then the situation is only worse with more complex combinations. What can a researcher do? This section considers analyzing groups of words together. For example, this includes lemmas, which consists of all the inflected forms of a word.

But grouping need not stop here. Instead of considering just one lemma, create a group of related lemmas. For example, instead of analyzing the use of the adjective *red* (along with the comparative forms *redder* and *reddest*), analyze color words as a group, which is done below with *The Call of the Wild*.

To do this, a list of such words is needed, but a thesaurus has this type of information, and both the *Moby Thesaurus* [122] and *Roget's Thesaurus* [107] exist online and are in the public domain.

Looking at sections 430–439 in *Roget's Thesaurus* [107], numerous color words are listed. Selecting the more common ones produces the following list: white, black, gray, silver, brown, red, pink, green, blue, yellow, purple, violet, and orange. One group of these words have the form *noun-colored*, for example, sulfur-colored. Some of the words have multiple meanings and are left out, for example, *yolk*. To find each word of a group, alternation works, as shown below.

```
\b(white|black|red|...|orange)
```

Finally, running the concordance program produces output 6.11, which shows the first 12 lines out of a total of 61. The most common color is *white* with 21 instances, then *red* with 14 instances. Hence this strategy worked because 61 lines is at least 3 times as frequent as any particular color in *The Call of the Wild*.

Output 6.11 Color words in *The Call of the Wild*. The first 12 lines out of 61 are shown.

```
 1 ult and turned over to a black-faced giant called Franc
 2 emonstrative, was a huge black dog, half bloodhound and
 3 ensions were realized.  "Black" Burton, a man evil-temp
 4 l wood moss, or into the black soil where long grasses
 5 stream he killed a large black bear, blinded by the mos
 6 eir backs, rafted across blue mountain lakes, and desc
 7 ious.  But for the stray brown on his muzzle and above
 8 re seen with splashes of brown on head and muzzle, and
 9  a middle-aged, lightish-colored man, with weak and water
10  the dark, and the first gray of dawn found them hitti
11 ne only he saw,--a sleek gray fellow, flattened agains
12 low, flattened against a gray dead limb so that he see
```

However, words are not the only lexical items that are analyzable with this technique. As noted in section 6.4.3, morphological structures are detectable by regexes, for example, analyzing adverbs ending in *-ly* as done earlier in this chapter. But there are many other grammatical forms, for example, gerunds, which are verb forms ending in *-ing* that can be used as nouns or adjectives, such as *running is an exercise* or *there is a running cat*.

Furthermore, there is a Perl module that can identify parts of speech, which is discussed in section 9.2.4. Using this, patterns involving types of words are possible, for example, finding two adjectives in a row.

The next section gives a number of references, which contain many examples. These provide many further ideas well suited for programming in Perl.

6.6 APPLICATIONS WITH REFERENCES

Much work has been done in corpus linguistics, and there are many examples in the academic literature of using concordancing techniques to analyze one or more texts. This section lists a few of these for the interested reader to pursue.

First, section 2.6 of Douglas Biber, Susan Conrad, and Randi Reppen's *Corpus Linguistics* [11], compares words that seem synonymous. This is essential for the lexicographer who needs to find all the different shades of meaning, and it can be used to investigate grammar, as well as how grammar interacts with words.

Specifically, section 2.6 analyzes the adjectives *big*, *large*, and *great*. Grammatically, these seem interchangeable, however, there are a variety of restrictions on how these are used. This analysis by Biber et al. has similarities with section 106 of *Practical English Usage* [114], and perhaps there is a link between these.

Section 3.2 of Biber et al. [11] gives another example of how concordancing gives insight into language. The authors study the distributional properties of nominalizations among registers. These are a way to form new nouns by adding an ending to existing words. For example, *nominalization* is a noun formed from the verb *nominalize* by adding *-tion* (plus a vowel change). As long as there are a reasonable number of well-defined patterns, finding these can be done by regexes.

In general, Biber et al. [11] is an excellent book for anyone interested in quantitative analysis of corpora. It has many practical examples and is quite readable. Another great book is *Corpora in Applied Linguistics* by Susan Hunston [59]. She gives numerous interesting examples of searching corpora for a variety of word patterns. For example, she defines a *frame* as three words in a row where the first and third are fixed, but the second is arbitrary. She lists several examples on page 49. But converting this pattern to a regex is straightforward, as shown in the example below (which ignores punctuation).

```
$word1 \b(\w+)\b $word2
```

Language teaching is another application of concordancing. At present, many people across the world want to take English as a Second Language (ESL) classes. This has increased the need for language references designed for nonnative speakers. In particular, learner dictionaries specifically for ESL students have been influenced by corpus linguistics. One key idea is ranking words in the order of frequency, which has been done several times in this book, for example, see table 6.2 or section 3.7.1.

Giant corpora have been developed to study language. The Cambridge International Corpus (CIC) is used by the language reference books published by Cambridge University Press [25]. An example of a dictionary using frequency information from the CIC is the *Cambridge Advanced Learner's Dictionary* (CALD) [121]. This book has three labels to broadly indicate how common a word is, for example, a word given as *essential* usually has a rate of more than 40 per million words.

Unfortunately, the CIC is proprietary, but a frequency analysis is done easily for any text available in electronic form. For example, if an ESL student wants to read *The Call of the Wild*, then table 6.2 is useful.

For more on using corpus linguistics for teaching, see chapters 6, 7 and 8 of Hunston [59]. These give concrete examples of how to apply this to teaching. The use of two language corpora is also discussed, for example, the French-English parallel corpus of *Le Petit Prince/The Little Prince* (a French novel by Antoine de Saint Exupéry).

An excellent book on language instruction is I. S. P. Nation's *Learning Vocabulary in Another Language* [80]. The focus of this book is how to teach vocabulary, and right away it addresses quantitative questions involving word frequencies. For example, chapter 1 starts off discussing how many words a student should know. Implicit in this question is the idea that a core vocabulary needs to include the highest frequency words. Finally, this book has many ideas of interest to the corpus linguist, for example, chapter 7 discusses principal components analysis.

Finally, *stylometry* is the analysis of one or more texts to determine quantitative measures indicative of the author's style. Although literary critics and historians have long done this by analyzing historical evidence along with close readings of the texts in question, stylometry is usually associated with computer analyses that look at a large number of variables. These are split into two types: first, textual features that are probably unconscious habits of the author; second, features which the author consciously tries to manipulate.

Some researchers prefer working with the first type. For example, an author probably does not consciously think about his or her use of function words. So the rate of usage of *up* probably reflects a writer's habitual style.

A famous example in the statistical literature is Frederick Mosteller and David Wallace's book *Applied Bayesian and Classical Inference: The Case of the Federalist Papers* [79]. Here the authors try to determine who wrote 12 disputed (at the time) texts among the *Federalist Papers*, which are a series of newspaper articles arguing that New York should ratify the United States constitution. This makes a great example because it is acknowledged that either James Madison or Alexander Hamilton wrote these 12 papers, so an analysis only needs to decide between these two. Moreover, both have many other written documents that are available for determining the writing style of each.

Mosteller and Wallace's analysis is detailed and thoughtful, and much attention is given to checking the assumptions of the statistical models used. The details are best left to their book, but note that much of their analysis focuses on finding function words that do a good job of distinguishing between Madison and Hamilton. Since the *Federalist Papers* are a joint effort (with John Jay), each author might have consciously tried to write in a common style. Hence it is important to focus on stylistic markers that were probably unconscious habits.

However, as a human reader, this type of analysis is not satisfying. For example, a person, asked why he or she enjoys *The Call of the Wild* does not mention the usage of the preposition *up* but instead discusses the exciting plot, how dogs think, and so forth.

Perhaps to reflect the reader's perspective, some researchers have measured textual characteristics that an author is certainly aware of and perhaps is trying to manipulate consciously. We consider one example of this.

In 1939 G. Udny Yule published an analysis of sentence lengths in *Biometrika* [128], which are analyzed to distinguish a pair of writers. Like Mosteller and Wallace, Yule is a statistician, so his analysis discusses the statistical issues involved. Finally, he applied his analysis to two texts with disputed authorships: *De Imitatione Christi* and *Observations upon the Bills of Mortality*. Sentence lengths are clearly something an author does think about, and it is believable that some writers might prefer different length sentences, on average.

On the whole, although a number of stylometric analyses have been done, the methods in print tend not to generalize well to other texts. For a great overview of this topic along with numerous examples, see Chapter 5 ("Literary Detective Work") of Michael Oakes' *Statistics for Corpus Linguistics* [82]. Also see the articles by Binongo and Smith [16] and Holmes, Gordon, and Wilson [57].

6.7 SECOND TRANSITION

We have reached a second transition in this book. Up to this point, the level of the statistics and mathematics is quite modest. The next two chapters, however, introduce topics that require a little more mathematical knowledge, although this is kept to a minimum. The emphasis is still on applications and practical problems, and the ideas behind the mathematics are explained.

In addition, the free statistical package R, which is introduced in section 5.5.1, is used to do calculations in chapters 7 and 8. The R code is explained, but like Perl, only certain parts are used in this book. If this taste of R piques your interest, there are free tutorials and documentation on the Web at `http://cran.r-project.org/`.

PROBLEMS

6.1   Voter registration lists are created by town clerks and registrars of voters, many of which exist, so much so that the task of obtaining all of them requires effort. This work load can be reduced by performing two stages of sampling. The first is a simple random sample of precincts, and the second is a simple random sample of registered voters within each precinct.

Is this a good idea for text sampling? For example, suppose that a researcher creates a list of different types of texts. Then picking a random subset of these types is the first stage of sampling. Then for each type, a random sample of texts is selected (say from a library catalog). It turns out that this design has been used.

The *Brown Corpus Manual* [46] describes the details of how the Brown corpus was created. In section 1, it says that the sampling design does have two phases. While the first phase (or stage) consists of picking categories of text, it says this is done subjectively using expert judgment as opposed to random selection. How does this compare to using a random selection of topics? Is one or the other technique superior? Once you have thought about this, go online and find this manual (the URL is in the bibliography) and compare your thoughts to the actual design details used.

6.2   Table 6.2 contains the word counts for Shelley's *Frankenstein* and London's *The Call of the Wild*. Using the programs in this chapter, recompute the word frequencies of these two novels, and compare your results to this table.

Now do the same task with a novel of your own choosing. When you compute your counts, how might these be checked?

6.3   Shelley's novel, *Frankenstein*, is analyzed using a concordance program in the book *Language and Computers* by Geoff Barnbrook [9]. For example, he points out that the monster created by Victor Frankenstein has no name, but he is referred to by a variety of terms.

For this problem, think about how one might try to find the words that refer to the monster in *Frankenstein*. Then check chapters 3 and 4 of Barnbrook's book to see how he analyzes this novel. With the concordancing programs developed in this chapter, you can reproduce his results for yourself. Moreover, his book has many additional text analyses to try.

6.4   Table 6.1 can be created by mimicking either program 4.3 or program 5.1. Using these as a model, create a program that counts the character frequencies of a file where the name of the file is put on the command line as follows.

```
perl character_frequencies.pl text.txt
```

6.5   Type in the Perl code for program 6.1 with code samples 6.2, 6.3, and 6.4. Once this runs, do the following problems.

   a) Table 6.1 reveals that there are underscores in the EnronSent corpus. Find out all the ways these are used. Note that many underscores in a row occur in this text.

   b) Table 6.1 reveals that square brackets are used in the EnronSent corpus. Find out how these are used. Were they all typed by the authors of the emails? Finally, remember that a square bracket has special meaning in a regex.

   c) Table 6.1 reveals that there are parentheses in the EnronSent corpus. How are these used?

   d) Find all the words with the character @ in the EnronSent corpus, and see how they are used. Since these are emails, one use is easy to guess.

6.6   In section 6.4.3, the form of adverbs is explored. For this problem try the suggestion given at the end of this section of removing the `not` in the `if` statement of code sample 6.5. Examine the resulting output to estimate the proportion of adverbs. Output 6.12 shows the first few words.

Output 6.12 Ten lines of output from the suggested adverb analysis in problem 6.6.

```
abasedly abdominally abjectly abnormally aborally
abrasively abruptly absently absentmindedly absolutely
absorbingly abstemiously abstractly abstrusely absurdly
abundantly abusively abysmally accidentally accordingly
accurately achingly acidly acoustically acquiescently
acridly actively actually acutely adamantly addedly
additionally adeptly adequately adjectivally
administratively admiringly admittedly adroitly adultly
advantageously adventitiously aerially aerodynamically
aeronautically affectedly affectingly affectionately
```

6.7   In code sample 6.9, why is `$word[$_[2]-1]` returned instead of `$word[$_[2]]`?

6.8   In section 2.2.2, the problem of finding phone numbers is discussed. The EnronSent corpus includes many of these as well as various other numbers, for example, ZIP codes, dates, times, prices, and addresses.

  a) Write a regex to find U.S. style phone numbers. In this corpus many styles are used. For example, there are company phone numbers that start with x and just give the last five digits. There are seven-digit phone numbers, as well as ones with area codes, and ones that start with the U.S. country code +1. Many numbers use dashes, but some use spaces or periods.

  b) How do you check how accurate your regex is? One idea is to run a promising regex and save the results. Then run a less restrictive regex that matches many more patterns, and then check if among the extra matches there are patterns overlooked by the promising regex.

  For example, to test a phone number regex, a pattern like `\d{3}\D\d{4}` is useful since it should match most numbers. However, there are false positives, for example, ZIP+4 codes. Applying this to the EnronSent corpus, what other false positives are there? Also, does it match all U.S. style numbers? What broader regex can be used to check this?

6.9   Adjectives have comparative and superlative forms. These are not quite straightforward because there are irregular forms and differences depending on the number of syllables in the adjective. See section 236c and sections 460 through 464 of the *Cambridge Grammar of English* [26] for more details.

For this problem, find a book on grammar and look up the rules for making comparative forms of adjectives. Write a Perl program that finds some of these. Remember that many words end in *-er* and *-est* that are not adjectives such as *reader* and *pest*. Remember that some adjectives use the words *more* and *most*. Finally, making a program that produces no errors is a monumental task, so part of the challenge of this problem is to decide on how much error is tolerable.

CHAPTER 7

MULTIVARIATE TECHNIQUES WITH TEXT

7.1 INTRODUCTION

Data is collected by taking measurements. These are often unpredictable, for one of two reasons. First, there is measurement error, and, second, the objects measured can be randomly selected as discussed in section 6.2. Random variables can model either type of unpredictability.

Text mining often analyzes multiple texts. For example, there are 68 Edgar Allan Poe short stories, all of which are of interest to a literary critic. A more extreme example is a researcher analyzing the EnronSent corpus. This has about a 100 megabytes of text, which translates into a vast number of emails.

Hence, a text miner often has many variables to analyze simultaneously. There are a number of techniques for this situation, which are collectively called *multivariate* statistics. This chapter introduces one of these, principal components analysis (PCA).

This chapter focuses on applications, and some of the key ideas of PCA are introduced. The goal is not to explain all the details, but to give some idea about how it works, and how to apply it to texts. Specifically, 68 Poe short stories are analyzed. These are from a five volume collected work that is in the public domain and is available online ([96], [97], [98], [99] and [100]).

These 68 stories are "The Unparalleled Adventures of One Hans Pfaall," "The Gold Bug," "Four Beasts in One," "The Murders in the Rue Morgue," "The Mystery of Marie Rogêt," "The Balloon Hoax," "MS. Found in a Bottle," "The Oval Portrait," "The Purloined Letter," "The Thousand-and-Second Tale of Scheherezade," "A Descent into the Maelström,"

"Von Kempelen and His Discovery," "Mesmeric Revelation," "The Facts in the Case of M. Valdemar," "The Black Cat," "The Fall of the House of Usher," "Silence – a Fable," "The Masque of the Red Death," "The Cask of Amontillado," "The Imp of the Perverse," "The Island of the Fay," "The Assignation," "The Pit and the Pendulum," "The Premature Burial," "The Domain of Arnheim," "Landor's Cottage," "William Wilson," "The Tell-Tale Heart," "Berenice," "Eleonora," "Ligeia," "Morella," "A Tale of the Ragged Mountains," "The Spectacles," "King Pest," "Three Sundays in a Week," "The Devil in the Belfry," "Lionizing," "X-ing a Paragrab," "Metzengerstein," "The System of Doctor Tarr and Professor Fether," "How to Write a Blackwood Article," "A Predicament," "Mystification," "Diddling," "The Angel of the Odd," "Mellonia Tauta," "The Duc de l'Omlette," "The Oblong Box," "Loss of Breath," "The Man That Was Used Up," "The Business Man," "The Landscape Garden," "Maelzel's Chess-Player," "The Power of Words," "The Colloquy of Monas and Una," "The Conversation of Eiros and Charmion," "Shadow – A Parable," "Philosophy of Furniture," "A Tale of Jerusalem," "The Sphinx," "Hop Frog," "The Man of the Crowd," "Never Bet the Devil Your Head," "Thou Art the Man," "Why the Little Frenchman Wears His Hand in a Sling," "Bon-Bon," and "Some Words with a Mummy." Although "The Literary Life of Thingum Bob, Esq." is listed in the contents of Volume 4, it is not in any of the five volumes.

These 68 stories are used as is except for the following. First, all the footnotes are removed except for the story "The Unparalleled Adventures of One Hans Pfaall," where Poe discusses other moon tales. Second, the XML tags <TITLE> and </TITLE> are placed around each story title. Third, each story has a notice marking the end of it, and these are removed.

The next section starts with some simpler statistical ideas that are needed for PCA. Fortunately, the amount of mathematics and statistics needed is not as much as one might fear.

7.2   BASIC STATISTICS

Section 4.4 introduces the mean and variance of a random variable as well as the sample mean and sample standard deviation of a data set. It is pointed out that these are easiest to interpret if the data has a bell shape (that is, the population is approximately a normal distribution). For an example, see figure 4.4.

Since language is generative, any group of texts can be considered a sample from a large population of potential texts. For example, Poe wrote about 68 short stories in his lifetime, but if he lived longer (he died at age 40) he would have written more. Undoubtably, he probably had many other ideas for stories, which he might have written given different circumstances such as if he were more financially successful during his life. Hence, we focus on sample statistics.

Suppose a data set has the values $x_1, x_2, ..., x_n$, where n represents the sample size. The sample mean is given in equation 7.1.

$$\overline{X} = \frac{1}{n} \sum_{i=1}^{n} x_i \qquad (7.1)$$

For bell-shaped data, the sample mean is a typical value of this data set. But the shape of the data set is an important consideration; for example, if the histogram of a data set is bimodal (has two peaks), the mean can be atypical.

Equation 7.2 for the sample variance is more complex. Note that the sum is divided by $n-1$, not n, so this is not quite a mean of the squared terms in the sum. However, if n is large, $n-1$ is close to n.

$$s_x^2 = \frac{1}{n-1} \sum_{i=1}^{n} (x_i - \overline{X})^2 \qquad (7.2)$$

The sample variance is a measure of the variability of the data. Thinking in terms of histograms, generally the wider the histogram, the more variable the data, and the least variable data set has all its values the same. In fact, no variability implies that s_x^2 equals zero. Conversely, if s_x^2 is zero, then every data value is the same. See problem 7.1 for an argument why this is true.

Note that s_x^2 measures the variability about $\overline{X}$. Equation 7.2 implies this is true because the only way x_i can contribute to s_x^2 is if it differs from $\overline{X}$. Note that if x_i is less than $\overline{X}$, this difference is negative, but squaring it makes a positive contribution. Other functions can be used to make all these differences nonnegative, for example, the absolute value. However, squaring has theoretical advantages; for example, it is easy to differentiate, which makes it easier to optimize sums of squares than, say, sums of absolute values.

For data analysis, the square root of the variance, s_x, is used, which is called the sample standard deviation. Note that $\overline{X}$ and s_x have the same units as the data set. For example, if the data consists of sentence lengths in terms of word counts, then $\overline{X}$ and s_x are word counts. If the data were sentence lengths in letter counts, then $\overline{X}$ and s_x are letter counts. Note that variance is in squared units. For example, the variance of a data set of times measured in seconds (s) is a number with units s^2, or seconds squared. The next section describes an important application of the sample mean and sample standard deviation.

7.2.1 *z*-Scores Applied to Poe

A *z-score* is a way to compute how a data value compares to a data set. It converts this value to a number, which is *dimensionless*, that is, there are no units of measurement left. Specifically, it measures the number of standard deviations a value is from the mean of its data set.

The formula for the *z*-score of x is given in equation 7.3. Since both the numerator and denominator have the same units, these cancel out.

$$z = \frac{x - \overline{X}}{s_x} \qquad (7.3)$$

As an example, we compute *z*-scores for word lengths of the 68 Poe short stories. In programming, once a task works for one particular example, it is often straightforward to apply it to numerous examples.

For computing $\overline{X}$, only a running count and sum are needed. Equation 7.2 for the sample standard deviation, however, requires knowing $\overline{X}$ first, so a program using it needs to go through the text twice. However, there is an equivalent form of this equation that only requires a running sum of the squares of the values. This is given in equation 7.4.

$$s_x^2 = \frac{\sum_{i=1}^{n} x_i^2 - \left(\sum_{i=1}^{n} x_i\right)^2 / n}{n-1} \qquad (7.4)$$

The words are identified by code sample 7.1, which removes the punctuation. Note that any apostrophes that start or end the word are removed. For instance, *Excellencies'pleasure* loses its apostrophe, which is not the case with *friend's equanimity*. However, the challenge of correctly identifying possessive nouns ending in *-s* is greater than the payoff, so it is not done. Compare this with program 5.2, which analyzes four Poe stories.

Code Sample 7.1 This code removes punctuation, counts words, and computes word lengths for each Poe story.

```
open (IN, "Poe5Volumes.txt") or die;

$nstory = -1;
while (<IN>) {
  chomp;
  if ( $_ =~ /<TITLE> *(.*) *<\/TITLE>/ ) {
    $name[++$nstory] = $1;
    print "$1\n";
  } else {
    $_ = lc;           # Convert to lower case
    s/{\*\d+}//g;      # Remove footnote symbols
    s/--+/ /g;         # Remove multiple hyphens
    s/(\W)-(\W)/$1$2/g; # Remove single hyphen dashes
    s/^-(\W)/$1/g;
    s/(\W)-$/$1/g;
    s/ +/ /g;          # Replace multiple spaces with one space
    s/[.,:;?"!_()*\[\]]//g; # Remove punctuation
    s/(\w)\'(\W)/$1$2/g; # Remove non-internal single quotes
    s/(\W)\'(\w)/$1$2/g;
    s/^\'//g;
    s/\'$//g;

    @words = split;
    foreach $word (@words) {
      ++$dict[$nstory]{$word}; # Word counts for each story
      ++$combined{$word};      # Overall word counts
      ++$len[$nstory][length($word)]; # Word lengths tallied
    }
  }
}
```

Code sample 7.2 uses the array of arrays @len of code sample 7.1 to compute the mean, variance, and standard deviation of the word lengths for the 68 Poe short stories. Note that the first for statement loops through all the stories, and the second one loops through all the words in each story. As claimed above, by using equation 7.4, only one pass through all the words is needed.

By adding code sample 7.2 to the end of code sample 7.1, the result produces 68 lines of output. Each has the following form, where the first number is the length of the story in words, the second is the sample mean, the third is the sample variance, and the fourth is the sample standard deviation.

```
THE GOLD-BUG, 13615, 4.305, 6.135, 2.477
```

Code Sample 7.2 Code to compute the sample mean, sample variance, and sample standard deviation for each Poe story. To run, append this to code sample 7.1.

```
for ($index=0; $index <= $#len; ++$index) {
   $n = 0;
   $sum = 0;
   $sum2 = 0;
   for ($value=1; $value <=  @{$len[$index]}-1; ++$value) {
      $n += $len[$index][$value];
      $sum += $len[$index][$value]*$value;
      $sum2 += $len[$index][$value]*$value**2;
   }
   $mean = $sum/$n;    # Compute sample mean
   $var = $sum2/($n-1) - $n/($n-1)*$mean**2;   # Variance
   $sd = sqrt($var);   # Compute sample standard deviation
   printf "%s, %5.0f, %.3f, %.3f, %.3f\n",
           $name[$index], $n, $mean, $var, $sd;
}
```

With these means and standard deviations, it is possible to compute z-scores of any word length for each story. Let us do this for a four-letter word. The z-score of 4 for "The Gold-Bug" is given in equation 7.5.

$$z = \frac{4 - 4.305}{2.477} = -0.123 \tag{7.5}$$

This means that for "The Gold-Bug," a word length of 4 is 0.123 standard deviations below the mean. This varies from story to story. The extreme z-scores are -0.0100 for "Why the Little Frenchman Wears His Hand in a Sling" and -0.3225 for "Metzengerstein." So four-letter words are all slightly below average for all the stories.

Although z-scores are computable for any data set, it is easier to interpret for approximately bell-shaped data. However, word lengths are not symmetric around the mean: there are fewer values less than the mean than are greater than it. For example, see output 3.4 for "The Tale-Tell Heart." This data shape is called *right skewed*. Nonetheless, there is only one peak; that is, it is *unimodal*. In addition, the longest word has 14 letters, so there are no extremely long words in this story. For such data, z-scores can still be useful.

Although z-scores are valuable themselves, they are also useful in computing correlations. This is the topic of the next section.

7.2.2   Word Correlations among Poe's Short Stories

For comparing two variables, units are a problem. For example, how should a physicist compare masses and times? One solution is to convert both variables to z-scores, and then compare these.

Another solution is the sample correlation coefficient. Equation 7.6 shows how to compute this, and notice that it is almost the mean of the product of the z-scores of each data value.

$$r = \frac{1}{n-1} \sum_{i=1}^{n} \frac{x_i - \overline{X}}{s_x} \frac{y_i - \overline{Y}}{s_y} \tag{7.6}$$

Correlations are used in a variety of statistical techniques, including PCA. It can be proved that the correlation r must satisfy equation 7.7.

$$-1 \leq r \leq 1 \tag{7.7}$$

Both $r = 1$ and $r = -1$ constrain the data to lie on a line when plotted. That is, both require that one variable is a linear function of the other. When $r = 1$, this has a positive slope, and $r = -1$ implies a negative slope. When $r = 0$, there is no linear relationship between the two variables. However, for all values of r, nonlinear relationships are possible.

For the first example, we analyze the frequencies of some common function words in each of the 68 Poe stories. It is likely that these counts are roughly proportional to the size of each story. If this is true, then these counts are positively correlated.

One way to detect a trend in the data is to plot two variables at a time in a scatter plot, which we do in R. Because this requires reading the data into R, it makes sense to have it compute the correlations, too, instead of programming Perl to do so. Although equation 7.6 is not that complicated, it is still easier to let a statistical software package do the work.

Code sample 7.3 computes a term-document matrix when it is combined with code sample 7.1. The open statement stores this matrix in the comma-separated file, Poe68.csv, which is sorted by the word frequencies of all 68 stories combined. Since this is a large file with 68 columns and over 20,000 rows, we consider just the top five words: *the, of, and, a,* and *to*. For how this is done in code sample 7.3, see problem 7.2.

Reading Poe68.csv into R is done with read.csv(). Remember that the greater than character is the command prompt for this package. The first argument is the filename, and note that a double backslash for the file location is needed. The second argument, header=T means that the first row contains the variable names.

The values are stored in data, which is called a *data frame*. The name data refers to the entire data set, and each variable within it is accessible by appending a dollar sign to this name, then adding the column name. For example, the counts for the word *the* are in data$the.

```
> data = read.csv("C:\\Poe68.csv", header=T)
```

The cor() function computes the correlations as shown in output 7.1. These are organized in a five by five table. Each entry on the main diagonal is 1, which must be true because any variable equals itself, which is a linear function with positive slope.

This matrix of correlations is symmetric about the main diagonal. For example, the correlation between *of* and *the* is the same as the correlation between *the* and *of*. So this matrix can be summarized by a triangular table of values. However, there are mathematical reasons to use the full matrix, which are discussed in section 7.3.

Looking at the off-diagonal values, all the correlations are above 0.90, which are large. Using the function pairs(), the positive trends are easily seen in figure 7.1, even though each individual plot is small.

```
> pairs(data, pch='.')
```

In figure 7.2, the counts of *of* and *the* are compared in one plot. In addition, the optimal prediction line is drawn. Output 7.2 gives the R commands to create both the plot and this line, which is called the *regression line*.

Code Sample 7.3 Creating a transposed term-document matrix for the 68 Poe stories and 5 most frequent words. This uses @dict from code sample 7.1.

```
sub byValues {
  $value = $combined{$b} <=> $combined{$a};
  if ($value == 0) {
    return $b cmp $a;
  } else {
    return $value;
  }
}

open (OUT, ">Poe68.csv") or die;
@sortedWords = sort byValues keys %combined;
$" = ',';
print OUT "@sortedWords[0..4]\n";

for $i ( 0 .. $#dict ) {
  $count = 0;
  for $word (@sortedWords) {
    if ($count < 4) {
      print OUT $dict[$i]{$word}+0, ",";
      ++$count;
    } else {
      print OUT $dict[$i]{$word}+0, "\n";
      last;
    }
  }
}

close(OUT);
```

Output 7.1 Example of computing correlations in R.

```
> cor(data)
          the        of       and         a        to
the 1.0000000 0.9708976 0.9036969 0.9043017 0.9467533
of  0.9708976 1.0000000 0.9261978 0.9219928 0.9419159
and 0.9036969 0.9261978 1.0000000 0.9194357 0.9146464
a   0.9043017 0.9219928 0.9194357 1.0000000 0.9467486
to  0.9467533 0.9419159 0.9146464 0.9467486 1.0000000
```

The function attach() makes the variables in data accessible by just using the column name. For example, data$the can be replaced with the. Hence plot(of,the) is a plot of the word counts of *of* and *the* for each of the 68 Poe stories.

The function lm() fits a linear model of the variable before the tilde as a function of all of them after it. So in output 7.2, the counts of *the* are modeled as a linear function of the *of*

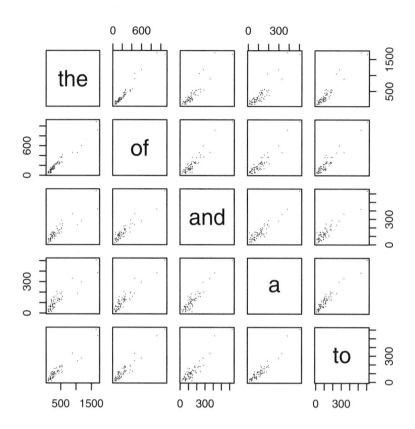

Figure 7.1   Plotting pairs of word counts for the 68 Poe short stories.

Output 7.2 Making a plot with the regression line added for the word counts of *the* versus *of*.

```
> attach(data)
> plot(of,the)
> lmofthe = lm(the ~ of)
> lines(of, fitted(lmofthe))
```

---

counts. The result is shown in output 7.3, which implies equation 7.8. Problem 7.3 shows how to get more information about the results of `lm()`.

$$\#\text{the} = -0.03825 + 1.66715 * (\#\text{of}) \tag{7.8}$$

The function `fitted()` returns the predicted values given by equation 7.8. Output 7.2 uses these to add the regression line using the command `lines()`, as shown below.

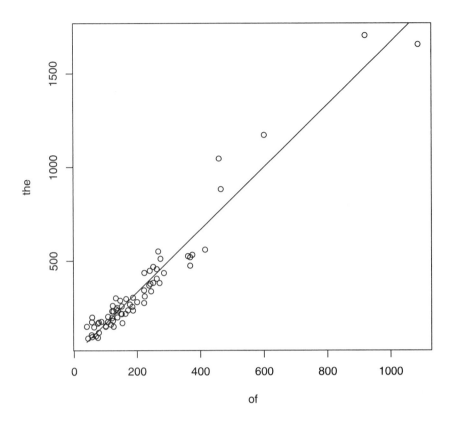

Figure 7.2   Plots of the word counts for *the* versus *of* using the 68 Poe short stories.

```
> lines(of, fitted(lmofthe))
```

The above discussion introduces the correlation. However, this computation is closely related to the cosine similarity measure introduced in section 5.4. The connection between these two techniques is explained in the next section.

7.2.3 Correlations and Cosines

This link between cosines and correlations is easy to show mathematically. Suppose the two variables X and Y have means equal to zero, that is, $\overline{X} = \overline{Y} = 0$. Then equation 7.9 holds true.

$$\cos(\theta) = \frac{\sum_{i=1}^{n} x_i y_i}{\sqrt{\sum_{i=1}^{n} x_i^2}\sqrt{\sum_{i=1}^{n} y_i^2}} = \frac{\frac{1}{n-1}\sum_{i=1}^{n} x_i y_i}{\sqrt{\frac{1}{n-1}\sum_{i=1}^{n} x_i^2}\sqrt{\frac{1}{n-1}\sum_{i=1}^{n} y_i^2}} = r \qquad (7.9)$$

Output 7.3 Fitting a linear function of the counts of *the* as a function of the counts of *of* for each Poe story. Output 7.2 computes lmofthe.

```
> lmofthe

Call:
lm(formula = the ~ of)

Coefficients:
(Intercept)             of
   -0.03825        1.66715
```

Of course, data rarely has mean zero. However, if x_i are measurements of any variable, then it is easy to show that $x_i - \overline{X}$ has mean zero. Note that this expression appears in the numerator of both the z-score (equation 7.3) and the correlation (equation 7.6).

Section 5.5.1 shows how to compute the cosines for the term-document matrix given in output 5.3. If this matrix is modified so that each column has mean zero, then the cosines for the modified matrix is exactly the same as the correlation matrix of the original, which is demonstrated in output 7.4. This uses the method shown in output 5.12.

Output 7.4 Example of computing cosines using matrix multiplication.

```
> out=scale(M)
> t(out) %*% out/7
          [,1]      [,2]      [,3]      [,4]
[1,] 1.0000000 0.8857338 0.6908841 0.8321416
[2,] 0.8857338 1.0000000 0.8157080 0.8667649
[3,] 0.6908841 0.8157080 1.0000000 0.9280992
[4,] 0.8321416 0.8667649 0.9280992 1.0000000
```

Output 7.5 The correlations of the columns of the term-document matrix M.

```
> cor(M)
          [,1]      [,2]      [,3]      [,4]
[1,] 1.0000000 0.8857338 0.6908841 0.8321416
[2,] 0.8857338 1.0000000 0.8157080 0.8667649
[3,] 0.6908841 0.8157080 1.0000000 0.9280992
[4,] 0.8321416 0.8667649 0.9280992 1.0000000
```

Hence it is no accident that any correlation is between -1 and 1 because it is equivalent to a cosine, which must be between -1 and 1. Although the data set in output 5.7 does not have zero mean, the cosine similarities and the correlations in output 7.5 are similar. In fact, the ranking of the six pairs of stories from most to least similar is the same for both.

As noted earlier, the correlation matrix is redundant because the upper right corner is a mirror image of the lower left corner. This means that the ith row and jth column entry is equal to the jth row and ith column. Symbolically, we denote the entries by subscripts, so this means $R_{ij} = R_{ji}$. Or written in terms of matrices, equation 7.10 holds.

$$R^T = R \tag{7.10}$$

Finally, correlations are not the only way to compute how two variables relate. The next section defines the covariance matrix, which is closely related to the correlation matrix.

7.2.4 Correlations and Covariances

The correlation between two variables is convenient because it is a pure number without the units of measurement of the data. However, sometimes it is useful to retain the original units, and there is a statistic corresponding to the correlation that does exactly this. It is called the *covariance*.

The formula for the covariance between two variables is given by equation 7.11. There are two ways to write this. First, Cov(X, Y), and, second, s_{xy}. Note that s_{xx} is just the variance of X because when $Y = X$, s_{xx} is the same as s_x^2 in equation 7.2.

$$s_{xy} = \frac{1}{n-1} \sum_{i=1}^{n} (x_i - \overline{X})(y_i - \overline{Y}) \tag{7.11}$$

Note that the units of s_{xy} are just the product of the units of X and Y, which can be hard to interpret. For example, if X is in feet, and Y is in dollars, then s_{xy} is in foot-dollars.

There is a close relationship between correlations and covariances, which is shown in equation 7.12. Comparing this to equations 7.11 and 7.6 shows that the right-hand side is indeed the correlation. Note that the inverse of $n - 1$ in front of s_{xy}, s_x and s_y all cancel out, like it does in equation 7.9.

$$r = \frac{s_{xy}}{s_x s_y} \tag{7.12}$$

Output 7.5 shows that cor() produces a correlation matrix in R. The function cov() similarly produces a covariance matrix, as shown in output 7.6 for the same matrix M used above.

Output 7.6 The covariance matrix of the term-document matrix M.

```
> cov(M)
        [,1]     [,2]     [,3]     [,4]
[1,]  68.98214 137.5714  86.2500 100.7500
[2,] 137.57143 349.7143 229.2857 236.2857
[3,]  86.25000 229.2857 225.9286 203.3571
[4,] 100.75000 236.2857 203.3571 212.5000
```

Finally, if the standard deviations of each column of M are computed, then dividing each row and column by its corresponding standard deviation produces the correlation matrix. That is, cor(M) is just a rescaled version of cov(M). See problem 7.4 for more details.

Note that the covariance matrix is also symmetric about its main diagonal. Although both the correlation and the covariance matrices can be summarized with fewer numbers, the next section shows why the square matrix form is useful, which requires some basic ideas from linear algebra.

7.3 BASIC LINEAR ALGEBRA

The last section notes that the correlation matrix for a set of variables is both square (the number of rows equals the number of columns) and symmetric about the main diagonal (the upper right corner is the mirror reflection of the lower left corner). It turns out that such matrices have special properties.

The study of matrices is the focus of *linear algebra*. It turns out that a fruitful way to understand a matrix, M, is to study how a vector $\mathbf{x}$ changes when multiplied by M to get $M\mathbf{x}$.

Square matrices have at least one nonzero vector that satisfies equation 7.13, where λ is a number. Such vectors are called *eigenvectors*, and the number λ is called the associated *eigenvalue*. For these vectors, matrix multiplication is equivalent to multiplication by a number.

$$M\mathbf{x} = \lambda\mathbf{x} \tag{7.13}$$

It can be proved that n by n correlation and covariance matrices have n real, orthogonal eigenvectors with n real eigenvalues. For example, see theorems 3.8 and 3.10 of *Matrix Analysis for Statistics* by Schott [108]. However, instead of theory, the next section discusses the concrete case of the 2 by 2 correlation matrix, which illustrates the ideas needed later in this chapter.

7.3.1 2 by 2 Correlation Matrices

For two variables, the correlation matrix is 2 by 2, and its general form is given in equation 7.14. Note that R is symmetric, that is, $R^{\mathrm{T}} = R$, which is true for any correlation matrix. Our goal is to find the eigenvectors with their respective eigenvalues.

$$R = \begin{pmatrix} 1 & r \\ r & 1 \end{pmatrix} \tag{7.14}$$

In general, an n by n correlation matrix has n eigenvectors, so R has 2. Call these $\mathbf{e_1}$ and $\mathbf{e_2}$. By definition, there must be two numbers λ_1 and λ_2 that satisfy equation 7.15.

$$R\mathbf{e_1} = \lambda_1\mathbf{e_1} \quad \text{and} \quad R\mathbf{e_2} = \lambda_2\mathbf{e_2} \tag{7.15}$$

Define the matrix E such that its first column is $\mathbf{e_1}$, and its second is $\mathbf{e_2}$ (E for *Eigenvectors*). Note that RE produces a matrix where the first column is $R\mathbf{e_1}$ and its second is $R\mathbf{e_2}$. However, these products are known by equation 7.15. Hence, equation 7.17 holds because postmultiplying by a diagonal matrix rescales the columns of the preceding matrix (see output 5.6 for another example of this). Let V be this diagonal matrix (V for *eigenValues*).

$$
\begin{aligned}
RE &= (R\mathbf{e_1} \ \ R\mathbf{e_2}) = (\lambda_1\mathbf{e_1} \ \ \lambda_2\mathbf{e_2}) \tag{7.16} \\
&= E\begin{pmatrix} \lambda_1 & 0 \\ 0 & \lambda_2 \end{pmatrix} = EV \tag{7.17}
\end{aligned}
$$

Using the notation of the preceding paragraph, we can rewrite equation 7.17 as equation 7.18. Note that E is not unique. If equation 7.15, is multiplied by any constant, then the result is still true. Hence, $\mathbf{e_1}$ can be multiplied by any nonzero constant and remains an eigenvector. One way to remove this ambiguity is to require all the eigenvectors to have length 1, which we assume from now on.

$$RE = EV \tag{7.18}$$

With eigenvectors of unit length, the cosine of the angle between two eigenvectors is the dot product. Note that the transpose of a product of matrices satisfies equation 7.19. For why this is true, see problem 7.5. Since vectors are also matrices, this equation still is true when N is a vector. Using these two facts, it is easy to show that for a correlation matrix, two eigenvectors corresponding to two different nonzero eigenvalues must be *orthogonal*, that is, the dot product is 0.

$$(MN)^{\mathrm{T}} = N^{\mathrm{T}} M^{\mathrm{T}} \tag{7.19}$$

To prove this, first note that equation 7.20 requires that $R^{\mathrm{T}} = R$ (this is the key property). Then compare equations 7.20 and 7.21. Because both start with the same expression, we conclude that equation 7.22 holds. If $\lambda_1 \neq \lambda_2$, then the only way this can happen is when $\mathbf{e_1}^{\mathrm{T}} \mathbf{e_2} = 0$, but this means that the cosine of the angle between these two vectors is zero. Hence these eigenvectors are orthogonal.

$$(R\mathbf{e_1})^{\mathrm{T}} \mathbf{e_2} = \mathbf{e_1}^{\mathrm{T}} R^{\mathrm{T}} \mathbf{e_2} = \mathbf{e_1}^{\mathrm{T}} (R\mathbf{e_2}) = \mathbf{e_1}^{\mathrm{T}} (\lambda_2 \mathbf{e_2}) = \lambda_2 \mathbf{e_1}^{\mathrm{T}} \mathbf{e_2} \tag{7.20}$$

$$(R\mathbf{e_1})^{\mathrm{T}} \mathbf{e_2} = (\lambda_1 \mathbf{e_1})^{\mathrm{T}} \mathbf{e_2} = \lambda_1 \mathbf{e_1}^{\mathrm{T}} \mathbf{e_2} \tag{7.21}$$

$$\Rightarrow \lambda_1 \mathbf{e_1}^{\mathrm{T}} \mathbf{e_2} = \lambda_2 \mathbf{e_1}^{\mathrm{T}} \mathbf{e_2} \tag{7.22}$$

In addition, since a vector with unit length implies that the dot product with itself equals 1, then equation 7.23 must hold. Let I be the identity matrix, that is, $I_{ii} = 1$ and $I_{ij} = 0$ for $i \neq j$. Then equation 7.23 is equivalent to equation 7.24, which holds since matrix multiplication consists of taking the dot product of the rows of the first matrix with the columns of the second matrix. However, the rows of E^{T} are the columns of E, so matrix multiplication in this instance is just taking the dot products of the columns of E, which satisfy equation 7.23. Finally, the second equality in equation 7.24 follows from the first, but proving this requires more mathematics (the concept of inverse matrices), and it is not done here.

$$\mathbf{e_i}^{\mathrm{T}} \mathbf{e_j} = \begin{cases} 1, & i = j \\ 0, & i \neq j \end{cases} \tag{7.23}$$

$$E^{\mathrm{T}} E = I \quad \text{and} \quad E E^{\mathrm{T}} = I \tag{7.24}$$

A key property of I is that equation 7.25 holds for all vectors $\mathbf{x}$. That is, multiplying vectors by I is like multiplying numbers by 1: the result is identical to the initial value.

$$I\mathbf{x} = \mathbf{x} \quad \text{and} \quad \mathbf{x}I = \mathbf{x} \tag{7.25}$$

With these facts in mind, we can reinterpret equation 7.18 as a way to *factor* the matrix R. Multiplying this equation on the right by E^{T} (order counts with matrix multiplication: see problem 7.6) and using equation 7.24, we get equation 7.26. Hence, R can be factored into a product of three matrices: the first and last contain its eigenvectors and the middle is a diagonal matrix containing its eigenvalues.

$$R = RI = R(EE^{\mathrm{T}}) = (RE)E^{\mathrm{T}} = EVE^{\mathrm{T}} \qquad (7.26)$$

With the theory above in mind, we consider a concrete example. By using the first two columns of the matrix M of output 5.3, we compare the use of male and female pronouns in Poe's "The Facts in the Case of M. Valdemar" and "The Man of the Crowd." This is done in output 7.7.

Output 7.7 Factoring the correlation matrix of the eight pronouns for the two Poe stories "The Facts in the Case of M. Valdemar" and "The Man of the Crowd."

```
> M2 <- matrix(c(19,9,7,13,22,0,1,2,27,5,10,11,55,0,4,0),8,2)
> cor(M2)
          [,1]      [,2]
[1,] 1.0000000 0.8857338
[2,] 0.8857338 1.0000000
> out = eigen(cor(M2))
> out
$values
[1] 1.8857338 0.1142662

$vectors
          [,1]       [,2]
[1,] 0.7071068  0.7071068
[2,] 0.7071068 -0.7071068

> out$vectors %*% diag(out$values) %*% t(out$vectors)
          [,1]      [,2]
[1,] 1.0000000 0.8857338
[2,] 0.8857338 1.0000000
```

The function `eigen()` computes the eigenvalues, which are stored in `out$values`, and the eigenvectors are stored in `out$vectors`. The last matrix product is the factorization of $R = EVE^{\mathrm{T}}$, which matches the output of `cor(M2)`.

Output 7.7 is one particular case of the 2 by 2 correlation matrix, but for this size, the general case is not hard to give, which is done in equation 7.27 through equation 7.30. This reproduces output 7.7 when $r = 0.8857338$. For example, the eigenvalues are $1 + r$ and $1 - r$, which equal `out$values`. Note that the second eigenvector in equation 7.28 differs from the second column of `out$vectors` by a factor of -1. However, this factor does not change the length of this unit vector, so the two answers are interchangeable.

$$R = \begin{pmatrix} 1 & r \\ r & 1 \end{pmatrix} \qquad (7.27)$$

$$E = \frac{1}{\sqrt{2}} \begin{pmatrix} 1 & -1 \\ 1 & 1 \end{pmatrix} \qquad (7.28)$$

$$V = \begin{pmatrix} 1+r & 0 \\ 0 & 1-r \end{pmatrix} \qquad (7.29)$$

$$R = EVE^{\mathrm{T}} \qquad (7.30)$$

Also note that the eigenvalues $1 + r$ and $1 - r$ are always different except when r is zero. Hence, the eigenvalues are always orthogonal when $r \neq 0$. However, if $r = 0$, then $R = I$, and by equation 7.25, all nonzero vectors are eigenvectors (with λ equal to 1). Hence, it is possible to pick two eigenvectors for $\lambda = 1$ that are orthogonal, for example, (0,1) and (1,0). Consequently, for all values $-1 \leq r \leq 1$, there are two orthogonal eigenvectors.

Furthermore, although this section considers the 2 by 2 case, equation 7.24 and the factorization given in equation 7.26 holds for any size correlation matrix. For example, cor(M) in output 5.3 can be factored as well, which is shown in output 7.8.

Output 7.8 Factoring the correlation matrix of the eight pronouns for four Poe stories.

```
> M = matrix(c(19,9,7,13,22,0,1,2,27,5,10,11,55,0,4,0,24,0,28,0,
+ 35,0,3,0,33,0,17,3,32,0,1,0),nrow=8,ncol=4)
> cor(M)
           [,1]      [,2]      [,3]      [,4]
[1,] 1.0000000 0.8857338 0.6908841 0.8321416
[2,] 0.8857338 1.0000000 0.8157080 0.8667649
[3,] 0.6908841 0.8157080 1.0000000 0.9280992
[4,] 0.8321416 0.8667649 0.9280992 1.0000000
> out = eigen(cor(M))
> out$vectors %*% diag(out$values) %*% t(out$vectors)
           [,1]      [,2]      [,3]      [,4]
[1,] 1.0000000 0.8857338 0.6908841 0.8321416
[2,] 0.8857338 1.0000000 0.8157080 0.8667649
[3,] 0.6908841 0.8157080 1.0000000 0.9280992
[4,] 0.8321416 0.8667649 0.9280992 1.0000000
```

Now we apply the matrix factorization of a correlation matrix R to texts. This is done in the next section with the multivariate statistical technique of principal components analysis.

7.4 PRINCIPAL COMPONENTS ANALYSIS

The ability to reduce a large number of variables to a smaller set is useful. This is especially true when dealing with text since there are numerous linguistic entities to count. Doing this, however, generally loses information. Hence, the goal is to obtain an acceptable trade-off between variable reduction and the loss of information.

Principal components analysis (PCA) reduces variables in a way that as much variability as possible is retained. This approach assumes variability is the useful part of the data, which is plausible in many situations. For example, none of Poe's 68 short stories has the word *hotdog*, so each story has 0 instances. Intuitively, this is not as informative as the word counts of *death*, which varies from 0 to 16.

The approach of PCA is simple. Suppose a data set has the variables x_1, x_2, ..., x_n. Then n new variables, call these c_1, c_2, ..., c_n, are constructed to satisfy the following four conditions. First, each component c_i is a linear function of the original x_i variables, so the system of equations 7.31 holds. This is written compactly in matrix notation as follows. Let **c** be the column vector containing c_1, c_2, ..., c_n; let **x** be the column vector containing x_1, x_2, ..., x_n; and let E be the matrix with row i and column j equaling e_{ij}. Then equation 7.32 holds.

$$
\begin{aligned}
c_1 &= & e_{11}x_1 + e_{12}x_2 + \cdots + e_{1n}x_n \\
c_2 &= & e_{21}x_1 + e_{22}x_2 + \cdots + e_{2n}x_n \\
c_3 &= & e_{31}x_1 + e_{32}x_2 + \cdots + e_{3n}x_n \\
&\vdots& \\
c_n &= & e_{n1}x_1 + e_{n2}x_2 + \cdots + e_{nn}x_n
\end{aligned} \tag{7.31}
$$

$$
\mathbf{c} = E\mathbf{x} \tag{7.32}
$$

Second, the vector $\mathbf{c}$ has unit length. That is, equation 7.33 holds.

$$
\mathbf{c}^\mathrm{T}\mathbf{c} = 1 \tag{7.33}
$$

Third, each pair of c_i and c_j ($i \neq j$) are uncorrelated. That is, the correlation matrix of $\mathbf{c}$ is the identity matrix, I. Fourth, the variances of c_1, c_2, ..., c_n are ordered from largest to smallest. These four conditions uniquely specify the matrix E, which is given in the next section.

7.4.1 Finding the Principal Components

There are two approaches to PCA. A researcher can work with either the correlation matrix or the covariance matrix. For the former approach, each variable must be converted to its z-scores first. If the latter is used, then the original data values are left alone. Below, both methods are shown, but the focus is on using the correlation matrix, R.

Equation 7.32 puts the PCA coefficients in the matrix E. This might seem like poor notation since E is also used in section 7.3.1 to denote the eigenvector matrix of R. However, it turns out that the columns of R are the PCA coefficients for the z-scores of the data. In addition, the eigenvectors of the covariance matrix are the PCA coefficients for the original data set. For more details on PCA using either the correlation or covariance matrices, see chapter 12 of Rencher's *Methods of Multivariate Analysis* [104].

Although R has a function called `prcomp()` that computes the principal components (PCs), the discussion in the preceding section also allows us to compute these directly using matrix methods. This link between PCA and eigenvectors is applied to a term-document matrices in the next section.

7.4.2 PCA Applied to the 68 Poe Short Stories

Code sample 7.3 gives Perl code to compute the word counts of the five most frequent words in the Poe short stories (namely, *the, of, and, a, to*). We use this term-document matrix for our first example.

Output 7.9 first reads in the file `Poe68.csv` by using `read.csv()`. Then `scale()` computes the z-scores of the word counts and puts these into the matrix, `Poe5z`, and `out` contains both the eigenvectors and eigenvalues of the correlation matrix (note that the correlation matrix of `Poe5` is the same as `Poe5z` since both use z-scores instead of the original data). Taking the product of `Poe5z` with the eigenvectors produces the PCs. As shown in this output, the correlation matrix of these is the identity matrix, up to round-off error. Finally, `out$vectors` are both the eigenvectors and the coefficients of the PCs.

This is also achievable with the function `prcomp()`, and output 7.10 gives the results. Note that the standard deviations are the square roots of the eigenvalues, and that the PCs

Output 7.9 Computing the principal components "by hand."

```
> Poe5 = read.csv("C:\\Poe68.csv", header=T)
> Poe5z = scale(Poe5)
> out = eigen(cor(Poe5))
> cor(Poe5z %*% out$vectors)
              [,1]         [,2]         [,3]         [,4]         [,5]
[1,]  1.0000e+00  2.0423e-16  4.6955e-17 -3.4085e-16  1.7078e-15
[2,]  2.0423e-16  1.0000e+00  1.1580e-16 -1.5070e-15  5.3763e-17
[3,]  4.6955e-17  1.1580e-16  1.0000e+00 -7.2411e-16 -3.1098e-15
[4,] -3.4085e-16 -1.5070e-15 -7.2411e-16  1.0000e+00 -2.0725e-15
[5,]  1.7078e-15  5.3763e-17 -3.1098e-15 -2.0725e-15  1.0000e+00
> out$vectors
              [,1]         [,2]         [,3]          [,4]         [,5]
[1,] 0.4479384  0.59665130  0.05283368  0.007829268  0.66370602
[2,] 0.4512716  0.37147278  0.19534916 -0.446395013 -0.64879280
[3,] 0.4419035 -0.49708875  0.70992974  0.213534608  0.08959248
[4,] 0.4446688 -0.50827600 -0.51029964 -0.492150216  0.20324283
[5,] 0.4502178  0.02394739 -0.44118177  0.716143373 -0.29871015
> out$values
[1] 4.71891565 0.11922068 0.09281803 0.04531961 0.02372603
```

are the same as the eigenvectors (up to signs). Setting `scale.` to true uses the correlation matrix. If it is false, then the covariance matrix is used instead.

Output 7.10 Computing the principal components with the function `prcomp()`. Compare to output 7.9.

```
> prcomp(Poe5, scale. = T)
Standard deviations:
[1] 2.1723065 0.3452835 0.3046605 0.2128840 0.1540326

Rotation:
          PC1         PC2         PC3          PC4         PC5
the -0.4479384  0.59665130 -0.05283368 -0.007829268  0.66370602
of  -0.4512716  0.37147278 -0.19534916  0.446395013 -0.64879280
and -0.4419035 -0.49708875 -0.70992974 -0.213534608  0.08959248
a   -0.4446688 -0.50827600  0.51029964  0.492150216  0.20324283
to  -0.4502178  0.02394739  0.44118177 -0.716143373 -0.29871015
```

The `summary()` function shows the importance of each PC in output 7.11. Remember that the first PC is constructed so it gets as much variability as possible, and the second PC gets as much of the rest of the variability as possible, and so forth.

So for these five words, the first PC is roughly proportional to the mean of the counts of the five words since all the weights are approximately equal (and ignoring the negative signs). This PC explains 94.4% of the variability, so the other four PCs are not very important.

Output 7.11 Using `summary()` on the output of `prcomp()`.

```
> summary(prcomp(Poe5, scale. = T))
Importance of components:
                          PC1    PC2    PC3     PC4     PC5
Standard deviation      2.172 0.3453 0.3047 0.21288 0.15403
Proportion of Variance 0.944 0.0238 0.0186 0.00906 0.00475
Cumulative Proportion  0.944 0.9676 0.9862 0.99525 1.00000
```

That is, although there are five variables in the data set, these can be summarized by one variable with little loss of variability.

These five words are the most common five words used by Poe in his short stories. In addition, they are all function words, so their counts are positively correlated with the size of the stories. Hence the first PC, which is nearly an average of these counts, captures this relationship.

Finally, note that the PC coefficients differ depending on whether the correlation or covariance matrix is used. This is shown in output 7.12, which computes the PCs using the covariance matrix. Although the coefficients differ, the first PC still explains the vast majority of the variability. So in either case, the five variables can be reduced to one.

Output 7.12 Computing the principal components using the covariance matrix. Compare to output 7.11.

```
> prcomp(Poe5, scale. = F)
Standard deviations:
[1] 386.70732  49.72679  33.45049  27.73959  19.53010

Rotation:
            PC1         PC2         PC3        PC4        PC5
the -0.7941645  0.5389676 -0.19301648  0.1662676 -0.1179679
of  -0.4576397 -0.2720821  0.76380101 -0.3537533  0.0894639
and -0.2301611 -0.5544725  0.02003543  0.7930616  0.1011827
a   -0.2080904 -0.4939688 -0.36128770 -0.3075355 -0.6982738
to  -0.2521764 -0.2898971 -0.49841993 -0.3516942  0.6930047
> summary(prcomp(Poe5, scale. = F))
Importance of components:
                          PC1     PC2      PC3      PC4      PC5
Standard deviation      386.71 49.7268 33.45049 27.73959 19.53010
Proportion of Variance   0.97  0.0160  0.00725  0.00499  0.00247
Cumulative Proportion    0.97  0.9853  0.99254  0.99753  1.00000
```

In general, since using the correlation matrix is equivalent to using the z-scores of the data, all the variables have comparable influence in the PCs. Using the covariance matrix, however, implies that the variables that vary most have the most influence. Either case is useful, so it depends on the researcher's goals on which to use.

The next section briefly looks at another set of word counts for Poe's stories. This time the variability is more spread out among the PCs.

7.4.3 Another PCA Example with Poe's Short Stories

In section 5.2.2, the pronouns *he, she, him, her, his, hers, himself,* and *herself* are analyzed in four Poe stories. In this section we apply PCA to these using all 68 Poe stories . The counts can be computed by replacing the end of code sample 7.3 with code sample 7.4. The idea is to use the pronouns as keys in the array of hashes, `@dict`.

Code Sample 7.4 Word counts for the eight pronouns are written to the file `Poe68.csv`. This requires `@dict` from code sample 7.1.

```
open (OUT, ">Poe68.csv") or die;
@pronouns = (he, she, him, her, his, hers, himself, herself);
$" = ',';
print OUT "@pronouns\n";

for $i ( 0 .. $#dict ) {
  for ($j = 0; $j < $#pronouns; ++$j) {
    print OUT $dict[$i]{$pronouns[$j]}+0, ",";
  }
  print OUT $dict[$i]{$pronouns[-1]}+0, "\n";;
}
```

Once the file `Poe68.csv` is created, read it into R using `read.csv()`. Then output 7.13 computes the PCA for these eight pronouns.

Again the first PC is approximately proportional to the average of the eight counts since the weights are all roughly the same. Unlike the preceding section, however, the first PC only explains 48% of the variability. Although the second PC also has weights comparable in absolute value, four of the signs are positive, and the other four are negative. Note that the former weights go with the feminine pronouns, and the latter go with the masculine!

Although this PCA uses a bag-of-words language model that ignores all syntactic information, it distinguishes between male and female pronouns. So using simplified models of language coupled with a computer can discover interesting language structures.

7.4.4 Rotations

Notice outputs 7.10, 7.12, and 7.13 include the word *Rotation* just before the PCs. This section explains why this is the case.

Rotations only change the orientation but not the shape of any object. For example, spinning a suitcase does not change its shape. Suppose there is a data set with n-variables, then an n-dimensional plot is possible with one dimension for each variable. As with objects, rotating these values changes the orientation but not the shape of the data.

Surprisingly, rotations in any number of dimensions are easy to describe mathematically. Any rotation in n-dimensions is representable by an n-by-n matrix, call it E, that satisfies the two properties given in equations 7.34 and 7.35.

$$E^\mathrm{T} E = I \qquad (7.34)$$

$$\det(E) = 1 \qquad (7.35)$$

Output 7.13 The PCA of eight pronouns in the 68 Poe short stories.

```
> prcomp(Poe8pn,scale.=T)
Standard deviations:
[1] 1.9120490 1.6130358 0.7344750 0.6298724 0.5934494 0.4763188
[7] 0.3940458 0.2676894


Rotation:
                PC1         PC2          PC3         PC4         PC5
he       0.3968662 -0.3427335  0.045274128 -0.11577301 -0.1014911
she      0.3268217  0.4252042 -0.227591982 -0.04400534 -0.4643040
him      0.3529773 -0.3315296  0.220014539 -0.68278920 -0.1961602
her      0.3587514  0.3994852  0.056188780  0.20883497 -0.4117217
his      0.3451026 -0.3829043 -0.002812392  0.34181970  0.1086482
hers     0.2689269  0.3702944  0.767368075  0.05003566  0.4041360
himself  0.4139825 -0.2422977 -0.152091419  0.50035210  0.1225839
herself  0.3458183  0.2996549 -0.531596742 -0.32426921  0.6131645
                PC6          PC7          PC8
he      -0.002695473 -0.835631212  0.03147343
she      0.125548208  0.055106112  0.65136565
him     -0.141524948  0.431439804 -0.07898856
her      0.014680992  0.004098073 -0.70369931
his      0.733970927  0.258364837  0.01302934
hers    -0.005662007 -0.031545737  0.18668159
himself -0.649088162  0.210372857  0.12580665
herself  0.062647567 -0.022856816 -0.14984397
> summary(prcomp(Poe8pn,scale.=T))
Importance of components:
                         PC1    PC2    PC3    PC4    PC5
Standard deviation     1.912  1.613 0.7345 0.6299 0.593
Proportion of Variance 0.457  0.325 0.0674 0.0496 0.044
Cumulative Proportion  0.457  0.782 0.8497 0.8992 0.943
                         PC6    PC7     PC8
Standard deviation     0.4763 0.3940 0.26769
Proportion of Variance 0.0284 0.0194 0.00896
Cumulative Proportion  0.9716 0.9910 1.00000
```

However, equation 7.34 is the same as equation 7.24. Equation 7.35 it a technical condition that rules out rotations coupled with mirror reflections. Note that det() is the determinant function, which is not discussed in this book, but see section 1.6 of Schott's *Matrix Analysis for Statistics* [108] for a definition.

If all the normalized eigenvectors of a correlation matrix are used as the columns of a matrix E, this is a rotation in n-dimensional space. So finding principal components is equivalent to rotating the data to remove all correlations among the variables.

Since rotation does not distort the shape of the data, a PCA preserves all of the information. Because of this, it is often used to create new variables for other statistical analyses. These new variables have the same informational content as the original ones, and they are uncorrelated.

Information is lost in a PCA only by picking a subset of PCs, but this loss is quantified by the cumulative proportion of variance. This allows the researcher to make an informed decision when reducing the number of variables studied.

The above discussion covers the basics of PCA. The next section gives some examples of text applications in the literature.

7.5 TEXT APPLICATIONS

7.5.1 A Word on Factor Analysis

The idea of taking a set of variables and defining a smaller group of derived variables is a popular technique. Besides PCA, factor analysis (FA) is often used. Some authors (including myself) prefer PCA to FA, but the latter is well established. Before noting some applications in the literature, this section gives a short explanation on why PCA might be preferred by some over FA.

PCA is based on the fact that it is possible to rotate a data set so that the resulting variables are uncorrelated. There are no assumptions about this data set, and no information is lost by this rotation. Finally the rotation is unique, so no input is needed from the researcher to create the principal components. However, FA is used to reduce the number of variables to a smaller set called *factors*. Moreover, it tries to do this so that the resulting variables seem meaningful to the researcher.

Although FA has similarities to PCA, it does make several assumptions. Suppose this data set has n variables. Then FA assumes that these are a linear function of k factors ($k < n$), which is a new set of variables. In practice, k factors never fully determine n variables, so assumptions must be made about this discrepancy. FA assumes that these differences are due to random error. Finally, any solution of an FA is not unique: any rotation of the factors also produces a solution. This allows the researcher to search for a rotation that produces factors that are deemed interpretable.

The above discussion reveals two contrasts between these two methods. First, PCA preserves information, but if FA is mistakenly used, then information is lost since it is classified as random error. Second, PCA produces a unique solution, but FA allows the researcher to make choices, which allows the possibility of poor choices.

Since natural languages are immensely complex, the ability of FA to allow researcher bias might give one pause. However, people are experts at language, so perhaps human insight is a valuable input for FA. There is much statistical literature on both of these techniques. For an introduction to PCA and FA, see chapters 12 and 13 of Rencher's *Methods of Multivariate Analysis* [104], which includes a comparison of these two methods. For an example of computing an FA in R, see problem 7.8.

The next section notes some applications of PCA and FA to language data sets in the literature. After reading this chapter, these references are understandable.

7.6 APPLICATIONS AND REFERENCES

We start with three non-technical articles. Klarreich's "Bookish Math" [65] gives a non-technical overview of several statistical tests of authorship, including PCA. In addition, the Spring 2003 issue of *Chance* magazine features the statistical analysis of authorship attribution. In general, this magazine focuses on applications and targets a wide audience, not just statisticians. Two of the four articles in this issue use PCA. First, "Who Wrote the

15th Book of Oz?" by Binongo [15] gives a detailed example of using PCA to determine if Frank Baum wrote *The Royal Book of Oz*. Second, "Stylometry and the Civil War: The Case of the Pickett Letters" by Holmes [56] also uses PCA along with clustering (the topic of chapter 8) to determine if a group of letters were likely written by George Pickett. Both of these articles plot the data using the first two principal components.

Here are two technical articles on applying PCA to text. First, Binongo and Smith's "The Application of Principal Component Analysis to Stylometry" [16]. This discusses PCA and has examples that include plots using principal component axes. Second, "A Widow and Her Soldier: A Stylometric Analysis of the 'Pickett Letters'" by Holmes, Gordon, and Wilson [57] has five figures plotting the texts on principal component axes.

Factor analysis can be used, too. For example, Biber and Finegan's "Drift and the Evolution of English Style: A History of Three Genres" [12] analyzes the style of literature from the 17th through the 20th centuries. The factors are used to show differences over this time period. Second, Stewart's "Charles Brockden Brown: Quantitative Analysis and Literary Interpretation" [112] also performs an FA, and plots texts using factor axes, an idea that is popular with both FA and PCA.

An extended discussion on FA as it is used in corpus linguistics is contained in Part II of the book *Corpus Linguistics: Investigating Language Structure and Use* by Douglas Biber, Susan Conrad, and Randi Reppen [11]. This book is readable and has many other examples of analyzing language via quantitative methods.

PROBLEMS

7.1 [Mathematical] Section 7.2 notes that the standard deviation is zero exactly when all the data values are zero. For this problem, convince yourself that the following argument proves this claim.

$$s_x^2 = \frac{1}{n-1} \sum_{i=1}^{n} (x_i - \overline{X})^2 \tag{7.36}$$

Consider equation 7.2, which is reproduced here as equation 7.36. First, if all the data have the same value, then $\overline{X}$ equals this value. Then $(x_i - \overline{X})$ is always zero, so s_x^2 is also zero.

Second, since a real number squared is at least zero, all the terms in the sum are at least zero. So if s_x^2 is zero, then each of the terms in the sum is zero, and this happens only when every $(x_i - \overline{X})$ is zero. Hence all the x_i's are equal to $\overline{X}$.

7.2 This problem shows how to exit a `for` loop before it terminates. This is used in code sample 7.3 to stop the inner `for` loop, which stops the `print` statement from writing more output to `Poe68.csv`.

Perl has the command `last`, which terminates a loop. For example, code sample 7.5 shows a loop that should repeat 10 times, but due to the `if` statement, it terminates in the fifth iteration, which is shown by the output.

Take code sample 7.5 and replace `last` by `next` and compare the results. Then replace `last` by `redo` and see what happens. Guess what each of these commands does and then look them up online.

Code Sample 7.5 The `for` loop is halted by the `last` statement when `$i` equals 5. For problem 7.2.

```
for ($i = 1; $i <= 10; ++$i) {
  print "$i ";
  if ($i == 5) { last; }
}

OUTPUT: 1 2 3 4 5
```

7.3   R is object oriented (OO), and many statistical operations produce an object, including `lm()`. In OO programming, working with objects is done with *methods*, which are functions. Here we consider the method `summary()`. Try the following yourself.

Output 7.14 Regression of counts for *the* as a function of counts for *and* in the 68 Poe short stories. For problem 7.3.

```
> data = read.csv("C:\\Poe68.csv", header=T)
> attach(data)
> lmtheand = lm(the ~ and)
> lmtheand

Call:
lm(formula = the ~ and)

Coefficients:
(Intercept)           and
     -48.01          2.91
```

Output 7.14 performs a regression where the counts of *the* are fitted as a function of the counts of *and* in the 68 Poe short stories. Compare these results to output 7.2, which is a similar analysis. Here `lmtheand` is an object, and typing it on the command line gives a little information about it. However, the function `summary()` provides even more, as seen in output 7.15. If you are familiar with regression, the details given here are expected.

If you investigate additional statistical functions in R, you will find out that `summary()` works with many of these. For example, try it with `eigen()`, though in this case, it provides little information. For another example, apply it to a vector of data.

7.4   At the end of section 7.2.4, it is claimed that the correlation matrix is a rescaled version of the covariance matrix, which can be shown by doing the following. First, divide the first row and column by the standard deviation of the first column of M, which is 8.305549. Second, divide the second row and column by the standard deviation of the second column of M, which is 18.70065. Do the same for the third and fourth rows and columns of M using 15.03092 and 14.57738, respectively.

This is also possible by using matrix methods. Convince yourself that output 7.16 is doing the same rescaling described in the preceding paragraph by doing the following steps.

Output 7.15 Example of the function `summary()` applied to `lmtheof` from output 7.14 for problem 7.3.

```
> summary(lmtheand)

Call:
lm(formula = the ~ and)

Residuals:
    Min      1Q   Median      3Q     Max
-248.396  -78.826   -9.244   43.952  537.456

Coefficients:
            Estimate Std. Error t value Pr(>|t|)
(Intercept) -48.0134    28.3608  -1.693   0.0952 .
and           2.9102     0.1697  17.147   <2e-16 ***
---
Signif. codes:  0 '***' 0.001 '**' 0.01 '*' 0.05 '.' 0.1 ' ' 1

Residual standard error: 133 on 66 degrees of freedom
Multiple R-Squared: 0.8167,     Adjusted R-squared: 0.8139
F-statistic:    294 on 1 and 66 DF,  p-value: < 2.2e-16
```

Output 7.16 Rescaling the covariance matrix by the standard deviations of the columns of the term-document matrix M for problem 7.4.

```
> M = matrix(c(19,9,7,13,22,0,1,2,27,5,10,11,55,0,4,0,24,0,28,0,
+ 35,0,3,0,33,0,17,3,32,0,1,0), nrow=8, ncol=4)
> cor(M)
            [,1]      [,2]      [,3]      [,4]
[1,] 1.0000000 0.8857338 0.6908841 0.8321416
[2,] 0.8857338 1.0000000 0.8157080 0.8667649
[3,] 0.6908841 0.8157080 1.0000000 0.9280992
[4,] 0.8321416 0.8667649 0.9280992 1.0000000
> solve(diag(sd(M))) %*% cov(M) %*% solve(diag(sd(M)))
            [,1]      [,2]      [,3]      [,4]
[1,] 1.0000000 0.8857338 0.6908841 0.8321416
[2,] 0.8857338 1.0000000 0.8157080 0.8667649
[3,] 0.6908841 0.8157080 1.0000000 0.9280992
[4,] 0.8321416 0.8667649 0.9280992 1.0000000
```

   a) First, enter matrix M into R and compute `sd(M)`. Applying `diag()` to this matrix selects the diagonal entries. Applying `solve()` to this result replaces the diagonal entries by their inverses. Confirm this.

   b) What happens to `cov(M)` when the following command is executed? Confirm your guess using R.

```
solve(diag(sd(M))) %*% cov(M)
```

c) What happens to `cov(M)` when the following command is executed? Confirm your guess using R.

```
cov(M) %*% solve(diag(sd(M)))
```

d) Combining the last two parts, convince yourself that the following command equals `cor(M)`.

```
solve(diag(sd(M))) %*% cov(M) %*% solve(diag(sd(M)))
```

7.5   [Mathematical] If matrix M has entries m_{ij}, and N has entries n_{ij}, then matrix multiplication can be defined by equation 7.37. Here $(MN)_{ij}$ means the entry in the ith row and jth column of the matrix product MN.

$$(MN)_{ij} = \sum_k m_{ik} n_{kj} \tag{7.37}$$

Taking a transpose of a matrix means switching the rows and columns. Put mathematically, A_{ij}^{T} equals A_{ji}. Hence the transpose of a matrix product satisfies equation 7.38.

$$(MN)_{ij}^{\mathrm{T}} = (MN)_{ji} = \sum_k m_{jk} n_{ki} = \sum_k n_{ki} m_{jk} = (N^{\mathrm{T}} M^{\mathrm{T}})_{ij} \tag{7.38}$$

Since equation 7.38 holds for all the values of i and j, we conclude that equation 7.39 is true. If this reasoning is not clear to you, then look this up in a linear algebra text, for example, Gilbert Strang's *Linear Algebra and Its Applications* [113].

$$(MN)^{\mathrm{T}} = N^{\mathrm{T}} M^{\mathrm{T}} \tag{7.39}$$

7.6   The order of matrices in matrix multiplication is important. In some cases, different orders cannot be multiplied. In others, different orders can produce different results. This is easily shown by trying it with some specific matrices. See output 7.17 for an example using the matrices defined in equations 7.40 and 7.41.

$$A = \begin{pmatrix} 1 & 2 & 3 \\ 5 & 6 & 7 \end{pmatrix} \tag{7.40}$$

$$B = \begin{pmatrix} 4 & 3 \\ 1 & 0 \\ -1 & -2 \end{pmatrix} \tag{7.41}$$

Output 7.17 Example of multiplying two matrices in both orders and getting different answers. For problem 7.6.

```
> A = matrix(c(1,2,3,5,6,7), c(2,3), byrow=T)
> B = matrix(c(4,3,1,0,-1,-2), c(3,2), byrow=T)
> A %*% B
      [,1] [,2]
[1,]    3   -3
[2,]   19    1
> B %*% A
      [,1] [,2] [,3]
[1,]   19   26   33
[2,]    1    2    3
[3,]  -11  -14  -17
```

In this case, AB is a 2 by 2 matrix, while BA is a 3 by 3 matrix. So these two products are not even the same size, much less identical matrices.

   a) Let M_1 be a four by four matrix with every entry equal to 1, and call the diagonal matrix in output 5.5, M_2. Compute the matrix products $M_1 M_2$ and $M_2 M_1$. How do these differ?

   b) Let M_3 and M_4 be defined by equations 7.42 and 7.43. Show that $M_3 M_4$ and $M_4 M_3$ give the same result.

$$M_3 = \begin{pmatrix} 1 & 0 & 0 \\ 0 & -2 & 0 \\ 0 & 0 & 3 \end{pmatrix} \tag{7.42}$$

$$M_4 = \begin{pmatrix} 2 & 0 & 0 \\ 0 & 2 & 0 \\ 0 & 0 & 1 \end{pmatrix} \tag{7.43}$$

   c) Let M_5 and M_6 be defined by equations 7.44 and 7.45. Show that $M_5 M_6$ and $M_6 M_5$ give the same results.

$$M_5 = \begin{pmatrix} 3 & 1 \\ 1 & 3 \end{pmatrix} \tag{7.44}$$

$$M_6 = \begin{pmatrix} 0 & 2 \\ 2 & 0 \end{pmatrix} \tag{7.45}$$

In general, matrices rarely satisfy $AB = BA$. If they do, they are said to *commute*. To learn what conditions are needed for two matrices to commute, see theorem 4.15 of section 4.7 of James Schott's *Matrix Analysis for Statistics* [108].

7.7   [Mathematical] Equation 7.46 is a two by two rotation matrix, which rotates vectors θ degrees counterclockwise.

$$\begin{pmatrix} \cos\theta & -\sin\theta \\ \sin\theta & \cos\theta \end{pmatrix} \tag{7.46}$$

   a) Verify that equation 7.46 satisfies equations 7.34 and 7.35.

b) Compute equation 7.46 for θ equal to $0°$. Does the result make sense, that is, does it rotate a vector zero degrees?

c) If equation 7.46 is applied to a specific vector, then it is easy to check that it really is rotated by the angle θ. Do this for θ equal to $45°$ applied to the vector $(1, 1)^T$.

d) Equations 7.47 and 7.48 shows two rotation matrices. Multiplying $M_1 M_2$ produces a rotation matrix with angle $\theta_1 + \theta_2$, which is given by equation 7.49. First, show that $M_1 M_2$ equals $M_2 M_1$. As interpreted as rotations, does this make sense? Second, the matrix product $M_1 M_2$ must equal M_3, so each entry of the matrix product equals the respective entry of M_3. Compute this and confirm that the results are the angle addition formulas for sines and cosines.

$$M_1 = \begin{pmatrix} \cos \theta_1 & -\sin \theta_1 \\ \sin \theta_1 & \cos \theta_1 \end{pmatrix} \tag{7.47}$$

$$M_2 = \begin{pmatrix} \cos \theta_2 & -\sin \theta_2 \\ \sin \theta_2 & \cos \theta_2 \end{pmatrix} \tag{7.48}$$

$$M_3 = \begin{pmatrix} \cos (\theta_1 + \theta_2) & -\sin (\theta_1 + \theta_2) \\ \sin (\theta_1 + \theta_2) & \cos (\theta_1 + \theta_2) \end{pmatrix} \tag{7.49}$$

7.8   This problem shows how to do a factor analysis (FA) in R using the Poe8pn data set. This requires specifying the number of factors beforehand. Output 7.18 has two factors, while output 7.19 has three. Although the factor loadings are a matrix, the default is to not print the values below 0.1. Also, the default rotation of `factanal()` is varimax, so it is used here.

Output 7.18 Example of a factor analysis using the Poe8pn data set used in the PCA of output 7.13. For problem 7.8.

```
> out=factanal(Poe8pn, factors=2)
> out$loadings
```

```
Loadings:
         Factor1 Factor2
he        0.939
she               0.930
him       0.817
her               0.960
his       0.853
hers              0.691
himself   0.801   0.222
herself   0.175   0.687
```

```
               Factor1 Factor2
SS loadings     2.958   2.793
Proportion Var  0.370   0.349
Cumulative Var  0.370   0.719
```

Output 7.19 Example of a factor analysis with three factors. For problem 7.8.

```
> out=factanal(Poe8pn, factors=3)
> out$loadings

Loadings:
        Factor1 Factor2 Factor3
he       0.938
she              0.972  -0.223
him      0.816
her              0.969   0.216
his      0.852
hers             0.657   0.269
himself  0.801   0.220
herself  0.170   0.687  -0.182

                Factor1 Factor2 Factor3
SS loadings       2.953   2.846   0.214
Proportion Var    0.369   0.356   0.027
Cumulative Var    0.369   0.725   0.752
```

Note that the first two factors for both models have nearly identical loadings. Recall that PCs are interpreted by considering which variables have large coefficients in absolute value, and the same idea is used for factors. Therefore, factor 1 picks out all the male, third-person pronouns, while factor 2 picks out all the female pronouns. Because the PCA performed in output 7.13 shows that PC2 also contrasts pronouns by gender, there are similarities between this FA and PCA.

For this problem, compute a third model with four factors. Compare the proportion of variability for the factors compared to the principal components of output 7.13. Finally, are there any other similarities between the features revealed by the factors and those by the principal components besides gender differences?

CHAPTER 8

TEXT CLUSTERING

8.1 INTRODUCTION

This chapter discusses how to partition a collection of texts into groups, which is called *clustering*. For example, a researcher analyzes a corpus of emails to find subsets having common themes. These are not known beforehand and are determined as part of the analysis. A related task called *classification* also partitions texts into groups, but these are known prior to the analysis. For example, there are commercial programs that classify incoming emails as either spam or nonspam.

These two tasks need different types of information. First, if the groups are unknown prior to the analysis, then a quantitative similarity measure is required that can be applied to any two documents. This approach is called *unsupervised* because computing similarities can be done by the program without human intervention.

Second, if the groups are known beforehand, then the algorithm requires *training* data that includes the correct group assignments. For example, developing a spam program requires training the algorithm with emails that are correctly labeled. A human provides these, so this approach is called *supervised*. However, creating or purchasing training data requires resources.

Because classification needs training data, which typically does not exist in the public domain, this chapter focuses on clustering. This only requires texts and an algorithm. As seen earlier in this book, there are plenty of the former available on the Web, and the latter exists in the statistical package R.

Practical Text Mining with Perl. By Roger Bilisoly
Copyright © 2008 John Wiley & Sons, Inc.

8.2 CLUSTERING

Similarity measures are introduced in section 5.7. Although cosine similarity or TF-IDF can be used, this chapter uses the simpler Euclidean distance formula from geometry, but once this approach is mastered, the others are straightforward to do.

8.2.1 Two-Variable Example of *k*-Means

We start by considering only two variables, so the data can be plotted. Once two-dimensional clustering is understood, then it is not hard to imagine similar ideas in higher dimensions.

The k-means clustering algorithm is a simple technique that can be extended to perform classification, so it is a good algorithm to start with. The letter k stands for the number of clusters desired. If this number is not known beforehand, analyzing several values finds the best one.

Let us consider a simple, made-up example that consists of two variables x and y. The data set is shown in figure 8.1, where it is obvious (to a human) that there are two clusters, which are in the northeast and southwest corners of the plot. Does k-means agree with our intuition?

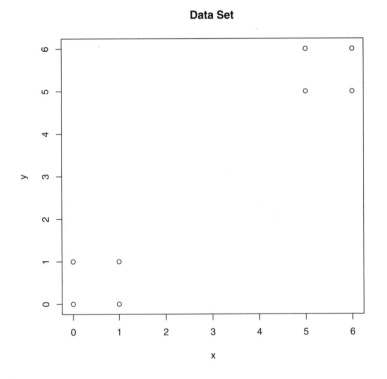

Figure 8.1   A two variable data set that has two obvious clusters.

Since k must be specified before k-means begins, this plot is useful because it suggests $k = 2$. There are 256 ways to partition eight objects data into 2 groups. In general, for k

groups and n data values, there are k^n partitions: see problem 8.1 for details. Unfortunately, this function grows quickly. With 100 data values and four groups, 4^{100} has 61 digits, which is enormous. Hence, any clustering algorithm cannot perform an exhaustive examination of all the possibilities.

For $k = 2$, k-means picks two data values at random, which become the initial "centers" of two regions, which are the sets of points in the plain closest to its center. For two, this creates two half-planes, where each point on the dividing line is exactly equidistant from the centers. Suppose that the points $(0,1)$ and $(1,1)$ are the initial centers.

It is well known from geometry that this dividing line is the perpendicular bisector of the line segment formed by these two points. This is best understood by looking at figure 8.2. This line is half-way between the points $(0,1)$ and $(1,1)$, and it is at right angles to this line segment. As claimed, the points in the left half-plain are closer to the point $(0,1)$, and those in the right half-plain are closest to the point $(1,1)$.

Perpendicular Bisector of the Line Segment (0,1) to (1,1)

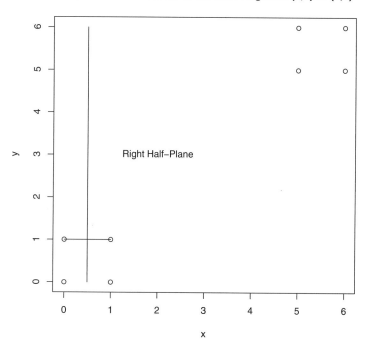

Figure 8.2   The perpendicular bisector of the line segment from $(0,1)$ to $(1,1)$ divides this plot into two half-planes. The points in each form the two clusters.

This line partitions the eight data points into two groups. The left one consists of $(0,0)$ and $(0,1)$, and the other six points are in the right one. Once the data is partitioned, then the old centers are replaced by the centroids of these groups of points. Recall that the centroid is the center of mass, and its x-coordinate is the average of the x-coordinates of its group, and its y-coordinate is likewise the average of its group's y-coordinates. So in figure 8.3, the two centroids are given by equations 8.1 and 8.2.

$$x = (0+0)/2 = 0, \quad y = (0+1)/2 = 0.5 \tag{8.1}$$

$$x = (1+1+5+5+6+6)/6 = 4, \quad y = (0+1+5+6+5+6)/6 = 3.83 \tag{8.2}$$

These two centroids are denoted by the asterisks in figure 8.3. The line segment between these centroids is not drawn this time, just the perpendicular bisecting line, which divides the data into two groups of four points: the two squares in the southwest and northeast corners of the plot that intuition suggests.

New Partition of Data

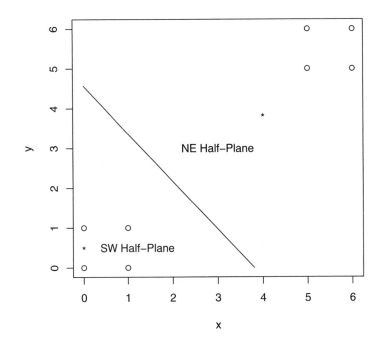

Figure 8.3   The next iteration of k-means after figure 8.2. The line splits the data into two groups, and the two centroids are given by the asterisks.

Note that the centroids of these two squares are (0.5, 0.5) and (5.5, 5.5). The new dividing line goes from (0, 6) to (6, 0), which cuts the region of the plot into southwest and northeast triangles. Hence the two groups have not changed, and so the k-means algorithm has converged. That is, the next iteration of centers does not change. The final answer is that the two groups are $\{(0,0),(1,0),(0,1),(1,1)\}$ and $\{(5,5),(5,6),(6,5),(6,6)\}$.

The above example captures the spirit of k-means. In general, the algorithm follows these steps for k groups, m variables, and n data values. First, k data points are selected at random and are designated as the k centers. Second, these centers partition all the data points into k subsets. The data points in any set are exactly those that are closer to its center than to any other center.

Third, the data points in each subset are averaged together to form the centroid, which is done for each of the coordinates. These centroids become the new centers. Fourth, steps two and three are repeated until the centers do not change anymore. Once this is achieved, then this partition of the data are the k clusters.

These steps can be implemented into Perl, but R already has the function kmeans(). The above example is repeated using R in the next section. Also, for more on making plots that partition the plane when there is more than two centers, see problem 8.2.

8.2.2 k-Means with R

Using R is much easier than hand computations, of course. The function kmeans() just needs a data matrix and the number of centers, that is, the value of k. Once the eight data points in figure 8.1 are put into the matrix data and k is set to 2, then R does the rest, which is shown in output 8.1.

Output 8.1 An example of k-means using the data in figure 8.1 and k set to 2.

```
> data = matrix(c(0,0,0,1,1,0,1,1,5,5,5,6,6,5,6,6),8,2,byrow=T)
> kmeans(data, centers=2)
K-means clustering with 2 clusters of sizes 4, 4

Cluster means:
  [,1] [,2]
1  0.5  0.5
2  5.5  5.5

Clustering vector:
[1] 1 1 1 1 2 2 2 2

Within cluster sum of squares by cluster:
[1] 2 2
```

As found by hand, the final centroids (denoted *cluster means* in the R output) are (0.5, 0.5) and (5.5, 5.5). The *clustering vector* labels each data point in the matrix data. That is, the first four points are in cluster 1, and the last four points are in cluster 2. This again agrees with the partition found by hand.

The *within sum of squares* is the sum of the squared distances from each point of a cluster to its center. For example, for group 1, which consists of the four points $\{(0,0), (0,1), (1,0), (1,1)\}$, the distance from each of these to the centroid, (0.5, 0.5) is $1/\sqrt{2}$. This distance squared is 0.5 for each point, so the sum is four times as big, or 2, which is the value given in the R output.

By looking at figure 8.1, setting k to 2 is obvious. However, kmeans() produces clusters for any value of k between 1 and n (these two extreme cases are trivial, so they are not allowed). Consider $k = 4$ where intuition suggests that each square splits into two opposite sides. However, there are two ways to do this for each square. For example, the southwest square can be split into $\{(0,0), (0,1)\}$ and $\{(1,0), (1,1)\}$, but $\{(0,0), (1,0)\}$ and $\{(0,1), (1,1)\}$ is also possible. Hence there are four ways all together to cluster this data set, or so says intuition. Output 8.2 puts this claim to the test.

Output 8.2 Second example of *k*-means using the data in figure 8.1 with 4 centers.

```
> data = matrix(c(0,0,0,1,1,0,1,1,5,5,5,6,6,5,6,6),8,2,byrow=T)
> out=kmeans(data, centers=4); out$cluster
[1] 2 4 2 4 1 3 1 3
> out=kmeans(data, centers=4); out$cluster
[1] 4 2 4 2 1 1 3 3
> out=kmeans(data, centers=4); out$cluster
[1] 2 2 3 3 4 1 4 1
> out=kmeans(data, centers=4); out$cluster
[1] 1 1 2 2 4 3 4 3
> out=kmeans(data, centers=4); out$cluster
[1] 2 2 3 1 4 4 4 4
```

Note that the semicolon allows multiple statements on the same line (as is true with Perl). Also, out$cluster contains the cluster labels. The first four cases agree with the argument made above using intuition. For example, the first result gives 2 4 2 4 1 3 1 3. This means that the first and third points, $\{(0,0),(1,0)\}$, compose cluster 2, and the second and fourth points, $\{(0,1),(1,1)\}$, are cluster 4, and so forth.

However, the fifth result makes cluster 4 the entire northeast square of points, and the southwest square is split into three clusters. Since this type of division occurred only once, kmeans() does not find it as often as the intuitive solution. However, this example does underscore two properties of this algorithm. First, its output is not deterministic due to the random choice of initial centers. Second, as shown by the fifth result, the quality of the solutions can vary.

Because the clusters produced by kmeans() can vary, the researcher should try computing several solutions to see how consistent the results are. For example, when centers=2 is used, the results are consistently the northeast and southwest squares (although which of these squares is labeled 1 varies). That this is false for centers=4 suggests that these data values do not naturally split into four clusters.

The next section applies clustering to analyzing pronouns in Poe's 68 short stories. The first example considers two pronouns for simplicity. However, several values of k are tried.

8.2.3 *He* versus *She* in Poe's Short Stories

The data values in figure 8.1 were picked to illustrate the *k*-means algorithm. This section returns to text data, and we analyze the use of the pronouns *he* and *she* in the 68 short stories of Edgar Allan Poe .

Since the counts for these two function words probably depend on the story lengths, we consider the rate of usage, which is a count divided by the length of its story. Although it is possible these are still a function of story length (see the discussion of mean word frequency in section 4.6 for a cautionary example), this should be mitigated.

These rates can be computed in Perl, or we can read the story lengths into R, which then does the computations. Both approaches are fine, and the latter one is done here.

Code sample 7.4 shows how to create a CSV file that contains the counts for the eight pronouns. Since *he* and *she* are included, they are extractable once read into R.

Code sample 7.1 creates a file with the number of words in each story. This results in an array of hashes called @dict that stores the number of times each word appears in each Poe story. Summing up the counts for all the words in a particular story produces the length of that story, which is done in code sample 8.1.

Code Sample 8.1 Computes the word lengths of the 68 Poe stories. This requires the array of hashes @dict from code sample 7.1.

```
open(SIZE, ">size.csv") or die;

for $i ( 0 .. $#dict ) {
  $sum = 0;
  foreach $x ( keys %{$dict[$i]} ) {
    $sum += $dict[$i]{$x};
  }
  print SIZE "$sum\n";
}
```

Assuming that the files Poe68.csv and size.csv have been created by code sample 7.4 and the combination of code samples 7.1 and 8.1, then these are read into R as done in output 8.3. Note that the rate is per thousand words so that the resulting numbers are near 1. Values this size are easier for a person to grasp.

Output 8.3 Computation of the rate per thousand words of the pronouns *he* and *she*.

```
> size = read.csv("C:\\size.csv",header=F)
> Poe8pn = read.csv("c:\\Poe68_pronouns.csv",header=T)
> attach(Poe8pn)
> heRate = he/size*1000
> sheRate = she/size*1000
> summary(heRate)
   Min. 1st Qu.  Median    Mean 3rd Qu.    Max.
  0.000   2.872   6.576   7.392   9.660  24.450
> summary(sheRate)
   Min. 1st Qu.  Median    Mean 3rd Qu.    Max.
 0.0000  0.0000  0.2527  1.3390  1.9390 11.5300
```

Since this data is two-dimensional, plotting heRate against sheRate shows the complete data set. This is done with the plot() function, as given below. Figure 8.4 shows the results.

```
> plot(heRate, sheRate)
```

Although the data points are not uniformly distributed, the number and location of the clusters are not intuitively clear. Now kmeans() proves its worth by providing insight on potential clusters.

The type option for plot() changes the symbol used to indicate points. Setting type="n" produces a blank plot, but the locations of the data points are remembered by R. The function text() then prints characters at these data point locations. These are the cluster labels produced by kmeans(), which is done in output 8.4, and figure 8.5 shows the resulting plot. Note that the function cbind() combines the vectors heRate and sheRate as columns into a matrix called heSheRate.

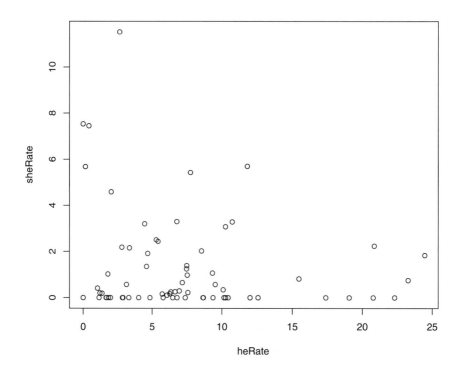

Figure 8.4   Scatterplot of `heRate` against `sheRate` for Poe's 68 short stories.

Output 8.4 Computation of two clusters for the `heRate` and `sheRate` data.

```
> heSheRate = cbind(heRate, sheRate)
> plot(heRate, sheRate, type="n")
> text(heRate, sheRate, kmeans(heSheRate,centers=2)$cluster)
```

Figure 8.5 shows that a group of stories with high rates of *he* is identified as a cluster. Since the computer is doing the work, investigating other values of k is easily done. Output 8.5 shows the code that produces figure 8.6. Note that the command `par(mfrow=c(2,2))` creates a two by two grid of plots in this figure.

As the number of clusters goes from two to three, the large cluster on the left in figure 8.5 (its points are labeled with 1's) is split into two parts. However, the cluster on the right (labeled with 2's) remains intact. Remember that the labels of the clusters can easily change, as shown in output 8.2, so referring to clusters by location makes sense.

Going from three to four clusters, the rightmost one is almost intact (one data value is relabeled), but a small cluster is formed within the two on the left. Nonetheless, the original three clusters are relatively stable. For k equals five and six, subdividing continues.

Now that R has done its work, it is up to the researcher to decide whether or not any of these clusters seem meaningful. We consider cluster 2 for $k = 6$. This has stories with high

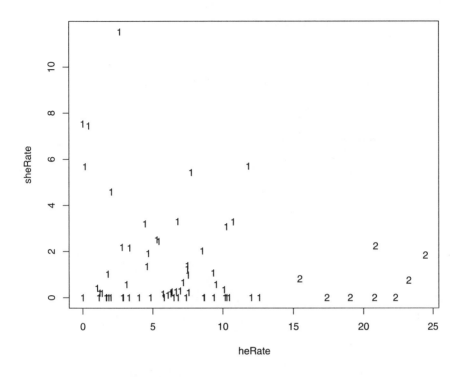

Figure 8.5   Plot of two short story clusters fitted to the heRate and sheRate data.

Output 8.5 Computation of three, four, five, and six clusters for the heRate and sheRate data.

```
> par(mfrow=c(2,2))
> plot(heRate, sheRate, type="n")
> text(heRate, sheRate, kmeans(heSheRate,centers=3)$cluster)
> plot(heRate, sheRate, type="n")
> text(heRate, sheRate, kmeans(heSheRate,centers=4)$cluster)
> plot(heRate, sheRate, type="n")
> text(heRate, sheRate, kmeans(heSheRate,centers=5)$cluster)
> plot(heRate, sheRate, type="n")
> text(heRate, sheRate, kmeans(heSheRate,centers=6)$cluster)
```

---

usages of *she* (above 4 per 1000 words), but low usages of *he* (below 3 per 1000 words). The titles printed out by code sample 7.1 are read into R by output 8.6, which prints out the ones corresponding to the cluster. For more on how this code works, see problem 8.3.

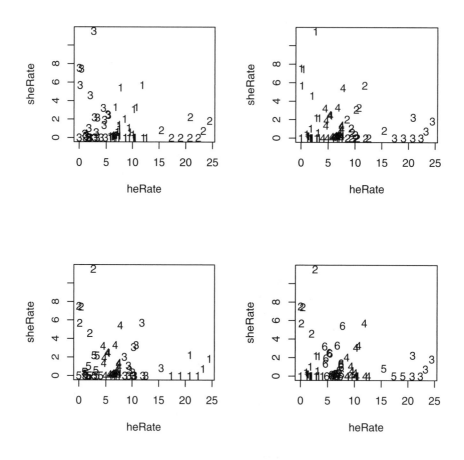

Figure 8.6   Plots of three, four, five, and six short story clusters fitted to the `heRate` and `sheRate` data.

Three of these stories are similar in their literary plots. "Eleonora," "Ligeia," and "Morella" are all told by a male narrator and are about the death of a wife (more precisely, in "Eleonora" the narrator's cousin dies before they can wed, and in "Morella," two wives in a row die). A human reader also thinks of "Berenice" since in this story the narrator's cousin also dies before they are to wed. It turns out that this story is not far from the above cluster (*he* occurs at 2.80 per 1000, but *she* only occurs at 2.18 per 1000). "The Spectacles" is about a man who falls in love and eventually marries, but this story is unlike the above four stories in that it is humorous in tone. Finally, "The Island of the Fay" is narrated by a man who sees a female fay (which is a fairy).

The above clustering is rather crude compared to how a human reader groups stories. On the other hand, the cluster considered did consist entirely of stories with narrators talking about a woman, though it does not capture all of them. Nonetheless, *k*-means is detecting structure among these works.

Output 8.6 Finding the names of the stories of cluster 2 in figure 8.6 for $k = 6$.

```
> poeTitles=read.csv("C:\\Poe 68 Titles.txt",header=F)
> out=kmeans(heSheRate, centers=6)
> plot(heRate, sheRate, type="n")
> text(heRate, sheRate, out$cluster)
> as.matrix(poeTitles)[out$cluster==2]
[1] "THE ISLAND OF THE FAY" "ELEONORA"        "LIGEIA"
[4] "MORELLA"               "THE SPECTACLES"
```

8.2.4   Poe Clusters Using Eight Pronouns

There is nothing special about two variables except for the ease of plotting, and k-means has no such limitation because it only needs the ability to compute the distance between centers and data values. The distance formula in n-dimensional space is given by equation 5.9 and is not hard to compute, so k-means is easily done for more than two variables.

To illustrate this, we use the pronoun data read into Poe8pn in output 8.3. There the variables heRate and sheRate are created, but by using matrix methods, it is easy to create rates for all eight variables at once. This is done in output 8.7, which also performs the k-means analysis with two clusters, and then plots these results for the first two pronouns, *he* and *she*. Note that heRate is the same as Poe8rate[,1], and that sheRate is the same as Poe8rate[,2]. This is easily checked by subtraction, for example, the command below returns a vector of 68 zeros.

```
heRate - Poe8rate[,1]
```

Output 8.7 The third-person pronoun rates in Poe's short stories clustered into two groups, which are labeled 1 and 2.

```
> Poe8rate=Poe8pn/size*1000
> out=kmeans(Poe8rate, centers=2); out$cluster
 1  2  3  4  5  6  7  8  9 10 11 12 13 14 15 16 17 18 19 20 21 22 23
 1  1  2  1  1  1  1  1  2  1  1  2  1  2  1  2  2  1  2  1  1  1  1
24 25 26 27 28 29 30 31 32 33 34 35 36 37 38 39 40 41 42 43 44 45 46
 1  1  1  1  1  1  1  1  1  1  1  2  2  2  2  2  2  1  1  1  2  2  1
47 48 49 50 51 52 53 54 55 56 57 58 59 60 61 62 63 64 65 66 67 68
 1  2  2  1  1  1  2  1  1  1  1  1  1  1  1  2  2  2  2  1  2  1
> plot(heRate, sheRate, type="n")
> text(heRate, sheRate, out$cluster)
```

The clusters computed in output 8.7 are plotted in figure 8.7. Note there are similarities with figure 8.5. For example, cluster 2 for both plots include all the stories with rates of the word *he* above 15 words per 1000. However, there are additional points in cluster 2 in figure 8.7, and these appear to be closer to the other cluster's center. However, remember that this only shows two of the eight variables, and so these 2's are closest to a center in 8 dimensions.

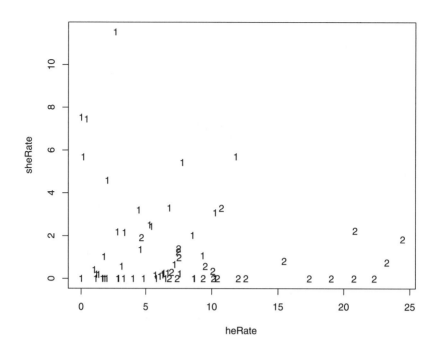

Figure 8.7   Plots of two short story clusters based on eight variables, but only plotted for the two variables `heRate` and `sheRate`.

The above example reveals one problem when working with 3 or more variables: visualization is hard to do. Since there are 8 variables in this data set, there is a total of 28 plots of 2 variables at a time. A sample of 4 more projections of the rates is plotted in figure 8.8.

All five plots in figures 8.7 and 8.8 show the same two clusters. They are all just different views of the eight-dimensional data projected onto planes defined by two axes corresponding to two pronoun rates. However, there are an infinite number of planes that can be projected onto, so these five plots are far from exhausting the possibilities. For an example of losing information by just looking at a few projections, see problem 8.4.

As the number of variables grows, this problem of visualization becomes worse and worse. And with text, high dimensionality is common. For example, if each word gets its own dimension, then all of Poe's short stories are representable in 20,000-dimensional space.

However, there are ways to reduce dimensionality. In chapter 7, the technique of PCA is introduced, which is a way to transform the original data set into principal components. Often a few of these contain most of the variability in the original data set. In the next section, PCA is applied to the `Poe8rate` data set.

8.2.5   Clustering Poe Using Principal Components

Output 7.13 shows a PCA of the eight third-person pronouns counts. Since 78.2% of the variability is contained in the first two principal components, and 84.97% are in the first three, using only two or three makes sense.

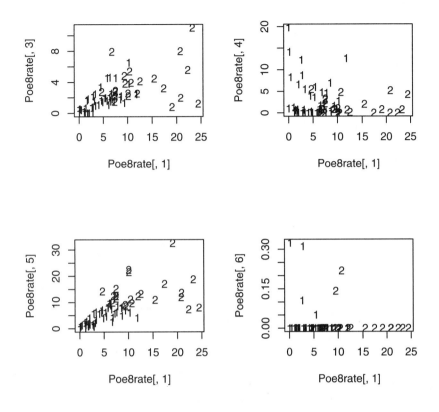

Figure 8.8 Four more plots showing projections of the two short story clusters found in output 8.7 onto two pronoun rate axes.

In this section we do a PCA of the eight pronoun rate variables computed earlier in this chapter, and then perform clustering using two of the PCs. These results are plotted and are compared with the clusters in the preceding section. In addition, we compare the PCA of the rates with the PCA of the counts. Any differences are likely due to the effect of story size.

Output 8.7 defines the matrix `Poe8rate`, which is the input to `prcomp()` in output 8.8. The cumulative proportions for the PCA model of the pronoun counts (see output 7.13) are reproduced below.

```
0.457 0.782 0.8497 0.8992 0.943 0.9716 0.9910 1.0000
```

Notice that the cumulative proportions of the rate PCs grow even slower, so the variability is more spread out. The other extreme is output 7.12, where the first PC has 97% of the variability. In this case, using just one is reasonable because little variability is lost. However, here the first PC has only 41.6% of it, so considering additional PCs is reasonable.

Output 8.9 gives the weights of the first five PCs of `Poe8rate`. Note that PC1 compares the male and female pronouns, and PC2 is close to an average of the pronoun rates. Compare

Output 8.8 Principal components analysis of the eight third-person pronoun rates for the 68 Poe short stories.

```
> out = prcomp(Poe8rate, scale=T)
> summary(out)
Importance of components:
                         PC1   PC2   PC3    PC4    PC5    PC6
Standard deviation     1.825 1.422 0.867 0.7876 0.7385 0.6165
Proportion of Variance 0.416 0.253 0.094 0.0775 0.0682 0.0475
Cumulative Proportion  0.416 0.669 0.763 0.8404 0.9086 0.9561
                         PC7    PC8
Standard deviation     0.4968 0.3227
Proportion of Variance 0.0309 0.0130
Cumulative Proportion  0.9870 1.0000
```

this to output 7.13, where the same interpretations hold except that the order is reversed, so controlling for story size by using rates increases the importance of gender in pronoun usage.

Since the later PCs still explain 33.1% of the variability, it is worth checking how interpretable they are. This is done by noting the largest weights in absolute value, and then considering their signs. For example, *she*, *her*, and *hers* have the biggest weights in PC3, where the first two are positive and the last one is negative. So this PC contrasts *she* and *her* with *hers*. Similarly, PC4 contrasts *him* with *his*.

The theory of statistics states that PCs partition variability in a certain way, but practical importance is a separate issue. Hence, collaboration with a subject domain expert is useful for interpreting statistical results. Consequently, to decide whether or not these PCs are interesting is a question to ask a linguist.

Output 8.9 The weights of the first five PCs of `Poe8rate` from output 8.8.

```
> out$rotation
                  PC1         PC2          PC3          PC4         PC5
he       0.3732562 -0.3707989  0.089331837 -0.01265033 -0.3708173
she     -0.3965089 -0.3789554  0.375093941  0.05746540 -0.1849496
him      0.3520300 -0.2794273 -0.181195197  0.72612489 -0.2388015
her     -0.4004131 -0.3699889  0.250578838 -0.13227136 -0.3614189
his      0.3928507 -0.2949958  0.109616655 -0.53150251  0.1136037
hers    -0.2608834 -0.2790116 -0.861791903 -0.24679127 -0.1807408
himself  0.3299412 -0.4193282  0.007583433 -0.15142985  0.3521454
herself -0.2965666 -0.4040092 -0.030729482  0.29232309  0.6863374
```

Now that the PC weights are computed, these create a new data set of eight uncorrelated variables. We use all eight PCs for clustering in output 8.10, although only the first two PCs are plotted in figure 8.9, which represents 66.9% of the variability.

However, clustering using only the first two PCs is also possible, which is done by replacing the second line of output 8.10 by the command below. Now the square brackets specify just the first two columns. This is left for the interested reader to try.

Output 8.10 Computing clusters by using all eight principal components.

```
> pca_poe8rate = scale(Poe8rate) %*% out$rotation
> out = kmeans(pca_poe8rate, centers=2)
> plot(pca_poe8rate[,1], pca_poe8rate[,2],type="n")
> text(pca_poe8rate[,1], pca_poe8rate[,2],out$cluster)
```

```
> out = kmeans(pca_poe8rate[,1:2], centers=2)
```

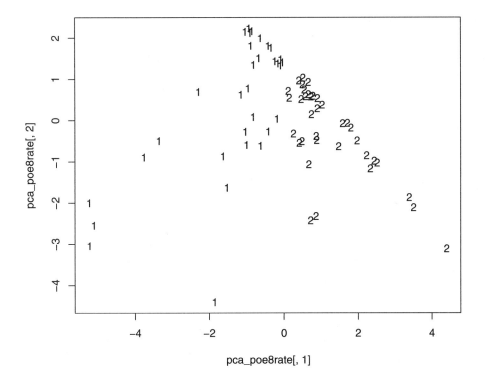

Figure 8.9 Eight principal components split into two short story clusters and projected onto the first two PCs.

As done in output 8.6, after the models have been run, the last step is to consider what is in each cluster. In this case, how have the Poe stories been partitioned? And as a human reader, do these two groups matter? This is also left to the interested reader.

Remember that `kmeans()` is just one type of grouping. The next section briefly introduces hierarchical clustering. However, there are many more algorithms, which are left to the references given at the end of this chapter.

8.2.6   Hierarchical Clustering of Poe's Short Stories

Clustering is popular, and there are many algorithms that do it. This section gives an example of one additional technique, hierarchical clustering.

Any type of clustering requires a similarity measure. The geometric (or Euclidean) distance between two stories is the distance between the vectors that represent them, which is used in this chapter. However, other measures are used, for example, the Mahalanobis distance, which takes into account the correlations between variables. So when reading about clustering, note how similarity is computed.

The example in this section uses hierarchical clustering and Euclidean distance applied to the Poe8rate data set . Doing this in R is easy because hclust() computes the former, and dist() computes the latter.

In hierarchical clustering the groups are summarized in a tree structure, which is called a *dendrogram* and resembles a mobile. The code to do this is given in output 8.11, and the results are given in figure 8.10.

Output 8.11 Computing the hierarchical clustering dendrogram for the 68 Poe stories.

```
> out = hclust(dist(Poe8rate))
> plot(as.dendrogram(out))
```

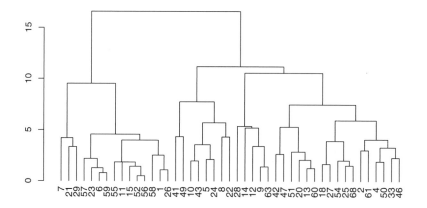

Figure 8.10   A portion of the dendrogram computed in output 8.11, which shows hierarchical clusters for Poe's 68 short stories.

This figure indicates distances on the *y*-axis. At the bottom of each branch of the tree there is a number that labels the story, for example, 1 stands for "The Unparalleled Adventures of One Hans Pfaall." The clusters are obtained by cutting a branch of the dendrogram. For example, stories 40 and 67 form a small cluster (these are second and third from the left in figure 8.10). Going a level further up the tree, the following is a cluster: 40, 67, 17, 53, 16, 37. In general, all the stories below any point of the dendrogram constitute a cluster, and it is up to the researcher to decide which ones are meaningful.

Unfortunately, the numbers at the bottom of figure 8.10 are small and crammed together due to the size of the tree. However, see problem 8.5 for another example using the transpose of `Poe8rate`. This finds the clusters among the eight pronouns.

This ends our discussion of clustering. The next section focuses on classification, and the chapter ends with references for further reading on this vast subject.

8.3 A NOTE ON CLASSIFICATION

Classification of texts is both practical and profitable. For example, email spam filters are big business. However, we do not cover this because it requires a training data set. The other examples in this book use text that is available over the Web and in the public domain. However, public domain collections of text that are already classified are rare.

In addition, many texts in this book come from famous writers, for example, Charles Dickens and Edgar Allan Poe, and almost all of their literary output is known. So training an algorithm on what they have written in order to classify newly discovered works is rarely needed.

When working with classification algorithms, researchers avoid overfitting because this usually generalizes poorly. However, literary critics often search for peculiarities of a specific text, or for the subtle interconnections of a group of texts. So overfitting a complete body of work can be profitable if it uncovers information interesting to a researcher. However, the results can be trivial, too, as seen in the example in the next section.

8.3.1 Decision Trees and Overfitting

A decision tree algorithm classifies objects by creating if-then statements of the following form.

```
If Property P is true, then classify object with Label L.
```

If a researcher uses words to classify texts without worrying about overfitting, then it is easy to identify any group of texts. This is a consequence of Zipf's law (see section 3.7.1) because it implies there are numerous words that only appear once in any collection of texts.

Here is an example of this using Poe's short stories. Suppose a rule is desired to select exactly the following: "The Balloon Hoax," "X-ing a Paragrab," "The Oblong Box," and "The Sphinx." These stories are arbitrary, and the idea below works for any group of Poe stories.

This is one rule that works. A Poe story is one of these four if and only if it has one of the following words: *authentic*, *doll*, *leak*, or *seventy-four*. This rule is created by examining a frequency list of words for all 68 stories put together. By Zipf's law this contains numerous words that appear exactly once. Among these, one word for each of these four stories is picked. There are many such words, so there are many rules like this, but few, if any, provide any insight into the literary similarities of this group.

In spite of this example, decision rule algorithms can be useful. For more information on this, look at the appropriate references in the next section. Finally, for some specific advise on finding the above rule using Perl, see problem 8.6, which reveals one trivial property that these four stories do share.

8.4 REFERENCES

This chapter is just an introduction to clustering. Many more techniques exist in the literature, and many functions to do clustering exist in R. For another introductory explanation of this, see chapter 8 of Daniel Larose's *Discovering Knowledge in Data* [69]. For clustering applied to the Web, see chapters 3 and 4 of Zdravko Markov and Daniel Larose's *Data Mining the Web* [77]. Both of these books give clear exposition and examples.

For clustering applied to language, start with chapter 14 of Christopher Manning and Hinrich Schütze's *Foundations of Statistical Natural Language Processing* [75]. Then try Jakob Kogan's *Introduction to Clustering Large and High-Dimensional Data* [66]. This book focuses on sparse data, which is generally true for text applications.

Clustering belongs to the world of unsupervised methods in data mining. For an introduction that assumes a strong statistical background, see chapter 14 of Trevor Hastie, Robert Tibshirani, and Jerome Friedman's *The Elements of Statistical Learning* [52]. This book also discusses a number of other data mining techniques. Sholom Weiss, Nitin Indurkhya, Tong Zhang, and Fred Damerau's *Text Mining* [125] also covers both clustering and classification, and also discusses the links between data mining and text mining.

There are many more books, but the above are informative and provide many further references in their bibliographies.

8.5 LAST TRANSITION

Chapters 4 through 8 each focus on different disciplines that are related to text mining. For example, chapter 5 shows how to use the technique of term-document matrices to analyze text. Moreover, chapters 2 through 8 give extensive programming examples.

Chapter 9, however, introduces three, short topics in text mining. These include brief programming examples that are less detailed than the rest of this book. These, along with references to books that deal with text mining directly, provide some parting ideas for the reader.

PROBLEMS

8.1 In section 8.2.1 it is claimed that for k groups and n data values, there are k^n partitions. This problem shows why this is the case.

    a) Any clustering is representable by a vector with n entries, each with a label of a number from 1 through k. In fact, this is how kmeans() indicates the clusters it has found; for example, see output 8.2.

        Suppose there are only two data values, hence only two entries in this vector. The first can have any label from 1 through k. For each of these, the second entry also can have any label from 1 through k. This makes k choices for the first, and for each of these, k choices for the second. So for both labels, there are k times k, or k^2, choices.

        Extend this argument for n entries, each having k choices. This justifies the claim made at the beginning of section 8.2.1.

    b) The above argument, unfortunately, is a simplification. For example, the third and fourth repetitions of kmeans() in output 8.2 represent the same clusters, but they are labeled with different numbers. Counting up the number of groups without duplications from changing labels requires a more complicated approach, which is not done here. For more information, see chapter 1 of Constantine's *Combinatorial Theory and Statistical Design* [32].

8.2 As discussed in section 8.2.1, for two centers, the plane is divided into two half-planes. For each, all the points in it are closer to its center than to the other center, and the dividing line between these is the perpendicular bisector of the line segment between the centers.

For three or more centers, the situation is more complex and requires a more sophisticated algorithm. The result is called a *Voronoi diagram*, which is interesting to see. Since there is an R function to do it, we consider an example here.

Like Perl, R also has packages that are downloadable, which provide new functions for the user. The most current information on how to do this is at the Comprehensive R Archive Network (CRAN) [34], so it is not described in this book. For this problem, go to CRAN and figure out how to perform downloads, and then do this for the package `Tripack` [105].

Then try running output 8.12, which creates the Voronoi diagram for a set of 50 random centers where both coordinates are between 0 and 1. That is, these are random points in the unit square. Your plot will resemble the one in figure 8.11, where the stars are the centers and each region is a polygon with circles at its corners.

Output 8.12 Creating a Voronoi diagram for a set of 50 random centers for problem 8.2.

```
> x = runif(50)
> y = runif(50)
> out = voronoi.mosaic(x, y)
> plot.voronoi(out)
```

8.3 This problem discusses how to select subsets of a vector in R. In output 8.6, story titles are printed that corresponded to one of the clusters found by `kmeans()`. This is accomplished by putting a vector of logical values in the square brackets.

Output 8.13 reproduces output 8.6 and, in addition, shows that the names of the stories are selected by TRUEs. In this case, these are the titles of the stories in cluster 2.

Output 8.13 Using a logical vector to select a subset of another vector for problem 8.3.

```
> poeTitles=read.csv("C:\\Poe 68 Titles.txt",header=F)
> out=kmeans(heSheRate,centers=4)
> plot(heRate, sheRate, type="n")
> text(heRate, sheRate, out$cluster)
> out$cluster==2
 [1] FALSE FALSE FALSE FALSE FALSE FALSE FALSE FALSE FALSE FALSE
[11] FALSE FALSE FALSE FALSE FALSE FALSE FALSE FALSE FALSE FALSE
[21]  TRUE FALSE FALSE FALSE FALSE FALSE FALSE FALSE FALSE  TRUE
[31]  TRUE  TRUE FALSE  TRUE FALSE FALSE FALSE FALSE FALSE FALSE
[41] FALSE FALSE FALSE FALSE FALSE FALSE FALSE FALSE FALSE FALSE
[51] FALSE FALSE FALSE FALSE FALSE FALSE FALSE FALSE FALSE FALSE
[61] FALSE FALSE FALSE FALSE FALSE FALSE FALSE FALSE
> as.matrix(poeTitles)[out$cluster==2]
[1] "THE ISLAND OF THE FAY" "ELEONORA"          "LIGEIA"
[4] "MORELLA"               "THE SPECTACLES"
```

Voronoi mosaic

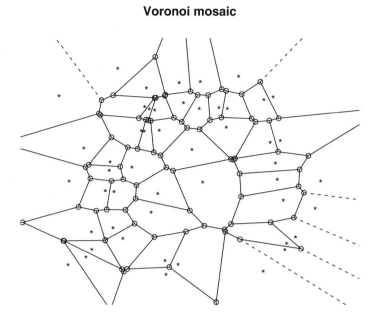

out

Figure 8.11   The plot of the Voronoi diagram computed in output 8.12.

Try this trick with simpler vectors using output 8.14 as a model. Note that the function `seq()` produces a sequence of values. Its first and second arguments are the starting and stopping values, and the third argument is the increment. Finally, the logical operators in R are the same as the numerical ones in Perl: `==` for equals, `>` for greater than, and so forth.

a) Construct a vector with the values 1 through 100 inclusive and then select all the multiples of 7. Hint: `%%` is the modulus operator, which returns the remainder when dividing an integer by another one.

b) Construct a vector with the values 1 through 100 inclusive. Select a sample such that every value has a 10% chance of being picked. Hint: try using `runif(100) < 0.10`. Note that `runif(n)` returns a vector containing n random values between 0 and 1.

c) Construct a vector with the values 1 through 100 inclusive. Take a random sample of size 10 using `sample()`.

d) Perform a random permutation of the numbers 1 through 100 inclusive. Hint: use `sample()`. This also can be done by using `order()` as shown in code sample 9.7.

8.4   Section 8.2.4 claims that a finite number of projections loses some information from the original data set. To prove this requires knowledge about calculus and the Radon transform. This problem merely gives an example of information loss when two-dimensional data is projected onto the x and y-axes.

Output 8.14 Examples of selecting entries of a vector. For problem 8.3.

```
> x = seq(1, 10, 1)
> x
 [1]  1  2  3  4  5  6  7  8  9 10
> x[x %% 3 == 0]
 [1] 3 6 9
> x[runif(10) > 0.50]
 [1]  1  5  6  7 10
> x[runif(10) > 0.50]
 [1]  1  2  4  5  6 10
> x[runif(10) > 0.50]
 [1] 1 2 7
> sample(x, 3)
 [1] 2 8 1
> sample(x, 3)
 [1] 7 2 3
> sample(x,length(x))
 [1]  9  4  8 10  1  6  3  7  5  2
> sample(x,length(x))
 [1]  2  4  1  3  5 10  8  7  6  9
```

Consider the four two-dimensional plots in figure 8.12. All have points distributed uniformly in certain regions. All the projections of these four plots onto either the x or y-axis produces a uniform distribution. In fact, these four plots suggest numerous other two-dimensional distributions with uniform projections. Hence two projections do not uniquely determine the two-dimensional distribution of the data.

Unfortunately, this problem only gets worse when higher dimensional data is projected onto planes. Nonetheless, looking at these projections is better than not using visual aids.

For this problem, generate the top two plots for this figure with R. Then produce histograms of the projections onto the x and y-axes using the following steps.

    a) For the upper left plot, the x and y-coordinates are random values from 0 to 12. These are produced by output 8.15. The projections of these points onto the x-axis is just the vector x. Hence `hist(x)` produces one of the two desired histograms. Do the same for the y-axis.

Output 8.15 Code for problem 8.4.a.

```
> x = runif(1000)*12
> y = runif(1000)*12
> plot(x, y)
> hist(x)
```

    b) For the upper right plot, the x and y-coordinates are either both from 0 to 6 or both from 6 to 12. These are produced by output 8.16. Use them to create the two desired histograms.

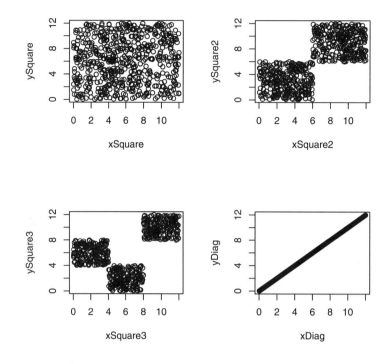

Figure 8.12 All four plots have uniform marginal distributions for both the *x* and *y*-axes. For problem 8.4.

Output 8.16 Code for problem 8.4.b.

```
> x = c(runif(500)*6, runif(500)*6+6)
> y = c(runif(500)*6, runif(500)*6+6)
```

8.5 When working with term-document matrices, it is common to focus on word distributions in texts, but there is another point of view. A researcher can also analyze the text distribution for a word, which emphasizes the rows of the term-document matrix. This provides insight on how certain words are used in a collection of documents.

After reading the material on hierarchical clustering in section 8.2.6, try to reproduce output 8.17 and figure 8.13 to answer the questions below. Hint: use output 8.11 replacing Poe8rate with its transpose.

  a) Which two pronouns are farthest apart according to output 8.17? Find these on the dendrogram.
  b) The pronouns *he* and *his* form a group as does *she* and *her*. Notice that the bar connecting the latter is lower than the one for the former. Find the distances between these two words for each pair to determine exactly how high each bar is.

Output 8.17 Distances between every pair of columns in Poe8rate. For problem 8.5.

```
> dist(t(Poe8rate))
                he      she     him     her     his    hers  himself
she        73.8112
him        57.5437 29.1106
her        73.9414 20.5586 40.1233
his        40.3734 76.7224 61.9131 77.5598
hers       77.5684 21.0204 26.1771 37.5787 79.3582
himself    71.1354 20.3757 20.5020 36.1270 72.6496  8.1322
herself    77.2866 20.2461 25.9152 36.9459 79.1043  1.3400   7.8749
```

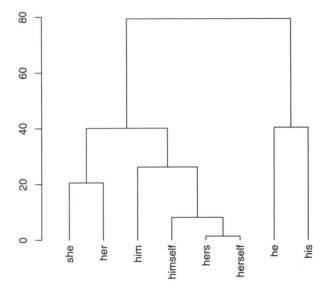

Figure 8.13   The dendrogram for the distances between pronouns based on Poe's 68 short stories. For problem 8.5.

c) It pays to think about why a result is true. For example, the main reason that *hers* and *herself* are close as vectors is that they both have many rates equal to zero, and even the nonzero rates are small. Confirm this with a scatterplot. However, two vectors with many zero or small entries are close to each other.

8.6   Section 8.3.1 gives an example of a rule that decides if a Poe story is one of four particular stories. For this problem, find the words that appear exactly once among all of his stories, and then identify which stories each word appears in.

Here are some suggestions. First, use code sample 7.1 to compute word frequencies for each story by itself and for all of them put together. The former are stored in the array of hashes `@dict`, the latter in the hash `%combined`.

Second, print out each of the words that appear exactly once in `%combined`, as well as the story in which it appears. The latter part can be done by a `for` loop letting `$i` go from 0 through 67. Then exactly one of these entries `$dict[$i]{$word}` is 1 for any `$word` found to appear exactly once in `%combined`. Finally, use the array `@name` to print out the title of this story.

The list just made allows any set of stories to be identified. For example, *authentic* appears only in "The Balloon Hoax," *doll* in "X-ing a Paragrab," *leak* in "The Oblong Box," and *seventy-four* in "The Sphinx." Hence, the rule given in the text works.

Finally, what do these four stories have in common? They are exactly the ones that contain the letter x in their titles.

CHAPTER 9

A SAMPLE OF ADDITIONAL TOPICS

9.1 INTRODUCTION

Chapters 2 through 8 all have a theme. For example, regular expressions and data structures underlie chapters 2 and 3, respectively, and chapter 8 focuses on clustering. This one, however, covers three topics in less detail. The goal is to give the interested reader a few parting ideas as well as a few references for text mining.

9.2 PERL MODULES

Not only is Perl free, there are a vast number of free packages already written for Perl. Because the details of obtaining these depends on the operating system, see The Comprehensive Perl Archive Network (CPAN) Web site `http://cpan.perl.org/` [54] for instructions on how to download them.

Perl packages are called *Perl modules*, which are grouped together by topic. Each name typically has two or three parts, which are separated by double colons. The first part usually denotes a general topic, for example, `Lingua`, `String`, and `Text`. The second part is either a subtopic or a specific module. For instance, `Lingua`'s subtopics are often specific languages; for example, `Lingua::EN` for English and `Lingua::DE` for German (DE stands for *Deutsch*). Our first example is from the former.

Practical Text Mining with Perl. By Roger Bilisoly
Copyright © 2008 John Wiley & Sons, Inc.

9.2.1   Modules for Number Words

Lingua::EN::Numbers [21] has a three-part name, where Lingua stands for language, and EN for English. The third part states what the package does in particular, and in this case, it involves numbers.

CPAN gives information about each module and tells us there are two functions in this one: num2en and num2en_ordinal. The former converts a number into English, for example, num2en(6) returns the string six. Not surprisingly, num2en_ordinal(6) returns the string sixth. An example of the former is given below.

Once a package has been downloaded to the correct place in the computer, the function use makes it accessible to the programmer. Code sample 9.1 and output 9.1 show how to invoke num2en. Note that at the end of the use command, the name of the desired function (or functions) are listed. Once these are declared, however, they are used like any other Perl function. Finally, if use attempts to access a module that has not been downloaded, then an error occurs that prints out a statement like, "Can't locate Lingua/EN/Numbers.pm in @INC ...." Note that the file extension pm stands for *Perl Module*.

Code Sample 9.1 Loading the module Lingua::EN::Numbers and then using the function num2en.

```
use Lingua::EN::Numbers num2en;

print num2en(-6), "\n", num2en(1729), "\n", num2en(1.23);
```

Output 9.1 Results from code sample 9.1.

```
negative six
one thousand seven hundred and twenty-nine
one point two three
```

As an aside, recall program 3.5, which makes an anagram dictionary from a word list. This is easily changed into an anagram dictionary for numbers. Are there two of these that are anagrams? The answer is yes, for example, *sixty-seven* and *seventy-six*. However, this just exchanges the words *six* and *seven*, that is, the same digits are used in both numbers. Are there two numbers that are anagrams, but their digits are not?

This task is much harder without this package. In general, when faced with a text mining challenge, first searching through CPAN for applicable modules is prudent. If there is a module there, then the programming is much easier. If no such module exists, and if you create a program yourself, then this is a chance to convert your code into a module and give back to the Perl community.

Since EN stands for *English*, perhaps number modules for other languages exist, and this is true. For example, Lingua::DE::Num2Word [60] translates numbers into German. This is done in code sample 9.2, which produces output 9.2.

There are other languages that have a numbers module, and the reader can search CPAN for these. The next module we consider provides lists of stop words in a variety of languages.

Code Sample 9.2 The analog of code sample 9.1 for German.

```perl
use Lingua::DE::Num2Word num2de_cardinal;

for ($i = 1; $i <= 3; ++$i) {
  print num2de_cardinal($i), ", ";
}

print "...\n";
```

Output 9.2 Results from code sample 9.2.

```
ein, zwei, drei, ...
```

9.2.2 The StopWords Module

Stop words are common function words that often do not add anything to a text analysis such as the prepositions *of* and *up*, which is discussed in section 6.3.1. However, one researcher's stop words is another's research topic. For example, when studying phrasal verbs, then prepositions are important.

The module Lingua::StopWords [102] provides an array of stop words for 12 languages. Code sample 9.3 shows how to obtain these for English and German, and output 9.3 shows the beginning of each list.

Code Sample 9.3 Example of the module Lingua::StopWords.

```perl
use Lingua::StopWords getStopWords;

$" = ',';

$reference = getStopWords('en'); # English
@stoplist = keys %{$reference};
print "@stoplist\n";

$reference = getStopWords('de');
@stoplist = keys %{$reference};  # German
print "@stoplist\n";
```

Note that the function getStopWords produces a hash reference. So @stoplist is created by dereferencing this, then applying keys to the result, which is then printed out.

Moving on, the module in the next section returns one last time to sentence segmentation. This is analyzed several times in chapter 2, and here is yet another solution.

9.2.3 The Sentence Segmentation Module

Sentence segmentation is done in sections 2.6 and 2.7.3. Lingua::EN::Sentence [127] also does this task. Code sample 9.4 applies this module to Edgar Allan Poe's "The Oval Portrait."

Output 9.3 The first few words of the English and German stoplists from code sample 9.3.

```
these,you,both,which,my,didn't,if,we'll,himself,him,own,doesn't,
he'll,each,yours,what,them,there's,your,again,but,too,and,why's,
over,shan't,of,here's, ...


einiger,habe,kann,deinen,da,anderr,meiner,dann,einer,meines,
hat,gewesen,eure,solche,ihre,mich,vom,sehr,also,allem,jener,
warst,alle,solchem,eures, ...
```

Code Sample 9.4 Example of the module Lingua::EN::Sentence, which does sentence segmentation.

```perl
use Lingua::EN::Sentence get_sentences;

$/ = undef; # Slurp mode
open(IN, "poe_oval_portrait.txt") or die;
$text = <IN>;
close(IN);

$reference = get_sentences($text);

foreach $x ( @{$reference} ) {
  print "$x\n\n";
}
```

Output 9.4 The first three sentences of Poe's "The Oval Portrait" found by code sample 9.4.

```
THE chateau into which my valet had ventured to make forcible
entrance, rather than permit me, in my desperately wounded
condition, to pass a night in the open air, was one of those
piles of commingled gloom and grandeur which have so long
frowned among the Appennines,
not less in fact than in the fancy of Mrs. Radcliffe.

To all
appearance it had been temporarily and very lately abandoned.

We established ourselves in one of the smallest and least
sumptuously furnished apartments.
```

As in the last section, the function get_sentences returns a reference to an array. This is dereferenced, and then the result is looped over by the foreach statement. Each entry is one sentence, of which the first three are shown in output 9.4.

All three modules considered above supply the programmer with new functions. However, there is another way to provide them, which is through the object-oriented programming paradigm. Although learning how to program this way requires effort, it is easy to use when provided by a module, which is shown in the next section.

9.2.4 An Object-Oriented Module for Tagging

Object-oriented (OO) programming emphasizes modular code, that is, breaking a large program into distinct pieces. How to program this way is not discussed here, but see Conway's *Object Oriented Perl* [33] for a detailed explanation. This section only gives one example of using an OO module.

When analyzing a text, knowing the parts of speech can be useful. For example, identifying verbs and prepositions helps an analysis of phrasal verbs. A program that labels words by their part of speech is called a *tagger*. The details of how this is done requires sophisticated language models. One approach uses hidden Markov models (HMM). For an example, see section 9.2 of the *Foundations of Statistical Natural Language Processing* [75]. However, using a tagger does not require knowing the theoretical details.

The key to using an OO module is the creation of *objects*. Although OO programming arose from the needs of software engineering, the core idea is simple. Objects are a way to group related subroutines together, and the latter are called *methods*.

The module Lingua::EN::Tagger [30] is a tagger, as its name suggests. Code sample 9.5 shows an example of how it is used. Note that $taggerObject is an instance of an object that has the method add_tags, which adds tags to text. The symbol -> points to a method, which is the same syntax used for references (see section 3.8.1). Hence, new is a method that creates the desired object. Output 9.5 displays the results.

Code Sample 9.5 Example of the object-oriented module Lingua::EN::Tagger, which is a parts-of-speech tagger.

```
use Lingua::EN::Tagger;
$taggerObject = Lingua::EN::Tagger->new;

$text = "He lives on the coast.";
$tagged_version = $taggerObject->add_tags($text);

print "$tagged_version\n";
```

Output 9.5 The parts of speech found by code sample 9.5.

```
<prp>He</prp> <vbz>lives</vbz> <in>on</in> <det>the</det>
<nn>coast</nn> <pp>.</pp>
```

These tags are similar to the ones in the Penn Treebank, which are widely known. For example, VBZ stands for the singular, third-person form of a verb, and note that these are XML style tags. Although code sample 9.5 looks a little different from the programs earlier in this book, it is straightforward to use.

This module also includes other methods, for example, get_sentences, which (like the module in the preceding section) segments sentences. Finally, before leaving modules, the next section mentions a few more of interest, although without examples.

9.2.5 Miscellaneous Modules

There are a vast number of modules in CPAN, and new modules are added over time. For the latest information, go to the CPAN Web site [54]. This section just mentions a few more examples to whet your appetite.

First, some of the modules are recreational. For example, `Acme::Umlautify` [101] takes text and adds umlauts to all the vowels (including *e*, *i*, and *y*). Perhaps this is silly, but it is all in good fun.

Second, there are many modules that start with `Math` or `Statistics`. For example, there are modules to work with matrices, so Perl can be used instead of R in chapter 5. There are also modules to compute statistical functions like standard deviations and correlations. For more on this see Baiocchi's article "Using Perl for Statistics" [8]. However, R can do many complex statistical tasks like `kmeans()` and `hclust()`, so it is worth learning, too. Finally, there is a module called `Statistics::R` that interfaces with R, so Perl can access it within a program and then use its output for its own computations.

Third, some of the modules are quite extensive and add amazing capabilities to a program, although only one is noted here. `LWP` [1] enables a Perl program to go online and directly access text from the Web, which is a text miner's dream come true. For example, like a browser, it can request the HTML code of a Web page and then store the results in a Perl variable, which is then available for use throughout the program. This module is complex enough that there is a book devoted to it: *Perl & LWP* by Burke [20].

Finally, just as Perl has modules available from CPAN, R also has downloadable libraries from the Comprehensive R Archive Network (CRAN) [34]. So before starting a major programming task, it is worth checking these two Web sites for what already exists. Remember that if you desire some capability enough to program it, then someone else probably felt the same way, and this person might have uploaded their work.

9.3 OTHER LANGUAGES: ANALYZING GOETHE IN GERMAN

All the texts analyzed in the earlier chapters are in English, but this only reflects my status as a monoglot. English uses the Roman alphabet with few diacritical marks, in fact, using no marks is common. Many languages also use the Roman alphabet, but with diacritical marks or extra letters. For example, German has the umlaut (which can be used with the vowels *a*, *o*, and *u*), and the double *s*, denoted *ß* in the lowercase, and called *Eszett* in German. In addition, there are other alphabets (Greek, Cyrillic, Hebrew, and so forth), and some languages use characters instead (for example, Chinese).

Thanks to the Unicode standard, a vast number of languages can be written in an electronic format, hence ready for text mining. However, languages are quite different, and an analysis that is useful in one might be meaningless in another.

As a short example, a frequency analysis of letters and words is done for the first volume of the German novel *Die Leiden des jungen Werthers* by Johann Wolfgang von Goethe. Although German and English are closely related in the Indo-European language tree, they also have numerous differences, and some of these are immediately apparent by looking at letter and word frequencies.

First we compute the letter frequencies for this novel. This is done with program 4.3 in section 4.2.2.1. Applying this to Goethe's novel produces table 9.1, which builds on output 4.2 by comparing the letter frequencies of Goethe's novel to those of Charles Dickens's *A Christmas Carol* and Poe's "The Black Cat."

Table 9.1 Letter frequencies of Dickens's *A Christmas Carol*, Poe's "The Black Cat," and Goethe's *Die Leiden des jungen Werthers*.

e: 14869	e: 2204	e: 14533
t: 10890	t: 1600	n: 9232
o: 9696	a: 1315	i: 7596
a: 9315	o: 1279	r: 5483
h: 8378	i: 1238	s: 5217
i: 8309	n: 1121	h: 5020
n: 7962	h: 985	t: 4862
s: 7916	r: 972	a: 4483
r: 7038	s: 968	d: 4307
d: 5676	d: 766	u: 3387
l: 4555	l: 684	l: 3161
u: 3335	m: 564	c: 3093
w: 3096	f: 496	m: 2714
c: 3036	c: 488	g: 2541
g: 2980	u: 471	w: 1708
m: 2841	y: 387	o: 1629
f: 2438	w: 358	b: 1538
y: 2299	p: 329	f: 1237
p: 2122	g: 292	z: 997
b: 1943	b: 286	k: 954
k: 1031	v: 152	v: 682
v: 1029	k: 80	ü: 568
x: 131	x: 33	ä: 494
j: 113	j: 16	ß: 421
q: 97	q: 13	p: 349
z: 84	z: 6	ö: 200
		j: 136
		q: 14
		Ü: 12
		y: 8
		x: 5
		Ä: 5
		Ö: 2

The third column is clearly longer than the other two, which has three causes. First, the umlauted vowels are distinct from the nonumlauted vowels. Second, the Perl function `lc` does not apply to capital, umlauted vowels. For example, the letters *ä* and *Ä* are counted separately. Finally, German has the *ß*, as noted above.

Moreover, the order of the letters in the third column is different than the first two columns (which are quite similar). The letter *e* is the most common in all three texts, and *t* is ranked second in the first two columns, but seventh in the third, and *n* is ranked second in Goethe, but seventh and sixth in the English texts. Looking at the infrequent letters, while *z* ranks last in English, it is much more common in German.

For a final, basic analysis of this German novel, we compute the word counts. Remember that section 2.4 discusses three problematic punctuations: dashes, hyphens, and apostrophes. Goethe certainly used dashes. However, there is only one case of two words connected with a hyphen: *Entweder-Oder*. Although compound words are plentiful in

German, these are combined without hyphens. Apostrophes are rare in German, but Goethe does use them for a few contractions, for example, *hab'* for *habe* and *gibt's* for *gibt es*. Note that German has many contractions that do not use an apostrophe, for example, *aufs* for *auf das*.

For finding the words in this novel, dashes are removed, hyphens are no problem, and there are apostrophes, but these are used for contractions, not quotations. Code sample 9.6 shows how the punctuation is removed. Note there is one problem with this: using `lc` does not change the case of capital umlauted vowels, but according to table 9.1, this only happens 19 times, so this complication is ignored.

Code Sample 9.6 How punctuation is removed from Goethe's *Die Leiden des jungen Werthers*.

```
while (<TEXT>) {
  chomp;
  $_ = lc;    # Change letters to lower case
  s/--/ /g;   # Remove dashes
  s/[,.";!()?:_*\[\]]//g;
  s/\s+/ /g; # Replace multiple spaces with one space
  @words = split(/ /);
  foreach $word (@words) {
    ++$freq{$word};
  }
}
```

Writing a program to print out the word frequencies has been done: see program 3.3. Output 9.6 shows the 10 most common words in the novel.

Output 9.6 The 10 most frequent words in Goethe's *Die Leiden des jungen Werthers*.

```
und, 700
ich, 602
die, 454
der, 349
sie, 323
das, 277
zu, 259
in, 216
nicht, 200
mich, 182
```

The most frequent word is *und* (*and*), which is also common in English (for example, see output 3.21, which shows that *and* is the second most frequent word in Dickens's *A Christmas Carol*). Second most frequent is *ich* (*I*). The first part of the novel is written as a series of letters from Werther (the protagonist) to his close friend Wilhelm, so it is not surprising that the first-person, singular pronoun is used quite often.

The most common word in English is *the*, and this is true in German, too. In fact, output 9.6 also shows that this is true in spite of the *und* at the top of the list. This happens because German has several inflected forms of the word *the*, which depends upon the case, grammatical gender, and number of the noun. Discussing the relevant German grammar is too much of a diversion, but table 9.2 gives an example of the different forms of *the* used with the word *Mensch* in Goethe's novel, which were found by concordancing. The lines shown are a subset of those produced by code samples 6.7, 6.8, and 6.10 used with program 6.1. All six lines shown have a form of *the* in front of *Mensch*, a masculine noun.

Table 9.2   Inflected forms of the word *the* in Goethe's *Die Leiden des jungen Werthers*.

7	lbst und alles Glück, das dem Menschen gegeben ist.
9	merzen wären minder unter den Menschen, wenn sie nicht – Gott wei
16	b' ich nicht – o was ist der Mensch, daß er über sich klagen darf
18	oldenen Worte des Lehrers der Menschen:"wenn ihr nicht werdet wie
27	Freund, was ist das Herz des Menschen! Dich zu verlassen, den ic
34	, was ich Anzügliches für die Menschen haben muß; es mögen mich ih

To get a total number of uses of *the* in German, the counts in table 9.3 must be summed. This totals 1450, which is much larger than the number of times *und* appears (only 700), so *the* is the most common word in this text. Note, however, German utilizes *the* in more ways than is true in English. For example, many forms (but not all) of relative pronouns match a form of *the*.

Table 9.3   Counts of the six forms of the German word for *the* in Goethe's *Die Leiden des jungen Werthers*.

	die	454
	der	349
	das	277
	den	164
	dem	138
	des	68
	total	1450

Even the simple analysis above shows that assumptions about English may or may not hold for German in spite of their close relationship. This suggests that fluency in the language of a text is important when doing text mining, which is just common sense.

Finally, corpora of other languages have been created, and these have been analyzed for various purposes. To name one example, *A Frequency Dictionary of German* [63] gives a list of just over 4000 words in order of frequency. Such a book is useful for beginning students of German.

9.4   PERMUTATION TESTS

In section 4.5, the bag-of-words model is discussed. This underlies the term-document matrix, the topic of section 5.4. Recall that this matrix has a column for every text and a row for every term. The intersection of each row and column contains the count of the number of times the term appears in that document. However, the term-document matrix of any permutation of a text is the same as the original text. That is, word order makes no difference.

Obviously, the bag-of-words model is incorrect. For example, much of the grammar in English restricts word order. On the other hand, the term-document matrix is useful because it performs well in information retrieval tasks. So the question becomes, when does word order matter in English?

To answer this assume that word order is irrelevant for a particular function, which is applied to many random permutations of a text. Then these values are compared to the value of the original. If the latter seems consistent with the permutation values, then this function probably does not depend on word order for this text. Hence, using a technique like the word-document matrix probably poses no problems in this situation. However, if this is not true, then ignoring word order probably loses information.

Note that looking at all permutations of a text is impossible. There are $n!$ permutations for n objects, and this means that even a 100-word text has $100! \approx 9.33262 \times 10^{157}$ different orders. Hence, analyzing a sample is the best a researcher can do.

Also note that the unit of permutation makes a big difference. For example, a character-document matrix (that is, counting characters in texts) preserves little information. Perhaps languages can be distinguished this way, for example, see table 9.1 for such a matrix comparing a German novel to two English novels. But it is unclear what else is discernible.

At the other extreme, taking a novel and changing the order of the chapters might be readable. For example, the chapters of William Burroughs's *Naked Lunch* were returned out of order by his publisher, but Burroughs decided to go ahead using this new order (see page 18 of Burroughs' *Word Virus* [22]).

The goal in the next two sections is to test this idea of comparing permutations to the original text. The next section discusses a little of the statistical theory behind it, and the section after gives two examples.

9.4.1   Runs and Hypothesis Testing

We start with a simple example to illustrate the idea of comparing the original value to the permutation values. Then this technique is applied to *A Christmas Carol* and *The Call of the Wild*.

Suppose the sequence of zeros and ones in equation 9.1 is given, and a researcher wants to test the hypothesis that these are generated by a random process where each distinct permutation is equally likely. Note that permutations do not change the number of 0's and 1's, and this is consistent with the bag-of-words model, which fixes the counts, but ignores the order.

$$111111111111110000000011111 \qquad (9.1)$$

The sequence in equation 9.1 does not seem random, but how is this testable? The metric used here is based on the number of *runs* in the data. The first run begins at the start and continues until the value changes. Where it does change is the start of the second run, which ends once its value changes again, which is the start of the third run, and so forth. So for the above sequence, there are three runs: the first twelve 1's, the next eight 0's, and the last five 1's.

Next, compute a large number of random permutations and for each of these, compute the number of runs. This generates a set of positive numbers, which can be summarized with a histogram. If three runs is near the left end of the histogram (so that most permutations have more), then this hypothesis of the randomness of the above data is unlikely. If three is a typical value near the center of the histogram, then this hypothesis is supported by this data. However, randomness is not proven since other measures might reveal that this hypothesis is unlikely.

The above procedure is straightforward to do in R. Code sample 9.7 defines a function that produces n random permutations, and counts the number of runs in each one. These are obtained by generating uniform random numbers and then using the order() function to find the permutation that sorts these numbers into order. Since the original values are random, the resulting permutation is random. This also can be done by using sample() (see problem 8.3.d). Finally, runs occur exactly when two adjacent values are not equal, and this is tested for and counted in the line that assigns a value to nruns, the number of runs. These results are stored in the vector values.

Code Sample 9.7 An R function that computes the number of runs for n random permutations of an input vector, x.

```
> runs_sim
function(x, n) {
# Computes n random permutations of x, a vector
# Returns the numbers of runs, one for each permutation
  values = matrix(0, 1, n)
  for (i in 1:n) {
    perm = x[order(runif(length(x)))]
    nruns = sum(perm[-1] != perm[-length(x)]) + 1
    values[i] = nruns
  }
  return(values)
}
```

Output 9.7 shows the code that produces a histogram of the number of runs for each of 100,000 random permutations. Clearly values around 13 are typical in figure 9.1, and since 3 occurs exactly once (applying sum to the logical test of equaling 3 returns 1, and 3 is the minimum value), the probability of such a low number of runs is approximately 1/100,000 = 0.00001.

Output 9.7 This produces a histogram of the number of runs after permuting the vector data 100,000 times using the function defined in code sample 9.7.

```
> data = c(rep(1,12), rep(0,8), rep(1,8))
> data
 [1] 1 1 1 1 1 1 1 1 1 1 1 1 0 0 0 0 0 0 0 0 1 1 1 1 1 1 1 1
> Counts_of_Runs = runs_sim(data,100000)
> hist(Counts_of_Runs)
> min(Counts_of_Runs)
[1] 3
> sum(Counts_of_Runs <= 3)
[1] 1
```

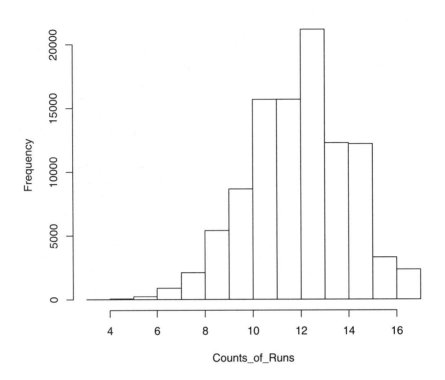

Figure 9.1   Histogram of the numbers of runs in 100,000 random permutations of digits in equation 9.1.

Since this probability estimate is extremely low, we conclude that the original data values are not consistent with the hypothesis of random generation. This result can be checked using the R package `tseries` [118], which has `runs.test()`. It reports a p-value equal to 0.0000072, which is quite close to the above estimate. With this example in mind, we apply this to texts in the next section.

9.4.2   Distribution of Character Names in Dickens and London

We apply the technique of the preceding section to names in a novel. Since the plot structure determines when characters appear or are discussed, this is not random, so it is an interesting test to see what an analysis of runs detects.

The first example uses the names Scrooge and Marley in Dickens's *A Christmas Carol*. First, note that a random permutation of all the words in the story induces a random permutation of these two names. Hence, it is enough to list the order these names appear in the novel, and then randomly permute these to do the analysis.

Concordancing using program 6.1 makes it easy to find and print out just these two names in the order they appear in the novel. To save space, let 0 stand for Scrooge and 1 for Marley. The Perl code is left for the reader as an exercise. The values are stored in the vector `scroogemarley`, and note that Marley is more common at the start, and then fairly infrequent for the rest of the novel.

Output 9.8 The 398 uses of *Scrooge* or *Marley* in *A Christmas Carol*. 0 stands for Scrooge, 1 for Marley.

```
> scroogemarley
  [1] 1 1 0 0 1 1 0 0 0 0 1 1 0 1 0 1 0 1 0 0 1 0 0 0 0 0 0 0 0
 [30] 0 0 0 0 0 0 0 0 0 0 0 0 0 0 0 0 0 0 0 0 0 0 0 0 0 0 1 0 1
 [59] 1 0 0 0 0 0 0 0 0 0 0 0 0 0 0 0 0 0 0 0 0 0 0 0 0 0 0 0 1
 [88] 0 1 1 0 1 0 1 0 0 0 0 0 0 1 1 0 0 0 1 1 0 0 0 1 0 1 0 1 0
[117] 0 0 0 0 0 0 0 0 0 0 0 0 0 0 0 0 1 0 0 0 0 0 0 0 0 0 0 0 0
[146] 0 0 0 0 1 0 0 1 0 0 0 0 0 0 1 0 0 0 0 0 0 0 0 0 0 0 0 0 0
[175] 0 0 0 0 0 0 0 0 0 0 0 0 0 0 0 0 0 0 0 0 0 0 0 0 0 0 0 0 0
[204] 0 0 0 0 0 0 0 0 0 0 0 0 0 0 0 0 0 0 0 0 1 0 0 0 1 0 0 0 0
[233] 0 0 0 0 0 0 0 0 0 0 0 0 0 0 0 0 0 0 0 0 0 0 0 0 0 0 0 0 0
[262] 0 0 0 0 0 0 0 0 0 0 0 0 0 0 0 0 0 0 0 0 0 0 0 0 0 0 0 0 0
[291] 0 0 1 0 0 0 0 0 0 0 0 0 0 0 0 0 0 0 0 0 0 0 0 0 0 0 0 0 1
[320] 0 0 0 0 0 0 0 0 0 0 0 0 0 0 0 0 0 0 0 0 0 0 0 0 0 0 0 0 0
[349] 0 0 0 0 0 0 0 1 0 0 0 1 0 0 0 0 0 0 0 0 0 0 0 0 0 0 0 0 1
[378] 0 0 0 0 0 0 0 0 0 0 0 0 0 0 0 0 0 0 0 0 0
```

Output 9.9 shows that there are 57 runs for the data shown in output 9.8. Then 10,000 permutations are applied, and the runs for each one is computed by `runs_sim()`. The results are plotted in the histogram shown in figure 9.2.

Output 9.9 The results of 10,000 permutations of the data in output 9.8.

```
> sum(scroogemarley[-1] != scroogemarley[-length(scroogemarley)])
[1] 57
> Counts_of_Runs = runs_sim(scroogemarley, 10000)
> min(Counts_of_Runs)
[1] 51
> max(Counts_of_Runs)
[1] 73
> sum(Counts_of_Runs <= 57)
[1] 68
> hist(Counts_of_Runs, 51:73)
```

First, it is obvious that tall and short bars alternate, where the former happens with odd values and the latter with even ones. This is not an accident because an odd number of runs only occurs when the first and last value in the vector are the same. For `scroogemarley`, there are 362 0's and 36 1's, hence the chances of the first and last values equaling 0 is quite high (about 83%).

Second, there are 68 cases where the number of runs are equal to or less than 57, which is the number of runs in `scroogemarley`. So the probability of seeing a result as extreme

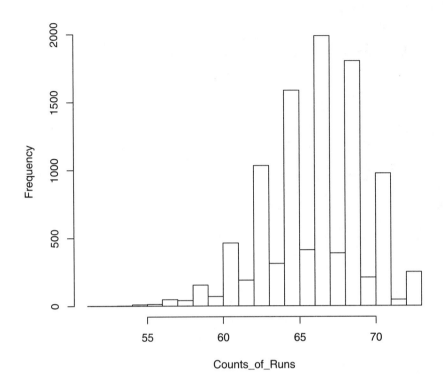

Figure 9.2   Histogram of the runs of the 10,000 permutations of the names Scrooge and Marley as they appear in *A Christmas Carol*.

or more extreme is about 68/10,000 = 0.0068, which is quite low. Hence we conclude that the distribution of the names Scrooge and Marley is not random.

A second example comes from *The Call of the Wild*. In this novel, Buck has a number of owners that come and go before he obtains his freedom at the end. Early in the story he is part of a dog-sled team run by Francois and Perrault, who are two French-Canadians. While they own Buck, they play a prominent role, and their names alternate much more than is true with Scrooge and Marley. See output 9.10, and note that Francois is represented by 0, Perrault by 1.

These two names appear 99 times, 60 for Francois and 39 for Perrault, a much more even division than the previous example. Redoing the above analysis, we see that the conclusion is different because the number of runs in the original sequence of names is 45, and there are 2831 permutations with this or less runs. A probability of 2831/10,000 = 0.2831, however, is not small. The histogram of the 10,000 runs is shown in figure 9.3. Note that it does not have alternating heights since the probability that a random permutation begins and ends with the same name is close to 50%.

Output 9.10 The appearance of the names Francois and Perrault in *The Call of the Wild*. Here 0 stands for Francois, 1 for Perrault.

```
> francoisperrault
 [1] 1 1 1 1 0 1 0 1 0 0 0 0 0 0 0 0 0 0 1 1 1 1 0 0 1 1 0 0 1
[30] 1 0 1 1 1 0 0 0 1 1 1 0 1 0 1 1 0 1 0 0 1 0 1 0 0 0 0 1 0
[59] 0 0 0 0 1 0 0 0 0 1 0 1 0 0 0 0 0 0 1 0 1 0 0 0 0 1 0 0
[88] 0 1 1 1 0 0 0 1 1 0 1 0
> sum(franperr[-1] != franperr[-length(franperr)])
[1] 45
> sum(Counts_of_Runs <= 45)
[1] 2831
```

Hence for Scrooge and Marley, the former is common because it is the protagonist's name. Marley's ghost appears at the start of the novel, but he is mentioned infrequently after that. However, for Francois and Perrault, these two characters work together as part of a team. Hence it is not surprising that there is a difference in the pattern of how each pair of names appears in their respective novels.

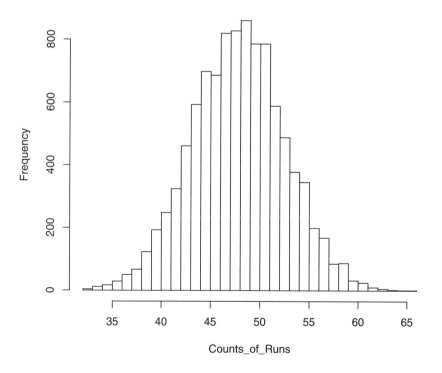

Figure 9.3 Histogram of the runs of the 10,000 permutations of the names Francois and Perrault as they appear in *The Call of the Wild*.

This book draws to an end. The next section gives some text mining references for the interested reader. Finally, I have enjoyed writing this book and hope that you have enjoyed reading and working through it.

9.5 REFERENCES

This book is an introduction to some of the important techniques of text mining. Many of these are from other research areas such as information retrieval and statistics, and references for these topics are given at the end of the respective chapters. This section lists a few books that focus on text mining itself.

Text mining grew out of data mining. A good introductory book on applying data mining to online texts is *Data Mining the Web* by Zdravko Markov and Daniel Larose [77]. Another introductory book on using Perl to interact with the Web is *Spidering Hacks* by Kevin Hemenway and Tara Calishain [53].

For an introduction to text mining, try *Text Mining* by Sholom Weiss, Nitin Indurkhya, Tong Zhang, and Fred Damerau [125]. Their emphasis is on creating quantitative summaries of one or more texts, then applying data mining techniques. Finally, a more advanced book is *The Text Mining Handbook* by Ronen Feldman and James Sanger [43].

Appendix A

Overview of Perl for Text Mining

This appendix summarizes the basics of Perl in these areas: basic data structures, operators, branching and looping, functions, and regular expressions. The focus is on Perl's text capabilities, and many references are made to code throughout this book.

The form of these code samples is slightly different than the ones in this book. To save space, the output is placed at the end of the computer code.

To run Perl, first download it by going to `http://www.perl.org/` [45] and following the instructions there. Second, type the statements into a file with the suffix `.pl`, for example, call it `program.pl`. Third, you need to find out how to use your computer's command line interface, which allows the typing of commands for execution. Fourth, type the statement below on the command line and then press the enter key. The output will appear below it.

```
perl program.pl
```

Remember that Perl is case sensitive. For example, commands have to be in lowercase, and the three variables `$cat`, `$Cat`, and `$CAT` are all distinct. Finally, do not forget to use semicolons to end each statement.

A.1 BASIC DATA STRUCTURES

A programmer must be able to store and modify information, which is kept in scalar, array, and hash variables. We start with scalars, which store a single value, and their names **always** start with a dollar sign. First, consider the examples in code sample A.1, which demonstrates Perl's two types of scalars, strings and numbers. If a string is used as a number, then Perl tries to convert it. Conversely, a number used as a string is always converted.

Code Sample A.1 Perl converting a string to a number and vice versa.

```
$x1 = "4";
$y1 = "5";
$z1 = $x1 + $y1; # Addition

$x2 = 4;
$y2 = 5;
$z2 = $x2 . $y2; # Concatenation

$x3 = "4";
$y3 = 5;
$z3 = $x3 . $y3;
$z4 = $x3 + $y3;

print "$z1, $z2, $z3, $z4\n";

OUTPUT: 9, 45, 45, 9
```

Code sample A.2 shows that the logical values true and false are represented by either strings or numbers. The values 0, '0', "0", '', "", (), and undef are false, and all other numbers and strings are true.

Code Sample A.2 Numbers and strings represent true and false.

```
if ( 0 )      { print "True "; } else { print "False "; }
if ( '0' )    { print "True "; } else { print "False "; }
if ( "0" )    { print "True "; } else { print "False "; }
if ( 7 )      { print "True "; } else { print "False "; }
if ( '7' )    { print "True "; } else { print "False "; }
if ( "7" )    { print "True "; } else { print "False "; }
if ( '' )     { print "True "; } else { print "False "; }
if ( "" )     { print "True "; } else { print "False "; }
if ( () )     { print "True "; } else { print "False "; }
if ( undef )  { print "True "; } else { print "False "; }

OUTPUT: False False False True True True False False False False
```

Code sample A.3 gives examples of references, which are hexadecimal numbers representing a memory location. These are created by placing a backslash in front of the scalar (or array or hash). References can be chained together, for example, a reference to another reference. A dereferencing operator is used to access the value in the memory location. For a reference to a scalar, this operator is ${}. Finally, references are used extensively in complex data structures such as arrays of hashes, as discussed in section 3.8.

Code Sample A.3 Examples of scalar references.

```
$x = 1729;
$xref = \$x;   # A reference to the value in $x
$xrefref = \$xref;   # A reference to a reference
$y = ${$xref};   # Dereferencing a reference
$zref = ${$xrefref};
$z = ${${$xrefref}};   # Two dereferences in a row
print "$x, $xref, $xrefref, $y\n$z, $zref";

OUTPUT: 1729, SCALAR(0x1832960), REF(0x1832984), 1729
        1729, SCALAR(0x1832960)
```

Examples of working with arrays are shown in code sample A.4. While scalars contain only one value, arrays have many. While scalars always start with a dollar sign, arrays as a whole always start with an *at* sign, for example, @array. An array is a collection of variables indexed by 0, 1, 2, ..., and these individual values are accessed as follows: $array[0], $array[1], $array[2], ... Note that each starts with a dollar sign.

Arrays can be defined by listing the values in parentheses, or created by a variety of functions, for example, split. They can be built up by functions, too, for example, push. If a scalar is set to an array, this does not produce a syntax error, in fact, the scalar is set to the number of entries it has. For example, $scalar in code sample A.4 has the value 5 because @array2 has five elements. Finally, an array of indices can be placed in the square brackets to select a subset.

Code Sample A.4 Making and modifying arrays.

```
@array1 = ("Katy", "Sam", 16);
$array1[3] = "Taffy";
@array2 = split(//, "Test");
push(@array2, "ing");
$scalar = @array2;
@indices = (0,0,1,0,2,1);
@array3 = @array1[@indices];

print "$array1[0], @array1, @array2[0], @array2\n";
print "$scalar, @array3\n";

OUTPUT: Katy, Katy Sam 16 Taffy, T, T e s t ing
        5, Katy Katy Sam Katy 16 Sam
```

References to arrays are illustrated in code sample A.5. These can be created by listing values between square brackets or by putting a backslash in front of an array name. To access the array, dereferencing must be done. Just as scalar names start with a dollar sign, and scalar dereferencing is done with ${}, arrays start with an *at* symbol and array dereferencing is done with @{}.

Code Sample A.5 Array references and dereferences.

```
$ref1 = [1,2,"Cat"];
@array1 = @{$ref1};

$ref2 = \@array1;
@array2 = @{$ref2};

print "$ref1, @array1, $ref2, @array2";

OUTPUT: ARRAY(0x18330b8), 1 2 Cat, ARRAY(0x1832be4), 1 2 Cat
```

Code sample A.6 has examples of hashes, which are like arrays except they are indexed by strings, not nonnegative integers. Hashes can be defined the same way as an array, but the odd entries are the keys (or indices), and the even entries are the values. A hash can also be created by setting it equal to an array. The functions keys and values return an array of keys and values, respectively.

Code Sample A.6 Working with hashes.

```
%hash = (Cat, 3, Dog, 4, Rabbit, 6);   # Quotes are optional
@array = %hash;
@keys = keys(%hash);
@values = values(%hash);

print "$hash{Cat}, $hash{Rabbit}, @array\n";
print "@keys, @values\n";

OUTPUT: 3, 6, Rabbit 6 Dog 4 Cat 3
        Rabbit Dog Cat, 6 4 3
```

References are made to hashes by either listing values between curly brackets or putting a backslash in front of a hash name as shown in code sample A.7. These are dereferenced by using %{}, and note that hash names and dereferencing both begin with a percent sign. Unlike scalars and arrays, hashes are not interpolated inside double quotation marks because hashes are unordered. Note that the two print statements do not list the hashes in the same order. However, a hash can be assigned to an array, which can be interpolated.

Finally, scalars, arrays, and hashes can be mixed together using references to form complex data structures. See section 3.8 for a discussion.

A.1.1 Special Variables and Arrays

Perl defines many variables that it uses for a variety of purposes. Table A.1 contains just a few of these along with examples of use (if any) in this book. For more information, read one of the books on Perl programming listed in section 2.8.

Code Sample A.7 Hash referencing and dereferencing.

```
$ref1 = {Cat, 3, Dog, 4, Rabbit, 6};
%hash1 = (Cat, 3, Dog, 4, Rabbit, 6);
$ref2 = \%hash1;
%hash2 = %{$ref1};
@array1 = %hash1;
@array2 = %hash2;

print "$ref1, @array1\n";
print "$ref2, @array2\n";

OUTPUT: HASH(0x18332f8), Rabbit 6 Dog 4 Cat 3
        HASH(0x18330e8), Rabbit 6 Cat 3 Dog 4
```

Table A.1   A few special variables and their use in Perl.

Name	Purpose	Example
$_	Default variable	Program 2.7
$1	Contents of leftmost parentheses	Program 3.3
$2	Contents of next parentheses	Code sample 2.31
@ARGV	Command line arguments	Code sample 2.17
@_	Subroutine arguments	Code sample A.20
$/	Separator for reading input file	Program 2.7
$/="";	Paragraph mode	Program 2.7
$/="\n";	Line-by-line mode	Default
$"	Separator for interpolation	Code sample 3.21
$`	Stores string before regex match	
$&	Stores regex match	
$'	Stores string after regex match	Code sample 2.25

A.2 OPERATORS

Operators are just functions, but they use special symbols and syntax. For example, addition is an arithmetic operator in Perl and is denoted by +, which is written in between numbers. The common mathematical operators in Perl are given in code sample A.8. Note that the percent sign is the *modulus* operator, which returns the remainder for an integer division.

Code sample A.9 demonstrates two string operators. The second uses the letter x and can be used with arrays, too.

In Perl, only the values 0, '0', "0", '', "", (), and undef are false, and all other numbers or strings are true. So logical operators work with both numbers and strings as shown in code sample A.10.

However, when Perl computes a logical true or false, it uses 1 and "" as seen in code sample A.11. To make the output more readable, the symbol printed between array entries is changed to a comma (by setting $" to this). Perl has two types of comparison operators: one for numbers, the other for strings. The former uses symbols (for example, == for numerical equality), while the latter uses letters (for example, eq for string equality). However, a

Code Sample A.8 Examples of mathematical operators.

```
$x = 2;
$y = 3;
$z = 8;

$answer[0] = $x + $y;    # Addition
$answer[1] = $x * $y;    # Multiplication
$answer[2] = $x - $y;    # Subtraction
$answer[3] = $x / $y;    # Division
$answer[4] = $x ** $y;   # Exponentiation
$answer[5] = $z % $y;

print "@answer";
OUTPUT: 5 6 -1 0.666666666666667 8 2
```

Code Sample A.9 Examples of two string operators.

```
$concat1 = 'abc' . '123';
$concat2 = "cat" . 123;
$mult = 'cat' x 3;
@array1 = (1, 2, 3) x 2;
@array2 = @array1 x 5;
@array3 = (@array1) x 2;
@array4 = 2 x (1, 2, 3);
@array5 = 2 x @array1;
@array6 = 2 x (@array1);

print "$concat1, $concat2, $mult\n";
print "@array1, @array2, @array3\n";
print "@array4, @array5, @array6\n";

OUTPUT: abc123, cat123, catcatcat
        1 2 3 1 2 3, 66666, 1 2 3 1 2 3 1 2 3 1 2 3
        222, 222222, 222222
```

comparison like 14 gt 3 is possible, but it changes both numbers to strings, and then does a string comparison, so in this case it is false because the string "14" precedes the string "3" when using alphabetical order. Finally, <=> and cmp are both comparison operators. If the first value is greater than the second, then 1 is returned; if the two values are equal, 0 is returned; and if the second value is greater than the first, −1 is returned.

Code sample A.12 gives a few miscellaneous operators. The regex matching operators return true and false: see section 2.7.2 for a discussion. The ++ operator increments the variable it is next to: if it is before the variable, then that variable in incremented before it is assigned, but if it is after the variable, then it is incremented after it is assigned. For example, compare the values of $answer[3] and $answer[4].

Code Sample A.10 Logical operator examples.

```
$answer[0] = 5 and 6;
$answer[1] = 5 && 6;
$answer[2] = 3 or "";
$answer[3] = 0 || "";
$answer[4] = 3 xor 5;
$answer[5] = ! '';
$answer[6] = not '';

$" = ',';
print "@answer\n";

OUTPUT: 5,6,3,,3,1,1
```

Code Sample A.11 Comparison operator examples.

```
$answer[0] = 14 > 3;
$answer[1] = 14 gt 3;
$answer[2] = "14" > "3";
$answer[3] = "14" gt "3";
$answer[4] = 25 < 7;
$answer[5] = 'cat' lt "dog";
$answer[6] = 22.24 < 3.99;
$answer[7] = 'cat' ge 'dog';
$answer[8] = 'cat' eq 'cat';
$answer[9] = 5 == 6;
$answer[10] = 5 <=> 6;
$answer[11] = 6 <=> 6;
$answer[12] = 7 <=> 6;
$answer[13] = 'cats' cmp 'dog';
$answer[14] = 'dog' cmp 'dog';
$answer[15] = 'rats' cmp 'dog';

$" = ',';
print "@answer\n";

OUTPUT: 1,,1,,,1,,,1,,-1,0,1,-1,0,1
```

Finally, the double period is the range operator, and it produces an array of numbers or strings. This is shown below where @array receives the elements 1 through 10. This also works with letters, for example, ('a'..'z') produces the lowercase alphabet.

```
@array = (1..10);
```

The above operators are not exhaustive, but they are useful in text mining. Next we review branching and looping in a program.

Code Sample A.12 . A few miscellaneous operators.

```perl
$text = "It's never too late ...";
$answer[0] = $text =~ /never/;
$answer[1] = $text !~ /never/;
$answer[2] = $text =~ /cat/;
$x = 6;
$answer[3] = ++$x;
$x = 6;
$answer[4] = $x++;
$answer[5] = $x;
$x = 6;
$answer[6] = --$x;

$" = ',';
print "@answer\n";

OUTPUT: 1,,,7,6,7,5
```

A.3 BRANCHING AND LOOPING

The ability to make decisions and to repeat portions of code is essential to programming. The `if` statement tests logical conditions, and examples are given in code sample A.13. A logical test is performed within parentheses, the outcome of which determines which block of code (contained in curly brackets) to execute. Note that the `if` can come after a statement. In this code sample, all the regexes are tested against the default variable $\_$, which can either be explicitly written or left out. To test another variable against the regex, it must be explicitly given.

Code Sample A.13 Examples of `if` statements.

```perl
$_ = "This is a test.";

if (/test/) { print "Match, "; }
if ($_ =~ /test/) { print "Match, "; }
print "Match, " if (/test/);

if ($_ =~ /test/) {
  print "Match, ";
} else {
  print "No Match, ";
}

OUTPUT: Match, Match, Match, Match,
```

An `if-elsif-else` statement allows more than one test, and two or more `elsifs` are permissible. See code sample A.14 for an example.

Code Sample A.14 Example of using `elsif` twice.

```
$_ = "This is a test.";

if ($_ =~ /cat/) {
  print "Matches cat ";
} elsif (/dog/) {
  print "Matches dog ";
} elsif (/bat/) {
  print "Matches bat ";
} else {
  print "No matches here ";
}

OUTPUT: No matches here
```

The `for` statement loops over a block of code, as seen in code sample A.15. The number of iterations is determined by a counter (the variable `$i` in the first example), or over a sequence of values like `0..9`, or over the elements of an array. Finally, although a programmer may prefer either `for` or `foreach` depending on the situation, these two statements are interchangeable.

Code Sample A.15 Examples of `for` loops.

```
for ($i = 0; $i <10; ++$i) {
  print "$i ";
}
print "\n";

for $i (0..9) {
  print "$i ";
}
print "\n";

@array = ('a'..'j');
for $i (@array) {
  print "$i ";
}

OUTPUT: 0 1 2 3 4 5 6 7 8 9
        0 1 2 3 4 5 6 7 8 9
        a b c d e f g h i j
```

It is also possible to use a hash in a `for` or `foreach` loop, which is seen in code sample A.16. However, the order is unpredictable since Perl determines how the hash is stored, which can differ from how it is constructed. A better approach is to iterate over the keys of the hash, which can be sorted as desired, for example, put into alphabetical order.

Code Sample A.16 Using a hash in a `for` loop.

```
%hash = (dog, 1, cat, 2, rabbit, 3);

for $i (%hash) { print "$i "; }

print "\n";
for $i (sort keys %hash) {
  print "$i $hash{$i} ";
}

OUTPUT: cat 2 rabbit 3 dog 1
        cat 2 dog 1 rabbit 3
```

The `while` loop is also enormously useful. For example, text files are usually read in by a statement of the following form.

```
while (<FILE>) { # code }
```

Here the filehandle within the angle brackets reads the file piece by piece (the default is line by line). The `while` statement can also iterate over all the matches of a regex, as seen in code sample A.17.

Code Sample A.17 Looping over the matches of a regex with `while`.

```
$_ = "This is a test.";

$vowels = 0;
while ( /[aeiou]/g ) {
  ++$vowels;
}
print "# of vowels = $vowels";

OUTPUT: # of vowels = 4
```

Finally, a `while` loop can test for all types of logical conditions. Code sample A.18 shows an example where the `while` loop executes like a `for` loop.

Code Sample A.18 A `while` loop executing like a `for` loop.

```
$i = 0;
while ($i < 10) {
  ++$i;
  print "$i ";
}

OUTPUT: 1 2 3 4 5 6 7 8 9 10
```

Sometimes, modification of the execution of a `for` or `while` is needed. There are three commands to do this; for example, when `last` is executed, the loop immediately ends, as seen in code sample A.19. Other statements to modify looping behavior are `next` and `redo`. See problem 7.2 for an example.

Code Sample A.19 Ending a loop with the statement `last`.

```
$text = "This is a test.";
@words = split(/ /, $text);
foreach $word (@words) {
  if ($word eq "a") { last; }
  print "$word ";
}
```

```
OUTPUT: This is
```

Another way to execute blocks of code is the subroutine. The analogous idea for a group of subroutines is called a module, but this topic is more advanced: see section 9.2.

The default in Perl allows subroutines to access and modify any variables in the main code. This can cause problems, especially if subroutines are reused in other programs. The solution is easy: make the variables in a subroutine local to that subroutine, which can be done with the `my` statement at the beginning for all the variables at once, as shown below.

```
my $variable1, @array1, %hash1;
```

The `my` statement can also be used the first time a variable is used, as shown in code sample A.20. Also see problem 5.5.

Code Sample A.20 Example of a subroutine. Note the use of `my`, which makes variables local to the subroutine.

```
sub letterrank {
  my $lcletter = lc($_[0]);
  if ( 'a' le $lcletter and $lcletter le 'z' ) {
    return ord($lcletter) - ord('a') + 1;
  } else {
    return '';
  }
}

$letter = 'R';
print "$letter has letter rank ", letterrank($letter), "\n";
print "$letter has letter rank ", &letterrank($letter), "\n";

OUTPUT: R has letter rank 18
        R has letter rank 18
```

In this code sample, the subroutine uses `return`, which returns a value back to the main program. Hence this subroutine is a function. Also note that after a subroutine is defined, then its name does not require an initial ampersand, although there is no harm in always using it. Also see problem 5.4.

The array @_ contains the subroutine arguments, so $_[0] is the first argument, $_[1] the second, and so forth. Finally, the function ord returns the ASCII rank of each character, which assigns 65 to *A*, 66 to *B*, ..., 90 to *Z*, and 97 to *a*, ..., 122 to *z*. So by changing each letter to lowercase and then subtracting the rank of *a* and adding 1, we get the desired letter rank (that is, *A* has rank 1, *B* has rank 2, and so forth.)

Functions break a complex task into a sequence of simpler tasks. The ability of functions to use other functions enables a programmer to create a hierarchy of them to do a task.

Finally, many functions are already built into Perl, or can be easily loaded into Perl, so before writing a subroutine, it is wise to check to see if it already exists by checking online. The next section discusses just a few of these.

A.4 A FEW PERL FUNCTIONS

Perl has many functions built into it and even more that can be downloaded. The Perl documentation online [3] or the Comprehensive Perl Archive Network (CPAN) [54] are great places to check for information. This section, however, only discusses some of these applicable to text mining.

First, table A.2 lists string functions with an example of where they are used in this book. Note that the inverse of ord is chr. Finally, note that reverse reverses a string when in scalar context as shown below. However, it reverses an array if it is in an array context as shown in table A.3, which has examples of array functions used in this book.

```
$answer = reverse("testing, testing");
```

Table A.2 String functions in Perl with examples.

Name	Purpose	Example
chomp	Remove trailing newline	Program 2.4
index	Find position of substrings	Code sample 2.13
join	Combine strings	Code sample 2.7
lc	Convert to lowercase	Code sample 3.15
ord	ASCII value	Code sample 3.38
pos	Position in string	Code sample 2.15
split	Split up strings	Code sample 2.2
sprintf	Create formatted string	Code sample 2.35
substr	Find substrings	Program 2.7

Second, since an array is easily converted into a hash, the functions in table A.3 are not unrelated to hashes. Table A.4, however, has functions for hashes only. Note that values is analogous to keys: the former returns an array of the values of a hash. In addition, there is the function each, which is shown in code sample A.21.

Third, there are many mathematical functions available in Perl. For example, the natural logarithm, log, and the square root, sqrt, are used in program 5.5. Perl has limited trigonometric functions unless the Math::Trig module is loaded with use, which is done in code sample 5.5.

Table A.3   Array functions in Perl with examples.

Name	Purpose	Example
grep	Apply regex to entries	Code sample 3.12
map	Apply a function to an array	Code sample 3.38
pop	Remove last entry	Code sample 3.11
push	Add new last entry	Code sample 3.11
reverse	Reverse an array	Code sample 3.16
shift	Remove first entry	Code sample 3.11
split	Output is an array	Code sample 2.2
sort	Sort an array	Code sample 3.14
unshift	Add new first entry	Code sample 3.11

Table A.4   Hash functions in Perl with examples

Name	Purpose	Example
exists	Test if key exists	Program 3.5
keys	Create array of keys	Code sample 3.22

Code Sample A.21 Example of the function `each`.

```
%hash = (cat, 3, dog, 3, rabbit, 6);

while ( ($key, $value) = each %hash ) {
  print "$key, $value; ";
}

OUTPUT: cat, 3; rabbit, 6; dog, 3;
```

Finally, the functions `open` and `close` manipulate external files. There are three modes for the former: input, overwriting, and appending. These are shown in code sample A.22 along with `close` and `die`, where the latter halts execution of the program if `open` fails to work.

The command line can be used to overwrite or append to a file as shown below. The character > overwrites, while >> appends. This completes our review of functions, and regular expressions are the topic of the next section.

```
perl program.pl > output.txt
perl program.pl >> output.txt
```

A.5 INTRODUCTION TO REGULAR EXPRESSIONS

Chapter 2 is devoted to regular expressions (also called regexes), which is central to text patterns, so reading it is essential. This section, however, just summarizes the regex syntax and refers the reader to illustrative examples in this book. Finally, table 2.3 summarizes some of the special symbols used.

Code Sample A.22 Three different ways to open a file for reading, overwriting, and appending.

```
open (INPUT, "test.txt") or die; # Rewrites file
while (<INPUT>) { # commands }
close (INPUT);

open (OUTPUT, ">test.txt") or die; # Rewrites file
print OUTPUT "Your Text";
close (OUTPUT);

open(OUTPUT, ">>test.txt") or die; # Appends to file
print OUTPUT "Your Text";
close(OUTPUT);
```

First, the syntax for matching a regex is as follows.

```
$text =~ m/$regex/;
```

There is also an operator for not matching.

```
$text !~ m/$regex/;
```

Note that the m is not required. Substitution has a similar syntax, but the s is required.

```
$text =~ s/$regex/string/;
```

Both matching and substitution have modifiers, which are placed after the last forward slash. Two useful ones are g for *global*, and i for case *insensitive*. See code sample 6.1 for an example of the former and code sample 3.35 for an example of the latter.

As shown above, variables are interpolated inside matching or substitution. An example of this is program 3.6. The qr// construct allows storing a regex in a variable; for example, see code sample 3.12.

Table A.5 lists the common special characters in regexes along with an example of a program that uses each one, if any. Note that the ^ also stands for character negation when it is the first character inside a pair of square brackets.

Table A.6 summarizes the syntax for how many times a pattern can appear in a regex. Note that all the examples in the table are greedy, but by adding a final question mark, these become nongreedy: ??, *?, +?, {m,n}?. See code sample 2.21 and program 5.2 for examples of *?.

Square brackets specify a collection of characters. Examples are seen in programs 3.3, 4.4, and 6.1. Parentheses form groups, for example, (abc)+ means one or more repetitions of the string "abc." The part of the regex within a set of parentheses is stored in the variables, $1, $2, $3, ... For two examples of this, see programs 3.7 or 5.1. To refer to matches within a regex, the backreferences \1, \2, \3, ..., are used. See code sample 3.12 for an example.

Finally, the idea of lookaround is discussed in section 2.7.3. These match conditions at a position as opposed to characters. This is a generalization of \b, which matches a word boundary, which is the condition that a letter is on one side of the position, but not on the other.

Table A.5   Some special characters used in regexes as implemented in Perl.

Name	Purpose	Example
\b	Word boundary	Program 6.1
\B	Negation of \b	
\d	Digit	Program 2.1
\D	Negation of \d	
\s	Whitespace	Program 4.4
\S	Negation of \s	
\w	Word character	Code sample 3.12
\W	Negation of \w	Program 3.3
.	Any character	Program 3.7
^	Start of line	Program 5.1
$	End of line	Section 3.7.2.1

Table A.6   Repetition syntax in regexes as implemented in Perl.

Name	Number of matches	Example
?	Zero or one	Program 2.1
*	Zero or more	Program 2.6
+	One or more	Program 2.9
{m,n}	At least m, at most n	Program 2.9
{m}	m	Program 2.1
{m,}	m or more	

For an in depth examination of regexes, start with Watt's *Beginning Regular Expressions* [124], and then you will be ready for Friedl's *Mastering Regular Expressions* [47].

Appendix B

Summary of R used in this Book

R is a statistical package that is open source and is distributed under the GNU General Public License (GPL). Like Perl, R is available free from the Web. To download it along with documentation and tutorials, see the instructions at The Comprehensive R Archive Network (CRAN) [34].

This appendix covers two topics. First, it reviews the basics of R. Second, for the functions used in this book, outputs and page numbers are given, so the interested reader can look up examples.

If your interest about R has been piqued, here are three good introductory books. First, Peter Dalgaard's *Introductory Statistics with R* [37]. Second, Michael Crawley's *Statistics: An Introduction Using R* [35], and, third, Brian Everitt and Torsten Hothorn's *A Handbook of Statistical Analyses Using R* [42].

B.1   BASICS OF R

This section describes bare basics of R. In this book, an R session consists of doing a task one step at a time using the command line. However, it has powerful statistical functions, and more can be written by the user, so one step can accomplish much.

Practical Text Mining with Perl. By Roger Bilisoly
Copyright © 2008 John Wiley & Sons, Inc.

B.1.1 Data Entry

The first task is entering the data. If there are only a few values, then these can be manually typed in as shown in output B.1. Note that the greater than sign is the command prompt, and after typing any command, pressing the enter key runs it.

Output B.1 Entering a scalar, vector, and matrices into R by typing.

```
> x = 4
> x
[1] 4
> y = c(1,0,0,3,1)
> y
[1] 1 0 0 3 1
> z1 = matrix(c(1,2,3,4,5,6,7,8,9,10),2,5)
> z1
     [,1] [,2] [,3] [,4] [,5]
[1,]    1    3    5    7    9
[2,]    2    4    6    8   10
> z2 = matrix(c(1,2,3,4,5,6,7,8,9,10),2,5, byrow=T)
> z2
     [,1] [,2] [,3] [,4] [,5]
[1,]    1    2    3    4    5
[2,]    6    7    8    9   10
```

In this output, x is a scalar, y is a vector, and both z1 and z2 are two by five matrices. The default is to treat a matrix as a collection of columns. Hence, the first column of z1 has 1 and 2, the second column 3 and 4, and so forth. However, byrow=T causes R to work with rows instead. For example, the first row of z2 has the numbers 1 through 5, and the second has 6 through 10.

Most data sets, however, are too large to enter by hand, so reading in data files is essential for any practical task. Assume that a file called test.csv has the data shown in table B.1. (CSV stands for *comma-separated variables*, and most software packages have an option to store data this way.)

Table B.1 Data in the file test.csv.

1,2,3,4,5
6,7,8,9,10

The function read.csv() reads this file as shown in output B.2. The option header=F means that the variable names are not contained in the file. When data is printed out, notice that names for each column are created so that the first column is V1, the second V2, and so forth.

There is a subtle distinction made in R between data frames and matrices. In output B.2, data is a data frame, not a matrix. The former has column variables, which have names. The latter acts like a matrix. For example, matrix multiplication works with it. See output B.3 for an example of how these two concepts differ.

Output B.2 Reading in a CSV file into a data frame.

```
> data = read.csv("c:\\test.csv", header=F)
> data
  V1 V2 V3 V4 V5
1  1  2  3  4  5
2  6  7  8  9 10
```

Output B.3 The function `read.csv()` creates a data frame, and `data.matrix()` changes a data frame to a matrix.

```
> data = read.csv("c:\\test.csv", header=F)
> data$V1
[1] 1 6
> data[,1]
[1] 1 6
> data %*% t(data)
Error in data %*% t(data) : requires numeric matrix/vector arguments
> data = data.matrix(data)
> data$V1
NULL
> data[,1]
1 2
1 6
> data %*% t(data)
     1   2
1  55 130
2 130 330
```

The columns of data can be accessed by using their names; for example, `data$V1` refers to the first column, which has the name `V1`. Matrices do not have column names, and entries, rows, and columns are accessed by using square brackets. Note that matrix multiplication does not work for a data frame.

A data frame can be converted to a matrix by the function `as.matrix()`. Moving on, the next section gives a short overview of the basic operators in R.

B.1.2 Basic Operators

Arithmetic operators in R are the same as Perl's except that exponentiation uses a caret. Also, vectors of the same size are combinable by the arithmetic operators, which is done by component-wise arithmetic. See output B.4 for examples. Note that dividing by zero produces `Inf`, which stands for *infinity*. Finally, matrices can be combined component-wise with arithmetic operators (not shown here).

The logic operators of R are the same as the numeric ones in Perl. See output B.5 for some examples using vectors. Note that the results are in terms of the logical values TRUE and FALSE.

Output B.4 Examples of arithmetic operators with scalars and vectors.

```
> x = c(1,2,3)
> y = c(2,0,-2)
> x - 4
[1] -3 -2 -1
> x/3
[1] 0.3333333 0.6666667 1.0000000
> x^2
[1] 1 4 9
> x + y
[1] 3 2 1
> x - y
[1] -1  2  5
> x * y
[1]  2  0 -6
> x / y
[1]  0.5  Inf -1.5
```

Output B.5 Examples of logic operators.

```
> x = c(1,2,3)
> y = c(2,0,-2)
> x == 2
[1] FALSE  TRUE FALSE
> x != y
[1] TRUE TRUE TRUE
> x > y
[1] FALSE  TRUE  TRUE
> x <= y
[1]  TRUE FALSE FALSE
```

B.1.3 Matrix Manipulation

This book uses basic matrix manipulations, which are summarized in this section. Matrices use square brackets for subscripts, which can be used to select submatrices, as shown in output B.6. Also see problem 8.3. Note that the colon operator generates a list of values, for example, 2:5 produces the values 2, 3, 4, 5. Also note that the function diag() returns the diagonal entries of any matrix (these are the entries [1,1], [2,2], [3,3], and so forth).

Pieces of vectors can be selected by using logical operators, as shown in output B.7. Finally, using logical operators for selecting pieces of a matrix also works, but the results are returned as a vector. For example, m1[m1>2] returns the values 4, 5, 3, 6 (notice the order of the results.)

Finally, the function t() returns the transpose of a matrix (this switches the rows and columns), and the operator %*% performs matrix multiplication: see section 5.5.1. Examples are shown in output B.8.

The next section summarizes the R functions used in this book and indicates where these are used.

Output B.6 Selecting submatrices of a matrix.

```
> m1 = matrix(c(1,2,3,4,5,6),2,3, byrow=T)
> m1
     [,1] [,2] [,3]
[1,]    1    2    3
[2,]    4    5    6
> m1[,1]
[1] 1 4
> m1[2,]
[1] 4 5 6
> diag(m1)
[1] 1 5
> m1[,2:3]
     [,1] [,2]
[1,]    2    3
[2,]    5    6
```

Output B.7 Selecting pieces of a vector.

```
> v = c(10:1)
> v
 [1] 10  9  8  7  6  5  4  3  2  1
> v[3]
[1] 8
> v[v>5]
[1] 10  9  8  7  6
> v[v<=3]
[1] 3 2 1
```

B.2 THIS BOOK'S R CODE

This section has tables that group R functions by purpose and indicate where each function is used in this text. Table B.2 shows R functions for matrices. Several of these create matrices: `as.matrix()`, `cbind()`, `diag()`, `matrix()`. In addition, `read.csv()` creates a data frame from a file, which can be converted into a matrix by `as.matrix()`. The operator `%*%` does matrix multiplication; `solve()` inverts matrices; and `t()` transposes them.

Table B.3 shows functions that perform statistical computations. Correlations and covariance matrices are computed by `cor()` and `cov()`, respectively. Clustering is done with `kmeans()` and `hclust()`. Fitting linear models, for example, a regression line, is done with `lm()`. Finally, `prcomp()` does principal components analyses (PCA), and `factanal()` does factor analyses.

Functions that produce graphical output are shown in table B.4. The function `plot()` creates a plot using Cartesian coordinates (the usual *x-y* plot). Text is added to a plot by using `text()`, and overlaying a line onto the plot is done with `lines()`. The function `par()` adjusts the plotting parameters; for example, it allows the creation of multiple plots

Output B.8 Examples of transpose and matrix multiplication.

```
> m1 = matrix(c(1,2,3,4,5,6),2,3, byrow=T)
> m1 %*% c(1:3)
      [,1]
[1,]   14
[2,]   32
> t(m1)
      [,1] [,2]
[1,]    1    4
[2,]    2    5
[3,]    3    6
> m1 %*% t(m1)
      [,1] [,2]
[1,]   14   32
[2,]   32   77
```

Table B.2   R functions used with matrices.

R Function	Purpose	Examples
%*%	Matrix multiplication	Output 5.4
%*%	Matrix multiplication	Output 5.7
%*%	Matrix multiplication	Output 7.17
as.matrix()	Convert to matrix	Output 8.6
cbind()	Combine columns	Output 8.4
diag()	Diagonal entries	Output 5.5
eigen()	Eigensystem	Output 7.7
eigen()	Eigensystem	Output 7.8
eigen()	Eigensystem	Output 7.9
matrix()	Create matrix	Output 5.3
matrix()	Create matrix	Output 5.8
matrix(byrow=T)	Create matrix	Output 5.11
read.csv()	Read in data file	Output 7.14
read.csv()	Read in data file	Output 7.9
read.csv()	Read in data file	Output 8.3
solve()	Invert a matrix	Output 7.16
t()	Transpose	Output 5.4
t()	Transpose	Output 5.7

in one graphic. Finally, plot.voronoi() plots a Voronoi diagram, but to use it, the package Tripack must be downloaded from the Web from CRAN [34].

Finally, table B.5 has miscellaneous R functions. First, as.dendrogram() takes the output from hclust() and makes it into a dendrogram when printed out. The R package Tripack has both voronoi.mosaic() and plot.voronoi(), which are used together to make plots of Voronoi diagrams. Data frames have named variables, and these are directly accessible by using attach() so that frame$var can be replaced by var. Note that summary() produces summaries of a variety of statistical outputs; that is, it recognizes the type of output, and then prints out the pertinent information.

Table B.3   R functions for statistical analyses.

R Function	Purpose	Examples
cor()	Correlation matrix	Output 7.5
cov()	Covariance matrix	Output 7.1
factanal()	Factor analysis	Output 7.18
factanal()	Factor analysis	Output 7.19
hclust()	Hierarchical clustering	Output 8.11
kmeans()	Clustering	Output 8.1
kmeans()	Clustering	Output 8.2
kmeans()	Clustering	Output 8.6
kmeans()	Clustering	Output 8.7
kmeans()	Clustering	Output 8.10
kmeans()	Clustering	Output 8.13
lm()	Fit a linear model	Output 7.2
lm()	Fit a linear model	Output 7.14
prcomp()	Principal components	Output 7.10
prcomp()	Principal components	Output 7.11
prcomp()	Principal components	Output 7.12
prcomp()	Principal components	Output 7.13
prcomp()	Principal components	Output 8.8

Table B.4   R functions for graphics.

R Function	Purpose	Examples
lines()	Add a line	Output 7.2
par()	Plot parameters	Output 8.5
plot()	Cartesian plot	Output 7.2
plot()	Cartesian plot	Output 8.4
plot()	Cartesian plot	Output 8.5
plot()	Cartesian plot	Output 8.6
plot.voronoi()	Plot Voronoi diagram	Output 8.12
text()	Add text to plot	Output 8.4
text()	Add text to plot	Output 8.5
text()	Add text to plot	Output 8.6

Table B.5 Miscellaneous R functions.

R Function	Purpose	Examples
as.dendrogram()	Creates dendrogram	Output 8.11
attach()	Directly access frame variables	Output 7.2
attach()	Directly access frame variables	Output 7.14
dist()	Compute distances	Output 8.11
dist()	Compute distances	Output 8.17
scale()	Compute z-score	Output 5.12
scale()	Compute z-score	Output 7.4
seq()	Produce a sequence	Output 8.14
sprintf()	Formatted print	Output 5.8
sqrt()	Square root	Output 5.5
summary()	Summarizes outputs	Output 7.11
summary()	Summarizes outputs	Output 7.15
summary()	Summarizes outputs	Output 8.3
voronoi.mosaic()	Create a Voronoi diagram	Output 8.12

Finally, remember that this appendix is just the beginning of what is possible with R. See the references at the beginning of this appendix for more information, or, even better, download R and its documentation from CRAN [34] and try it for yourself.

References

1. Gisle Aas and Martijn Koster. LWP, Version 5.808, 1995. URL: http://search.cpan.org/~gaas/libwww-perl-5.808/lib/LWP.pm, November 15, 2007.

2. Alan Agresti. *Categorical Data Analysis*. Wiley Interscience, New York, New York, 2nd edition, 2002.

3. Jon Allen. Perl 5.8.8 Documentation, 2007. Supported by The Perl Foundation. URL: http://perldoc.perl.org/, September 16, 2007.

4. Tony Augarde. *The Oxford A to Z of Word Games*. Oxford University Press, New York, New York, 1994.

5. Tony Augarde. *The Oxford Guide to Word Games*. Oxford University Press, New York, New York, 2003.

6. R. Harald Baayen. *Word Frequency Distributions*. Springer Verlag, New York, New York, 2001.

7. Lee Bain and Max Engelhardt. *Introduction to Probability and Mathematical Statistics*. PWS-Kent Publishing Company, Boston, Massachusetts, 1989.

8. Giovanni Baiocchi. Using perl for statistics: Data processing and statistical computing. *Journal of Statistical Software*, 11:1–75, 2004.

9. Geoff Barnbrook. *Language and Computers: A Practical Introduction to the Computer Analysis of Language*. Edinburgh University Press, Edinburgh, United Kingdom, 1996.

10. Michael W. Berry and Murray Browne. *Understanding Search Engines: Mathematical Modeling and Text Retrieval*. Society for Industrial and Applied Mathematics, Philadelphia, Pennsylvania, 2nd edition, 2005.

11. Douglas Biber, Susan Conrad, and Randi Reppen. *Corpus Linguistics: Investigating Language Structure and Use*. Cambridge University Press, New York, New York, 1998.

12. Douglas Biber and Edward Finegan. Drift and the evolution of english style: A history of three genres. *Language*, 65:487–517, 1989.

13. Roger Bilisoly. Concatenating letter ranks. *Word Ways*, 40:297–9, 2007.

14. Roger Bilisoly. Anasquares: Square anagrams of squares. *The Mathematical Gazette*, 92:58–63, 2008.

15. José Nilo G. Binongo. Who wrote the 15th book of oz? an application of multivariate analysis to authorship attribution. *Chance*, 16:9–17, 2003.

16. José Nilo G. Binongo and M. W. A. Smith. The application of principal component analysis to stylometry. *Literary and Linguistic Computing*, 14:445–466, 1999.

17. Rens Bod, Jennifer Hay, and Stefanie Jannedy, editors. *Probabilistic Linguistics*. MIT Press, Cambridge, Massachusetts, 2003.

18. Dmitri A. Borgmann. *Beyond Language: Adventures in Word and Thought*. Charles Scribner's Sons, New York, New York, 1967.

19. Gary Buckles, 2007. Personal Communication, September 25, 2007.

20. Sean M. Burke. *Perl & LWP*. O'Reilly & Associates, Sebastopol, California, 2002.

21. Sean M. Burke. Lingua::EN::Numbers, Version 1.01, 2005. URL: http://search.cpan.org/~sburke/Lingua-EN-Numbers-1.01/lib/Lingua/EN/Numbers.pm, November 15, 2007.

22. William S. Burroughs. *Word Virus: The William S. Burroughs Reader*. Grove Press, New York, New York, 2000. Edited by James Grauerholz and Ira Silverberg.

23. Cambridge International Corpus, 2007. By the Cambridge University Press. URL: http://www.cambridge.org/elt/corpus/default.htm, November 14, 2007.

24. Cambridge Learner Corpus, 2007. By the Cambridge University Press. URL: http://www.cambridge.org/elt/corpus/learner_corpus.htm, November 14, 2007.

25. English language teaching: Cambridge dictionaries, 2007. By Cambridge University Press. URL: http://www.cambridge.org/elt/dictionaries/index.htm.

26. Ronald Carter and Michael McCarthy. *Cambridge Grammar of English*. Cambridge University Press, New York, New York, 2006.

27. *The Chicago Manual of Style*. The University of Chicago Press, Chicago, Illinois, 14th edition, 1993. Created by the Chicago Editorial Staff.

28. Tom Christiansen and Nathan Torkington. *Perl Cookbook*. O'Reilly Media, Sebastopol, California, 2nd edition, 2003.

29. CiteSeer: Scientific Literature Digital Library, 2007. Hosted by Penn State's College of Information Sciences and Technology, URL: http://citeseer.ist.psu.edu/cs, November 16, 2007.

30. Aaron Coburn, Maciej Ceglowski, and Eric Nichols. Lingua::EN::Tagger, Version 0.13, 2007. URL: http://search.cpan.org/~acoburn/Lingua-EN-Tagger-0.13/Tagger.pm, November 15, 2007.

31. William W. Cohen. Enron Email Dataset, 2007. URL: http://www.cs.cmu.edu/ enron/, November 21, 2007.

32. Gregory M. Constantine. *Combinatorial Theory and Statistical Design*. John Wiley & Sons, New York, New York, 1987.

33. Damian Conway. *Object Oriented Perl*. Manning Publications, Greenwich, Connecticut, 1999.

34. The Comprehensive R Archive Network, 2007. URL: http://cran.r-project.org/index.html, November 14, 2007.

35. Michael J. Crawley. *Statistics: An Introduction Using R*. John Wiley and Sons, New York, New York, 2005.

36. David Cross. *Data Munging with Perl*. Manning Publications, Greenwich, Connecticut, 2001.

37. Peter Dalgaard. *Introductory Statistics with R*. Springer Verlag, New York, New York, 2002.

38. Alligator Descartes and Tim Bunce. *Programming the Perl DBI*. O'Reilly & Associates, Sebastopol, California, 2nd edition, 2000.

39. Charles Dickens. *A Christmas Carol*. Number 46 in Project Gutenberg Releases. Project Gutenberg, 2006.

40. Albert Ross Eckler. *Word Recreations: Games and Diversions from Word Ways*. Dover Publications, New York, New York, 1979.

41. Ross Eckler. *Making the Alphabet Dance: Recreational Wordplay*. St. Martin's Press, New York, New York, 1996.

42. Brian S. Everitt and Torsten Hothorn. *A Handbook of Statistical Analyses Using R*. Chapman and Hall/CRC, New York, New York, 2006.

43. Ronen Feldman and James Sanger. *The Text Mining Handbook: Advanced Approaches in Analyzing Unstructured Data*. Cambridge University Press, New York, New York, 2006.

44. William Feller. *An Introduction to Probability Theory and Its Applications, Volume I*. John Wiley and Sons, New York, New York, 3rd edition, 1968.

45. The Perl Foundation. The Perl Directory, 2007. URL: http://www.perl.org/, September 16, 2007.

46. W. N. Francis and H. Kucera. *Brown Corpus Manual*. Brown University, Providence, Rhode Island, revised and amplified edition, 1979. Available online at http://icame.uib.no/brown/bcm.html, December 31, 2007.

47. Jeffrey Friedl. *Mastering Regular Expressions*. O'Reilly Media, Sebastopol, California, 3rd edition, 2006.

48. David A. Grossman and Ophir Frieder. *Information Retrieval: Algorithms and Heuristics*. Springer Verlag, New York, New York, second edition, 2004.

49. Gerald J. Hahn and William Q. Meeker. *Statistical Intervals: A Guide for Practitioners*. Wiley-Interscience, New York, New York, 1991.

50. John Haigh. *Taking Chances: Winning with Probability*. Oxford University Press, New York, New York, 2003.

51. Michael Hammond. *Programming for Linguists: Perl for Language Researchers*. Blackwell Publishing, Malden, Massachusetts, 2003.

52. Trevor Hastie, Robert Tibshirani, and Jerome Friedman. *The Elements of Statistical Learning: Data Mining, Inference, and Prediction*. Springer Verlag, New York, New York, 2001.

53. Kevin Hemenway and Tara Calishain. *Spidering Hacks: 100 Industrial-Strength Tips and Tools*. O'Reilly Media, Sebastopol, California, 2003.

54. Jarkko Hietaniemi. The Comprehensive Perl Archive Network (CPAN), 2007. Supported by The Perl Foundation. URL: http://cpan.perl.org/, September 16, 2007.

55. Douglas R. Hofstadter. *Gödel, Escher, Bach: An Eternal Golden Braid*. Basic Books, New York, New York, 1979.

56. David I. Holmes. Stylometry and the civil war: The case of the pickett letters. *Chance*, 16:18–25, 2003.

57. David I. Holmes, Lesley J. Gordon, and Christine Wilson. A widow and her soldier: A stylometric analysis of the 'pickett letters'. *History and Computing*, 11:159–179, 1999.

58. John E. Hopcroft, Rajeev Motwani, and Jeffrey D. Ullman. *Introduction to Automata Theory, Languages and Computation*. Addison-Wesley Publishing, Reading, Massachusetts, 2nd edition, 2000.

59. Susan Hunston. *Corpora in Applied Linguistics*. Cambridge University Press, New York, New York, 2002.

60. Richard Jelinek and Roman Vasicek. Lingua::DE::Num2Word, Version 0.03, 2002. URL: http://search.cpan.org/~rvasicek/Lingua-DE-Num2Word-0.03/Num2Word.pm, November 15, 2007.

61. Samuel Johnson. *Samuel Johnson's Dictionary*. Levenger Press, Delray Beach, Florida, 2004. Introduction and edited by Jack Lynch.

62. Samuel Johnson. *A Dictionary of the English Language (Facsimile of 1755 First Edition on DVD-ROM)*. London, London, United Kingdom, 2005. Introduction by Eric Korn and essay by Ian Jackson.

63. Randall L. Jones and Erwin Tschirner. *A Frequency Dictionary of German: Core vocabulary for learners*. Routledge, New York, New York, 2006.

64. Daniel Jurafsky and James H. Martin. *Speech and Language Processing: An Introduction to Natural Language Processing, Computational Linguistics and Speech Recognition*. Prentice-Hall, Upper Saddle River, New Jersey, 2nd edition, 2008.

65. Erica Klarreich. Bookish math. *Science News*, 164:392–4, 2003.

66. Jacob Kogan. *Introduction to Clustering Large and High-Dimensional Data*. Cambridge University Press, New York, New York, 2007.

67. Brigitte Krenn and Christer Samuelsson. The linguist's guide to statistics - don't panic, 1997. URL: http://citeseer.ist.psu.edu/krenn97linguists.html.

68. Amy N. Langville and Carl D. Meyer. *Google's PageRank and Beyond: The Science of Search Engine Rankings*. Princeton University Press, Princeton, New Jersey, 2006.

69. Daniel T. Larose. *Discovering Knowledge in Data: An Introduction of Data Mining*. Wiley-Interscience, Hoboken, New Jersey, 2005.

70. Mark D. LeBlanc and Betsey Dexter Dyer. *Perl for Exploring DNA*. Oxford University Press, New York, New York, 2007.

71. Laura Lemay. *Sams Teach Yourself Perl in 21 Days*. Sams, Indianapolis, Indiana, 2nd edition, 2002.

72. Stephen O. Lidie and Nancy Walsh. *Mastering Perl/Tk*. O'Reilly & Associates, Sebastopol, California, 2002.

73. University of Pennsylvania Linguistic Data Consortium. Linguistic Data Consortium (LDC), 2007. URL: http://www.ldc.upenn.edu/, November 21, 2007.

74. Longman. *Longman Dictionary of American English*. Addison Wesley Longman Limited, New York, New York, 2nd edition, 2002.

75. Christopher D. Manning and Hinrich Schütze. *Foundations of Statistical Natural Language Processing*. MIT Press, Cambridge, Massachusetts, 1999.

76. Bill Mark and Raymond C. Perrault. Cognitive Assistant that Learns and Organizes (CALO), 2007. URL: http://www.ai.sri.com/project/CALO, November 21, 2007.

77. Zdravko Markov and Daniel T. Larose. *Data Mining the Web: Uncovering Patterns in Web Content, Structure and Usage*. Wiley-Interscience, Hoboken, New Jersey, 2007.

78. Tony McEnery, Richard Xiao, and Yukio Tono. *Corpus-Based Language Studies: An Advanced Resource Book*. Routledge, New York, New York, 2006.

79. Frederick Mosteller and David L. Wallace. *Applied Bayesian and Classical Inference: The Case of The Federalist Papers*. Springer Verlag, New York, New York, 1984.

80. I. S. P. Nation. *Learning Vocabulary in Another Language*. Cambridge University Press, New York, New York, 2001.

81. National Center for Biotechnology Information (NCBI), 2007. Supported by the National Library of Medicine and National Institutes of Health. URL: http://www.ncbi.nlm.nih.gov/, September 16, 2007.

82. Michael P. Oakes. *Statistics for Corpus Linguistics*. Edinburgh University Press, Edinburgh, United Kingdom, 1998.

83. Jon Orwant. *Perl 5 Interactive Course: Certified Edition*. Waite Group Press, Corte Madera, California, 1997.

84. Jon Orwant, Jarkko Hietaniemi, and John Macdonald. *Mastering Algorithms with Perl*. O'Reilly & Associates, Sebastopol, California, 1999.

85. David D. Palmer. SATZ – an adaptive sentence segmentation system. Technical report, Computer Science Division, University of California at Berkeley, 1994. Report No. UCB/CSD-94-846, URL: http://citeseer.ist.psu.edu/132630.html, January 27, 2008.

86. Georges Perec. History of the lipogram. In *Oulipo: A Primer of Potential Literature*. Dalkey Archive Press, Normal, Illinois, 1998.

87. Georges Perec and Gilbert Adair. *A Void*. David R Godine, Publisher, Boston, Massachusetts, 2005.

88. Edgar Allan Poe. The Black Cat. In *The Works of Edgar Allan Poe, Volume 2*, number 2148 in Project Gutenberg Releases. Project Gutenberg, 2000.

89. Edgar Allan Poe. The Facts in the Case of M. Valdemar. In *The Works of Edgar Allan Poe, Volume 2*, number 2148 in Project Gutenberg Releases. Project Gutenberg, 2000.

90. Edgar Allan Poe. Hop Frog. In *The Works of Edgar Allan Poe, Volume 5*, number 2151 in Project Gutenberg Releases. Project Gutenberg, 2000.

91. Edgar Allan Poe. Maelzel's Chess-Player. In *The Works of Edgar Allan Poe, Volume 4*, number 2150 in Project Gutenberg Releases. Project Gutenberg, 2000.

92. Edgar Allan Poe. The Man of the Crowd. In *The Works of Edgar Allan Poe, Volume 5*, number 2151 in Project Gutenberg Releases. Project Gutenberg, 2000.

93. Edgar Allan Poe. A Predicament. In *The Works of Edgar Allan Poe, Volume 4*, number 2150 in Project Gutenberg Releases. Project Gutenberg, 2000.

94. Edgar Allan Poe. The Tell-Tale Heart. In *The Works of Edgar Allan Poe, Volume 2*, number 2148 in Project Gutenberg Releases. Project Gutenberg, 2000.

95. Edgar Allan Poe. The Unparalleled Adventures of One Hans Pfaall. In *The Works of Edgar Allan Poe, Volume 1*, number 2147 in Project Gutenberg Releases. Project Gutenberg, 2000.

96. Edgar Allan Poe. *The Works of Edgar Allan Poe, Volume 1*. Number 2147 in Project Gutenberg Releases. Project Gutenberg, 2000.

97. Edgar Allan Poe. *The Works of Edgar Allan Poe, Volume 2*. Number 2148 in Project Gutenberg Releases. Project Gutenberg, 2000.

98. Edgar Allan Poe. *The Works of Edgar Allan Poe, Volume 3*. Number 2149 in Project Gutenberg Releases. Project Gutenberg, 2000.

99. Edgar Allan Poe. *The Works of Edgar Allan Poe, Volume 4*. Number 2150 in Project Gutenberg Releases. Project Gutenberg, 2000.

100. Edgar Allan Poe. *The Works of Edgar Allan Poe, Volume 5*. Number 2151 in Project Gutenberg Releases. Project Gutenberg, 2000.

101. Phillip Pollard. Acme::Umlautify, Version 1.01, 2004. URL: http://search.cpan.org/~bennie/Acme-Umlautify-1.01/lib/Acme/Umlautify.pm, November 15, 2007.

102. Fabien Potencier and Marvin Humphrey. Lingua::StopWords, Version 0.08, 2004. URL: http://search.cpan.org/~creamyg/Lingua-StopWords-0.08/lib/Lingua/StopWords.pm, November 15, 2007.

103. S. James Press. *Applied Multivariate Analysis*. Dover Publications, New York, New York, 2005.

104. Alvin C. Rencher. *Methods of Multivariate Analysis*. Wiley-Interscience, New York, New York, 2nd edition, 2002.

105. R. J. Renka, Albrecht Gebhardt, Stephen Eglen, Sergei Zuyev, and Denis White. The Tripack Package, 2007. R package available from CRAN at http://cran.r-project.org/index.html.

106. John A. Rice. *Mathematical Statistics and Data Analysis*. Wadsworth and Brooks, Pacific Grove, California, 1988.

107. Peter Mark Roget. *Roget's Thesaurus*. Number 22 in Project Gutenberg Releases. Project Gutenberg, 1991.

108. James R. Schott. *Matrix Analysis for Statistics*. Wiley-Interscience, New York, New York, 2nd edition, 2005.

109. Randal L. Schwartz, Tom Phoenix, and brian d foy. *Learning Perl*. O'Reilly & Associates, Sebastopol, California, 4th edition, 2005.

110. Abraham Sinkov. *Elementary Cryptanalysis: A Mathematical Approach*. Mathematical Association of America, Washington, D.C., 1998.

111. Richard A. Spears. *NTC's Dictionary of Phrasal Verbs and Other Idiomatic Verbal Phrases*. National Textbook Company, Chicago, Illinois, 1993. Division of NTC Publishing Group.

112. Larry L. Stewart. Charles brockden brown: Quantitative analysis and literary interpretation. *Literary and Linguistic Computing*, 18:129–138, 2003.

113. Gilbert Strang. *Linear Algebra and Its Applications*. Brooks Cole, Pacific Grove, California, 4th edition, 2005.

114. Michael Swan. *Practical English Usage*. Oxford University Press, New York, New York, 2005.

115. Steven K. Thompson. *Sampling*. Wiley-Interscience, New York, New York, 2nd edition, 2002.

116. James Tisdall. *Beginning Perl for Bioinformatics*. O'Reilly Media, Sebastopol, California, 2001.

117. James Tisdall. *Mastering Perl for Bioinformatics*. O'Reilly Media, Sebastopol, California, 2003.

118. Adrian Trapletti. The tseries Package, 2007. R package available from CRAN at http://cran.r-project.org/index.html.

119. Peter Wainwright, Aldo Calpini, Arthur Corliss, Simon Cozens, Juan Julian Merelo-Guervos, Aalhad Saraf, and Chris Nandor. *Professional Perl Programming*. Wrox Press Ltd., Birmingham, United Kingdom, 2001.

120. Larry Wall, Tom Christiansen, and Jon Orwant. *Programming Perl*. O'Reilly & Associates, Sebastopol, California, 2000.

121. Elizabeth Walter and Kate Woodford, editors. *Cambridge Advanced Learner's Dictionary*. Cambridge University Press, New York, New York, second edition, 2005.

122. Grady Ward. *Moby Thesaurus*. Number 3202 in Project Gutenberg Releases. Project Gutenberg, 2002.

123. Grady Ward. *Moby Word Lists*. Number 3201 in Project Gutenberg Releases. Project Gutenberg, 2002.

124. Andrew Watt. *Beginning Regular Expressions*. Wrox-Wiley, Hoboken, New Jersey, 2005.

125. Sholom M. Weiss, Nitin Indurkhya, Tong Zhang, and Fred J. Damerau. *Text Mining: Predictive Methods for Analyzing Unstructured Information*. Springer Verlag, New York, New York, 2005.

126. Dominic Widdows. *Geometry and Meaning*. CSLI Publications, Stanford, California, 2004.

127. Shlomo Yona. Lingua::EN::Sentence, Version 0.25, 2001. URL: http://search.cpan.org/~shlomoy/Lingua-EN-Sentence-0.25/lib/Lingua/EN/Sentence.pm, November 15, 2007.

128. G. Udny Yule. On sentence-length as a statistical characteristic of style in prose: With application to two cases of disputed authorship. *Biometrika*, 30:363–390, 1939.

Index